FOUNDATIONS OF
EDUCATIONAL PSYCHOLOGY

Nature's Gifts to Man

FOUNDATIONS OF
EDUCATIONAL PSYCHOLOGY

Nature's Gifts to Man

BY

PETER SANDIFORD

PROFESSOR OF EDUCATIONAL PSYCHOLOGY
AND DIRECTOR OF THE DEPARTMENT OF
EDUCATIONAL RESEARCH IN THE
UNIVERSITY OF TORONTO

LONGMANS, GREEN AND CO.

NEW YORK · LONDON · TORONTO

1938

LONGMANS, GREEN AND CO.
114 FIFTH AVENUE, NEW YORK
221 EAST 20TH STREET, CHICAGO
88 TREMONT STREET, BOSTON

LONGMANS, GREEN AND CO. LTD.
39 PATERNOSTER ROW, LONDON, E.C. 4
17 CHITTARANJAN AVENUE, CALCUTTA
NICOL ROAD, BOMBAY
36A MOUNT ROAD, MADRAS

LONGMANS, GREEN AND CO.
215 VICTORIA STREET, TORONTO

SANDIFORD

FOUNDATIONS OF EDUCATIONAL PSYCHOLOGY

FIRST EDITION

PRINTED IN THE UNITED STATES OF AMERICA

TO

IZAK LEON KANDEL

FRIEND AND SCHOLAR

This Book is Affectionately Dedicated

PREFACE

THIS volume is the first of a series designed to give a general survey of the foundations of Educational Psychology. It follows closely the first part of the course we provide in the University of Toronto for advanced students of education. The field covered by this book is approximately the one which was called by Thorndike "The Original Nature of Man." The second volume will deal with the "Psychology of Learning." Since we expect our students to obtain for themselves material that is commonly found in college text-books, this work confines itself to a discussion of fundamental principles and to the more interesting of the problems raised by modern researches. In other words, the aim of the work is to place the student on a solid foundation; later specialization should enable him to build securely his part of the super-structure.

We have designated seven rather long discussions by the terms Introduction and Chapters. Probably Sections would be a better term as they are extended treatments of topics into which our course is conventionally divided. Each chapter, therefore, contains enough material for several weeks of work. Indeed, some instructors could use each of them as the basis of a short course. Because the course works well in Toronto, we are publishing it in the hope that other institutions may profit from our labors. Naturally, I have drawn upon material published in an earlier work of mine, but this book represents a different treatment of the subject made necessary by the rapid growth of the science within recent years.

For permission to use excerpts from copyrighted books, we are grateful to many authors and publishers. Acknowledgments of our specific indebtedness are made at appropriate places in the text.

My colleague, Dr. C. B. Conway, has undertaken the onerous task of preparing the drawings which adorn the text. Miss Kathleen Hobday, the Secretary of the Department of Educational Research, prepared the manuscript for the Press. To both of these, I render grateful thanks.

PETER SANDIFORD

University of Toronto

CONTENTS

INTRODUCTION

THE NATURE OF EDUCATIONAL PSYCHOLOGY

PAGE

Psychology Becoming a Science 1
Scientific Method and Principles 11
The Schools of Psychology 16
The Divisions of Psychological Studies 29
The Nature of Educational Psychology 32

CHAPTER I

HEREDITY AND ENVIRONMENT

Man's Place in Nature 36
Heredity and Environment 40
The Theory of the Gene 44
Mendelism 54
Variation in Human Beings 64
Studies of Heredity and Environment 71
Social Heredity 130

CHAPTER II

INDIVIDUAL DIFFERENCES FOUND IN HUMAN NATURE

Galton's Pioneering Work 136
Types of Individual Differences 137
Differences Due to Remote Ancestry or Race 138
Differences Due to Nearer Ancestry or Family 148
Differences Due to Sex 149
Differences Due to Maturation 162
Variation within the Individual 176
Extreme Individual Differences in Man 178
Individual Differences in Sensitivity 192
Individual Differences in Motor Reactions 193
Variability, Training and Age 196
Educational Provision for Individual Differences 199

CHAPTER III

THE FOUNDATIONS OF BEHAVIOR

PAGE

The Meaning of Behavior 205
Organismic Behavior 215
Protoplasmic Behavior 219
The Physiological Gradient 221
Variable and Non-Variable Behavior 225
The Mechanisms of Behavior 226
Effectors 227
The Endocrine Glands 228
Receptors 235
Connectors 240
The Autonomic Nervous System 243
The Nervous Impulse 246
Lashley's Mass Action 251

CHAPTER IV

NON-VARIABLE OR UNLEARNED BEHAVIOR: REFLEXES, INSTINCTS AND EMOTIONS

The Nature of Unlearned Behavior 257
The Forms of Non-Variable Behavior 261
Criteria of Native Responses 280
Methods Used in Securing Lists of Unlearned Reactions . . 284
Watson's Activity Stream 293
Responses with a Proven Biological Foundation 295
Instinct and Emotion 295
The Conditioning of Reflexes 298
The History of the Study of Emotions 305
The Nervous System and Emotions 311
Theories of Emotion 316
Experimental Studies of Emotional Expression 320
Emotional Levels and Outlets 325

CHAPTER V

INTELLIGENCE: ITS NATURE AND MEASUREMENT

Intelligence is Innate 333
Intelligence Develops Precociously 334
The Nature of Intelligence 337

PAGE

The Multi-focal and Bi-focal Theories of Intelligence . . . 338
Other Theories of Intelligence 344
The Kinds of Intelligence 346
The Attributes of Intelligence 347
How Intelligence Came to be Measured 351
Important Contributions to Mental Testing, by Countries . 357
Development of Intelligence Tests after Binet 359
The Standardization of Tests 363
The Evaluation of Test Scores 367
The Growth of Intelligence 369
The Distribution of Intelligence 377
The Uses of Intelligence Tests 383
The Results of Intelligence Testing 388

CHAPTER VI

PERSONALITY: ITS NATURE AND MEASUREMENT

The Meaning of Personality 394
The Relationship of Character, Temperament and Disposition
to Personality 401
The Elements of Personality 402
Sample List of Personality Types 406
The Problem of a Scientific Basis for Personality Types . . 412
Personality and the Environment 422
The Growth of Personality 425
The Measurement of Personality 432
The Most Significant Elements in Personality 442
Other Problems in Regard to Personality 445

INDEX 453

LIST OF ILLUSTRATIONS AND DIAGRAMS

FIGURE   PAGE

1. The Evolutionary Tree of Man from Early Mammals to the Present Day 39

2. Cell Division of the Egg of *Ascaris* (a parasitic round-worm) 46

3. Development, Maturation and Fertilization of Gametes 48

4. Crossing over of Chromosomes 50

5. Results of Crossing Grey Body and Long Wings with Black Body and Vestigial Wings 51

6. A Back Cross of First Filial Generation, F_1, with Parent 52

7. Crossing over of Factors for Long Wings (V) and Vestigial Wings, (v) 52

8. Results from Back Cross when 17% of Crossing over occurs 53

9. Diagrammatic Representation of a Typical Mendelian Experiment with Round and Wrinkled Peas . . . 56

10. Diagram A, illustrating the Behavior of Chromosomes in Mendel's Cross of Round and Wrinkled Peas. Diagram B, illustrating the Behavior of F_1 Generation when Inbred 58

11. Diagram exhibiting the Di-hybrid Ratio 9, 3, 3, 1 in the F_2 Generation 59

12. Curve showing the Theoretical Frequency of Heads turning up when 10 coins are tossed 1024 times . . . 67

13. Distribution Curve for the Stature of 8585 Adult Males in the United Kingdom 69

14. A Normal Surface of Frequency 69

15. The Wedgwood-Darwin-Galton Family 74

16. Weight Record of the Dionne Quintuplets 125

17. Height Record of the Dionne Quintuplets 126

18. Mental Growth Curve of Normal Infant from Four to Twenty-four Months 172

FIGURE   PAGE

19. Mental Growth Curves of Superior and Sub-normal
    Children 173

20. Psychograph of an Intellectually Superior Pupil . . . 178

21. Comparative Psychograph, showing Intellectual Corre-
    spondence and Variations within the Individuals of
    two sets of Twins 179

22. Hearing Loss of 1000 Individual Ears of Toronto Public
    School Pupils 184

23. Chart of the Auditory Sensation Area showing the Num-
    ber of Distinguishable Tones 185

24. Audiogram demonstrating Variation in Hearing Loss for
    Tones of Various Pitches 186

25. Graph of Scores of Goitrous and Non-Goitrous Girls in a
    Steadiness Test 195

26. Typical Forms of Neurons 241

27. Path of Conduction from a Sense Organ to a Muscle . 242

28. Simple Reflex Arc of three Neurons 242

29. General Arrangement of the Autonomic Nervous System 245

30. Production of a di-phasic "Action Current" 248

31. Relation between Stimulus, Sensory Message and Sensation 251

32. Diagrammatic representation of the Variable and Non-
    variable Elements in Behavior, and their Phylogenetic
    and Ontogenetic Development 260

33. Stereotropic Orientations of Young Rat or Mouse . . 264

34. The Activity Stream (Watson) 294

35. Diagram of the Mid-section of the Cat Brain showing
    "the Seat of the Emotions" 313

36. Diagram showing the Phylogenetic Relations of the
    Thalamus and Cortex in Emotional Control . . . 315

37. Luria's Method of combining Jung's Word-association
    Technique with Voluntary and Non-voluntary Move-
    ments of the Hands 326

38. Diagram showing the Relationships existing among Levels,
    Widths and Areas of Intellect 350

39. Curves showing the Growth of Intelligence from Birth to
    Maturity 370

40. Curve of Growth of Intelligence when measured by
       CAVD.   371

41. Mental Growth on the Binet Tests measured in equal
       Units   372

42. Curves of Mental Growth for Normal, Subnormal, and
       Supernormal Children   373

43. Distributions of I.Q.'s of Rural and Urban Groups . .   378

44. Diagram showing the Distribution of I.Q.'s in a Normal
       Population   380

45. Composite Curve for the Sixth Grade, based upon Eleven
       Single Curves   381

46. Composite Curve for the Ninth Grade, based upon Eleven
       Single Curves   381

47. Composite Curve for the Twelfth Grade, based upon Ten
       Single Scores   382

48. Composite Curve for College Freshmen, derived from
       Eleven Single Examination Scores   383

LIST OF TABLES

TABLE   PAGE

I. Subdivisions of the Order Primates 37

II. Mendel's F_2 Generations Showing the Proportion of Dominant to Recessive Phenotypes . 57

III. A List of Well-Known Mendelian Characters in Plants and Animals 61

IV. The Theoretical Frequency of Heads That Will Turn Up When 10 Coins Are Tossed 1024 Times 66

V. The Stature of 8585 Adult Males of the Population of the United Kingdom, Arranged According to Place of Birth 68

VI. Some Correlations of Twins and Siblings in Six Mental Traits 101

VII. Some Coefficients of Correlation of Siblings . 102

VIII. Resemblances of Twins in Intelligence . . . 103

IX. Standard Deviations and Standard Errors of Estimate of I.Q.'s of Merriman's Twins. . . 105

X. Coefficients of Correlation Found in Various Tests Given to Twins of the Same and of Opposite Sexes 106

XI. Coefficients of Correlation of Physical Traits of Twins 107

XII. Resemblances of Twins in General Intelligence 109

XIII. Resemblance of Younger Twins and Older Twins 109

XIV. Resemblances of All Twin Pairs in Native and Acquired Traits 110

XV. Comparison of *Dissimilar* Twins in *Similar* Environment with *Similar* Twins in *Similar* Environment 112

XVI. Comparison of *Similar* Twins in *Similar* Environment with *Similar* Twins in *Dissimilar* Environment 113

XVII. Comparison of *Dissimilar* Twins in *Similar* Environment with *Similar* Twins in *Dissimilar* Environment   114

XVIII. Summary of Twin Resemblances in Motor Skills Compared with Resemblances in Other Traits   115

XIX. Basic Scores and Differences for Nineteen Pairs of Separated Identical Twins   118

XX. Correlations for Three Groups of Twins . .   121

XXI. Finger Pattern Types, and Ridge Counts read from Left to Right, and Total Quantitative Values for Each Hand of the Quintuplets .   123

XXII. A Series of Nine Values Determined from the Finger Patterns in the Dionne Family . .   124

XXIII. Mental Test Scores of Quintuplets   127

XXIV. The Bach Family   129

XXV. Comparison of Negro and White by Means of the Binet Tests   144

XXVI. Negro and White School Children Tested by Group Tests   144

XXVII. I.Q.'s of Samples of Racial Groups from Various Sources   145

XXVIII. Combined Point Scale Scores for Klineberg's Ten European Groups   147

XXIX. M-F Scores of Male Groups   154

XXX. M-F Scores of Female Groups   157

XXXI. Some Findings Regarding Sex Differences . .   163

XXXII. Increase in Brain-Weight with Age   168

XXXIII. The Age of the Eruption of the Permanent Teeth. A Scale for Measuring Anatomical Age   174

XXXIV. Deaf-Mutes and Blind in Canada   182

XXXV. Distribution of Deafness Among Toronto Public School Pupils   183

XXXVI. Distribution of Scores of Goitrous and Non-Goitrous Girls in a Steadiness Test . . .   194

TABLE   PAGE
XXXVII.   The Ratio of Longevity to Adolescence . . . 211
XXXVIII. The Effectors of the Body 227
XXXIX.   Table of Human Reflexes 267
XL.   General Grouping of Animal Activities . . . 271
XLI.   Forms of Self-Maintaining Protective Behavior
          Toward Enemies 273
XLII.   Forms of Parental Behavior 274
XLIII.   Forms of Social Behavior 275
XLIV.   Scores in *Army Alpha* Made by the Population
          of a Community, Classified by Age . . . 375
XLV.   Distribution of I.Q.'s in a Normal Population . 379
XLVI.   Physical and Psychic Dispositions 408

FOUNDATIONS OF
EDUCATIONAL PSYCHOLOGY

INTRODUCTION

THE NATURE OF EDUCATIONAL PSYCHOLOGY

Psychology Becoming a Science.— Almost a casual glance at any modern text in psychology reveals the fact that the subject is becoming more and more scientific. Compared with the texts of a generation ago, the recent ones contain far more material derived from carefully conducted experiments. Far less space is devoted to hair-splitting, metaphysical discussion than was formerly the case. Though the old topics — memory, perception and so forth — may still find a place, the treatment each receives is now very different. There are still many 'schools' of psychology, but each school apparently is anxious to be regarded as scientific. So true are these statements that it is no exaggeration to say that psychology since 1900 has progressed scientifically more than it did in the previous 2000 years. The story of this belated spurt will now be briefly given.

Although psychology as a separate branch of study is almost as old as astronomy, chemistry or physics, its progress has been far less rapid and today, as hinted above, it may still be regarded as in its swaddling clothes. When Aristotle wrote *De Anima* (on the soul as connected with the body), it was probably as scientific as his *Physica Auscultatio, De Cælo, Meteorologica* or other writings. Yet present-day physics, astronomy and even meteorology seem somehow to be far more scientific than psychology. Why is this, and why is it possible to say with truth that psychology as taught today is mainly the history of its development — what this or that man did or when this or that theory was evolved? There seem to be two main reasons — first, the peculiar way in which the subject evolved; and second, the inherent difficulties of the science itself.

Psychology is old, dating back to the time of Aristotle and beyond, but the name is comparatively new. Rudolf Goeckel (*Lat.* Goclenius) published a book in 1590 which bore the title *Psychologia*. This word, compounded of *psyche* (soul) and *logos* (word, talk about, science of), fitted the subject so well that it has been retained. *Soul* in the twentieth century has a somewhat narrow theological connotation. Not so the *psyche* of the Greeks. The *psyche* was the essence or true being of an organism; it was the cause and principle of its life. Without a soul the body was merely a corpse. In modern terminology, the Greek *psyche* included the notions of both mind and soul; it exhibited both aspects, although it was an indivisible unity. With the passage of time each of these two aspects was increasingly emphasized so that by the time the Middle Ages was reached, they had largely become separate disciplines — the philosopher (or psychologist) studying the one, the theologian the other. Psychology, during this period, tended to change from the study of the soul to the study of the mind.

Mind, however, as a subject of study was almost as elusive and difficult as the soul. There was obviously some connection between mind and body, but the relation between them remained an unsolved riddle. Gradually the phenomenon of mind known as consciousness was selected for special investigation and psychology became the study of consciousness. Consciousness, which has many meanings, can best be regarded as awareness. When conscious we are aware of the happenings in the world around us; when unconscious, as in a dreamless sleep, we are not aware of anything.

But consciousness, studied by introspective techniques, was almost as elusive a term as mind itself. Certainly it was as intangible. So gradually an aspect of consciousness, rather than consciousness itself, was selected for study. This aspect was behavior, by which is meant the doings or reactions of an organism. Obviously when we are conscious we do things, we react, we behave. Now behavior is far more promising as the core of psychological studies. Other persons besides ourselves can observe our behavior. It opens up the possibility of objective study, even of experimental treatment and measurement. Moreover, undoubted scientists — biologists and physiologists — spend their time in studying special aspects of the behavior of organisms, including man himself. Why should not the objective study of the behavior of organisms be regarded as the province of psychology? There are certain obvious limitations and even more obvious losses by restricting the subject in this way. The dividing lines between psychology on the one hand and physiology and biology on the other, are difficult to draw. We neglect some of the most important elements in our lives, namely, our subjective reactions to music, art, people, and literature. But there are also gains. Animal behavior as well as human behavior can be studied; and the behavior of such queer human beings as the feebleminded and the insane can be brought within the sphere of psychology. Psychology, almost perforce, gradually became the study of behavior.

Summing it up we may say with Woodworth[1]: "First psychology lost its soul, then it lost its mind, then it lost consciousness; it still has behavior of a kind." (p. 2)

It must not be supposed that these historical changes in emphasis were sharp and abrupt. Historical changes seldom are; they are usually made gradually and one period overlaps another. So in regard to psychology one cannot say, for instance, that from St. Augustine to Descartes psychology was the science of the mind, or rather, of the mental aspects of the soul; or that psychology as the study of behavior began with the inauguration of Wundt's psychological laboratory in 1879, or with the opening year of the twentieth century. The fact of the matter is, that although some definitions have become outmoded, they have all persisted to the present day. Thus most Roman Catholic psychologists still define their field as the science of the soul. There are others who regard with horror the work of the "rat-runners" and protest vigorously against the inclusion of their findings within the corpus of the subject. Such a one was the late Professor Titchener of Cornell. For him and his school, the only legitimate method of psychological study was that of introspection by trained introspectionists. But despite many schools of psychology, much eclecticism, and a considerable body of "middle-of-the-roaders," the main trend in psychol-

[1] R. S. Woodworth, *Psychology, a Study of Mental Life,* 1929.

ogy today is towards an objective science. Experimentation is almost universal and in course of time the subject seems destined to become as scientific as biology now is. It is still a very young science, but it is a lusty one and growing vigorously.

The question that naturally arises is "why did psychology lag so much behind physics, chemistry, astronomy and medicine in becoming an objective science?" These four subjects were made over in the sixteenth and seventeenth centuries. Physics as an experimental science was founded by Galileo (1564–1642), Robert Boyle (1627–91) and others. Scientific medicine was greatly furthered by Harvey's (1578–1657) discovery of the circulation of the blood and by Van Leeuwenhoek's (1632–1723) invention of the microscope. Boyle and his co-workers, Hooke (1635–1703) and Mayow (1643–79), changed alchemy into chemistry and placed it on a firm foundation of experiment. Astronomy developed out of astrology through the work of Copernicus (1473–1543), Kepler (1571–1630) and Newton (1642–1727). But psychology remained a branch of philosophy until the end of the nineteenth century and the divorce of the two is still far from being absolute. However, even the experimental sciences had their growing pains; for, unlike Pallas, they did not spring full panoplied from the head of Jove; they grew gradually in many heads. Even as late as 1794, the great French chemist, Lavoisier, was guillotined, partly because he was an aristocrat, but also because he taught such nonsensical doctrines as that when things burn they gain in weight.

Science, like any other scholarly pursuit, weighs evidence and tries to find out whether a thing is proved or not. When is a thing proved? Obviously enough, proof in mathematics is more easily demonstrated than in any other branch of learning. It may be secured for all time by one man, providing his premises be granted. When Lindemann, in 1882, published his proof of the non-possibility of squaring a circle, this one solution established the case forever. Similarly, it has been proved that the trisection of an angle is an impossibility, providing we use, of course, only compasses and ruler. If, therefore, some crank now writes to an editor to say that he has succeeded in squaring a circle or trisecting an angle, his manuscript may be deposited gently in the waste-paper basket without a single qualm or misgiving.

But a single person's *ipse dixit* in physics or chemistry is insufficient to establish a case. Rather must he give an account of his experimental set-up, his findings, and his conclusions. If his findings and conclusions are confirmed by a number of other skilled workers in the field, then, and not till then, are they regarded as authentic. Such repetition in physics and chemistry is comparatively easy; the material dealt with is inorganic and easily controlled. It should, however, be noted that both physics and chemistry are based on measurement and on mathematics, the science of pure number.

As we pass to the biological sciences, for example to zoology and botany, we get further removed from the foundation of mathematics; we move into an area where the variables are more difficult to control. We have reached the field of organisms, and truths about organisms are more difficult to establish than truths about inorganic matter. Still the ideal of research is essentially the same as in physics or chemistry since it is the isolation and investigation of the single variable.

Psychology may be regarded as the next step further removed from mathematics. Here we are largely dealing with human beings, and these, even to a greater extent than plants and sub-human animals, simply refuse to "stay put." This is the basis of the claim that research in psychology is so much more difficult than research in chemistry, in physics, or in the biological sciences; it is, in fact, the most difficult kind of research of the single-variable type that we have today.

This difficulty in research, this difficulty in establishing a truth, largely explains the dilatoriness in the development of a science of psychology. But there are other contributing factors. Psychology was studied and kept alive by philosophers and theologians. Neither of these branches of learning lends itself to experimental treatment. The method used was that of introspection and again the introspective method does not lend itself to experimental control. As a scientific method, introspection is subject to the following weaknesses:

(1) In introspection, the mind is asked to attend to its own workings. It is as if we asked the kettle of boiling water to describe the boiling, or the zinc and sulphuric acid the fizzing that takes place when they are brought together. "The mind in watching its own workings," says Stout,[2] "must necessarily have its attention divided between two objects — on the one hand the mental operation which is to be observed, and on the other, the object to which this mental operation is directed." (p. 18)

(2) Before mental states can be described they must first happen. Nobody can describe his feelings of anger before the state of anger has occurred. Introspection, therefore, is always retrospection; it describes memories of events that are either past or passing away.

(3) If an observation of a state of mind is made, the very act of observing tends to change it. Thus if a psychologist says to himself "I am angry; I must observe this anger very carefully," the calmness and deliberation necessary to such observation will inevitably dissipate the anger. It destroys or at least changes the object it is examining. As James[3] states: "The attempt at introspective analysis in these cases is, in fact, like seizing a spinning-top to catch its motion, or trying to turn up the gas quickly enough to see how the darkness looks." (p. 244)

(4) Mental states change so quickly that only the slower changes can be observed; the quicker ones elude introspective observation. For instance, nobody has been able to observe introspectively what really happens when we feel the meaning of a word we want to write and then write it. What my mental processes are as I write this sentence are beyond my powers of introspective analysis, and, for that matter, those of everybody else in a similar situation.

(5) It is not given to everybody to introspect either easily or well. Certainly one cannot place much reliance on the introspections of imbeciles or the insane. And judging from results, introspectionists as a class have been those who analyzed and reasoned rather easily, hence their over-emphasis of such processes as analysis, reasoning, and judgment, and

2 G. F. Stout, *Manual of Psychology*, 1898.
3 W. James, *Principles of Psychology*, I, 1908.

the comparative neglect of other mental operations equally frequent and valuable.

(6) Introspection, being a very special kind of observation, is possible, as seen above, only to the normal or supernormal individual. Some maintain that it is possible only to the trained introspectionist. Introspection is a task not to be undertaken by the man in the street. And even the trained introspectionist may lapse into the vulgar error of seeing *things* as the common run of humanity naïvely sees them, and fail to observe his mental content during the seeing. When the introspectionist thus backslides, he is guilty of the "stimulus error," a minor vice from which nobody really frees himself.

(7) Physiological actions within the body, certain reflexes, posture habits and others that have become automatic, seldom enter into consciousness at all. Some of them can never be made to do so. They therefore escape the notice of the introspectionist, although nobody would dare to deny their importance in life. And if modern psychoanalysis is to be believed, many states observed in consciousness are the results of unconscious causes whose actual nature is still obscure and unknown. Man rationalizes his behavior to a most extraordinary extent; he can find excellent reasons for doing anything he wants to do. Yet introspection failed to discover these twists in mental states; it was objective analysis that first disclosed them. When we do things because "we feel we must," the cause for them is always hidden and never forms part of the "content of consciousness" with which the introspectionist is constrained to deal. The mental states discoverable by introspection, therefore, must give but a partial and one-sided picture of mental life. Frequently the picture is distorted and quite out of focus.

(8) The essence of a science is controlled observation under experimental conditions. Scientific results are of such a nature that they are verifiable by the reconstruction of the original conditions. But mental states which introspectionists observe are unique events; they are never repeated in identically the same form. The argument, of course, must not be pushed too far, for the observations used in physics and chemistry have a subjective element — there is always an observer when a thing is observed. But the introspection-

ist does not observe things naïvely as the scientist does, otherwise he is guilty of the "stimulus error" as noted above; he is interested in the miracle which takes place when things are observed.

And what is this miracle? Suppose I am looking at the landscape. From trees, houses, water, reflected waves of light of different wave-lengths reach my eye and are focused on my retina. Complicated chemical reactions are set up in my rods and cones, and energy, probably in the form of a wave, is transmitted along my optic nerve. So far, the physicist, chemist and physiologist can give a reasonable, certainly an understandable, account of the successive happenings. But when the stimulating current or wave reaches the central nervous system the miracle happens. I see trees, houses, water, and I know from previous experiences that I am seeing trees, houses and water. In other words, I see a landscape and not waves; and my previous experiences with landscapes modify my impressions of the present one. At this stage the chemist, physiologist and physicist lose interest in the phenomena, but the introspectionist wants to find out more about these mental happenings. Obviously, the observer gets more from the same light waves than the camera does.

The illustration is over-simplified. The observer not only sees a landscape, but concomitantly hears rustling noises from the leaves and sounds from the running water. Temperature effects may be registered, for the day may be cold or hot. In the observation and analysis of these mental states the introspectionist is interested while the natural scientist is not. The physicist and chemist accept the phenomena as facts and give no further thought to them.

It is obvious that the observation of this miracle is a difficult task. It may be that it is so difficult that it will never repay the time and energy spent upon it. Some creditable results have been obtained, and Woodworth[4] makes out a good case for the "method of impression." However, a careful study of his examples shows that success has been reached only when experimental controls have been introduced. Vague introspective observations never land the observer anywhere. Moreover, the method of impression starts

---

[4] R. S. Woodworth, *Contemporary Schools of Psychology*, 1931, pp. 18-22.

with the premise of the natural scientist that the sense-organs of different individuals function in much the same fashion. They may not. A color-blind person sees reds and greens differently from a normal person, but we are usually safe in saying that if two observers looking at a bluish-green color report it as bluish-green, then they are getting similar experiences.

Thus we may say that introspectionists are dealing with unique events and since science tries to deal in common-sense fashion with repeatable events, introspectionist psychology yields results of doubtful scientific validity. Even the results from the "method of impression" may be difficult to interpret, for there is no impartial judge to whom we may turn. If I say "When I am angry, I feel so and so," and another equally competent observer says "No, your description is wrong; when I am angry I feel thus and thus," who is to judge of the truth between us? But if we adopted the method of the objective psychologist and made observations of angry behavior, we could reach a scientific conclusion about the redness or whiteness of the face, the clenching of the fists, the lowering of the eyebrows, the baring of the teeth and so on. We might even experiment with anger and arrange situations which arouse anger in a subject and then observe his reactions. This objective type of study has undoubtedly produced results of great and undisputed value and is rapidly usurping the place that the subjective method held for so long.

(9) Introspection, as we have seen, deals solely with the mental states of normal or superior beings; those of the defective, insane and other abnormals are beyond its ken. The very valuable contribution of abnormal psychology could never have been made if the method of introspection had been rigidly adhered to. Yet objective observations of insanity and hysteria have shown that these abnormalities are but extreme and unbalanced developments of characteristics and functions which form integral parts of normal human behavior. As for animals, introspection could not possibly have anything to do with them. Yet it is from the field of animal learning that a new world has been opened up which is proving of the utmost importance for human education, especially in the fields of motivation, maturation and learn-

ing. Introspection missed the great truth that behavior in animals is graded on the evolutionary scale. Man at the top of the scale exhibits forms of behavior differing not particularly in kind but mainly in degree from those below him.

(10) If an introspective psychology written about 1900, say, Stout's *Manual of Psychology*, be compared with the writings of a schoolman of the Middle Ages, say, St. Thomas Aquinas, no great differences are to be found. One is just about as subtle as the other and nobody can say which is the truer. In other words, little progress, if any, had been made in over 600 years. A non-progressive method digs its own grave.

The foregoing criticisms surely dispose of the claim made by introspectionists that theirs is the only method of psychological observation. Introspection, at its best, gives relatively uniform results only when the observations are of a comparatively simple nature. Apparently all observers agree that when a bright light, say a glowing electric bulb, is looked at for a short time and the eyes then turned upon a dark background, a "positive after-image" of the filament appears. But with "negative after-images," such as one gets by looking steadily at a colored spot for thirty seconds and then turning the eyes upon a plain grey background, there is less unanimity of opinion. And the more complex the mental process, the more variable the data of introspection become. It may also be freely granted that certain sorts of information, and very important sorts of information, can only be obtained by introspection. These should be freely used by the individual gaining them, but they should not be used as a part of the body of science. The pleasure that one derives from reading a book is largely sealed from the objective observer, but is well known to the reader himself. But the reader's statements about his pleasure do not yield reliable data for science. The scientific person observing a reader would make careful records of what the man reads. In the last analysis we judge a man's pleasure in reading by the kind and quantity of the reading that he does. He may report that he loves reading Shakespeare, but if his Shakespeare becomes dusty on his shelves, while detective stories are read almost continuously, we are apt to mistrust his statement, although it may have been made in perfectly good faith. If a man says, "I can add a column of 100 figures in 10 seconds," he is reporting a self-observation which is easily verified, not an introspection.

Introspection can seldom if ever be made to give consistent or verifiable results. For this reason, and also because of the inherent difficulties of introspection summarized above, scientific psychology is gradually abandoning the method and turning more and more to the securing of objective data from controlled observation and experiment.

Contrasting modern scientific and objective psychology with the introspective psychology of an earlier time we may sum up the matter in the following way:

(1) Modern psychology links up the behavior of human beings with that of lower organisms.

(2) Modern psychology is objective and experimental in its methods; its conclusions and generalizations are open to verification by other workers.

(3) Modern psychology includes in its study young and old, normal and abnormal, human beings and sub-human animals, and is not restricted, as the older psychology was, to subjective observations by supernormal persons.

(4) Modern psychology aims to predict and control. Every science, of course, aims to predict and control, but psychology is unique in aiming to predict and control behavior, especially the behavior of human beings. The data obtained from animals are most useful when they are used comparatively in the elucidation of the vexed problem of human behavior.

Scientific Method and Principles.— Psychology can justify its claim to inclusion within the body of sciences in one way and in one way only. It must demonstrate beyond a shadow of doubt that it adheres rigidly to the methods and principles which science has pragmatically established throughout the ages. Some of these have been touched upon previously, but a more elaborate summary must now be made.

(1) Science finds an explanation within its own data; it does not appeal to gods or demons or to any "unknown X" outside itself. A hurricane to a savage may be a manifestation of the wrath of a god or a demon who must be appeased. To the scientist it is due to movements of air which are

caused by great differences of pressure. These differences in turn are caused by unequal heatings and other causes. In the development of a science, the right explanation may not present itself immediately, and outside agencies or explanations may be invoked. Thus the working of a pump was once ascribed to the fact that "Nature abhorred a vacuum." This explanation is, of course, non-scientific since it invokes the aid of an agency, Nature, which lies outside the phenomenon under observation. Freud's invocation of a censor and so on, as explanations of peculiar forms of behavior, are modern examples of an ancient folly.

(2) Science is dependent upon factual data from crucial observations. Observations may be of a more or less general nature or they may be controlled by means of an experimental set-up. A scientific experiment is nothing more nor less than a device for controlling or making crucial observations. This it does by limiting the field of observation and by introducing the principle of the single variable. The observations must be for the sole purpose of settling some problem or resolving some difficulty. When we go for a walk we are usually observant but not scientifically observant. We haven't a problem which can be solved by a crucial observation. But if we walk over a country-side and wish to learn whether or not it was once glaciated, we must look for moraines, striated rocks, pot-holes and other crucial evidences of glaciation. If we do this, we become scientifically observant; in fact, we turn ourselves into geologists because we are seeking the solution of a geological problem.

In the psychological field, casual observation shows that babies sometimes exhibit signs of fear — moving away from objects, puckering up the face and crying. The psychologist as a scientist wants to find out more about the phenomenon of fear. What causes the fear? Through experiment he limits the field. The blanket on which the baby is lying is jerked suddenly. Does the baby show fear? A loud noise is made by hammering iron near a placid baby. Does he show fear? If one baby reacts to insecurity of position or to noise, will other babies react also? The more carefully the experiment is controlled — that is, the more rigidly extraneous and non-essential factors are excluded — the greater the confidence that can be placed in the results. It may be that neither the noise nor the sudden jerk causes the baby to cry; he may be frightened by the presence of a strange face. As a matter of fact it would be exceedingly difficult to establish the truth or untruth of such a statement as the following: "Babies under 6 months of age can be made to show fear in one or both of two ways: either by a sudden change of position (loss of security) or by a sudden loud noise."

(3) Science, being dependent on objective observations under controlled conditions, is verifiable, since similar or fairly similar conditions may again be established. Thorndike's cat experiments have been repeated by Adams. Sometimes Thorndike's findings and conclusions were verified; sometimes they were not. The psychologist as scientist asks: "Were the conditions exactly the same or was there deviation from them? Were the deviations significant? The cats could not be the same, but were they around the same age? Were they healthy? Did they receive the same treatment?" If these and other questions cannot be satisfactorily answered, the experiment must be repeated until the truth about the matter appears.

(4) Science is sceptical — it doubts and questions everything. Some of its doubts and suggestions for experiments have offended the feelings of some people. Thus Galton offended his generation by suggesting a controlled experiment to test the efficacy of prayer; and more recently the professor who baptized one member of his set of identical twins and left the other without the benefits of baptism undoubtedly shocked a great many of his contemporaries. All the same, the advice to students to "go around with a question mark on the shoulder instead of a chip" is perfectly sound from the standpoint of science. Some beliefs, like that in the homing instinct of dogs and birds have been put to test, though not very successfully. But the perennial story in the newspaper of the dog that came home from a distance of 100 miles can be countered by turning to the "lost and found" column where there are usually a dozen instances of dogs lost on the same day by wandering a block or two from home.

(5) Science tries to predict and control. As Bertrand Russell[5] pertinently says:

[5] B. Russell, "Science" in *Whither Mankind*, edited by C. A. Beard.

"Hitherto, the practical applications of science have been mainly directed to modifications of our material environment. . . While we alter the environment to suit ourselves, we do not much alter ourselves to suit each other. The reason is, of course, that the sciences that deal with the formation of human character are far less developed than those which deal with the inanimate world. This, however, is rapidly changing. It is highly probable that in a hundred years we shall have acquired the same control over the characters of children that we now have over physical forces. . . But what men will make of these powers when they come to possess them, it would be rash to prophesy. Doubtless they will make something which, to our inherited standard of values, would seem horrible; but to them, one must suppose, it will seem good." (pp. 71-72)

The prediction and control of the behavior of human beings is beset by many pitfalls and fraught with great difficulties, yet it is a task to which the scientific psychologist must consecrate his life.

(6) Science tries to arrive at the truth. Truth is an elusive thing, but as far as science is concerned it reduces itself to a question of probability. It can usually be expressed in terms of chance. The chances that the law of gravitation is true may be many billions to one, but the chances that persons with I.Q.'s of 140 and upward will never be convicted and sent to prison are undoubtedly much smaller. One of the difficulties which confronts the psychologist is that he is dealing with truths that are far from absolute and are at the same time difficult to establish. The chances that King George V was once King of England are infinitely great, but what are the chances of a child of five showing anger when thwarted in some way or other? Many of the truths of psychological science are accepted because they seem to be the best under the circumstances, or because they seem to be more probable than not.

(7) Science works in accordance with certain principles which, however, are under considerable fire at the present time. These are:

(a) the principle of the *uniformity of nature*. By this is meant that the course of events in nature is uniform. Of course, as stated in this fashion, it is palpably false, or there would be no need of science. As interpreted by the scientist it means that there is order in nature but it has to be looked for. If we seek it in the correct way we shall find it. Nature may be simple and we are apt to infer that it is so because all the discoveries so far made seem to indicate an underlying simplicity. However, nature may be complex and that we have not discovered it to be so is due to the fact that the complexities are always harder to discover than the simplicities. In psychology many of the generalizations and laws so far disclosed seem to be of a simple kind; but this may be an illusion and due simply to our inability to unravel the complexities;

(*b*) the principle of *causation*, namely, that every event has a cause, or that every event is the effect of some antecedent cause. A is said to cause B when one (or both) of the following conditions is fulfilled: — when B varies as A is changed; or when B disappears when A is removed. This principle is under even heavier fire than the principle of uniformity or orderliness of nature. In some branches of science it must be discarded, for, as Heisenberg has shown in his principle of indeterminacy, "if a system is small, we cannot observe it without producing a serious disturbance; we cannot, for instance, know both the position and the speed of a particle at one and the same time." Despite this, the psychologist still arranges his life and work in accordance with cause and effect. If Tommy mis-spells the word "receive" there is some cause for this effect. Can the effect be linked to a cause? If so, the psychologist has explained or found a reason for the mis-spelling;

(*c*) the principle of *parsimony* or *economy of hypothesis*. This principle occurs in many guises. Occam[6] asserted that "entities are not to be multiplied more than is necessary." In modern terms it means that carrying an analysis further than is necessary to give the required result is wasted effort. Karl Pearson[7] said, "we ought not to look for new causes to account for any group of phenomena until we have shown that no known cause is capable of explaining it." (p. 92) In much the same form the principle was stated by Hamilton[8] who said, "neither more, nor more onerous, causes are to be assumed than are necessary to account for the phenom-

---

[6] Quoted by A. D. Ritchie, *Scientific Method*, 1923, p. 114.
[7] K. Pearson, *Grammar of Science*, 2nd ed.
[8] Quoted by Karl Pearson, *Grammar of Science*, 2nd ed., p. 537.

ena." The statement of the principle which finds most acceptance among psychologists is Morgan's.[9] It runs: "In no case may we interpret an action as the outcome of the exercise of a higher psychical faculty if it can be interpreted as the outcome of the exercise of one which stands lower in the psychological scale." (p. 53) More recently, Nelson[10] has formulated the principle of parsimony as follows: "Of any set of rival explanations, a more parsimonious one is more probable than a less parsimonious one, provided that all other factors relevant to the probability of the rival explanations are equally favorable to them all." He shows that the Multiplicative Axiom of the calculus of probabilities justifies the principle.

Whatever the form the principle takes, the implication is that nature is essentially simple and orderly. So if we interpret the hazing of the freshman by the sophomore as an indulgence in sadistic cruelty when it can be more simply explained as an example of herd behavior, we sin against the principle of parsimony.

The Schools of Psychology.— Mahomet claimed that everything necessary for salvation was to be found in the Koran. In the writings of the various schools of psychology — structuralism, functionalism, behaviorism, psychoanalysis — the beginner is apt to find similar claims. Like the man who was asked to define orthodoxy and heterodoxy and replied, "orthodoxy is my doxy; heterodoxy is the other fellow's doxy," the psychologist is apt to believe that his school represents the truth, the whole truth, and nothing but the truth.

If, however, we remember that psychology is a new science that broke from parental philosophy only yesterday, we shall find a reason for the many and vigorous schools of psychology. Has not philosophy many schools? Psychology is new and the various schools approach their problems from different angles. May not this varied attack be a blessing in disguise, and may not a fuller and truer synthesis develop from these various contributions of partial truths? It would be a great mistake to discourage the evangelical fervor of the gestaltist or behaviorist as he devises new experiments to support his point of view; his factual results are useful and

9 C. L. Morgan, *An Introduction to Comparative Psychology.*
10 E. J. Nelson, "A Note on Parsimony." *Philos. of Science,* III, 1, pp. 62-66.

permanently valuable even if his conclusions are somewhat biased and distorted. It took the biologist a long time to arrive at the stage when he could examine evidence dispassionately. As the science of psychology matures it is probable that the differences will become less acute. There is some evidence that agreements rather than differences are becoming increasingly emphasized.

Psychological investigation, as we have seen, is the hardest kind of scientific investigation. It is difficult to secure reliable psychological data. But with more experimental data of a reliable nature at our command, the truth will begin to appear. So the existence of controversial schools need not daunt the beginner, but he should be cautioned against giving unqualified allegiance to any one school. The one that seems to be least offensive to the scientist is the objective approach. It is the one emphasized in this book, and has been deliberately selected because the objective approach has proved successful in other fields.

Curiously enough, the theory of mind held by the psychologist does not determine the school to which he belongs. Apparently one can be a good psychologist without any deep philosophical belief as to the nature of mind. But psychologists, being recently philosophers, have put forward many theories of mind. Among these theories may be found the following:

(1) *The dual aspect theory,* sometimes called monodualism or dual monism. Warren bravely upheld this theory and probably the majority of living psychologists believe in it. Mind and body are looked upon as two aspects of a single process, or as two entities which are two aspects of a third entity. When we see things we have a perception. This perception is one aspect (mental) of a single process, the other aspect (physical) being the activity of the eye, optic nerve and brain. These two aspects are complementary to each other.

(2) *Physical monism,* sometimes called materialism or mechanism. The physical monist ignores mind because, being non-physical, we can do nothing with it. He reduces mind to matter. He believes in behavior, for, as he maintains, scientific analysis reveals no other basis for belief in existence. He is content to remain within the field of his

own behavior — his sensory behavior which is a reality. This physical monism seems best adapted to behaviorism; in fact a behaviorist of the Watsonian variety must almost of necessity adopt it.

(3) *Psychophysical parallelism.* This view, which postulates two non-interacting entities, body and mind, was held by Titchener and his school, although it did not greatly affect their psychology. There were bodily events, A, B, C, and mental events, α β γ; study α β and γ and leave A, B and C severely alone. Body is body and mind is mind, and ne'er the twain shall meet.

(4) *Psychophysical interaction.* The two entities, body and mind, interact. A caused α, B caused β and so on. In general, Bentley in America and the psychoanalysts of Europe are interactionists.

(5) *Emergent evolution.* This theory is associated with the names of Bergson and G. B. Shaw. It emphasizes time as well as space in any statement of reality. Time carries the past into the present, but there is no repetition, rather a continual creation of what is new. In psychology, the theory stresses the fact that different qualities of mind emerge at the various levels of animal evolution, or as G. B. Shaw puts it (in *Back to Methuselah*), the Life-Force manifests itself in higher and lower "potentials," which conflict with one another for all the world as if they were really different and antagonistic forces. To Bergson, intelligence and instinct are not different in degree but in kind; and perception and memory are antithetic.

(6) *Psychical monism,* or *idealism.* According to this theory, mind is the ultimate reality and body can be reduced to mind. The theory has had a long and interesting history. It was developed along slightly different lines by Plato, Locke, Berkeley, Leibnitz, Hegel and Kant, but throughout the ages we find that the idealistic philosophers held consistently to the view that mind was pre-eminent over the body and that ideas were the only things known to us. Prince is a modern psychologist whose writings uphold this theory of mind. It is, of course, the exact converse of epiphenomenalism.

(7) *Epiphenomenalism.* This theory, a modern variant of materialism, was named and expounded by T. H. Huxley.

Mental events are caused by physical events and always succeed them in time. The physical changes in the brain cause an immediate and continuous stream of momentary processes or psychical elements in the stream of consciousness. Hence the name; consciousness was an epiphenomenon of brain activity. But it is the brain, not the mind, that registers activities and associates them together. Mind is a superimposed, somewhat shadowy effect of the activities of the sensory and nervous system. Indeed, Huxley compared mind to the whistle of the locomotive and to the shadows cast by the moving parts of a machine. Mind, like the body, evolves; it came into existence when the physio-chemical activities of neural protoplasms became sufficiently complex to produce or to be accompanied by consciousness. It is thus a theory of mind which appeals greatly to the biologist.

(8) Hollingworth's view of *nature as a continuum*, ranging from the physical to the mental, though unnamed as a specific theory of mind, should be noted. No sharp lines can be drawn between the mental and the physical. The theory is important for cue reduction as an explanation of learning; when learning takes place the system moves, as it were, towards the mental end of the scale.

Returning now to our discussion of the schools or systems of psychology, we find that they fall naturally into two groups. In the first group are the systems which are atomistic in character and analytic in method. They seek for the irreducible elements of mind and behavior. They tend to be associationist in outlook for they try to discover how the whole is constructed from its elements. Structuralism, behaviorism and the bond psychology (reaction-hypothesis) of Thorndike belong to this first group. The second group comprises all those systems which emphasize the functioning of the organism as a whole. Gestalt, functionalism and the new organismic psychology are representative systems belonging to the second group. They tend to decry analysis and maintain that the organism works and reacts as a whole; and that this whole is greater than the sum of its parts. This is no new doctrine. Even a house is greater than the sum total of its bricks; but in stressing the essential wholeness of mind or behavior the members of this group have performed a valuable service. The gestaltists, in particular, claim that in the growth and development of the organism and in its behavior, the whole is prior to the part. Behavior is not the building up of a complex whole from simple elements, but it starts from a simple, loosely organized whole and gradually becomes differentiated and specific. Though the lines of demarcation between the two groups are not as sharply drawn as some of the polemical literature of the day would lead us to suppose, nevertheless in the field of learning the cleavage is both wide and deep. The organismic group see the whole boy kicking a football; the bond psychologists tend to analyze the boy's action into its elements and recombine them in such a way that the boy's skill in football immeasurably improves.

It would be out of place to give a detailed description of each of the major schools; a brief summary of their chief characteristics must suffice.

(1) *Structuralism* or *existentialism*. This is the oldest school of psychology. Although the members of this school may fail to agree on the ultimate elements of mind, they are unanimous in asserting that the only way to discover them is by means of introspection. Brentano thought that ideas, feelings and judgments were the elements of mind; Titchener's elements were sensations, simple feelings, and images. Sensations have some or all of the following properties — quality, duration, intensity, extensity and vividness. Elementary sensations may become patterned into blends, fusions and mosaics. The workers in this school interest themselves in the psychology of sensation and imagery and have collected, by means of the method of impression, a large amount of valuable data. Titchener was the chief representative of the school in America; Ward and Stout in England. The school is gradually decreasing in importance and seems destined to become obsolescent within the next generation.

(2) *Organismic psychology*. This school is so new that it is difficult to say exactly where it stands. It has grown up within schools of education of the more adventurous and radical type in response to a demand for a psychological foundation for progressive, child-centered forms of education. In essence, it is an offshoot of gestalt psychology, but

draws its support mainly from biological experiments. It takes its stand on the obvious "fact of the unified, organic nature of human response" (Rugg). Many biologists and physiologists have noted that "the whole organism contributes to the response," among them being Cannon, Sherrington, Child, Lashley, Jennings and Coghill, and it is their findings that are so freely drawn upon by the organismic psychologists. The integrated curriculum of the child-centered school needed an integrated organism and "the organism responding as a whole" supplied this need. Although not explicitly stated, the Thorndikean bond psychology is the chief object of attack. So far its chief contributions have been to find support for school theory and practices of the following types:

1. Emphasis upon
   (*a*) Maturation as prerequisite to fruitful experience.
   (*b*) The importance of interest and purpose and goal-directed activity in learning.
   (*c*) The effects of success and failure on personality rather than solely in relation to efficiency of learning.
   (*d*) The importance of integrative experience as opposed to disintegrating pressures.

2. Criticism of
   (*a*) Repetitive activity — over-emphasis upon drill.
   (*b*) Naïve dependence on departmentalized teaching.
   (*c*) Over-use of failure, grades, and other extrinsic devices for motivation.
   (*d*) Over-teaching, coupled with under-emphasis upon pupil activity.
   (*e*) Emphasis upon method and teaching technique rather than upon pupil experience and content development.
   (*f*) Over-confidence in regimented curriculum participation, i.e., in a fixed curriculum.
   (*g*) Naïve acceptance or rejection of psychological tests and measures.
   (*h*) Rule-of-thumb techniques of teaching.

3. Suggestions for positive changes
   (*a*) Selection of units of work, and direction they should take.
   (*b*) Correlation and fusion of materials.
   (*c*) Development of project and problem teaching.

(d) Sequential unification of the entire experience pattern developed as a curriculum.

(e) Development of group activities which safeguard individual initiative and allow for individual differences, and yet develop social understanding.

(f) Development in guidance workers of more complete understanding of the individual and society, through broader training in educational sociology and social psychology.

(g) Better training for the adjustive phases of guidance, including training in mental hygiene and clinical psychology.

(h) Association in school supervision of psychiatrically trained social workers.

(i) Increased recognition of the importance of activity in line with the individual's developed and developing interests and goals.

(j) Development by counselors of skill in helping individuals to define and develop worth-while, integrating purposes and goals.[11]

To such a program most educational psychologists could give allegiance. It suffers, as so many American school programs seem to suffer, from a worship of change for change's sake. The old must be bad because it is old; the new must be good because it is new. The aim of education becomes the development of personality; knowledge, skills, achievements of any kind are relegated to a subordinate position.

The organismic psychologists do not realize that they will have to discover *how* the organism *works* as a whole, and if they ever find a solution it will probably be through such time-honored devices of the atomistic schools as analysis and experimentation. One cannot find out how a railway engine works by watching it move as a whole; one has to trace the force of the steam as it acts on the various parts. Similarly, human behavior must be analyzed and traced back to its elements. In its present stage of development, organismic psychology seems to be a new type of vitalism or mysticism with "maturation" and "sequential unification of the entire experience pattern" as the unknown X's. In practice, it leads to scurrying in seven different directions at once, since nothing

11 Stanford *Conference on Curriculum and Guidance*, 1936, pp. 29-30.

in regard to the educational process can be fixed or predicted in advance. Organismic psychologists scorn the work of Thorndike and fail to realize that he stated: "It is a general law of mental action that the response to any external situation will depend upon the condition of the person as well as upon the nature of the situation." When they can point to as much real progress in education as the Thorndikean school has achieved in the past thirty years, they will give us cause to take them very seriously. At present, despite protests, organismic psychology seems not only to describe itself in a mystical terminology but also to support in practice a superficial and sloppy kind of teaching. The safest plan is that of science which analyzes, experiments, measures and secures dependable data. Organismic psychology seems to be returning to a metaphysical speculation which we hoped was a thing of the past.

(3) *Functionalism.* This school is associated with the University of Chicago, since five of its chief exponents — Dewey, Angell, Moore, Mead, and Carr — were members of the staff of that institution. Dewey rebelled against the atomism of the structural school. In an important article, "The Reflex Arc Concept in Psychology,"[12] he combated the view that the stimulus initiated the activity and maintained that the "sensory stimulus, central connection and motor responses shall be viewed, not as separate and complete entities in themselves, but as divisions of labor, functioning factors within the single concrete whole, now designated the reflex arc." (p. 358) The significance of both stimulus and response lies in the part they play in co-ordination. Sensation and response are integrally related; neither has meaning alone. A response may be the stimulus for further activity. Activity implies both organism and environment. Functional psychology studies mental activity as a part of the whole biological activity, which, in turn, is part of organic evolution. Functionalists therefore are interested in co-ordinations — in adaptations of organisms to their environments. In these adaptations, mind is a forceful, dynamic agent. Consciousness, a product of organic evolution, becomes a biological tool for the maintenance of life. Adjust-

---

[12] J. Dewey, "The Reflex Arc Concept in Psychology." *Psychol. Review*, III, 4 (July, 1896), pp. 357-370.

ment is an important principle of functionalism, but since we must adjust to something, we adjust to environment. The queer and insane adjust, but their adjustments seem crazy to us. The answer seems to be that adjustments must be judged pragmatically; if they work, they are good. The series, reflexes → instincts → habits → intelligence, together with the central nervous system, are of chief interest to the functionalist. Most of his experiments lie within the field of habits and learning — forms of adjustment to the environment.

(4) *Watsonian behaviorism.* It seems necessary to prefix the adjective to the term behaviorism, since there are many behaviorists, objective psychologists, who fail to follow Watson to the limit. Watson maintains that the behaviorist finds no evidence for "mental existences" or "mental processes" of any kind, and hence he would make "a clean sweep of all the rubbish called consciousness." For Watson,[13] "psychology is that division of natural science which takes human behavior — the doings and sayings, both learned and unlearned, of people as its subject matter. It is the study of what people do from even before birth until death." (p. 4) Through systematic observation and experimentation, it attempts to formulate the laws and principles which underlie man's reactions. Included in these reactions are the language reactions, for *saying* is behaving. Even thinking is but subvocal talking. The inclusion of language makes behaviorism not unlike other forms of psychology which admit introspection as a method; and Watson's case is considerably weakened by admitting verbal report into the category of psychological methods. Had he restricted himself to the objective analysis of the behavior of muscles and glands he would have strengthened behaviorism as a science, though he would have made it difficult to distinguish his new science from that of physiology. With respect to the problem of heredity and environment, Watson is a strong environmentalist and thus breaks with many psychologists of the Thorndikean type, who recognize that hereditary factors influence behavior in a multitude of ways. "Give me a dozen healthy infants, well-formed, and my own specified world to bring them up in," says Watson, "and I'll guarantee to take any one at random and train him to become any type of specialist I might select

[13] J. B. Watson, *Psychology from the Standpoint of a Behaviorist,* 3rd ed. 1929.

— doctor, lawyer, artist, merchant-chief and, yes, beggar-man and thief, regardless of his talents, penchants, tendencies, abilities, vocations, and race of his ancestors" (p. 104),[14] which, of course, is a nonsensical boast. An imbecile may be healthy and well-formed but any and every method of training would fail to make him into a reasonably good doctor or lawyer. Perhaps Watson would guarantee to change the sex of his subject and all that it implied in his forms of behavior! Watson might now reply that he could change sexual behavior by the administration of suitable hormones, but this discovery was subsequent to the time of his boast. His method of training the child or animal is that of establishing conditioned reflexes. The reflex is the functional element of behavior, but to Watson must be given the credit for extending the concept of conditioning to include the emotions. The demonstration of the possibility of conditioning and unconditioning emotions is Watson's most important contribution to education. Finally, let it be said that although every psychologist has his fling in criticizing Watson, every one has been forced to read him and take him seriously into consideration. Psychology is far more scientific today than it would have been had Watson not lived.

(5) *Gestalt psychology.* This originated in Germany in Wertheimer's laboratory around 1912 and has been developed and elaborated by Koehler and Koffka. The chief American adherents to the school are Wheeler and Perkins, and Ogden. It is organismic in outlook; in fact it started in a revolt against the atomism of the traditional psychology. It claims that there are no simple and elemental stimuli or responses. Instead, there are natural autonomous wholes at all levels of the cosmic scale, involving their own intrinsic principles of patterning. In perception, every figure has a ground. Atomism, the bundle hypothesis, must be discarded. However, it has been charged that gestalt psychology deals with large chunks instead of small ones. Gestaltists claim that learning takes place by means of "insight" and that the laws of learning, as propounded by Thorndike and others, are both inadequate and misleading. When they assert that children are active when learning and not merely passive recipients of environmental stimuli, they are on surer ground.

[14] J. B. Watson, *Behaviorism*, 1924.

Gestaltists protest the constancy hypothesis — a one-to-one fixed relation between the stimulus and response; they protest associationism in all its forms and disregard the concept of attention. They have contributed greatly to our knowledge of perception; and educational psychology has profited from their labors. They, however, tend to be evangelical in their methods of spreading their gospel. They erect men of straw and demolish them with great gusto. As Wyatt[15] points out — traditional psychology had already taught that it is a function of mind to discriminate and select from its data (figure and ground); to unify experience (concept of wholeness); to be ever reaching to a higher discrimination level (precision definition, prägnanz, i.e., the most typical form for an organization to assume and towards which every structure tends — circle is simplest and commonest); to anticipate or pre-perceive (closure); and to interrelate presented data (Innigkeit).

In the field of atomism, their protests are of a later date, and no more vigorous than those of James (stream of consciousness) and Dewey (reflex-arc concept). Their neglect of analysis — the traditionally fruitful method in science — is inexcusable. All in all, the differences between gestalt and other systems are probably not so great as gestaltists think them to be. Anyhow, it is high time that the likenesses among the various schools were emphasized; up to the present the differences have received most attention.

(6) *The Psychoanalytical school.* There is some doubt whether this should be regarded as a school of psychology or a theory of personality. Whether school or theory, Freud was undoubtedly its founder. The variations introduced by Freud's quondam disciples, Adler and Jung, are frankly built on his foundation.

Freud is essentially a medical man interested in the treatment of mental disorders. Two of his teachers, Bernheim and Charcot, used hypnotism as a therapeutic agent. Breuer, a collaborator with Freud, discovered that mentally ailing patients were improved if they were allowed to "talk it out" while in a state of hypnosis. The cathartic effect of the confessional has long been known, and this talking out cure developed into Analysis. There is a marked resemblance be-

---

[15] Wyatt, "The Gestalt Enigma." *Psychol. Review*, 1928, XXV, pp. 298-310.

tween Freud's view of mind and Herbart's — the dynamic, vitally active qualities of ideas; two thresholds — the statical and the dynamical; the power possessed by ideas below the dynamical threshold of influencing those above the threshold; and so on. The terminology is Herbart's, but, under new names, these concepts are found in Freud. Analysis in Freud's hands is a method of discovering repressed ideas (complexes) which, in some unknown fashion, influence the behavior of those unfortunate enough to possess them. He seeks to discover the source or occasions of wrong conditionings; to recall the incidents which led to the wrong adjustments; and to replace these by normal attitudes and values. The repressed ideas are generally connected with sex. These, being socially inacceptable, since they could not be allowed free representation in ordinary consciousness, are consigned by the "censor" to the nethermost regions of the mind. But it must be remembered that time and space influence our moral standards. Kissing, for example, among the natives of East Africa is regarded as a horrifying and obscene act. In dreams and hypnotic states, these repressed ideas may thrust their way upward and reach the threshold of consciousness. They may also cause slips of the tongue or the pen. Hence, psychoanalysis pays great attention to the interpretation of dreams and unconscious lapses in language. The expression of these repressed ideas and desires in dreams is frequently symbolic and the psychoanalyst must learn to interpret the signs.

Most of the above tenets and principles must sound fantastic to the psychologist trained in other schools, for many of them can be explained equally well and in simpler fashion by well-established psychology. Memories, for instance, are stored in changes of the body, and the best hypothesis is that they are stored chiefly as changes in the nervous system. They are associated in time, and some memory associations are more accessible than others. The unconscious need not be regarded as the abode of repressed ideas and desires, but as a name for those neural patterns, unlearned and learned, which influence our conscious activities in a very definite way. However, Freud has done well to stress the importance of the emotional life for all of us; and the need for understanding and training our emotions and feelings, especially during the early years of childhood. His main contribution to psychology, therefore, is essentially a genetic one.

Adler differs from Freud in assigning chief place not to sex, but to the will to power. According to him, man's fundamental tendency is a craving for completeness, security and superiority. The child tends to develop inferiority complexes because he lives in a world surrounded by superior beings on whom he is bound to depend. Inferiority complexes lead to many disturbances of behavior; the subject may, for instance, try to hide a feeling of inferiority by boastful and other extravagant forms of conduct.

Jung places hunger and self-preservation, in general, ahead of sex; sex, he claims, is always secondary to the maintenance of the self. Jung divides mankind into two major types — the introvert and the extravert. By combining introversion and extraversion with (a) sensation, (b) thinking, (c) feeling, (d) intuition, he gets eight types. In the extravert, the *libido* is turned outwardly. The extravert tends to be shallow-minded, to do the obvious thing. He seldom innovates but follows the crowd; he is a "good mixer" and is unhappy if left to his own devices and thoughts. The actor and the teacher must have some of the characteristics of the extravert if they are to be successful. The introvert, on the other hand, turns his libido inwardly; he lives in a world of his own, distrusting everything and everybody; in fact, he is uneasy in society of any kind. The scientist and the inventor are typical introverts.

The fact of the matter is that these types are too sharply drawn. Even the extravert may have his introversive moments and the introvert his extraversive ones. Our moods and temperaments change from hour to hour. Sometimes we are introverts, sometimes extraverts; frequently, and probably for most of the time, we are simply neutral.

From the foregoing brief summary, it will be seen by the discerning reader that the psychoanalytical is among the least scientific of the schools of psychology. It seems to attract the charlatan rather than the seeker for truth. Although it has enriched the vocabulary with a number of words — complex, introvert, extravert, censor, transference, trauma, etc. — it has probably passed the peak both of its usefulness and development, and will gradually become an interesting episode in the history of psychology.

The Divisions of Psychological Studies. — Under working conditions, the division of the field of psychology becomes empirical rather than philosophical or rational. Thus an educational psychologist may give allegiance to the gestalt school, to the behavioristic or to any other, but since he concentrates his efforts on the educational situation of the schoolroom, it is this factor which determines his designation among his colleagues. Wheeler and Thorndike, for example, are both known as educational psychologists, though they belong to different schools of psychology. The divisions, then, are of practical use in mapping out the fields of psychological studies.

The diagram given below, which is a modification of one first designed by Yerkes,[16] (p. 17) represents the main divisions of psychology, as studied today. The divisions of physiological and experimental psychology are unrepresented, but as these are as much methods as independent areas, no particular harm

Psychology {
Normal —— Adult —— Human —— Individual —— Pure
Abnormal —— Young —— Animal —— Group —— Applied
Child   or   or Social   Educational
Developmental Comparative or Folk   Vocational
Genetic   Medical
                                               Legal

is done by omitting them. Each term in the upper line is contrasted with the one immediately below it — normal with abnormal; human with animal; and pure with applied. The lines and cross-lines indicate to some extent the various combinations which are to be found. Thus, "normal," "young," "humans," can be studied as "individuals," or in "groups" in order to establish the principles of a "pure" science of psychology. Plain or general psychology is represented by all the words of the upper line — normal, adult, human, individual and pure. It is, however, among the various combinations represented in the lower line that the greatest activity is to be found today — in animal psychology, in developmental psychology, and in the applications of psychology to the solution of educational and vocational problems.

[16] R. M. Yerkes, *Introduction to Psychology*, 1911.

A brief description of some of the divisions may help to make the matter a little clearer.

(*a*) *General human psychology.* This is the normal adult human psychology studied with the single motive of discovering scientific truth. It is "pure" in the sense that it seeks to discover the general laws which are found to operate in normal human behavior. The line of demarcation between normal and abnormal is difficult to draw and is usually a matter of expediency or convenience. General psychology describes behavior as it actually exists among the members of species today, without reference to the way in which this behavior evolved.

(*b*) *Abnormal psychology* deals with the abnormal behavior of organisms, i.e., with actions showing marked deviations from the central tendency of the group. The supernormals deviate positively and the subnormals negatively from this average. Abnormal psychology is especially interested in the study of the feebleminded (aments) — those exhibiting imperfectly developed forms and ranges of behavior; and the insane (dements) — those whose forms of behavior have degenerated with the passing of time. Because the dements have once been normal (indeed, many of them are frequently supernormal in the earlier parts of their lives), they are usually classified separately. In recent times the supernormal in intellect — the geniuses among us — have begun to receive deserved attention. Another class — the subnormals in moral and social behavior — cause us so much trouble in the world that psychologists have literally been forced to study them.

(*c*) *Developmental psychology.* It is rather difficult to distinguish among child, genetic and developmental psychology; in fact the newer developmental psychology seems to have completely absorbed the older child psychology. Genetic psychology is the systematic study of behavior by the genetic method, that is, in terms of the origin and evolution of behavior, either in the individual or the species. It asks such questions as: how do memory powers come to be? how do they change with increasing age? Child psychology may best be regarded as the branch of genetic psychology specially concerned with the development of younger children. Developmental psychology, as its name implies, tries to find out how the infant becomes an adult. The task is far from easy, for we are apt to impute to the child thoughts, motives, feelings and so forth similar to those we adults experience, and this may not be the case. If, however, the behavior of children over a period of years is studied in strictly objective fashion, no great harm can result.

(*d*) *Animal psychology*, since it is mainly studied from the comparative standpoint, is frequently called comparative psychology. It is a purely experimental branch and has a great and rapidly increasing literature. It studies the behavior of sub-human animals and notes how behavior changes as the scale of evolution is ascended.

(*e*) *Individual* or *differential psychology* is the psychology of individual differences. Individuals differ in their behavior according to race, sex, intelligence and the like. These differences may have greater psychological significance than the likenesses. It is the province of individual psychology to investigate and interpret them. The term individual psychology has unfortunately been used by Adler to describe his particular brand of psychology — the investigation of individual differences in the mode of striving toward the superiority goal — so it is perhaps best either to use the phrase "psychology of individual differences" or "differential psychology" to describe the field.

(*f*) *Social* or *group psychology* deals with the behavior of the individual as he is influenced by the society or group of which he forms a part. Our behavior is modified by group life; we respond to the behavior of others; some forms of behavior only come into being because of human association; these are the phenomena which social psychology studies. It is frequently confused with sociology, which, however, is simply a study of groups as groups, of human institutions of every kind. Folk psychology is a specialized branch of social psychology in which the origins and elaborations of various forms of social behavior are studied. Emphasis is usually placed on the customs of the more primitive races.

(*g*) *Applied psychology*. The main subdivisions of this branch of psychology are educational, vocational, medical and legal psychology. The applied psychologist applies the findings of research to the practical situations of life. He is interested in the avoidance of waste; in the economy of human energy, cost and effort. He generally asks "What is the use of this, or what is its value in this particular situation?" In education he is interested in such topics as economy in learning, permanence of learning, and fatigue; in the field of vocations he is interested in advertising, management, and guidance. Applied psychology finds its highest development on the North American continent where the genius of the people leads them to demand practical results. It should, however, be noted that applied psychology is dependent upon the research of the pure scientist whose only desire is to know and to understand.

The Nature of Educational Psychology.— We are now in a position to describe in some detail the nature of educational psychology. It is, as we have seen, a major branch or subdivision of applied psychology. Its subject-matter is the behavior of human beings undergoing the process of education. Generally speaking, it deals with the young rather than the old, and with the learning situations of the school rather than those of the wider environment. However, to these general statements there are many exceptions. Adult learning is a proper topic for the educational psychologist, and the psychology of play and of athletics is a subdivision of educational psychology. Its main subdivisions are:

(1) *The original nature of man.* This branch tries to discover what traits, powers, or capacities a child possesses which may be used as the basis of an educational training. The inheritance of these traits, their variability, etc., are topics of interest to the educational psychologist. So also are his bodily mechanisms of behavior — his sensory, neural and motor equipment; his reflexes, instincts, emotions and other unlearned or non-variable forms of behavior; his native intelligence; his personality and, in general, all the parts of his heredity that are concerned with learning. Intelligence and personality are coming to be regarded as separate branches in their own right.

(2) *The psychology of learning,* or, as it is more generally called, *the learning process.* Given the original nature of man, this second great branch of the subject inquires how the teacher can best arrange educational situations so as to bring about desired responses. The laws of learning and theories of learning are formulated from a study of specific acts of

learning. The rate, progress, and limits of improvement are investigated with a view to discovering the factors which underlie economical learning. The permanence of learning, fatigue, possibilities of transfer from one learning situation to another are topics which are generally included in this branch of the subject.

Besides the above general topics, there are some that have been erected into sub-branches of the psychology of learning. The most important of these are:

(*a*) *The measurement of achievement.* As achievement of pupils is generally regarded as a fair measure of teaching success, the problem of measuring achievement through the techniques of tests and examinations becomes important. Probably in no field does the educational psychology of to-day differ from that of a generation ago as in the field of tests and measurement. Teachers of an earlier generation assumed the validity and reliability of their examinations; today their lack of both these qualities is known to the veriest tyro. Despite much serious and excellent research, the problems raised by "measurement" are still far from being settled.

(*b*) *The psychology of special subjects.* Having discovered the laws and principles underlying learning in general, they may be applied to the case of special subjects such as reading, writing, arithmetic, spelling, algebra, modern languages and other branches of the course of study. The data on some of these subjects, for example, reading and arithmetic, are so extensive that a person could spend half a lifetime in getting merely a nodding acquaintance with them.

(*c*) *Educational statistics.* This is properly not a branch of the learning process at all, for statistics are statistics whether they be used for educational psychology, economics, or any other field of learning. But in the treatment of variable educational measurements much original statistical work has been done. The results of educational experiments are now found so frequently in statistical form that, unless the student has a knowledge of statistical technique, a whole world of information remains a *terra incognita* to him.

(3) *Child study, genetic psychology and developmental psychology.* These three are intimately related and overlap each other to a considerable extent. Child study is the oldest and developmental psychology the youngest of the three.

Child study restricts itself to younger children; genetic and developmental psychology follow the individual from birth to death. All investigate the development of behavior in the maturing individual. Since subjects for investigation must of necessity be mainly drawn from the schoolroom, these branches may rightfully be regarded as falling within the scope of educational psychology. The emphasis, of course, is upon the changes which take place as the organism grows older, but since these changes are also important for the educational psychologist, no great harm is done in regarding these branches as part of the legitimate field of educational psychology. In developmental psychology we should expect an investigator to be interested in such problems as: How do the language responses mature in children? When do the various emotional and instinctive responses normally make their appearance and what are the best methods of bringing them under social control?

Our survey is ended. If the reader has grasped the fact that modern psychology is a bio-social science, objective and experimental in method, and occupying a field of its own; that it is therefore not a branch of philosophy, or sociology, or anatomy or physiology; and that educational psychology cultivates an important portion of the field, namely, the one concerned with learning in every aspect and extension, he will be prepared to profit from the exposition which follows.

REFERENCES

Adams, J. *The Herbartian Psychology Applied to Education*. Boston, Heath, 1899. Pp. iv + 284.

Bills, A. G. *General Experimental Psychology*. New York, Longmans, 1934. Pp. x + 620.

Boring, E. G. *A History of Experimental Psychology*. New York, Century, 1929. Pp. xviii + 699.

Brett, G. S. *A History of Psychology*. 3 vols. London, Allen and Unwin, 1912 and 1921. Pp. xx + 388, 394, 322.

Brown, W. *Mind and Personality: an Essay in Psychology and Philosophy*. New York, Putnams, 1927. Pp. x + 356.

Dunlap, K. *Elements of Psychology*. St. Louis, Mosby, 1936. Pp. 499.

Gray, J. S. *Psychological Foundations of Education*. New York, American Book Co., 1935. Pp. xiii + 534.

Heidbreder, Edna. *Seven Psychologies*. New York, Century, 1933. Pp. ix + 450.

James, W. *Principles of Psychology.* 2 vols. New York, Holt, 1908. Pp. xii + 689, vi + 704.

Jung, C. G. *Psychological Types.* New York, Harcourt Brace, 1926. Pp. xii + 654.

LaPiere, R. T. and Farnsworth, P. R. *Social Psychology.* New York, McGraw-Hill, 1936. Pp. xii + 504.

Leary, D. B. *Modern Psychology: Normal and Abnormal.* Philadelphia, Lippincott, 1928. Pp. xii + 441.

McDougall, W. *Body and Mind.* London, Methuen, 1911. Pp. xix + 384.

Müller-Freienfels, R. *The Evolution of Modern Psychology.* New Haven, Yale University Press, 1935. Pp. xvi + 513.

Murchison, C. (Ed.) *A Handbook of Child Psychology.* Worcester, Clark University Press, 1931. Pp. xii + 711.

Murchison, C. (Ed.) *A Handbook of General Experimental Psychology.* Worcester, Clark University Press, 1934. Pp. xii + 1125.

Poffenberger, A. T. *Applied Psychology.* New York, Appleton, 1929. Pp. xx + 586.

Ritchie, A. D. *Scientific Method: an Inquiry into the Character and Validity of Natural Laws.* London, Kegan Paul, 1923. Pp. viii + 204.

Ritchie, A. D. *The Natural History of Mind.* London, Longmans, 1936. Pp. viii + 286.

Sarton, G. *Introduction to the History of Science,* Vol. I. Baltimore, Williams and Wilkins, 1927. Pp. xi + 839.

Stout, G. F. *Manual of Psychology.* London, University Tutorial Press, 1898. Pp. xvi + 661.

Ward, J. *Psychological Principles.* Cambridge, University Press, 1918. Pp. xiv + 478.

Warren, H. C. (Ed.) *Dictionary of Psychology.* Boston, Houghton Mifflin, 1934. Pp. x + 372.

Watson, J. B. *Psychology from the Standpoint of a Behaviorist.* 3rd ed. Philadelphia, Lippincott, 1929. Pp. xvii + 458.

Weiss, A. P. *A Theoretical Basis of Human Behavior.* Columbus, R. G. Adams, 1929. Pp. xvii + 479.

Woodworth, R. S. *Contemporary Schools of Psychology.* New York, Ronald Press, 1931. Pp. vi + 232.

CHAPTER I

HEREDITY AND ENVIRONMENT

Man's Place in Nature.— Even a somewhat superficial examination of the animals of the world would disclose the fact that man is differentiated from all the rest by (*a*) his upright carriage and bipedal locomotion; (*b*) his manual dexterity — his invention and use of tools, including fire; (*c*) his great cranial capacity compared with the size of his body; and (*d*) his use of language.

When, in 1863, T. H. Huxley used the title "Man's Place in Nature" to describe a series of lectures and papers he had prepared to refute Richard Owen's views regarding the origin of species, the place of man in nature was far from clear. Many regarded him as a special creation but little lower than the angels and few indeed were prepared to accept his kinship with the rest of the animal world. Darwin's task in *The Origin of Species* (1859) had been the collection of evidence which led him to conclude that species were not special acts of creation but "originated by means of natural selection, or through the preservation of favored races in the struggle for existence." Huxley's task was to assemble a line of anatomical, physiological and other forms of evidence which showed that man is separated from the brutes by a structural barrier no greater than that which separates one brute from another. Continuous creation, rather than separate and special creations, seemed to be nature's rule. However, Huxley never was quite satisfied with the Darwinian principle of natural selection and never wholly accepted it as the cause of the origin of new species. He thought it a valuable hypothesis and the only general one regarding the origin of species that had any scientific value. He was inclined to think, rightly as it has since turned out, that "transmutation" may take place without "transition." A struggle for existence there certainly was, but the gradual adjustment of the organism to its environment was an unproved hypothesis.

To Huxley, with his wonderful clarity in exposition, we owe, more than to any other leader, the dissemination of knowledge regarding man's origins and the place he occupies in the world of nature. Huxley patiently expounded to his generation that man was first of all a vertebrate (phylum); that he was a placental mammal (class); that he belonged to the primates (order); that he was an anthropoid or pithecoid (sub-order); that he was part of the family hominidae; and that *homo sapiens* occupies but a single genus and a single species. The various subdivisions of the primates are shown in Table I.

TABLE I. SUBDIVISIONS OF THE ORDER PRIMATES

Order	Sub-Order	Family
Primates	Pithecoids	Platyrrhines
		1. Hapalidae
		2. Cebidae
		Catarrhines
		1. Cercopithecidae
		Macaques
		Baboons
		Mangabeys
		Mandrills
		etc.
	Tarsoids	2. Hylobatidae
		Gibbons
		Siamangs
		3. Pongidae
		Gorillas
	Lemuroids	Chimpanzees
		Orangs
		4. Hominidae
		Man

In his comprehensive work, Dr. Elliott[1] has shown that the recent primates are composed of 57 genera and 593 species, of which the whole of one genus and one species is taken up by man. In other words, there are 593 terminal twigs to the 57 branches of the simian tree with man representing one of the twigs on a single branch.

Why has man been assigned to this unique position? The evidence is far too voluminous to cite here. But in addition to the abundant older findings of comparative anatomy, paleontology, physiology, embryology, etc., there has been ac-

[1] D. G. Elliott, *A Review of the Primates*, 3 vols., 1913.

cumulated recently confirmatory data from blood reactions, behavior patterns, measures of intelligence, and even from the diseases and parasites of the primates.[2]

As to man's ascent to his present high position on the tree of evolution, the following would seem to be true. It can be generally assumed that in the cretaceous period of the mesozoic era, primitive pro-simians arose, and that these divided into lemuroids and tarsoids. During the eocene epoch of the cenozoic era a group of these tarsoids evolved into primitive monkeys. These, in turn, evolved into two groups — the New World platyrrhine (broad-nosed) monkeys and the Old World catarrhine (narrow-nosed) monkeys. By oligocene times, the ancestral forms of the anthropoid apes had arisen from the Old World stem. Branching from this parent stem in oligocene times we find the gibbon; and, later, in miocene times, the orang, chimpanzee and gorilla. In this miocene epoch the basic human stock was also evolved, though *homo* himself did not appear until late pliocene times. With one possible exception (Piltdown man), all the fossil remains of man have been found in quaternary deposits, though some of them undoubtedly take us back to the earliest pleistocene. Apparently the most primitive genus is represented by *pithecanthropus* whose remains were found by Dubois in the pleistocene deposits of Java. Apparently this now extinct genus, found in a fairly late deposit, represents a degenerate descendant of a still more primitive form of man. Piltdown man (*eoanthropus*) or rather woman, found in what may possibly be declared as a pliocene deposit of Sussex, England — a female with a human brain and the jaw of an ape — undoubtedly stands above the recently discovered Peking man (*sinanthropus*), as *sinanthropus* in turn stands above *pithecanthropus*. Yet it must never be forgotten that *pithecanthropus* walked erect on his hind legs even though his teeth and brain were only half-way human.

The ancestry of modern man is somewhat uncertain. It is generally assumed that he is not the descendant of the stocks represented by the Neanderthal and Rhodesian skulls, and that he is more closely related to Cro-magnon man, though probably not in a direct line of descent. (See Fig. 1)

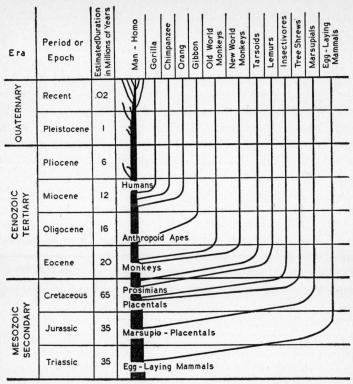

Fig. 1. The Evolutionary Tree of Man from Early Mammals to the Present Day.

It is perhaps fair to say that man was certainly on the earth and using tools and fire during the whole of the million years of the pleistocene epoch, and that the neandertaloid stock probably dates back far into the pliocene. Early man's culture was not very advanced, since the old stone age (*paleolithic*) persisted until around 70,000 years ago. In *neolithic* times the stone and bone implements became more refined and finally gave way to copper tools, apparently introduced into Eurasia about 6000 years ago. Copper in turn gave way to bronze (about 4900 years ago) and bronze to iron (about 3400 years ago). With the introduction of bronze we reach the historical period and the beginnings of great and important civilizations.

The interest of the educational psychologist in this story of ancient man and his forebears lies in the fact that in the anthropoid apes we have at our disposal, as it were, living fossils of what ancient man must have closely resembled. Through a study of animal behavior, and especially of the behavior of man's closest relatives, the chimpanzee and go- rilla, we get an inkling of the hidden sources of some of man's queer kinks. Babies, for example, can support their weight with a one-hand grasp at the age of a few days, but this reflex grasp disappears after about 120 days. Again, many of man's emotional reactions are extremely primitive and can only be interpreted in the light of his origins. The fact that man, alone of all the animals, has achieved language is apt to make us exaggerate his unique achievements among the animal creation, and forget that, without language, he would be in- ferior in many ways both to the gorilla and chimpanzee.

Heredity and Environment.— A person at any stage of his life is the product of two factors — heredity and environ- ment. The older he is, the greater the opportunity that en- vironment (or experience) has had of modifying him. So if we consider ourselves going backward in time and becoming younger we find, in regard to our make-up, heredity increas- ing in importance as environment decreases. If we are part of all that we have met, then it is obvious that the younger we are the less we have met. Is the baby, then, at birth "pure" heredity uncontaminated by anything of an environ- mental nature? Of course not, for the baby prior to birth has lived in a fluid environment for about forty weeks. If, therefore, we traced the growth of the baby backward over this period of forty weeks, we should find him eventually one cell big — a *zygote* or fertilized ovum about one-hundred and twenty-fifth of an inch in diameter. This zygote, formed from the union of two *gametes* (germ cells), a *sperm* and an *ovum*, contains all the hereditary potentialities that will ever be subsequently realized by the organism. This speck of pro- toplasm, which marks the beginning of the human being as an independent organism, is one of the most wonderful par- ticles of matter in the universe, for it contains, potentially, all the characters — mental, moral, and physical — that the adult human being will subsequently display. Certain it is that nobody has been able to *add* to the potentialities of any organism after the zygote stage, though an unfavorable en- vironment might prevent many of its potentialities from becoming actualities. Heredity, therefore, may be considered fixed and complete at the zygote stage and may be defined as *the sum total of the potentialities possessed by an organism in the zygote stage of its existence.* This definition breaks sharply with those which regard heredity as a force moulding the offspring in the likeness of the parent; and also with those which regard heredity as the antithesis of variation. Heredity is certainly not a force; nor does it consist solely in the resemblances exhibited by offspring and parent.

The definition we have given recognizes (*a*) the cellular structure of organisms and (*b*) the genetic continuity between successive generations. When we study heredity we try to discover the lines or genetic continuities between successive generations; the degree of likeness or unlikeness exhibited by parent and offspring; and the influence on the individuals of the materials which they receive from their parents at the beginning of their lives.

But an organism must live in some environment. The new-born baby needs food, air, exercise and stimulation of its various sense organs. This environment, changing from moment to moment, may usefully be regarded as the factor which stimulates the development of hereditary potentialities, or kills them off, or even leaves them severely alone. Thus *heredity and environment are correlative factors,* each one is inconceivable without the other. They are as necessary to each other as the engine and the gas of the motor car, or the figure and background in gestalt psychology.

There is, however, the widespread but mistaken belief that a change in environment will lead to a change in heredity, and that these changes are transmissible to offspring. Up to the present time, the only proven hereditary changes that have been caused by environmental agencies are those in germ cells which have been bombarded by X-rays or gamma-rays. In such cases, the offspring are frequently monstrosities of various kinds, but they are truly the result of environmental factors. They represent, in fact, a very special kind of inheritance of acquired characters. However, forty years of experimentation upon plants, animals, and human beings have failed to supply the crucial evidence that somatically acquired characters have produced specific changes of the same kind in the germ cells.   Morgan[3] has summarized the findings of Griffith, Detlefsen, McDougall, Pavlov, Kammerer, Guyer and Smith, Harrison, etc., and concludes against them.   He argues that "if such effects are transmitted, and especially if these are pre-eminently adaptive ones, there is every reason to suppose that evidence of such transmission should be obtainable — in fact should be abundantly apparent to anyone making careful observations."   But obviously they are not, for scores of people have endeavored to secure the evidence and have failed every time.

If the above views are correct, then heredity represents the more or less fixed element in the situation, and environment the flexible factor.   By improving the environment of an individual, the better hereditary potentialities will undoubtedly be developed, but since there is no transmission of acquired characters, the improvement will be limited to one generation.   Stock or race should be emphasized if we take the long view; progress will be slow, for race remains remarkably constant from generation to generation, despite marked changes in environment.   But if we want quick returns we should plump for environment.   These changes produced by improvement of the environment are frequently of an outstanding character, for only under very favorable conditions is there more than a mere fraction of nature's potentialities which become realities.   The eugenists are right so far as they stress the importance of stock, for, as every farmer knows, if one desires well-favored offspring the best procedure is to start with first-class parents.   The social service workers are also right in that an improvement in environment may lead immediately to marked advances in behavior.

Education is an environmental factor; and the most important correlative of heredity that man has devised.   Its effects, like all environmental acquirements, are limited to one generation.   A parent cannot pass on his knowledge to his children as he passes on his goods and bank balance.   That sometimes he seems to do so is because of social heredity — his goods and money enable the children to live in a superior environment in which such hereditary possibilities as they possess are given a better chance for development.   There is,

[3] T. H. Morgan, "The Mechanism and Laws of Heredity," in C. Murchison, (Ed.), *A Handbook of Experimental Psychology*, 1934.

however, the possibility that the superior heredity of the parent has been passed on to the children, in which case the credit for the children's success should be laid at the door of heredity.

Imagine two equally intelligent children, one of whom is taught to read, the other not. The differences between them, due to these differing environments, will be pronounced. One may become the greatest scholar of his generation; the other must remain an illiterate in a world of letters. But in the next generation things would tend to even up once more; the children of both the reader and the non-reader will be born with the potential ability to read just as their parents were before them.

Now imagine two equally stupid children, morons for example, one of whom is sent to a good school and the other not. With infinite trouble the moron who receives a training may be taught to read and write, but because he is a moron, he cannot put his reading and writing to much use. Education can make him into a better moron than the other, but it cannot make him normal. And, as before, in the next generation things will even up again. The children of both will tend to be stupid.

At first glance this may seem an unduly pessimistic doctrine for the teacher. He cannot change the hereditary possibilities of his pupils; he must take them as he finds them and make the most of them. Even if he succeeds in lifting them to the highest plane possible, all the work has to be done over again in the next generation. But the non-inheritance of acquired characters has its hopeful side. Even the most rabid environmentalist would hardly claim that everything that teachers have done in the past has been safe and wise. And the non-transmissible feature of education ensures that our mistakes will not be perpetuated. Every generation, as it were, starts with a clean educational slate. One hesitates to imagine what the human race would be like today if every indent made on the plastic nature of youth in the past had been faithfully transmitted to succeeding generations. The human race would be bowed down with the burden of error that it had unwittingly accumulated.

Teachers as a rule cannot become technical students of heredity, but each can try to discover the innate capacities of his pupils. Observations of parents will enable him to make shrewd guesses as to the probable capacities of his pupils. Tests of various kinds will add to his knowledge and help him in preparing the educational environment most suitable for their unique combinations of natural gifts. In these and in other ways, the wide-awake teacher can profit from the lessons of heredity.

The Theory of the Gene.— Before this theory can be understood certain discoveries in biological science must be noted. The first of these is Schleiden and Schwann's discovery (1839) that all organisms are composed of cells. In 1858, Virchow proved that all cells come from pre-existing cells by a process we now call *mitosis* or division. In 1873, chromosomes were discovered independently by Anton Schneider, Flemming, Bütschli and others, and named chromosomes by Waldeyer in 1888.

Each cell is a compartment full of living matter or *protoplasm*, which is centered in a spherical kernel or nucleus. The protoplasm surrounding the nucleus is called *cytoplasm*, that of the nucleus itself, *nucleoplasm*. The nucleus is the part of the cell most concerned with the transmission of hereditary characters. In it is found the dense network known as *linin*, on which is the *chromatin*, so called because it stains easily with aniline dyes. When a cell has grown so big that it must divide or die, the chromatin material, which is thread-like, contracts, thickens and finally divides up into fragments known as *chromosomes*. These chromosomes are elongated bodies having the shape of rods, beads or bent threads. The number, size and shape of chromosomes is definite for each species of animals and plants.[4] All chromosomes exist in cells in pairs. Each chromosome is made up of unitary elements arranged in linear fashion and known as *genes;* and each gene of a chromosome is paired with a gene in the corresponding member of the pair of chromosomes. This correspondence is indicated by naming the members of a pair *homologous* chromosomes. The genes may be re-

---

[4] The chromosomes being clumped and twisted together are very difficult to count accurately. However, it is generally agreed that the following are correct : man 48 chromosomes ; ascaris 4 ; drosophila 8 ; pea 14 ; evening primrose 14 ; wheat 14, 28 and 42 ; guinea pig 16 ; onion 16 ; salamander 24 ; trout 24 ; monkey 54 ; potato beetle 36 ; mouse 40 ; cotton 56 ; corn 20 ; nightshade 72 ; tobacco 48 ; cattle 60 ; sheep 60 ; goat 60 ; horse 60 ; pig 38 and in some types 40.

garded as the elements of heredity. They are minute organic particles about the size of a large organic molecule and are capable of reproduction. Genes have been photographed, mapped, and drawn to scale from direct observation. They were mapped before they were seen, but the drawings and photographs of the genes of the giant chromosomes of the salivary glands of the fruit fly (*drosophila melanogaster*) confirm in every detail the positions of the genes on the chromosomes which were assigned to them in the mapping.[5]

Summing up our present knowledge of the properties of genes we may say:

(1) Genes are minute organic particles of the order of magnitude of a large organic molecule.

(2) Genes possess the essential property of living matter in that they are able to reproduce themselves.

(3) Differentiated organisms have a large number of genes. The best estimate for *drosophila* whose genes are best known, puts this number at 2500. In man, the number must be enormous, but any estimate at this time must be a pure guess.

(4) Every cell of every organism usually contains a full set of genes, and usually in an unchanged condition.

(5) While a cell may live without a full complement of genes, a majority of the genes is essential for the vital functioning of any cell.

The genes, therefore, are the ultimate elements of heredity, although there is some evidence which indicates that they are composed of even smaller units. The chromosomes are groupings of these elemental genes which go into inheritance together. Either the chromosomes or the genes can be regarded as the bearers of heredity.

In Fig. 2, a typical cell division (mitosis) is shown graphically. Just before the cell divides, the chromatin material of the nucleus collects into a slender ribbon which coils about within the nucleus (A). This band becomes thicker and breaks into four approximately equal segments — the four chromosomes. At this stage the nuclear membrane dissolves away (B). The *centrosome* divides into two parts and each part takes its station on opposite sides of the chromo-

⁵ C. B. Bridges, "Salivary Chromosome Maps," *Journal of Heredity*, XXVI, 2 pp. 60-64.

somes which are arranged equatorially with respect to them
(C). The centrosomes and their spindles exert a pull or
attraction of some form which leads to each chromosome
splitting longitudinally down the center. Since each gene

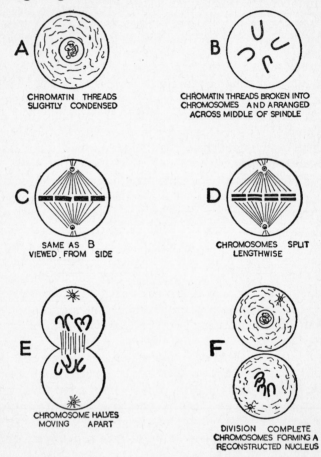

Fig. 2. Cell Division of the Egg of *Ascaris* (a parasitic roundworm).

in the chromosome is split in half we get two chromosomes
with identical contents (D). The two sets of chromosomes
are now drawn apart. The cell begins to divide and one
complete set of chromosomes goes to each of the daughter
cells (E). The division of the cells is next completed by
the growth of a dividing cell wall. The chromosomes then
reverse processes (B) and (A), becoming joined to form the

chromatin coil which finally dissolves and becomes enclosed once more within a nuclear membrane. The centrosome, however, remains outside the nucleus (F). Thus two new cells have arisen from the old one, and each contains the same number of chromosomes as the old one.

It is of interest to inquire whether or not we are dealing with the same sets of chromosomes in successive divisions of the cell. Since the chromosomes lose their identity and disappear for a time in the nucleus of the young cell, nobody can be sure that they remain intact from division to division. The reappearance in similar shape and form leads one to suppose that they retain their identity throughout the cycle. The argument is strengthened when we note that if there is accidental doubling of the chromosomes in a cell at any stage, this double number is continued in successive divisions.

There is no difficulty in understanding that, in the multiplication of cells to form a multi-celled organism, each cell has identical hereditary contents. Each somatic cell of a human being, and there are billions of them, has the same number of chromosomes, namely 48 or 24 pairs. But organisms derived from germ cells add their contents together at the instant of fertilization and therefore the chromosomes are added together. Weismann, as early as 1887, saw this difficulty, and stated that there must be some reduction in the hereditary elements when germ cells are formed, or reproduction by means of sperms and ova would be a physical impossibility. His shrewd observation has since been confirmed. It is now known that in the formation of sperms and ova from the parent germ cells, there is a reduction division, and at the end of this process each sperm or ovum contains exactly half the number of chromosomes of the parent cell. Thus each sperm and ovum of man contains 24 single chromosomes, not 24 pairs.

The process is illustrated schematically in Fig. 3. In the figure, the chromosomes contributed by the male parent are shaded, those of the female parent are left unshaded. The germ cells prior to *maturation* do not differ in any important respect from other (somatic) cells. They multiply as other cells do, and during division suffer no reduction in the number of chromosomes (see *spermatogonia* and *oögonia* in Fig. 3). Just before the final processes take place, these germ cells enlarge enormously, the spermatogonia from twenty to thirty times their original size; the oögonia to hundreds and even thousands of times their former size. These enlarged cells are now called *primary spermatocytes* and *primary oöcytes*. The homologous chromosomes now

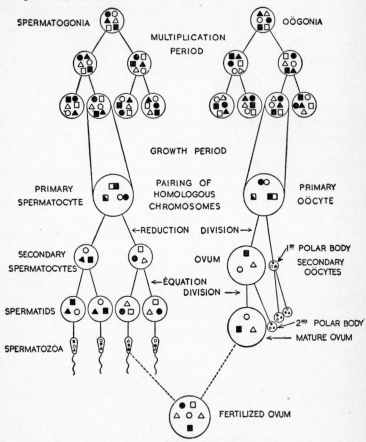

Fig. 3.   Development, Maturation and Fertilization of Gametes
(*Gametogenesis* or *Meiosis*).

come together in pairs and unite, probably mixing their contents, and then draw apart again. The very important *reduction division* now takes place. The two *secondary spermatocytes* which are formed from each primary spermatocyte obtain only one-half the original number of chromosomes (in the diagram, 3 instead of 6). The next step is known as the *equation division*. Each chromosome splits longitudinally as in ordinary cell division and the *spermatids* thus formed contain the reduced number of chromosomes (3). These spermatids elongate, become much smaller, and grow whip-like tails which propel the mature reproductive cells, now called *spermatozoa*, through the fluid in which they swim. The stages through which the oöcytes pass are similar to those of the spermatocytes, except that in their case, only one egg in four matures. The others are lost as polar bodies which are non-functional. The ovum, owing to the fact that it carries large quantities of food material, is enormously greater than the sperm. The union of a sperm with an ovum to produce the fertilized ovum or zygote brings together the full number of chromosomes once more (6 in this case). While there are minor differences in the process of egg and sperm formation among the different organisms, the process is essentially the same, namely, a means of securing that the gametes contain half the number of chromosomes that ordinary cells possess.

The chromosomes pass as units, wholes, from parental cells to daughter cells during the process of division, and from gametes to zygotes during fertilization. This, of necessity, means that the genes of a particular chromosome are linked in inheritance. *Linkage groups*, discovered by experimental breeding, are always found to correspond with the number of chromosome pairs which may be seen under suitable conditions through a microscope. Thus in *drosophila melanogaster* (fruit fly) with four pairs of chromosomes, over 400 mutants have been discovered and these fall into four, and only four, linkage groups. These linkage groups are:

(1) Sex-linked characters — about 150 of these. So called because the mutant characters show certain relations to sex.
(2) Body characters — about 120 of these.
(3) A second group of body characters — about 130 of these.
(4) A small group involving three characters — eyeless, bent wings, shaven or with reduced hairs.

Each of the above groups goes into inheritance together and no mutant character is duplicated.[6] (see pp. 10-14)

[6] T. H. Morgan, *The Theory of the Gene*, 1926.

However, in some cases, the percentages obtained by breeding do not correspond to theoretical expectations. *Crossing over* takes place. There is still linkage, but a great many genes may be involved in a crossing over which is quite orderly in character. What takes place can be seen in Fig. 4. Twisting chromosomes become attached at some point, then

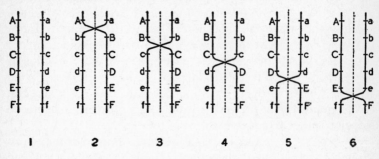

1   2   3   4   5   6

Fig. 4.   Crossing over of Chromosomes.

A separated from F 5 times
A   "   "   E 4   "
A   "   "   D 3   "
A   "   "   C 2   "
A   "   "   B 1 time
B   "   "   C 1   "
B   "   "   D 2 times, etc.

That is, the farther apart, the greater the chance of the genes becoming separated by crossing over. *Note:* Number 4 represents the maximum amount of crossing over, namely 50 per cent.

break, and recombine in such a manner that whole sections are transposed to the opposite member of the homologous pair.

Linkage and crossing over are of enormous importance, for they have made possible the mapping of the genes. Sturtevant, apparently, was the first to suggest that crossing over might lead to this possibility. He assumed (*a*) that the genes were arranged in linear order on the chromosomes, and (*b*) the further apart genes are the greater their chances of crossing over. (See Fig. 4.)   By counting the cross-overs from a given breeding experiment, the relative distance of the genes responsible for the characters may be obtained. The following example, taken from Morgan, illustrates the point:

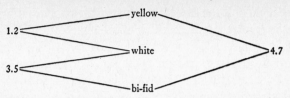

Flies showing yellow wings are crossed with flies showing white eyes. Crossing over occurs in 1.2 per cent of cases. Yellow and white are then placed on a scale 1.2 units apart. Crossing over between white eyes and bi-fid wings is 3.5 per cent. Is the 3.5 per cent in the direction of yellow wings or away from it? To test this, breed yellow wings and bi-fid wings. The cross-overs total 4.7 per cent (not 2.3 per cent), so the genes for bi-fid and yellow wings must be on opposite sides of the gene for white eyes. (see p. 24)

In Figs. 5, 6, 7 and 8 are shown a crossing over which involves 17 per cent of the offspring. The example is taken from an experiment by Morgan. It is found in *drosophila* that grey body and long wings are dominant to black body and vestigial wings, and that members of each pair normally remain in close association during breeding. In the diagrams, b stands for black, v for vestigial, B for grey and V for long.

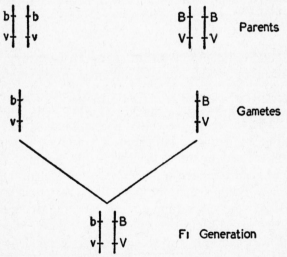

Fig. 5. Results of Crossing Grey Body and Long Wings with Black Body and Vestigial Wings. All F_1 generation have Grey Body and Long Wings.

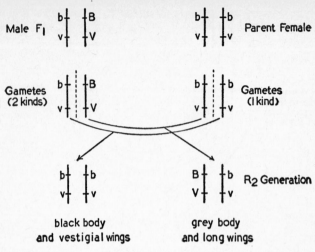

Male F₁

Gametes
(2 kinds)

Parent Female

Gametes
(1 kind)

R₂ Generation

black body
and vestigial wings

grey body
and long wings

Fig. 6. A Back Cross of F₁ with Parent. (If there is no crossing over, then we should expect 50 per cent of offspring to have Black Body and Vestigial Wings and 50 per cent Grey Body with Long Wings. Actually only 41.5 per cent of each kind appear. There has been a crossing over.) See Figs. 7 and 8.

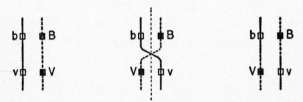

Fig. 7. Crossing over of Factors for Long Wings, (V), and Vestigial Wings, (v).

In this way, the hundreds of genes composing the four linkage groups (chromosomes) of *drosophila* have been plotted. Since the results from breeding support the theory of the linear order of the genes, it is the one now accepted. In the giant salivary chromosomes of *drosophila*, the actual genes can be seen strung on twisted fibrils in a linear order, thus confirming the shrewd guess that they were thus arranged on the chromosomes.

We may sum up the theory of the gene by the following statements:

(1) Chromosomes are made up of connected elements known as genes. Both chromosomes and genes exist in homologous pairs.

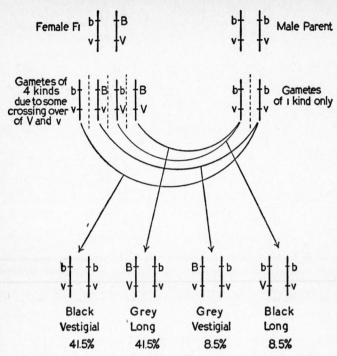

Fig. 8. Results from Back Cross when 17 per cent of
Crossing over occurs.

(2) Germ cells contain one-half the number of chromosomes (and therefore one-half the number of genes) of body cells. Each germ cell, as it were, is a half cell, containing a single set of chromosomes and genes.

(3) Chromosomes — different linkage groups — assort independently. Thus, tall peas may have round or wrinkled seeds. The shape of the ripe peas is independent of the size of the plant.

(4) Chromosomes frequently exhibit the phenomenon of crossing over. This crossing over is not irregular but orderly; and from the percentages of cross-overs, the relative position of the genes of a given linkage group may be determined. This crossing over furnishes evidence of the linear order of genes, confirmation of which has been secured by sight of them under the microscope in the giant chromosomes of the salivary gland of *drosophila*.

(5) All the known data of inheritance secured by experimental breeding fit in with the above propositions.

Mendelism.— Strictly speaking, this topic should have come before the discussion of the gene hypothesis, since Mendel's work was prior to that of Morgan and his school. But it was the work on *drosophila* that supplied a rational and scientific explanation of mendelian phenomena and supports the order of treatment in this volume. If the theory of the gene has been understood, mendelism should present no difficulties.

Mendel's name is now among those of the immortals in science. His scientific output was small, but of excellent quality. He alone of his generation saw clearly that to solve the problem of hybridization it was necessary to reduce the problem to that of a single variable which should be studied intensively. His contemporaries hybridized at large and lost their bearings in a mass of conflicting data secured from general observation. Secondly, he had the scientific acumen to see that the problem could be solved only in quantitative terms and not by general impressions, hence he counted the various forms his hybridization experiments produced.

Johann Gregor Mendel (1822–1884) was born of yeoman stock in Czechoslovakia and died as the Abbot of the Augustinian Monastery of Brünn. Early in his professional life he taught physics and natural history in the Modern School of Brünn. From the first, he was an indefatigable investigator and spent most of his spare time among his bees and flowers. His work on the crossing of peas was commenced in 1856 and in 1865 his results were given to the world in his now famous paper, *Versucheüber Pflanzenhybriden* (Experiments in Plant-Hybridization). His main conclusion, that what is handed on in inheritance is not a general impression of a plant type, but a number of individual characters (hereditary factors, genes) each of which is separately transmitted, and that these individual characters compose the new type, just as the separate stones combine to form a new mosaic pattern — this was a mixture of mathematics and botany which fell on uncomprehending ears. Not until 1900, when De Vries, Correns, and Tschermak each independently rediscovered Mendel's laws, was the value of his researches appreciated. Perhaps, in 1866, when his paper was actually published in the *Proceedings of the Natural History Society of Brünn,* the scientific and religious worlds were too preoccupied with the Darwinian controversy regarding the origin of species to devote much time to the work of an obscure scientist who grew peas in a monastery garden. True, Nägeli, a profound scientist, learned of the researches by correspondence with Mendel, but failed to realize their importance. Reference to the paper was made by Focke in 1881, but the impression seems to have been general that experiments in hybridization, such as Mendel had carried out, led to no definite conclusions.

Mendel was fortunate in the selection of characters that he studied. Peas contain seven pairs of chromosomes. Each pair apparently carries one of the sets of genes which determines one of the seven characters that Mendel selected for study. So his findings were necessarily clear-cut and unambiguous. The seven pairs of contrasted characters which Mendel selected as appropriate for his experiments were as follows:

(1) Roundness and wrinkledness of the ripe seed.
(2) Yellowness or greenness of the cotyledons.
(3) Greyness or whiteness of the seed coat.
(4) Inflation or constriction (between seeds) of the ripe pods.
(5) Greenness or yellowness of unripe pods.
(6) Position of flowers — axial or terminal.
(7) Tallness or dwarfness of the mature plant.

(*Note:* The first named character is *dominant* in each pair; the second one is *recessive*.)

The following may be regarded as a typical mendelian experiment; in fact it is one that Mendel himself made (see above). References are to Fig. 9. If a pea (WW) which has a wrinkled skin when dried is sown and crossed with a pea (RR) which is round when dried, the resultant peas of the first filial generation (F_1) are all round (Rw). Not a single wrinkled pea appears. If, now, these (F_1) peas are sown and self-fertilized, or crossed indiscriminately among themselves, the resultant crop (F_2), if counted, is found to have three times as many round peas as wrinkled ones. The wrinkled peas of this generation are homozygous or pure, that is, on sowing and self-fertilizing they produce none but wrinkled peas. But the round peas are of two kinds. One-third of them, or 25 per cent of the (F_2) crop, are homo-

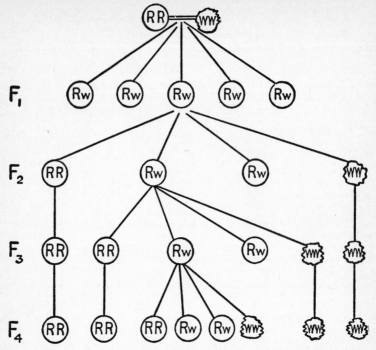

Fig. 9. Diagrammatic Representation of a Typical Mendelian Experiment with Round and Wrinkled Peas. "Roundness" is dominant and "Wrinkledness" is recessive.

zygous and breed true with respect to roundness. The other two-thirds, or 50 per cent of the (F_2) crop, are heterozygous and behave exactly as the (F_1) crop did; they produce round and wrinkled peas in the proportion of 3 to 1. Of this (F_3) crop, one-third of the round peas and the whole of the wrinkled peas are "pure"; two-thirds of the round are "impure" as before. And as long as the experiment is continued, the same kind of results is obtained.

Mendel's actual figures are shown in Table II.

In Fig. 10 is shown, in the light of our knowledge of the behavior of chromosomes and genes, how the 1, 2, 1 ratio is obtained.

Mendel carried his researches further and included experiments in which two and sometimes three contrasting pairs of characters were borne by the same plants. He thus got his famous 9, 3, 3, 1 and 27, 9, 9, 9, 3, 3, 3, 1 ratios. The

Differentiating Pairs of Characters (First Named is Dominant)	Total Specimens Raised		Number of		Ratio of Dominants to Recessives	Ratio Determined From a Count of
	Plants	Seeds	Dominants	Recessives		
1. Roundness and wrinkledness	253	7324	5474	1850	2.96:1	Seeds
2. Yellow & green cotyledons	285	8023	6022	2001	3.01:1	Seeds
3. Grey and white seed coat	929	——	705	224	3.15:1	Plants
4. Inflated and constricted pod	1181	——	882	299	2.95:1	Plants
5. Green and yellow unripe pods	580	——	428	152	2.82:1	Plants
6. Axial and terminal flowers	858	——	651	207	3.14:1	Plants
7. Tallness and dwarfness	1064	——	787	277	2.84:1	Plants

9, 3, 3, 1 ratio is shown diagrammatically in Fig. 11. In this figure, which shows the results of crossing a tall-round with a dwarf-wrinkled parent and breeding from the hybrid, we find that 9 will be tall and round, 3 will be tall and wrinkled, 3 will be dwarf and round, and 1 will be dwarf and wrinkled. Further, only 1, 6, 11 and 16 will breed true; the other twelve would split into various types on further breeding.

A useful exercise for the reader would be to construct a diagram showing the 27, 9, 9, 9, 3, 3, 3, 1 tri-hybrid ratio. If to the tall-round and dwarf-wrinkled parents dealt with above we add a third pair of unit characters, say yellow and green, the tri-hybrid ratio would be observed in the F₂ generation. It would consist of 27 tall round yellow, 9 tall round green, 9 tall wrinkled yellow, 9 dwarf round yellow, 3 tall wrinkled green, 3 dwarf round green, 3 dwarf wrinkled yellow, 1 dwarf wrinkled green.

From his experiments, Mendel was able to state his two laws of inheritance. A third one regarding dominance, which his contrasting characters in peas exhibited so beautifully, is now considered of minor importance. The two laws may be stated as follows:

1. *Segregation or purity of the gametes.* The reproductive cell can contain only one of two alternative characters; or the factors for two alternative characters (*allelomorphs*) are always separated from one another when gametes are formed, so that only one of them appears in any gamete.

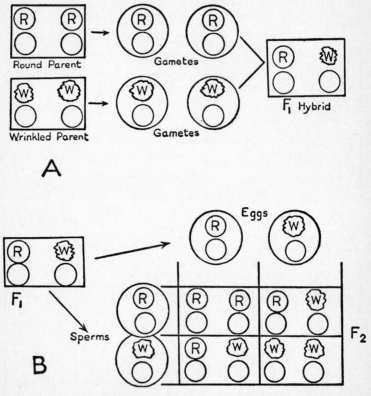

Fig. 10, A. and B.   Diagram A, illustrating the Behavior of Chromosomes in Mendel's Cross of Round and Wrinkled Peas. (Rectangles represent nuclei of zygotes; large circles, gametes; small circles, chromosomes.) Diagram B, illustrating the Behavior of F_1 Generation when Inbred. (Note the 3:1 *phenotype* ratio and the 1:2:1 *genotype* ratio.)

The gamete, for example, can contain the character for roundness or wrinkledness, but not both. If two gametes, each containing the factor for wrinkledness unite to form a zygote, the resultant pea will be wrinkled; if each contains the factor for roundness, the pea will be round; if one contains the factor for roundness and the other the factor for wrinkledness, the pea will be round, owing to the dominance of the factor for roundness (see Figs. 10 and 11).

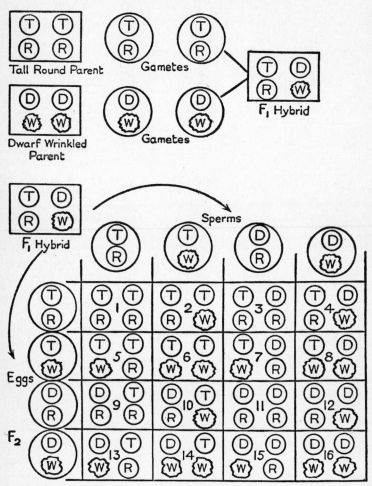

Fig. 11. Diagram exhibiting the Di-hybrid Ratio 9, 3, 3, 1 in the F_2 Generation.

2. *Independent assortment of unit characters or allelomorphic factors.* The behavior of the factors for any one pair of characters is without effect on the distribution of the members of any other pair; the factors undergo random assortment. Thus, in peas, roundness and wrinkledness are

independent of the nature of the plant as a whole. The plant, for example, may be tall or dwarf, but the roundness or wrinkledness of the ripe peas is unaffected by the size of the plant. In other words, roundness and wrinkledness, tallness and dwarfness are factors which assort themselves independently in inheritance.

Mendel recognized that dominance may be incomplete (as in the cross of a red flowered and white flowered four o'clock, *Mirabilis Jalapa*, which is pink), but never encountered it. Every one of his seven contrasting pairs of characters exhibited dominance and recessiveness in marked fashion and, therefore, he tended to over-emphasize them. But they are far from being as universal a phenomenon as Mendel supposed.

After the re-discovery of Mendel's laws in 1900, mendelism dominated biology. Thousands of experiments were made on plants and many additional mendelian characters were discovered. The next step forward was to extend the experiments to quick-breeding animals, such as rats, mice, guinea pigs, and rabbits. The inheritance of characters in cattle, pigs, poultry was also noted or experimented with. This led to the discovery of such well-known and sometimes useful mendelian characters as are shown in Table III.

The next natural step to take was to observe man himself, since it is scarcely *convenable* to submit him to breeding experiments. And one of the first characters observed and treated statistically was the inheritance of eye-color in man. It was soon seen that the pigmented iris is dominant over the unpigmented one (blue and grey). If the usual procedure of allowing capital letters to stand for the dominant character (in this case Pigmentation) and small letters for the recessive be followed, then the six possibilities in regard to inheritance of eye-color are shown schematically below:

	Parents	*Offspring*	
(1)	PP × PP	4PP	(all pigmented)
(2)	PP × pp	4Pp	(all pigmented)
(3)	PP × Pp	2PP + 2Pp	(all pigmented)
(4)	Pp × Pp	PP + 2Pp + pp	(¾ pigmented)
(5)	Pp × pp	2Pp + 2pp	(½ pigmented)
(6)	pp × pp	4pp	(none pigmented)

TABLE III. A LIST OF WELL-KNOWN MENDELIAN CHARACTERS
IN PLANTS AND ANIMALS

Plant or Animal	Dominant Character	Recessive Character
Wheat and Barley	Beardless ; non-immune to rust	Bearded ; immune to rust
Maize	"Starch" seed	"Sugar" seed
Mice	Colored coat	Albino coat
	Normal mouse	Dancing mouse
Rabbits	Short fur	Angora fur
Cattle	Hornlessness	Horns
Poultry	Brown eggs ; broodiness	White eggs ; non-broodiness
Guinea pigs	Black coat ; short fur	Albino coat ; angora fur
Fruit fly	Pink eye ; several scores of other characters	White eye ; several scores of other characters
Peas	Tallness ;	Dwarfness ;
	Roundness ;	Wrinkledness ;
	Yellow cotyledons ;	Green cotyledons ;
	Grey seed coat ;	White seed coat ;
	Inflated pods ;	Constricted pods ;
	Green unripe pods ;	Yellow unripe pods ;
	Axial flowers	Terminal flowers
Wood snail	Bandless shell	Banded shell

It will be seen that children of blue-eyed parents are bound
to have blue eyes (6), and that it is possible for a blue-eyed
child to be born of brown-eyed parents (4).

Other mendelian characters in man are the following:

Albinism — a recessive.
Brachydactyly (stub fingers) — a dominant.
White blaze of hair (piebaldism) — a dominant.
Huntington's chorea — a dominant.
Haemophilia (bleeding) — a sex-linked character.
Red-green color-blindness — a sex-linked character.
One form of night-blindness (inability to see in twilight) — a sex-
linked character.

Of more doubtful authenticity are — hair color, notorious
family characteristics such as the Hapsburg lip, woolly hair

like the negro's, cataract, aniridia, enlarged spleen, shape of nose, shape of head, polydactylism, deafmutism, feeblemindedness, musical ability, artistic ability in writing and painting, some forms of insanity, nomadism, hare lip, cleft palate, myopia, gout, tendency to produce twins, types of blood, and scores of other traits mostly of a pathological nature. If they are inherited, the gene pattern must frequently be very complex and has certainly not been determined.[7]

Color-blindness, which is of interest not only to the teacher but to society at large, is a sex-linked character. What is meant by a sex-linked character? In man we have seen that the somatic cells contain 48 chromosomes (24 pairs) and the germ cells 24. Of the 24 pairs, 23 are perfectly homologous, but the 24th pair differs in male and female. The female cells contain two X chromosomes; the male cells one X chromosome and one Y chromosome. This Y chromosome is considerably smaller than the X chromosome, somewhat of a runt in fact, and it is obvious that the genes of the X chromosomes cannot be matched by those of the Y. Any defect in the non-matched part of the X chromosome will show in the male. Such a defect is color-blindness. If we represent the female by 23X and the male by 23X, thereby meaning that
23X   23Y
in the female there are 23 pairs *plus* one pair of X chromosomes, and that in the male there are 23 pairs plus one X chromosome and one Y chromosome, and if, further, we represent an X chromosome which is defective for reds and greens by ⊠, we can draw up a table of possible inheritances of color-blindness. They are as follows:

(1)	23 X	+	23 ⊠......	23 ⊠	+	23 ⊠	+	23 X	+	23 X
	23 X		23 Y	23 X		23 X		23 Y		23 Y
	female		male	female		female		male		male
	normal		color-blind	bearer		bearer		normal		normal

(2)	23 ⊠	+	23 X......	23 ⊠	+	23 X	+	23 ⊠	+	23 X
	23 X		23 Y	23 X		23 X		23 Y		23 Y
	female		male	female		female		male		male
	bearer		normal	bearer		normal		color-blind		normal

[7] See files of the *Journal of Heredity*.

(3) 23 ☒ + 23 ☒...... 23 ☒ + 23 ☒ + 23 ☒ + 23 X
  23 X 23 Y   23 ☒ 23 X 23 Y : 23 Y
  female male female female male male
  bearer color-blind color-blind bearer color-blind normal

(4) 23 ☒ + 23 X...... 23 ☒ + 23 ☒ + 23 ☒ + 23 ☒
  23 ☒ 23 Y   23 X 23 X 23 Y 23 Y
  female male female female male male
 color-blind normal bearer bearer color-blind color-blind

(5) 23 ☒ + 23 ☒...... 23 ☒ + 23 ☒ + 23 ☒ + 23 ☒
  23 ☒ 23 Y   23 ☒ 23 ☒ 23 Y 23 Y
  female male female female male male
 color-blind color-blind color-blind color-blind color-blind color-blind

In a sense, it requires two doses of color-blindness (2 X's to be affected) to produce color-blindness in a female, while one dose (one X affected) is sufficient to cause color-blindness in a male. Consequently, color-blindness is found in males about ten times as frequently as in females, the percentages of serious defect being about 4 per cent and 0.4 per cent respectively. However, later investigations place the percentage of color-blindness in males at about 9 per cent. Haemophilia is inherited in a similar fashion — female bearers pass it on to one-half their sons. It should, however, be noted that recent researches on color-blindness show that the situation is more complex than the above explanation indicates.

Thus we see that mendelian phenomena are easily explained on the gene or factorial hypothesis and the tendency today is for mendelism to sink into the background. The gene theory explains fully why there is such a variety in human nature, and why two individuals are never exactly alike. When it is remembered, (1) that there are 24 chromosomes present in each human sperm and ovum, and that by combination these will give rise to more than a million possible kinds of germ-cells in the (F_1) generation; (2) that the number of combinations which two such sets of germ-cells may produce through fertilization is enormously greater; and (3) that each chromosome is made up of a large, though unknown number of genes, we begin to understand why two identical human beings are unknown; and why variations are distributed according to the law of chance.

Variation in Human Beings.— Heredity, as we have seen, is a great stabilizing factor; it results not only in the continuation of species, but also in the continuation of family characteristics. Everyone is familiar with the saying that "like tends to beget like," and everyone should also be familiar with the truism that the likenesses between offspring and parent are never perfect. There are always *variations*. Technically speaking, a variation is a filial departure from the parental type which is founded on a germinal change. The important part of the definition is that which insists on the germinal change. Variations are due to changes in genes and are therefore heritable. They can be passed on from one generation to another. Modifications, or acquired characters, unlike true variations, are non-heritable. They are impressed upon the organism from without, while variations are expressed from within. Modifications are changes in the structure acquired in the lifetime of the individual as a direct result of environment — chiefly injury, training and use. In this sense education is an acquired character, and is not directly passed on to the next generation. What is passed on is the potentiality which enables the next generation to receive on the average an education approximately equivalent to that which the parent received.

The causes of variations are to be sought in differences in gene structure. In experimental breeding, as in Morgan's work with *drosophila,* the gene changes which produce heritable variations have been traced. Some variants, especially in plants, are produced by the addition or subtraction of chromosomes; some by changes in the genes themselves. Many of the new types prove to be vigorous and able to perpetuate themselves in any normal environment. Other types are not fitted to survive. Selective elimination in the Darwinian sense occurs on a vast scale in nature, on a scale of vastness hitherto unsuspected.

Variations may be classified in many ways. Three classifications that are frequently met with are:

(1) *Meristic* and *Substantive.* Meristic variations have to

do with changes from the average in the number of parts. Polydactylism in man is a meristic variation. Substantive variations are concerned with the structure or size of an organism or parts thereof. Height, weight and eye-color in man are substantive variations.

(2) *Phenotypic* and *Genotypic*. This is the usual biological classification. Phenotypic variations are really modifications or acquired characters and are non-heritable. The enlarged muscles of the oarsman or blacksmith are phenotypic variations. Similarly, a heterozygous round pea (with hidden recessive wrinkledness) and a homozygous round pea are phenotypically alike; they cannot be distinguished by their shapes. Genotypic variations are true variations in the light of our definition. Heterozygous and homozygous round peas, while phenotypically alike, are genotypically different, as can be shown by breeding them. The genotypic variations are caused by contributions either from the sperm or the ovum.

(3) *Continuous* and *Discontinuous*. Discontinuous variations are usually called mutations. Height, weight, skin color, etc., in man are usually continuous variations. Mutations arise suddenly and are heritable, often becoming the starting point of new strains or species. Without variation there could be no evolution. Darwin thought a minute variation might possess survival value and become the dominant racial type or species. He was wrong in thinking that phenotypic variations could produce new types. We now know that the variations must be germinal in character, must be of the genotypic kind, if they are to possess value for evolution.

Variations are of great interest to the educator. Practically every measurement he makes on children, whether it be of height, weight, intelligence or morality, is a variable one. These variable measures, he soon discovers, tend to obey laws. Thus he finds that if he measures a large number of unselected, homogeneous individuals for a given trait, his measures are seen to be distributed according to the *curve of chance* or *probability curve*. The probability curve plays such an important part in educational psychology that it should be discussed further.

First, as to the nature of the curve of chance or probability curve. If ten coins are tossed 1024 times, and the numbers of heads which turn up counted, a record closely approximating Table IV will result.

TABLE IV. THE THEORETICAL FREQUENCY OF HEADS THAT WILL TURN UP WHEN 10 COINS ARE TOSSED 1024 TIMES

No. of Heads	Frequency of Occurrence
0	1
1	10
2	45
3	120
4	210
5	252
6	210
7	120
8	45
9	10
10	1
	Total 1024

The most frequent number of heads is 5; while 4 and 6, 3 and 7, 2 and 8, 1 and 9, 0 and 10 appear with equal but decreasing frequency as we pass from the middle to the ends of the table. If now we plot a curve by placing the number of heads on one axis (x axis) and frequency of occurrence on the other axis (y axis), we get a curve, Fig. 12, which if smoothed would resemble a bell in shape. If 100 coins had been tossed 100,000 times, the likeness to a bell would have been closer. Since the number of heads that turn up is obviously the result of chance, the curve so obtained is known as the curve of chance or probability curve. The area or surface the curve of chance encloses is known as the *normal surface of frequency*, since it represents an area that normally appears when chance alone determines it.[8]

That variable traits, such as height of adult men in any

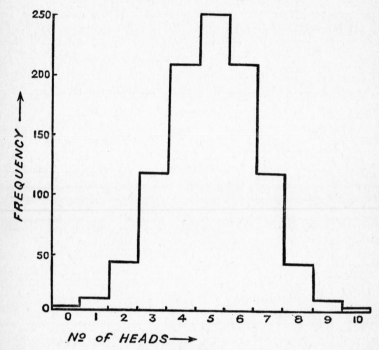

Fig. 12. Curve showing the Theoretical Frequency of Heads turning up when 10 coins are tossed 1024 times.

race, approximate a distribution closely resembling that obtained from tossing coins can be shown from any comprehensive series of records. Common observation shows that men

[8] For those who are mathematically inclined, it might be stated that the formula for the probability curve is

$$\gamma = \gamma_0 e^{\frac{-x^2}{2\sigma^2}}$$

where e is the base of naperian logarithms whose value is 2.7182818 and γ_0 is the maximum ordinate of the normal probability curve, and may be obtained from the formula

$$\gamma_0 = \frac{N}{\sigma\sqrt{2\pi}} = \frac{N}{2.5066\sigma}$$

cluster around the average in height, extremely tall or short men being comparatively rare. The figures of Table V, taken from the Anthropometric Committee of the British Association (p. 256), show this quite plainly.

TABLE V. THE STATURE OF 8585 ADULT MALES (AGE FROM 23 TO 50) OF THE POPULATION OF THE UNITED KINGDOM, ARRANGED ACCORDING TO PLACE OF BIRTH

Height Without Shoes		Number of Men within Said Limits of Height Place of Birth				Total
Inches	Metres	England	Scotland	Wales	Ireland	
57	1.448	1	—	1	—	2
58	1.474	3	1	—	—	4
59	1.499	12	—	1	1	14
60	1.525	39	2	—	—	41
61	1.550	70	2	9	2	83
62	1.575	128	9	30	2	169
63	1.601	320	19	48	7	394
64	1.625	524	47	83	15	669
65	1.653	740	109	108	33	990
66	1.677	881	139	145	58	1223
67	1.702	918	210	128	73	1329
68	1.728	886	210	72	62	1230
69	1.754	753	218	52	40	1063
70	1.779	473	115	33	25	646
71	1.804	254	102	21	15	392
72	1.830	117	69	6	10	202
73	1.855	48	26	2	3	79
74	1.881	16	15	1	—	32
75	1.906	9	6	1	—	16
76	1.931	1	4	—	—	5
77	1.957	1	1	—	—	2
Total........		6194	1304	741	346	8585

In Fig. 13, is shown the distribution curve of the measurements given in Table V. This form of diagram is called a *frequency polygon*. That of Fig. 12 is known as a *histogram* or *column diagram*. Both curves really tell the same story. A perfect or theoretical normal surface of frequency is shown for comparison in Fig. 14.

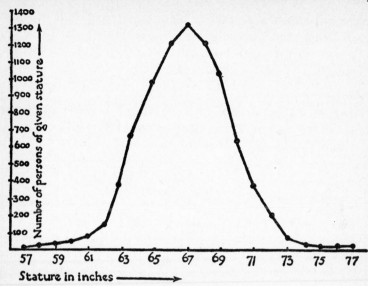

Fig. 13. Distribution Curve for the Stature of 8585 Adult Males in the United Kingdom.

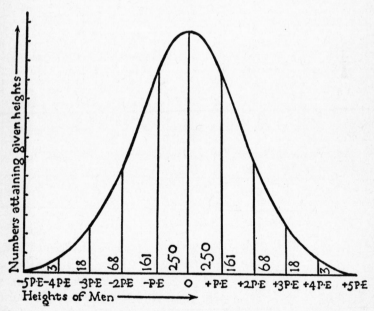

Fig. 14. A Normal Surface of Frequency. The Theoretical Distribution of 1000 Cases is shown.

Every known variable trait (speed in addition, ability to memorize, general intelligence, general morality, speed in typewriting, ability in handwriting, size of leaves, length of tentacles) whether of human beings, animals, or plants, tends to be distributed among unselected members of any homogeneous group according to the curve of chance. So constantly is this condition found that if a trait, measured over a sufficiently large number of individuals gives a skew distribution, we instantly begin to inquire the cause of it. Most frequently, in educational measures, we find that selection has been at work; that the sample we have taken is not a fair representation of the total population. Sometimes the skew distribution is the true one. Thus weights of adult men are skewed to the right; the curve of distribution is pulled out towards the right because in any sample of adult men cases of excessively fat ones will be found.

The study of the simultaneous variation of two or more variates is assuming great importance in educational psychology. This is known as *correlation*, and is due principally to the labors of Galton and Pearson. It is well known, for instance, that height tends to vary with weight; that the taller person tends to be the heavier. But the relation is never perfect, or we should find the tallest individual always the heaviest. The measure used to express this relation, this concomitant variation, is known as the *coefficient of correlation*. It is used so extensively in psychological and educational research that much of the literature remains a closed book to those who do not know its meaning and significance.

The discovery of variability in educational and biological measurements has marked a great step forward in educational psychology. Formerly, educators were apt to talk about "types" and the "average man." Though we hear less about visiles, audiles and tactiles than we used to do, there is still a great deal of nonsense talked about personality types. The fact of the matter is that there is no type in nature unless mediocrity is regarded as a type, and the "average man" is a mere fiction of statistics. Instead of thinking of a pupil as belonging to any exclusive type, we now try to deal systematically with his special combination of capacities, achievements and personality traits, and, in this way, try to secure for him an educational treatment that will develop his socially approved powers to the highest possible point. Similarly, we no longer regard instincts, habits and behavior patterns as immutably fixed, but as changing and varying their forms from day to day. In other words, the concept of development implies the concept of variability. Even our handwriting varies and if we signed our cheques without any variation in signature, the banker would be rightfully suspicious of forgery.

This does not mean, of course, that group education is impossible. The curve of chance shows us that in regard to any specific trait, most pupils cluster fairly closely around the average. The middle two-thirds can be given group teaching in most subjects without doing them any serious injustice. It is the upper and lower sixths of our distributions that cause the trouble, but the recognition of these greater variations has led to search for educational practices which will deal with them fairly. The older education stressed uniformity; the newer is running to seed trying to deal with every single variation in a pupil, whether it is important or not. The older education was stereotyped; the newer education has over-emphasized the individual at the expense of the social group to which he belongs.

Finally, we may note that it can be shown experimentally that variability in educational achievement would be increased if the opportunities now available for a small, favored section of the population were extended to everybody; and, *vice versa*, by forcing the small, well-endowed group to accept the mental pabulum provided for the masses we should decrease the variability in educational achievement.[9] If, therefore, marked variability rather than uniformity in educational attainment is a desirable thing for any community, the conclusion that we should provide the members with the highest possible form of education, is inescapable. A truly democratic education would eliminate as far as possible environmental differences in education, and fix the general level as high as possible.

Studies of Heredity and Environment.— If, as we have maintained, heredity and environment are correlative or interdependent factors, studies which attempt to evaluate the

[9] L. Hogben, *Nature and Nurture*, 1933.

relative contributions of these factors must be exceedingly difficult to make. And such has proved to be the case. Even in studies of identical twins, there is room for discussion as to how much of the resemblances that are found is due to the fact that twins live in a very similar environment; and whether or not the differences found among children reared in orphan homes are to be attributed to the differences of environment that are inevitable even in such surroundings. Yet all the studies so far made point in one direction — to heredity as being of very great if not of supreme importance. Environment, however, contributes positively, and he would be a bold person indeed who would set a limit to the immediate changes which might be brought about by regulating the environment, especially education.

The studies under consideration might usefully be classed under seven heads:

(1) Studies of family histories — noted and notorious.
(2) Studies of the factors, both hereditary and environmental, but chiefly environmental, which seem to contribute to the eminence of groups of various kinds, such as men of science, literary men, eminent women and clever pupils.
(3) Studies of foster children.
(4) Studies of children living in a similar environment, such as orphans and canal-boat children.
(5) Studies of related groups of people, such as twins, siblings and others.
(6) Studies of the inheritance of special traits in man, mendelian or otherwise (discussed earlier in the chapter).
(7) Studies of the children produced by the marriages of first cousins, and of marriages of persons even more closely related. So far as the author is aware, no studies of children from cousin-marriages have been done. The studies so far made of the pharaohs of Egypt and of the rulers of the Incas are inadequate.

(1) *Family histories.* Only those families which can be easily traced through adequate documentation and are therefore noted in some way or other, and those which have been studied by doctors, psychologists and sociologists because of their degeneracy or infamy, fall into this class. The information they give regarding heredity or environment is very

unreliable, and, in general, the task of separating the contributions of heredity from those of environment has proved insuperable. The pedigree of the Wedgwood-Darwin-Galton family, worked out by Karl Pearson and published in a series of plates supplementary to Vol. I of his monumental work entitled *Life, Letters and Labour of Francis Galton,* traces the ancestral ramifications of a very famous family. I have re-drawn part of the family tree to show the inheritance of scientific ability (see Fig. 15). The remarkable feature of the chart is that it shows five Darwins in direct line of descent who have been elected Fellows of the Royal Society. While environmental opportunity has undoubtedly played a great part in securing this remarkable result, it is nevertheless unlikely that if any unselected individuals had enjoyed the Darwin family atmosphere and training, they would have been equally eminent. The Darwins, Galtons and Wedgwoods were able stock and undoubtedly this excellence contributed to the scientific eminence the family enjoyed.

F. A. Woods[10] studied the royal families of Europe. This study was selected because there is usually a mass of fairly reliable data about such people. They enjoy a favorable environment, in which each member has the advantage of great care and attention, and usually of a good education and training. If environment is the more powerful factor, then the heir to a throne should show superiority over his brothers and sisters, since his training is generally conducted with greater care. Further, the members of a given family reared in different countries should show differences due to inequalities of environmental influence. If, on the other hand, heredity is the more potent, then heirs to thrones should show no marked superiority over their relatives; and family ability should show itself no matter where the family lived.

Woods found 671 members of royal families from the sixteenth century (eleventh for the Spanish Royal Family) to the present time, who could be used in his study. About each of these he read the easily available biographical material and then rated them on a scale of ten for intellect (671 cases) and for morality (608 cases). On the scale for intellect, 1 represented feeblemindedness; 10, such intellectual power

---

[10] F. A. Woods, *Mental and Moral Heredity in Royalty,* 1906.

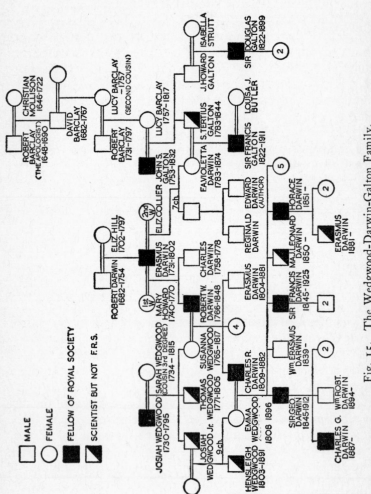

Fig. 15.   The Wedgwood-Darwin-Galton Family.

as was shown by William the Silent, Frederick the Great and Gustavus Adolphus. He tried to make the step intervals equal, and following the law of chance, clustered his ratings around the central tendency. The ratings for morality were similarly made. It is obvious that these ratings, being subjective, are open to error. To forestall this criticism, Woods printed his detailed ratings. If the reader disagrees with them, he can make his own and see if he comes to other conclusions. Nobody has suggested that Woods' ratings are biased, although it is very probable that they are subject to a family aura effect. This would tend to make the resemblances too high. On the other hand, chance inaccuracies would tend to make them too low.

Let us now try to answer our questions. With respect to primogeniture and superiority of intellect, the following are the results:

Grades of intellect➡→	1	2	3	4	5	6	7	8	9	10
Total number in each grade	7	21	41	49	71	70	68	43	18	7
Successive inheritors	5	14	26	31	49	38	45	23	8	4
Per cent	71	67	63	64	69	54	67	54	67	57

The heirs to thrones are not concentrated in the upper grades, hence their superior training has not contributed unduly to the raising of their intelligence. The younger sons made neither a poorer nor a better showing. These findings support the hereditarian argument.

Secondly, the able people, groups 9 and 10, are not distributed at random among the whole group but tend to be clustered in certain families, chief of which are those of Frederick the Great of Prussia, Gustavus Adolphus of Sweden, Isabella of Spain, and William the Silent of Holland. It matters not where the members of these families are domiciled; they tend to exhibit great ability. And similarly for mediocre and inferior intellects. The families of the houses of Hanover, Saxe-Coburg-Gotha, Reuss, Denmark, Saxony, Savoy and Orleans are essentially mediocre; those of Russia and Spain exhibit weaknesses that approach degeneracy. Again, the facts support the hereditarian interpretation.   Additional support to this explanation is given by the following correlations:

In intellect: r
    Offspring and fathers.. .30
    Offspring and grandfathers.. .16
    Offspring and great-grandfathers........................... .15

In morals:
    Offspring and fathers.. .30
    Offspring and grandfathers.. .175

With respect to morality, Woods is inclined to attribute greater potency to environment than he is in the case of intellect.   Some of his statements, however, are contradictory. He found that his ratings for intellect and morality correlated positively (.34 ± .04) and this is both interesting and comforting.

His final conclusion is, "The upshot of it all is, that as regards intellectual life, environment is a totally inadequate explanation.   If it explains certain characters in certain instances, it always fails to explain as many more; while heredity not only explains all (or at least 90 per cent) of the intellectual side of character in practically every instance, but does so best when questions of environment are left out of the discussion.   Therefore, it would seem that we are forced to the conclusion that all these rough differences in intellectual activity which are susceptible of grading on a scale of ten are due to predetermined differences in the primary germ-cells." (p. 286)

R. L. Dugdale, a prison commissioner of New York State, in making his rounds of the prisons, was struck by the frequency of a particular family name on the rolls.   He decided to investigate this family and found that the members were all descendants of a single degenerate and nomadic hunter of the northern part of the state who was born sometime between 1720 and 1740.   It took him three years to trace the various members of this family, and the families into which they married.   Calling them all by the fictitious name of Jukes,[11] he gave to the world the first of a long line of studies of notorious families.

[11] R. L. Dugdale, *The Jukes*, 1877.

The founder of the family was Max Jukes, a shiftless hunter and fisher. Two of his sons married two sisters of a very degenerate family consisting of six sisters. The study traces the descendants of these two marriages, together with those of three other sisters — Ada, who was, however, known to the community among whom she lived as "Margaret, the mother of criminals," Bell, a viciously immoral woman, and Clara, who married a licentious person who was known to have shot a man.

This study, carefully made, soon became a classic of its kind. After Dugdale's death, the original records, which fortunately had not been destroyed, fell into the hands of Dr. A. H. Estabrook in 1911. Learning the real name of the family, Estabrook was able to trace its history from 1877 onwards. He worked on the problem between 1912 and 1915, visiting as many members of the family as could then be discovered. He found them scattered over fourteen states of the United States. *The Jukes in 1915* is the fruit of Estabrook's investigation.

Summarizing the findings of both studies, his own and Dugdale's, Estabrook writes as follows:

"Dugdale studied 709 persons, 540 being of Juke blood and 169 of 'X' blood who married into the Juke family. He estimated that the Juke family would consist of 1200 persons, were it possible to have traced all the lines of descent from the original six sisters. Of the 709 whom he studied, 180 had either been in the poorhouse or received outdoor relief to the extent of 800 years (an average of 4½ years each). There had been 140 criminals and offenders, 60 habitual thieves, 7 lives sacrificed by murder, 50 common prostitutes, 50 women venereally diseased contaminating 440 persons, and 30 prosecutions in bastardy. The total cost to the state of New York of this one group of mental and social degenerates was estimated, for a period of 75 years beginning in 1800, at $1,308,000.

"In the present investigation, 2820 people have been studied, inclusive of all considered by Dugdale; 2094 were of Juke blood and 726 of 'X' blood who married into the Juke family; of these 366 were paupers, while 171 were criminals; and 10 lives have been sacrificed by murder. In school work 62 did well, 288 fairly well, while 458 were retarded two or more years. It is known that 166 never attended school; the school data for the rest of the family were unobtainable. There were 282 intemperate and 277 harlots.

The total cost to the state has been estimated at $2,093,685." (pp. 1-2)[12]

The spreading of the Jukes from their original habitat, forced on them by the closing of the cement works which gave many of them employment, has tended to improve their status. Is this improvement due to heredity, or to environment, or both? The facts can be interpreted in all three ways. The best answer, in the light of the facts, seems to be as follows. The Jukes of admittedly bad stock were undoubtedly improved when they moved to a better environment. This rise in the social scale enabled them to marry into better families. The blood of these better families, in turn, contributed to the betterment of the Juke stock and in a more permanent way than education and environment were able to contribute. Dissemination has improved the Juke stock, but at a terrible expense to the communities into which they have migrated. The fact that so many of the 1258 descendants living in 1915 found it impossible to adjust themselves socially to the new environments weakens the claim that environment working alone can improve the stock; the responses of an individual are also dependent upon his constitution. As Davenport[13] pertinently remarks, "Environment affords the stimulus; heredity determines largely the nature of the reacting substance; the reaction, or behavior, is the resultant or product of the two."

Similar studies of the Nams, Zeros, Dacks, Ishmaels, Sixties, Hickories, Hill Folk, Piney Folk, and the rest, show that the bulk of the trouble lies in the fact that "like tends to beget like." All of these families showed hereditary mental defect.

Two other studies of families, one very famous, the other notorious, should be noted. They have one feature in common, namely, that a distant paternal ancestor left two lines of descendants by different mothers, one in each case being very able. While the differences between the two lines cannot wholly be ascribed to heredity, one cannot help thinking that the germ plasm of the able maternal ancestor had a deal

---

[12] A. H. Estabrook, *The Jukes in 1915*, 1916.
[13] C. B. Davenport, in preface to Estabrook's *The Jukes in 1915*.

to do with it. The two studies are by *Goddard*[14] and *Winship*.[15]

The common ancestor in the *Kallikak* family was Martin Kallikak (name fictitious), a young soldier of the Revolutionary War. During the campaign, Martin had an illegitimate son by a nameless, feebleminded girl, from whom 480 individuals have descended in direct line. This line has never been an asset to the world. On the contrary, 143 of these descendants are known to have been feebleminded, and only 46 have been found normal. The rest are unknown or doubtful. Thirty-six have been illegitimate, 33 sexually immoral, 24 confirmed alcoholics, 3 epileptics, 3 criminals, 8 keepers of houses of ill-fame, and 83 children so feeble that they died in infancy.

After the war, Martin settled down and married a woman of good stock, and from the union 496 descendants have been traced. All of these, except two, were of normal or supernormal mentality and morality, holding positions as lawyers, doctors, teachers, traders, governors, professors and presidents of colleges and universities. This line of children apparently could not turn out badly in any environment; nobody ever had to build an asylum or prison to accommodate them. The other line, bearing the same name and living on the same soil, apparently could not turn out well; they were a perennial charge on the community in which they lived. After examining the evidence, Dr. Goddard concludes: "The fact that the descendants of both the normal and the feebleminded mothers have been studied and traced in every conceivable environment, and that the respective strains have been true to type, tends to confirm the belief that heredity has been the determining factor in the formation of their respective characters."

The sceptic may ask — how did Dr. Goddard's field workers determine the mentality of obscure people who lived a hundred and more years ago? What would have been the histories of the families had the children in the respective lines been able to exchange home environments? We know from other studies that it is likely that the degenerate family

[14] H. H. Goddard, *The Kallikak Family*, 1914.
[15] A. E. Winship, *Jukes-Edwards; a Study in Education and Heredity*, 1900.

would have improved in a better environment, and the excellent family would have degenerated in a poorer environment, but we do not know to what extent we create our own environments.   And that is the important consideration.

Dr. Winship, in his study of the Edwards, adduces a similar line of evidence.   Elizabeth Tuttle (or Tuthill), a New England woman of great beauty and wonderful intellect, but of unstable morals, married, in 1667, Richard Edwards, an erudite lawyer of Hartford, Connecticut, and bore him a son, Timothy Edwards (the father of Jonathan Edwards) and four daughters.   In 1691, Richard Edwards was divorced from his wife on the grounds of her adultery and other immoralities.   He subsequently married Mary Talcott, average in intellect and ordinary in appearance.   There were three sons and two daughters of this second marriage.   None of Mary Talcott's descendants rose above mediocrity or established an abiding reputation.   But the descendants of the first marriage — all of whom carried the reproductive plasm of Elizabeth Tuttle — present a wonderful array of eminent men and women.   Besides Timothy Edwards, a pastor of great learning, and his son Jonathan, one of the world's greatest intellects, pre-eminent as a theologian and president of Princeton University, there are among them Jonathan Edwards, Jun., president of Union College; Timothy Dwight, president of Yale; Sereno Dwight, president of Hamilton; Theodore Dwight Woolsey, president of Yale for 25 years; Daniel Tyler, a general in the American Civil War and founder of the iron industries of Alabama; Timothy Dwight 2nd, president of Yale 1886–1898; Theodore William Dwight, founder and head of the Columbia Law School; Merrill Edward Gates, president of Amherst; Catharine Maria Sedgwick, the authoress; Charles Sedgwick Minot, the eminent embryologist and biologist of the Harvard Medical School; Winston Churchill, the American novelist; Mrs. Theodore Roosevelt, a woman of great intellect; Aaron Burr, vice-president of the United States; Morrison R. Waite, Chief Justice of the United States; Henrietta Frances, wife of Eli Whitney, who helped her husband in his invention of the cotton gin; Robert T. Paine, one of the signers of the Declaration of Independence; the Marchioness of

Donegal, a distinguished woman of Ireland; the Fairbanks brothers, manufacturers of weighing scales; Bishop Vincent, founder of the Chautauqua movement and father of George Vincent, former head of the Rockefeller Foundation; Grover Cleveland and Ulysses S. Grant, presidents of the United States.

From Jonathan Edwards and his brilliant wife, Sarah Pierrpont, forming only one branch of this family, have descended (to year 1900) 1394 persons, among whom were 13 college presidents, 295 college graduates, 65 college professors, 60 physicians, 100 clergymen, 75 army or navy officers, 60 prominent authors, 100 lawyers, 30 judges, 80 public officials, 3 congressmen, 2 United States senators, and 1 vice-president of the United States.

The evidence, then, from family histories tends to point in one way, namely, towards heredity as an extremely potent factor in achievement. They cannot settle the problem, since heredity and environment are so inextricably mixed that a non-determinist could twist the argument so that all the above facts were brought to support his side in the discussion. Evidence from family histories is not crucial; we must extend our studies in other directions.

(2) *Studies of groups of eminent persons.* Although studies of this type cannot settle the problem of the relative contributions of heredity, they present a line of evidence which is often environmentalist in character and serves as a useful antidote to those which present the hereditarian view. For our first two studies, we shall take the complementary researches of *De Candolle* [16] and *Galton.* [17]

De Candolle's *Histoire des Sciences et des Savants depuis deux Siècles* was intended to be a reply to Galton's *Hereditary Genius* published in 1869. In it, De Candolle tried to show that environment was the chief factor in the production of scientific genius. For his subjects he selected the past and present associates and corresponding members of the Academy of Sciences, Paris (founded 1666); the corresponding members of the Royal Society, London (founded 1662); and the foreign members and correspondents of the Royal

[16] Alphonse de Candolle, *Histoire des Sciences et des Savants depuis deux Siècles,* 1873.
[17] Francis Galton, *English Men of Science,* 1874.

Academy, Berlin (founded 1700). This was an excellent and impartial selection of scientists, and they were eminent enough to be the subject of many written records. In all, the members studied were 212 for Paris, 235 for London, and 105 for Berlin. His method, unlike Galton's which was to trace and count family connections, was to concentrate on an analysis of the environmental factors which seem to have been influential in developing scientific genius. He concluded that the following influences were favorable to the progress of the sciences, and hence to the development of scientific genius. The following is a somewhat literal translation:

1. A considerable proportion of the people belonging to the rich and leisured classes relative to those who needs must work constantly in order to live, and especially to those who work at unskilled manual labor.
2. A considerable number of intellectual men of easy circumstances who are willing to devote their lives to non-lucrative scientific pursuits.
3. An ancient culture of the spiritual side of one's nature directed for several generations into right channels.
4. Immigration of intelligent families having a taste for non-lucrative intellectual work.
5. Existence of several contiguous families having favorable traditions towards science and to intellectual occupations of every kind.
6. A good system of education, especially secondary and higher education, organized independently of politics and religion.
7. Abundant material means in the shape of libraries, laboratories, observatories, and so forth, for the pursuit of science.
8. Public curiosity for truth rather than fiction.
9. Freedom to express or publish any opinion, at least on scientific subjects, without its being attended with any serious consequences.
10. Public opinion favorable to science and to scientists.
11. Liberty to exercise any profession, to follow none at all and to travel.
12. Religion not placed on an authoritative basis.
13. Clergy the friends of education.
14. Clergy not restricted to celibacy.
15. Habitual employment of one of the three principal languages — English, French, German — with as full a knowledge of non-native tongues as possible.

16. Small independent countries or a confederation of the same.
17. Situated in the temperate zone.
18. Proximity to civilized countries.
19. A large number of scientific societies or academies.
20. The habit of traveling and especially of sojourning abroad.

De Candolle, a Swiss, finds that in proportion to her population, Switzerland has produced more men of science than either France, England, Germany, Russia or America, and attributes it to the fact that she possesses more of the above favorable factors than any other country. In regard to factor 14, he states that the following, among scores of others, would not have been born had celibacy held sway, for all were sons of Protestant ministers, deans or pastors — Agassiz, Berzelius, Boerhave, Brown (Robert), Clausius, Encke, Euler, Fabricius, Grew, Haustein, Jenner, Linnaeus, Schimper, Schweizer, Wallis, Wollaston, Young, Emerson, Hallam, Hobbes, Müller, Sismondi, Addison, Jonson, Lessing, Richter, Swift, Thomson, Wilkie and Wren. The list could easily be extended. Undoubtedly, more eminent offspring have been born to Protestant ministers than chance alone would dictate, and the process continues to the present day. The reader will undoubtedly have noted that De Candolle's method determined the nature of his findings. He was looking for environmental factors and found them in abundance.

Galton, however, was not satisfied with the study; he thought that De Candolle had failed to consider many important aspects of the question. He therefore decided to make a further study which would closely parallel that of De Candolle's. For his subjects he took the Fellows of the Royal Society who possessed one or more of the following additional qualifications: (1) had earned a medal for scientific work; (2) had presided over a learned society, or a section of the British Association; (3) had been elected to the Council of the Royal Society; (4) was a professor in some important college or university. On this basis, he secured 180 subjects to whom he sent a questionnaire consisting of "seven huge quarto pages." He asked questions about ancestors, children and other relations, date and place of birth of each, education, size of head, personal estimates of energy of body, energy of mind, independence of judgment, special talents, mental peculiarities and a host of other things, and requested them to supply factual data wherever possible. He apparently received usable replies from 120 of them.

In working up his material, he used the technique of an earlier study, *Hereditary Genius,*[18] in which he computed the number of eminent relatives of eminent persons. He found that, among these British scientists, talent tended to concentrate in families such as the Alderson, Bentham, Carpenter, Darwin, Dawson-Turner, Harcourt, Hill, Latrobe, Playfair, Roscoe, Strachey, Taylor and Wedgwood families.

Taking the grandfathers and uncles of his 120 scientists, he found there were a total of 660, of whom 13 were eminent according to his criterion. Since Britain produced annually only 50 people of this degree of eminence, this group of 13 was equivalent to a quarter of the annual output. Next taking the brothers and male cousins of his group of 120, he found a total of 1450, of whom 8 were eminent. Stating the findings in another way, he found that for 100 scientific men there were 28 notable fathers, 36 brothers, 20 grandfathers and 40 uncles. Consequently, he concluded that nature (stock) had something to do with eminence in science, and that De Candolle had overlooked this factor in his study.

Other studies worthy of serious consideration in this group are those of *Ellis, Cattell, Odin* and *Terman.*[19] Space pre-

[18] The findings of *Hereditary Genius* are here given for comparison:

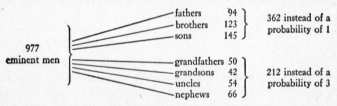

[19] Havelock Ellis, *A Study of British Genius*, Rev. Ed., 1926.

J. McK. Cattell, "A Statistical Study of Eminent Men," *Pop. Sci. Mo.*, Feb., 1903.

J. McK. Cattell, "The Scientific Men of the World," *Sci. Mo.*, XXIII, pp. 468-471.

J. McK. Cattell, "A Statistical Study of American Men of Science," *Science*, 1906, N.S., 24, pp. 732-742.

J. McK. Cattell, "The Distribution of American Men of Science in 1927," *American Men of Science*, IV, pp. 1118-1129.

J. McK. Cattell, "Families of American Men of Science," *Pop. Sci. Mo.*, 1915, 86, pp. 504-515.

A. Odin, *Genèse des grands hommes, gens de lettres français modernes*, 2 vols., 1895.

L. M. Terman, *Genetic Studies of Genius, Vol. I, Mental and Physical Traits of a Thousand Gifted Children*, 1925.

cludes any extended analysis of these works. Suffice it to mention that Ellis's *Study of British Genius* and Cattell's "A Statistical Study of Eminent Men" follow somewhat similar plans. Cattell selected his 1000 most eminent men that have appeared in the world, by taking six biographical dictionaries and averaging the space devoted to each person; his thousand men were those who were given most space. Ellis, for his selection of 1030 subjects (975 men and 55 women), used the "Dictionary of National Biography," eliminating royalties, hereditary nobles, villains and others whose inclusion had been determined by considerations other than that of intellectual eminence. The nature of Ellis's investigations can be understood from his chapter headings. These include — Nationality and Race, Social Class, Heredity and Parentage, Childhood and Youth, Marriage and Family, Duration of Life, Pathology, Stature, and Pigmentation. Not being statistically inclined, Ellis is apt to attribute the differences he finds to racial elements (Anglo-Danish running to mathematics), whereas they can be equally well regarded as due to the influences of the extremes of a normal distribution of talent.

Cattell has made many studies of a statistical character of American men of science. In the 1906 study, he found that Boston and Massachusetts were the intellectual center of the country, while the southern states had produced but little scientific talent. He states:

"The inequality in the production of scientific men in different parts of the country seems to be a forcible argument against the view of Dr. Galton and Professor Pearson that scientific performance is almost exclusively due to heredity. It is unlikely that there are such differences in family stocks as would lead one part of the country to produce a hundred times as many scientific men as other parts. The negroes may have a racial disqualification, but even this is not proved. The main factors in producing scientific and other forms of intellectual performance seem to be density of population, wealth, opportunity, institutions, and social traditions and ideals. All these may be ultimately due to race, but, given the existing race, the scientific productivity of the nation can be increased in quantity, though not in quality, almost to the extent that we wish to increase it." (pp. 734-735)

However, in his 1927 study, he finds that other centers of talent have arisen, notably Illinois, Iowa, Missouri and Minnesota. The residence of scientific men is determined by the rise of great universities and other institutions of learning and research, consequently he finds that Massachusetts has lost heavily, while New York, Illinois, Minnesota and California have gained enormously.

This explains his oversight, in 1906, of the fact that able men place themselves in environments congenial to their talents. At that time, Harvard was the one great American university and attracted talented people. With the rise of the universities of Columbia, Chicago and California; and with the development of scientific departments in Washington and of research institutions connected with industry, there were bound to be vast migrations of scientific men. Similar studies in twenty years' time will show that California, for instance, has been the birthplace of much of the scientific talent which will be found at that date. Instead of this fact supporting the environmentalist argument, it really supports the hereditarian, since the able people who have been attracted to California will have their able children born in that State.

The same oversight is exhibited in *Odin's* otherwise excellent study. Literary men in France live in towns and cities, and their children are born there. Only in centers of population can the average writer manage to earn a living. However, this research, as Ward (who devotes almost one-half of his *Applied Sociology* to a discussion of Odin's work) states, is "a perfect example of the heuristic method," and should be read by all serious students of the subject. The part that environment plays in the production of literary men is strikingly shown.

Terman's study of a thousand gifted children in California is one of the best of its kind. Of these pupils, 643 constituted the main experimental group about whom the fullest amount of information was collected, although a total of 1444 actually came under consideration after sifting about a quarter of a million children. The standard for inclusion in the gifted group was set at 140 I.Q., but for various reasons 22 cases slightly below this standard were included. This standard was reached by about 1 child out of 200. The average I.Q.'s were as follows:

	Boys	*Girls*	*Total*
Number	352	291	643
Mean I.Q.	151.42	151.21	151.33
S.D.	9.86	10.57	10.19

The data collected for each child included:

1. Two intelligence tests (Stanford-Binet and National A).
2. A two-hour educational test (Stanford Achievement).
3. A fifty-minute test of general information in science, history, literature and arts.
4. A fifty-minute test of knowledge of and interest in plays, games and amusements.
5. A four-page interest blank filled out by the children.
6. A two-months reading record kept by the children.
7. A sixteen-page home information blank filled out by the parents, including ratings on 25 traits.
8. An eight-page school information blank filled out by the teachers, including ratings on the same 25 traits as were rated by the parents.
9. When possible, ratings of the home on the Whittier Scale for home grading.

As would naturally be expected, 85 per cent were accelerated for their age in their progress through school. They were superior in all fields of accomplishment, having mastered subjects 40 per cent above the average, though their promotions were only 14 per cent above the average. In fact, they were on the average two to three grades below that which corresponds to their *mental* age, or they were retarded about one-quarter of their *actual* age. Their mean information quotient for nature study, science, literature, history and arts was 155 for boys and 147 for girls. The average gifted child of seven read more books in two months than the average child read up to fifteen years of age. The gifted child of nine years had reached a level of character development corresponding roughly to that of unselected children of 14 years. In regard to physical and mental health, and physique, these gifted children were distinctly above normal, which is contrary to popular belief.

However, it is their heredity that we are most interested in. How many intellectually superior relatives had these 643 children? Twelve of them had a parent or grandparent in *Who's Who*. There were 35 other relatives also reported. Of the 62 members of the Hall of Fame, 14, or 22.6 per cent, were known to be related to one or more of the main gifted group. These relatives were John Adams, John Quincy Adams, Charlotte Cushman, Henry Ward Beecher, Samuel L. Clemens, Benjamin Franklin, Ulysses S. Grant, Elias Howe, Andrew Jackson, Henry W. Longfellow, Harriet B. Stowe, George Washington, J. Greenleaf Whittier, and Roger Williams. At least one Hall of Fame relative was reported for 15 children, or 2.3 per cent of the entire number. Among the 58 relatives eminent enough to be included in standard dictionaries of biography, are 6 signers of the Declaration of Independence, 2 presidents and 2 vice-presidents of the United States, 4 generals, 6 writers, 2 inventors, 4 statesmen, 3 artists, and 2 supreme court judges. From these facts, Terman concluded that "they give considerable support to Galton's theory as to the hereditary nature of genius."

For the other side of the argument, the environmental, it should be stated that these gifted children came from superior homes. The average parent rated on a par with a "librarian" on the Barr scale of occupational intelligence. Ratings of 192 homes of the gifted children on the Whittier Scale for home grading showed home conditions of a superior nature, and especially superior on the item of "parental supervision." The median income was $3333, the mean $4705. Twenty-five per cent of the children had at least one parent with a university degree, and 17 per cent of the parents held degrees. The divorce rate of parents was 5.24 per cent, and 1.9 per cent were separated. These rates were much lower than those for the general population of the United States. The environmentalist can therefore argue that these superior home conditions were the cause of the excellent showings of the gifted children.

Eight years later a follow-up of about 90 per cent of the original group showed that, on the whole, these children were maintaining their relative superiority over the average members of the community. There was some loss in I.Q.

status, and 5 per cent of the gifted boys and 2 per cent of the gifted girls had presented more or less serious behavior or personality problems, which is probably not one-half the number that might normally have been expected.

The groups *Bagley* [20] studied were states of the United States. His method was to list the states in order of educational opportunities and provisions, and compare them with similar lists made for intelligence and various aspects of morality. More specifically, he compared the school ratings obtained by use of Ayres' "Index Numbers for State School Systems" with — (1) ratings obtained on the Army Alpha Intelligence Test; (2) infrequency of homicide; (3) infrequency of venereal disease; (4) inverse ratings as the birth states of federal prisoners. The coefficients of correlation were:

	r
School rating and Army Alpha	.72
School rating and infrequency of homicide	.55
School rating and infrequency of venereal disease	.57
School rating and inverse ratings of federal prisoners	.51

These coefficients, though somewhat low, are all positive and all point to the same conclusion, namely, that the better the schooling a state provides, the higher will be the intelligence and morality of its citizens. Bagley frankly admits that he "has an axe to grind" and apparently makes out a good case for environment. But he does not realize that his facts may be made to support the deterministic position. For example, California stands high in intelligence and in the rating for its educational system. Bagley would say that the school system made the high intelligence, whereas it is just as logical to say that the Californians, being intelligent, took good care to provide an excellent system of schools for their children.

Similarly, his interpretation of *Gordon's* [21] findings with respect to canal-boat children and gypsy children overlooks the fact that all intelligence tests are measures of achievement and that they posit equal opportunities for learning on the part of the testees. Gordon's results, namely, that

[20] W. C. Bagley, *Determinism in Education*, 1925.
[21] Hugh Gordon, *Mental and Scholastic Tests among Retarded Children ; an inquiry into the effects of schooling on various tests*, 1923.

younger children on canal boats have higher I.Q.'s than older ones, and similarly for gypsy children, are exactly what any intelligence tester would have expected. The older children, to a greater extent than the younger, have lacked just that equality of opportunity for learning that the tests pre-suppose. After all, Beethoven would never have written his symphonies if reared in an African forest, but, potentially, he would still have been a Beethoven.

With *Burt's*[22] evidence — "that to the complete score of adolescent children measured by the Binet tests, native intelligence contributed thirty-three per cent; general experience or the informal education of everyday life, eleven per cent; and formal schooling, fifty-four per cent" — Bagley is more unfortunate, since Burt misinterpreted a regression equation. All findings based on this misinterpretation, therefore, fall to the ground.

Bagley's surmise that horizontal growth (due to education) may bring about a significant access of vertical growth (native intelligence) has never been proved. If it were true, we could, theoretically, turn idiots into geniuses, but, so far, nobody has ever been able to make them anything else but good idiots; nobody has ever succeeded in making an idiot into a normal person.

Despite these obvious defects, Bagley's *Determinism in Education* is the best collection of data supporting the environmentalists' position that has been assembled, and should be read as an antidote against the extreme hereditarian position.

There are many other good studies of groups, but their findings must forever be inconclusive, since the method they employ fails to separate the contributions of heredity and environment. Far more promising are the studies of twins, sibs, orphans and foster children. Some of these will now be mentioned.

(3) *Studies of foster children.* The importance of studies of this kind lies in the fact that they enable us to evaluate the contribution of environment to mental growth. Suppose that a child living in an inferior environment is transferred to a superior one in a foster home. Comparisons of changes in I.Q., for instance, can be made with his real brothers or

---

[22] C. Burt, *Mental and Scholastic Tests*, 1921.

sisters living in the old home, and with foster brothers and sisters living in the new home. If the superior environment improves his mentality relatively to his real brothers and sisters left behind in the inferior environment, then the change can rightfully be attributed to environment. There are many possible pitfalls in studies of this kind, and it is sometimes difficult to avoid all of them. Two excellent investigations, which have avoided the more obvious snags, are open to our consideration. They are commonly known as the *Chicago* and *Stanford studies*.[23]

The studies, unfortunately, are not exactly parallel. The Chicago study involved more cases, but investigated colored and white, and adoptions at rather late ages. The Stanford study was more austere and limited its cases to legal adoptions before the age of twelve months (average 3) of children of white, English-speaking, non-Jewish parents. Practically all had spent at least five years in the foster home, since the study was limited to foster children between 5 and 14 years of age. A control group, comprising parents and true offspring, was used for comparative purposes.

In the *Chicago* group of 401 cases (367 white and 34 colored), there were found 74 children who had been tested for intelligence before adoption. After four years' stay in the foster home they were tested again and the following results obtained:

Average I.Q. before placement at the average age of 8 years..   91.2
Average I.Q. after average stay of 4 years in foster home......   93.7

Gain in I.Q...   2.5
True gain in I.Q. after correcting for age............................   7.5

The 74 cases were next divided into two groups — from superior foster homes and from inferior foster homes. The following tells the story:

[23] Frank N. Freeman, Karl J. Holzinger, and Blythe C. Mitchell, "The Influence of Environment on the Intelligence, School Achievement and Conduct of Foster Children," *27th Yearbook, N.S.S.E., Part I,* 1928, pp. 103-217.

Barbara S. Burks, "The Relative Influence of Nature and Nurture upon Mental Development; a Comparative Study of Foster Parent-Foster Child Resemblance and True Parent-True Child Resemblance," *27th Yearbook, N.S.S.E., Part I,* 1928, pp. 219-316.

Gain in I.Q. of children in superior foster homes.................. 5.3
True gain in I.Q. of children in superior foster homes.......... 10.4
Gain in I.Q. of children in inferior foster homes.................... .1
True gain in I.Q. of children in inferior foster homes.......... 5.0

Thus a superior environment is effective in increasing the I.Q. in four years by 5.4 points. Comparing the younger (those who had lived in the foster home between the ages of 6 and 10) with the older (10 to 14), the younger were found to have improved 10.2 I.Q. points, and the older only 4.6 points. This shows that environment has greater influence upon the young than upon the old. Confirmation of the reality of environmental influence on the change in I.Q.'s is found in the fact that "a newly committed group of 137 children not yet placed in homes had a mean C.A. of 9-3 and mean I.Q. of 88.6. The 260 legitimate *foster* children, with mean C.A. of 12-2, had a mean I.Q. of 94.1. The difference of 5.5 points I.Q. can probably be ascribed to environment."

In the *Stanford* study, "a group of 214 foster children, whose average inheritance was judged to be close to normal or slightly above, had an average I.Q. of 107. The average environment of their foster homes was markedly superior, and the conclusion was drawn that 5 or 6 points of the excess over 100 I.Q. could be explained by environment." Thus the two studies agree closely with reference to the increase of I.Q. by improvement of environment.

Dr. Barbara Burks collected in summary form the information given in the two studies regarding the correlation between I.Q. and environment (pp. 318-319). This summary is reproduced below:

Correlation Between I.Q. and Environment

(*a*) *Home ratings and foster I.Q.*

Chicago Study

Pre-Test Group

	r	P.E.
Home rating and I.Q. (74 cases at time of placement)....	.34	.07
Home rating and I.Q. (74 cases after 4 years)..........	.52	.06
Home rating and I.Q. (51 cases, with negroes and children outside range 5 to 14 eliminated)....................	.36	.08
Home rating and I.Q. (the above cases after 4 years)....	.57	.06

Home Group

Home rating and I.Q. (304 cases who have been in homes
at least 4 years).................................. .47 .03
Home rating and I.Q. (156 cases placed under 2 years).. .52 .04
Home rating and I.Q. (59 cases "for which there was
practically no information on the parentage")......... .51 .06
Home rating and I.Q. (273 cases with negroes and children outside range 5 to 14 eliminated).............. .49 .03
Home rating and I.Q. (104 cases placed under 2, with
negroes and children outside range 5 to 14 eliminated). .50 .05

Stanford Study
Foster Group

Culture index and I.Q................................ .25 .05
Whittier index and I.Q............................... .21 .04
Multiple *r*, environment and I.Q.................... .35 .05

(b) *Foster parent intelligence and I.Q.*

Chicago Study
Home Group

Otis score of foster family and I.Q. (180 cases).......... .37 .04
Otis score of foster mother and I.Q. (255 cases)........ .28 .04
Mid-foster parent and I.Q. (169 cases)................ .39 .04
Mid-foster parent and I.Q. (112 cases with negroes and
children outside range 5 to 14 eliminated)........... .47 .05
Mid-foster parent and I.Q. (132 cases placed under 2 years) .39 .05
Mid-foster parent and I.Q. (104 cases of above with negroes
and children outside range 5 to 14 eliminated)....... .50 .05

Stanford Study
Foster Group

M.A. of foster father and I.Q. (178 cases)............. .07 .05
M.A. of foster mother and I.Q. (204 cases)............ .19 .05
M.A. of mid-foster parent and I.Q. (174 cases)......... .20 .05

(c) *Home ratings, true parent intelligence, and true child's I.Q.*

Chicago Study

Home rating and I.Q. (36 true children in foster-own
group)... .47 .09
Mid-parent intelligence and I.Q. (28 true children in
foster-own group) .... .35 .11

Stanford Study

Culture index and I.Q. (101 true children in Control
Group)... .44 .05
Whittier index and I.Q. (104 true children in Control
Group)... .42 .05
Mid-parent intelligence and I.Q. (100 true children in
Control Group)................................... .52 .05

If the cultural level of the foster children approximated, with the passing of time, the cultural level of the home into which they were adopted, the influence of environment would be indicated. The fact that the correlation was raised from .34 to .52 in 4 years (Chicago) shows this to be the case.

Another line of evidence regarding the influence of environment, is that the correlation between the intelligence of a foster child with an own child in the same family was found in the Chicago study to be .34. This resemblance may be attributed to the fact that the children have been reared in the same environment, but the element of selective placing (choice of children resembling one's own children) cannot be overlooked.

Of even greater significance is the fact that siblings reared in different foster homes had a resemblance in intelligence represented by .34 (Chicago study reduces this to a true one of .25). Siblings reared together are found to have a coefficient of correlation for intelligence of .50. Different environments, therefore, tend to make children less alike.

Dr. Burks, by the use of ingenious statistical techniques upon the Stanford data, came to the following conclusions (pp. 308-309):

"1. Home environment contributes about 17 per cent of the variance in I.Q.: parental intelligence alone accounts for about 33 per cent.

2. The total contribution of heredity (i.e. of innate and heritable factors) is probably not far from 75 or 80 per cent.

3. Measurable environment one standard deviation above or below the mean of the population does not shift the I.Q. by more than 6 to 9 points above or below the value it would have had under normal environmental conditions. In other words, nearly 70 per cent of school children have an actual I.Q. within 6 to 9 points of that represented by their innate intelligence.

4. The maximal contribution of the best home environment to intelligence is apparently about 20 I.Q. points, or less, and almost surely lies between 10 and 30 points. Conversely, the least cultured, least stimulating kind of American home environment may depress the I.Q. as much as 20 I.Q. points. But situations as extreme as either of these probably occur only once or twice in a thousand times in American communities." (pp. 308-309)

The final conclusion from these studies is that although environment may increase or decrease intelligence as measured by intelligence tests by as much as 20 points, the contribution of heredity is about four times as potent as that of home environment.

(4) *Studies of people living in similar environments — orphans, gypsies, canal-boat children and criminals.* Common opinion usually attributes a tremendous power to an institutional environment. The English Public School, for instance, is supposed to put a stamp upon its product which can be recognized the world over. The Princeton man or the Harvard man is supposed to be recognizable everywhere as a product of a particular university atmosphere. The avowed aim of education, which is a specialized part of the greater environment, is to produce intelligent, loyal and upright citizens. When it fails to accomplish this purpose, society feels justified in blaming both schools and teachers.

Children reared in an orphanage for one-quarter of their lives, and having lived in it for at least three years, would appear to be suitable subjects for study. These children have eaten the same meals, been taught by the same teacher, gone to bed and got up at the same times, and, generally speaking, have enjoyed many similar experiences. If environment can mould them into a pattern, then the pattern should be apparent. *Wingfield* [24] could not detect any specific pattern. Orphans in orphanages were no more alike than unselected children living at home. Unfortunately, owing to his use of a faulty statistical technique, he did not prove his case. What he should have done was to test paired groups inside and outside the orphanage over a period of years and determine whether or not there were differential rates of progress.

Gordon's study of gypsies (82 cases) and canal-boat children (76 cases) has been mentioned. He showed conclusively that an inferior educational development depressed the mentality of canal-boat children, as measured by an intelligence test, by an average of 20 I.Q. points (90 to 70) between the extremes of 4 to 6 years on the one hand and 12 to 22 years on the other. This amount approaches the maximum amount assigned to environment by Barbara Burks.

[24] A. H. Wingfield, *Twins and Orphans : the Inheritance of Intelligence*, 1928.

The gypsy children showed similar but less marked decline of mentality with age. His conclusion (p. 87) can be accepted by both hereditarians and environmentalists:

"In conclusion, it is quite evident that, although the mental tests do undoubtedly test some kind of ability or abilities, such abilities are not developed without schooling or its equivalent, and as a consequence, the tests do not evaluate them apart from schooling, except *perhaps* in the case of children under six or seven years of age."

Goring's[25] study of the English convict is one of the most careful statistical studies ever made. Indeed, Karl Pearson describes it as "epoch-making." Although the main study is anthropological in character and conclusively refutes the theory of Lombroso that the criminal constitutes a type (unless defective physique may be said to constitute a type), an important chapter is devoted to the influence of heredity on the genesis of crime. The first finding of the study of the inheritance of a criminal diathesis shows that "the percentage of criminal offspring increases progressively according to whether neither parents, the mother only, the father only, or both parents, are criminal; and, secondly, that the percentage of criminal offspring becomes steadily greater as the age of the children increases to 14 and 23. The first relation bears resemblance to the result obtained by Pearson for the family influence of tuberculosis, and contrasts interestingly with the relation that would have been expected upon a mendelian hypothesis of criminal inheritance."

| | Offspring affected | | |
Parents affected	*Expected Mendelian %*	*% Tubercular. K. Pearson's Memoir*	*% Criminals. The Present Work*
Both	100	57	60.7
One	50	29	53.8
Neither	25	21	47.3

[25] Charles Goring, *The English Convict ; a Statistical Study*, (abridged edition), 1919.

The second relation is shown by the following summary from 73 families with criminal parentage:

Mean age of family	No. of families	Criminals (males)	Non-criminals (males)	Totals	Ratio of criminals to non-criminals
Under 23	43	54	103	157	1 to 1.91
23—30	15	24	31	55	1 to 1.30
31—40	10	16	9	25	1 to .56
41—	5	7	3	10	1 to .43
Totals	73	101	146	247	1 to 1.38

Goring found that environment (contagion) had apparently small effect on criminality. This finding is contrary to

Character or Condition	Source of Statistics	Computer and Locus	Minimum Values	Maximum Values	Probable Values
Stature	Pearson, Family Research	Lee & Pearson, Biometrica VII, 578.	.49	.51	.51
Span			.45	.46	.46
Forearm			.41	.42	.42
Eye-color	Galton, Family Research	Lee & Pearson, Phil. Trans. 195A, 106.	.44	.55	.50
Pulmonary Tuberculosis	Cunley Sanatorium	K. Pearson, Drapers' Research Memoirs.	.40	.60	.50
Pulmonary Tuberculosis	Criminals	C. Goring, Drapers' Research Memoirs	.43	.62	.50
Insane Diathesis	Dr. Urquhart's Data	Dr. Heron, Eugenics Lab. Memoirs, III.	?	.65	.53
Insane Diathesis	Criminals	C. Goring, Drapers' Research Memoirs.	?	?	.47
Hereditary Deafness	Dr. Fry's Data	E. Schuster, Biometrica IV, 466.	.45	.62	.54
Criminal Diathesis	Criminals	C. Goring, this work	.54	.68	.60

general expectation, but if it is to be refuted, it must be refuted by data collected as carefully as those of Goring's. A criminal diathesis, revealed by the tendency to be convicted and imprisoned for crime, is inherited at much the same rate as are other physical and mental qualities and pathological conditions in man. In support of this statement, Goring gives the above "Table of Parental Inheritance." (p. 268)

(5) *Studies of blood relations — twins, siblings and others.* Studies of this kind are extremely important. In the first place, we can compare twins with siblings and others of lesser genetic similarity who have been exposed to the various kinds of environment. If it could be proved that, no matter what the environment in which they lived, the nearer people were in blood (genetic) relationship, the closer they resembled each other in intelligence, achievement and behavior, then the potency of heredity would be indicated. Secondly, from studies of similar or identical twins reared in different environments from a very early age, we get an almost crucial test for the relative powers of heredity and environment. Not quite, however, for identical twins have enjoyed a common intra-uterine environment and it is always possible for the environmentalist to ascribe the similarities to this common environment. The case for the environmentalist would be weakened if it were found that identical twins remained alike the rest of their lives, despite differing environments. If, further, these differing environments were more effective in changing siblings than twins, the hereditarian case would be strengthened. Conversely, if the effect of different up-bringings were to cause identical twins to become different in their personalities, or if the changes were as great for siblings as for twins, then the case for environment would be strengthened.

For more than fifty years it has been recognized that nature provides, in the form of twins, material for the study of inheritance which is of immense importance. Moreover, twins are of two kinds — monozygotic (uni-ovular, similar or identical), and dizygotic (multi-ovular, dissimilar or fraternal) — and this adds value to nature's experimental set-up. Only the monozygotic twins are true twins; the dizygotic are multiple births or siblings born at the same time, as occurs normally in the births of pups and kittens. It is of interest to note that the tendency to dizygotic twinning is hereditary; monozygotic twinning is not. That there are these two kinds of twins is seen not only from common observation, but also from a study of fetal membranes, finger prints, hair whorls, birthmarks and the like. So far as identical genetic make-ups are concerned, monozygotic twins are the best representatives that can possibly be secured. They are always of same sex, since sex is determined at the moment of fertilization. This forced identity in sex enables us to estimate how frequently identical twins relative to fraternal twins are born. If all twins were fraternal, then the ratios of boy boy, girl boy, and girl girl twins would be 1, 2, 1. Actually, from Nichols'[26] and Cobb's[27] combined figures, the ratios approach 1:1:1. If this were the case, then it would mean that one out of three twin births was of the monozygotic type. The true proportion, calculated from the subjoined data, is found to be almost exactly one in four.

	Males	*Mixed*	*Females*
Number	235,615	265,291	230,335
Ratios	89	100	83

The proportion of twin to single births is greater than is usually supposed. In Canada, 1 birth in 89 is a twin birth; in the United States, 1 in 93; in some countries the ratio is lower than 1 in 100. For the world at large, it probably approaches one per cent, so that one person in fifty is born a twin. If the twinning ratio is 1:n, then the triplet ratio is 1:n^2; the quadruplet ratio 1:n^3. The figures so far published agree fairly well with the calculated ratios — twins 1:100; triplets 1:100^2; quadruplets 1:100^3. At the time of writing the Dionne quintuplets are alive. Assuming the

[26] J. B. Nichols, *Memoirs of the American Anthropological Association, Vol. I,* 1907.
[27] Margaret Cobb, "Evidence bearing on the Origin of Human Twins from a Single Ovum," *Science*, April, 1915.

same independent factor at work, they represent $1:100^4$ or $1:100,000,000$ births. This does not seem to place them in a unique position regarding births, but we must remember that most quintuplets are still-born, and many may not be recorded in the medical journals.

The literature on twins is assuming enormous proportions, so it will be possible to give only a few representative studies. These are not necessarily the most scientific, but they represent the historical development of techniques.

The first important study was made by *Galton*.[28] He used a questionnaire method and stated his results in anecdotal form. From his eighty returns of close similarity, thirty-five were sufficiently detailed to be of use. These were compared with 25 dissimilar pairs. Some of his anecdotes are quite amusing. Thus —

"A married first, but both twins met the lady together for the first time, and fell in love with her there and then. A managed to see her home and to gain her affection, though B went sometimes courting in his place, and neither the lady nor her parents could tell which was which."

Galton was clearly aware of the two kinds of twins in man (the only animal, by the bye, which produces both kinds), and his treatment of evidence was so restrained that the study can still be read with profit. His conclusion was as follows:

"There is no escape from the conclusion that nature prevails enormously over nurture when the differences of nurture do not exceed what is commonly to be found among persons of the same rank of society and in the same country. My fear is, that my evidence may seem to prove too much, and be discredited on that account, as it appears contrary to all experience that nurture should go for so little."

Next in historical order we have *Thorndike's* study of twins.[29] Although the study was made before the days of intelligence tests, he subjected his twins to the best objective

---

[28] Francis Galton, "History of Twins," in *Inquiries into Human Faculty and its Development*, 1883.

[29] E. L. Thorndike, *Measurement of Twins*, 1905.

measurements at his disposal — 8 physical and 6 mental measurements. The physical measurements included height; width of head; cephalic index (breadth to length of head); circumference of head; length of forearm; and so forth. The mental tests were the A test; *a-t* and *r-e* tests; misspelled word test; addition; multiplication; and opposites. The argument he used may be put down in tabular form as follows:

Heredity	*Environment*
If heredity is the stronger, then—	If environment is the stronger, then—
(1) The resemblances of twins should be greater than the resemblances of siblings.	(1) The resemblances of twins should equal the resemblances of siblings.
(2) The resemblances of younger twins should equal the resemblances of older twins.	(2) The resemblances of younger twins should be less than the resemblances of older twins.
(3) The resemblances of twins in traits modified by education should be equal to the resemblances of traits that have not been so modified.	(3) The resemblances of twins in traits modified by training and education should be greater than the resemblances of traits that have not been so modified.

His findings, on the whole, supported the hereditarian contentions. Some of his results are given in Table VI.

TABLE VI. SOME CORRELATIONS OF TWINS AND SIBLINGS IN SIX MENTAL TRAITS (Thorndike)

Tests	*All Twins*	*All Siblings*	*Twins 9-11 years*	*Twins 12-14 years*
Cancellation of A's	.69	.32	.66	.73
Cancellation of *a-t*, and *r-e*	.71	.29	.81	.62
Mis-spelled words	.80	—	.76	.74
Addition	.75	—	.90	.54
Multiplication	.84	—	.91	.69
Opposites	.90	.30	.96	.88
Averages	.78	—	.83	.70

In Table VII we give a selection of sibling coefficients found by Pearson.

TABLE VII. SOME COEFFICIENTS OF CORRELATION OF SIBLINGS
(Pearson)

Character	Boys: brother & brother	Girls: sister & sister	Both sexes
Stature	.51	.54	.55
Span	.55	.56	.52
Forearm	.49	.51	.44
Eye-color	.52	.45	.46
Hair color	.59	.51	.56
General health	.49	.56	.62
Head length	.50	.43	.46
Head breadth	.59	.62	.54
Head height	.55	.52	.49
Cephalic index			.49
Vivacity	.47	.43	.49
Assertiveness	.53	.44	.52
Introspection	.59	.47	.63
Popularity	.50	.57	.49
Conscientiousness	.59	.64	.63
Temper	.51	.49	.51
Ability	.46	.47	.44
Handwriting	.53	.56	.46
Averages	.53	.51	.52

Arguing from his own and Pearson's results (in which, it must be remembered, Pearson found similar correlations for both mental and physical traits), Thorndike concluded: "The facts then are easily, simply and completely explained by one simple hypothesis: namely, that the natures of the germ cells — the conditions of conception — cause whatever similarities and differences exist in the original natures of men, that these conditions influence body and mind equally, and that in life the differences in modification of body and mind produced by such differences as obtain between the environments of present-day New York City public school children are slight." Finally, he concluded that "the mental likenesses found in the cases of twins and the differences found in the case of non-fraternal pairs, when the individuals compared belong to the same age, locality and educational system, are due, to at least nine-tenths of their amount, to original nature." Probably a better and more conservative appraisal of the results would be — that the potential or hereditary traits of siblings, unlike twins, and like twins represent a series increasing in similarity. Even under the influence of possibly dissimilar environments these potential traits develop into a similar series of increasing likenesses. But environment causes slight differences to appear even when the heredities are as identical as those of monozygotic twins.

While Thorndike was working on twins, Binet was perfecting the first intelligence test. By the time the 1920's were reached, intelligence tests had become a valuable tool in the hands of the experimenter. In 1924, *Merriman*[30] was able to use three fairly reliable tests of intelligence in studying twins, and to compare his findings with the estimates of teachers. His findings are given in Table VIII.

TABLE VIII. RESEMBLANCES OF TWINS IN INTELLIGENCE
(Merriman) (Pearson *r*'s)

Pairs compared	Stanford-Binet I.Q.	Army Beta scores	N.I.T. scores	Teachers' Estimates
All pairs 5-9 yrs.	.809±.032	.784±.049	.797±.034	.686±.057
All pairs 10-16 yrs.	.757±.037	.664±.054	.875±.017	.373±.081
All twin pairs	.782±.025	.841±.022	.891±.011	.512±.053
Like-sex pairs 5-9 yrs.	.882±.028	.921±.025	.946±.012	.788±.053
Like-sex pairs 10-16 yrs.	.865±.027	.842±.036	.865±.022	.568±.083
All like-sex pairs	.867±.020	.908±.017	.925±.009	.654±.053
Girl-girl pairs 5-9 yrs.	.915±.026	.709±.112	.965±.009	.913±.030
Girl-girl pairs 10-16 yrs.	.814±.05	.896±.032	.919±.021	.521±.123
All girl-girl pairs.	.857±.029	.866±.033	.928±.012	.645±.071
Boy-boy pairs 5-9 yrs.	.800±.078	.934±.049	.921±.041	.534±.161
Boy-boy pairs 10-16 yrs.	.890±.034	.747±.080	.895±.027	.715±.089
All boy-boy pairs.	.877±.030	.938±.015	.925±.018	.605±.090
Unlike-sex pairs 5-9 yrs.	.774±.064	.519±.147	.753±.066	.681±.090
Unlike-sex pairs 10-16 yrs.	.298±.137	.643±.091	.834±.044	.072±.141
All unlike-sex pairs.	.504±.081	.732±.056	.867±.025	.266±.102

[30] Curtis Merriman, "The Intellectual Resemblances of Twins," *Psychological Review, Monograph Supplement 33*, 1924.

Merriman concludes from his study that —

(1) Environment appears to make no significant difference in the amount of twin resemblance. Older twin pairs are no more alike than younger twin pairs.

(2) Twins suffer no intellectual handicap.

(3) The data show that there are two types of twins, because (*a*) the correlation of like-sex pairs is higher than unlike-sex pairs; (*b*) sibling data, when compared with twin data, show that the correlations for siblings are much nearer the unlike-sex twin data than the like-sex twin data; (*c*) all the curves and curve-fitting tests indicate clearly a difference between like- and unlike-sex pairs; the study of verbal reports on "similar pairs" tends strongly to show that curve differences are to be largely accounted for by the like-sex pairs that show great intellectual and physical similarity, and that presumably belong to the duplicate type.

Except in the case of his Stanford-Binet I.Q.'s, Merriman did not eliminate the age factor from his results. Children of eight years, for example, show resemblances just because they have eight years of growth in common. Further, in the case of the Stanford-Binet I.Q.'s, which according to Merriman's data, show older twins to be less alike than younger ones, there is the possibility of (*a*) increasing unreliability of the I.Q. with age, and (*b*) increasing variability of the I.Q. with age, accounting for the difference. Shen[31] calculated the standard deviations of the I.Q.'s and also their standard errors of estimates from Merriman's data and showed that the older twins were a more variable group, except the unlike-sex pairs, which gave especially low correlations for the older children. Shen's results are given in Table IX.

It should be noted that the standard errors of estimate are remarkably regular, being about 3 points greater for the older groups of twins. This points to the fact that on the whole older twins are slightly less alike than younger twins, thus contradicting slightly the environmentalist argument, which makes them more alike the older they become.

Lauterbach's study[32] is more comprehensive than Merri-

[31] Eugene Shen, "The Intellectual Resemblances of Twins," *School and Society*, XXI, 542, May, 1925.

[32] C. E. Lauterbach, "Studies in Twin Resemblances," *Genetics*, X, 6, 1925.

TABLE IX. STANDARD DEVIATIONS AND STANDARD ERRORS OF ESTIMATE OF I.Q.'S OF MERRIMAN'S TWINS (Shen)

Pairs compared	*No. of pairs*	r	σ	$\sigma\sqrt{1-r^2}$
All twin pairs	105	.782	15.1	9.4
Pairs 5-9 yrs.	47	.809	13.0	7.6
Pairs 10-16 yrs.	58	.757	16.3	10.6
Like-sex pairs	67	.867	16.5	8.2
Like-sex 5-9 yrs.	29	.882	13.4	6.3
Like-sex 10-16 yrs.	38	.865	18.2	9.1
Girl-girl pairs	40	.857	15.9	8.2
Girl-girl 5-9 yrs.	19	.915	15.0	6.1
Girl-girl 10-16 yrs.	21	.814	15.4	9.0
Boy-boy pairs	27	.877	16.6	8.0
Boy-boy 5-9 yrs.	10	.800	9.7	5.8
Boy-boy 10-16 yrs.	17	.890	19.6	8.9
Unlike-sex pairs	38	.504	12.4	10.7
Unlike-sex 5-9 yrs.	18	.774	12.2	7.7
Unlike-sex 10-16 yrs.	20	.298	11.6	11.1

man's, but is open to criticism on the same grounds, namely, that he failed to make allowances for similarities due to age, or to take into account the variabilities of the groups he tested. He used twenty-one tests or measurements on 210 sets of twins. The tests employed were the Terman Group Test of Mental Ability; the National Intelligence Test; the Thorndike-McCall Reading Scale; the Courtis Standard Research Tests in Arithmetic, Series B; Memory span for digits; Discrimination of lines and ovals; O-Test for speed of movement; Kansas City Handwriting Scale; Height, standing and sitting; Weight; Cephalic index; Color of eyes and hair; Whorl of head hair; Handedness; and Palm Patterns.

He was specially interested in features which might be used to identify monozygotic twins — sex, features, texture and coloration of skin, color of hair and eyes, height, weight, cephalic index, right- and left-handedness, friction ridges of hands, whorl of hair, and birth marks. It had been supposed that those features, such as right- and left-handedness, hair-whorls on crown of head, friction-ridges, etc., which could show symmetry reversal, would be reversed in twins produced from a single ovum, but he was unable to obtain confirmatory evidence. Later studies have shown that mirror-imaging is commoner among monozygotic twins than among either dizygotic twins or siblings, but it is far from being in the nature of 100 per cent. For example, left-handedness is several times as common in identical twins as in the general population.

In the summary of his findings given in Tables X and XI, *a* and *b* stand for male, *x* and *y* for female. Thus *ab* and *xy* are boy twins and girl twins respectively, while *ax* are twins of opposite sex.

TABLE X. COEFFICIENTS OF CORRELATION FOUND IN VARIOUS
TESTS GIVEN TO TWINS OF THE SAME AND OF OPPOSITE SEXES
(Lauterbach)

Test	Same sex, ab & xy	Different sexes, ax
I.Q.	.77	.56
Reading Quotient	.59	.56
Arithmetic, accuracy	.69	.35
Arithmetic, speed	.70	.39
Memory for digits	.40	.25
Handwriting, quality	.69	.37
Handwriting, speed	.83	.41
Averages	.67	.41

Some of Lauterbach's conclusions are the following:

(1) Older twins show no greater degree of resemblance than younger twins. This is in conformity with the findings of Thorndike (1905) and Merriman (1924), and favors the argument that heredity is more potent than environment.

(2) Like-sex pairs of twins show a greater degree of resemblance than unlike-sex pairs. These differences in degrees of simi-

larity are attributed by Merriman to the circumstance of origin (monozygotic or dizygotic). The facts seem to favor the theory.

(3) Twins show a greater degree of resemblance than other sibs. It has also been shown that single-birth sibs are more nearly alike than parents and children; and parents and children than cousins. The inference follows that the closer the relationship, the greater the resemblance.

(4) Unlike-sex pairs show a degree of resemblance about equal to that of single sibs. A fraternal relationship is thus indicated.

(5) There is no evidence to warrant the assumption that twins are intellectually handicapped. (*Note:* Since Merriman's average I.Q. was 96, and Lauterbach's 95, it would seem as if twins were slightly handicapped. Wingfield and others have confirmed this finding.)

(6) The monozygotic origin of quadruplets among armadillos has been established by Newman. By analogy, twins among other vertebrates, including man, may have a similar genesis.

TABLE XI. COEFFICIENTS OF CORRELATION OF PHYSICAL TRAITS OF TWINS (Lauterbach)

Trait	*Like-sex* ab & xy	*Unlike-sex* ax	*Younger Twins* 90-156 *months*	*Older Twins* 157-238 *months*
Height, standing	.80	.53	.61	.65
Height, sitting	.73	.59	.60	.58
Weight	.89	.50	.59	.64
Cephalic Index	.67	.59	.72	.61
Averages	.77	.55	.63	.62

(7) The dissection of conjoined twins, and X-ray examinations of their anatomy, favor the theory of the monozygotic origin of twins by fission in the fertilized ovum.

(8) An examination of the fetal membranes of twins at birth has frequently revealed a single placenta and a single chorion. Embryologists maintain that such a condition is the result of genesis from a single ovum.

(9) Sex ratios among twins favor the theory of two types of twins, the actual ratio being approximately 1:1:1, whereas if they were only one type, it ought by the law of chance to be 1:2:1.

(10) Merriman has shown statistically that a distribution of the intelligence quotients of a twin population represents two types of population, and he concludes that these two types are determined by one-egg and two-egg genesis.

The next important study, historically speaking, is Wingfield's *Twins and Orphans*.[33] The underlying idea of this study was to compare twins, representing similar heredities, with orphans living in an orphanage, representing similar environments. Except that the statistical work on orphans was jumbled (a mistake that is found in many other studies), since he calculated the correlation between children paired at random, Wingfield's is a sound study. He used both intelligence and achievement tests, several of each, in fact, and took into account the effect of age on the amount if resemblance was found, and also the variability of his measurements.

Tests were given to 102 sets of twins, and to 29 orphans who had spent a minimum of three years and at least one-quarter of their lives in the same orphanage. The tests used were:

(1) The National Intelligence Test, Scale A, Form 1.
(2) The Multi-Mental Scale of McCall.
(3) The Stanford Achievement Test — a battery of nine subtests.
(4) The British Columbia Test in the Fundamentals of Arithmetic.
(5) The Morrison-McCall Spelling Scale.

Since in twin data it is impossible to determine which should be considered the X variable and which the Y variable, the Otis formula[34] was used instead of the Pearson in

[33] A. H. Wingfield, *Twins and Orphans*, 1928.

[34] $r = 1 - \frac{1}{2}\left(\frac{\sigma d^2}{\sigma y^2}\right)$

where σd = tandard deviation of the difference between the scores of each twin pair for the trait measured.

and σy = standard deviation of the scores of all children in general for the same trait.

calculating the coefficients of correlation. For comparing the resemblances, the standard error of estimate $\sigma \sqrt{1 - r^2}$ was used. The smaller the standard of estimate, the greater is the resemblance among the individuals comprising the group. Tables XII, XIII and XIV give the main results.

TABLE XII. RESEMBLANCES OF TWINS IN GENERAL INTELLIGENCE (Wingfield)

Group	No. of Pairs	Raw r	r for Constant Age		Standard Error of Estimate	Mean Difference in I.Q.'s
All twin pairs	102	.76	.75±.029	13.5	8.92	9.65
Unlike-sex pairs	26	.62	.59±.086	12.9	10.40	12.00
Like-sex pairs	76	.83	.82±.025	13.6	7.79	8.50
Fraternal pairs	57	.72	.70±.045	12.6	9.03	11.74
Identical pairs	45	.91	.90±.019	14.3	6.23	6.23

TABLE XIII. RESEMBLANCE OF YOUNGER TWINS (45 PAIRS) AND OLDER TWINS (50 PAIRS) (Wingfield)

Test	Twins 8-11 years			Twins 12-15 years		
	Raw r	r for Constant Age	Standard Error of Estimate	Raw r	r for Constant Age	Standard Error of Estimate
General Intelligence (I.Q.)	.73	.71±.047	8.09	.78	.77±.038	9.16
Stanford Achievement (E.Q.)	.73	.64±.060	8.13	.90	.87±.023	5.35
Stanford Achievement (A.Q.)	.82	.82±.033	3.95	.72	.72±.046	5.10
Arithmetic	.94	.89±.022	2.70	.85	.73±.045	4.00
Spelling	.89	.85±.029	4.18	.89	.85±.026	4.41
Averages		.78	5.41		.79	5.6

From Wingfield's results (marked with an asterisk) and from the averages of other workers we get the following correlations for intelligence arranged in order of decreasing genetic relationship:

Group

* Physically identical twins (predominantly uni-ovular)........ .90
* Like-sex twins... .82
* Fraternal twins (all twins *minus* physically identical)........ .70
* Unlike-sex twins (multi-ovular)...................................... .59
  Siblings .... .50
  Parent-child .... .31 †
  Cousins .... .27
  Grandparent-grandchild .... .15

† *Note :* Both Pearson and Jones found $r = .50$.

TABLE XIV. RESEMBLANCES OF ALL TWIN PAIRS IN NATIVE AND ACQUIRED TRAITS (Wingfield)

1. E.Q.'s (Stanford Achievement) I.Q.'s (General Intelligence) Difference	$r = .76 \pm .029$ (94 pairs) $r = .75 \pm .029$ (102 pairs) $= .01 \pm .041$
2. A.Q.'s (Stanford Achievement) I.Q.'s (General Intelligence) Difference	$r = .83 \pm .021$ (94 pairs) $r = .75 \pm .029$ (102 pairs) $= .08 \pm .036$
3. Arithmetic Scores I.Q.'s (General Intelligence) Difference	$r = .78 \pm .028$ (88 pairs) $r = .75 \pm .029$ (102 pairs) $= .03 \pm .04$
4. Spelling Scores I.Q.'s (General Intelligence) Difference	$r = .85 \pm .019$ (92 pairs) $r = .75 \pm .029$ (102 pairs) $= .10 \pm .035$

Some of Wingfield's conclusions are as follows:

(1) There is no significant difference in the amount of resemblance in mental traits between younger and older twins.

(2) Twins are no more alike in those traits upon which the school has concentrated its training than in general intelligence.

(3) Environment is inadequate to account for the mental resemblance of twins.

(4) Like-sex pairs of twins show a greater degree of resemblance in intelligence than unlike-sex pairs.

(5) Unlike-sex pairs of twins have approximately the same degree of resemblance in intelligence as siblings. (*Note:* Resemblances are slightly greater for unlike-sex pairs.)

(6) There are two distinct types of twins because: (*a*) the like-sex group, which must partly consist of a number of uni-ovular, or identical pairs, shows a higher degree of mental resemblance than the unlike-sex group; (*b*) physically identical pairs show a higher degree of resemblance than fraternal pairs; (*c*) the degree of resemblance of siblings in mental traits is nearer to that of unlike-sex pairs than to that of like-sex pairs. This bears out the contention that unlike-sex pairs are, from the genetic standpoint, really siblings that are born at the same time; (*d*) members of fraternal pairs of twins show, on the whole, greater diversity in school grades than members of physically identical pairs. This latter group is probably composed largely of uni-ovular twins.

(7) Twins as a group are very slightly below (2 to 3 per cent) the average of the population in general intelligence, but show about the same variability as unselected children.

(8) There is an increasing degree of resemblance in general intelligence among human beings with an increasing degree of blood relationship among them. *Ergo*, general intelligence is an inherited trait.

Hirsch's [35] study of twins introduces an interesting variation in technique. He carefully selected his twins, securing the following three groups:

(*a*) Very *similar* twins of the same sex living together in a *similar* environment.

(*b*) *Dissimilar* twins of the same sex living together in a *similar* environment.

(*c*) Very *similar* twins who live (apart) in *dissimilar* environments.

From the data secured from these groups he was able to make the following comparisons:

(1) Contrast (*b*) and (*a*) — *dissimilar* twins in *similar* environment with *similar* twins in *similar* environment. Differences attributed to heredity.

[35] N. D. M. Hirsch, *Twins : Heredity and Environment*, 1930.

(2) Contrast (*a*) and (*c*) — *similar* twins in *similar* environment with *similar* twins in *dissimilar* environments. Differences due to environment.

(3) Contrast (*b*) and (*c*) — *dissimilar* twins in *similar* environment with *similar* twins in *dissimilar* environments. Differences due to heredity.

The tests and measurements included: height, weight, head length, head width, cephalic index; hair, eye, skin coloration; individual and pair photographs; handwriting; drawing ability; Otis arithmetic test; manual and motor ability; disease history; teacher estimate; Pintner-Cunningham mental test; Otis primary mental test; Dearborn A mental test; Terman mental test; and personal estimates, from the twins themselves, of their emotional character and interests.

The results are summarized in Tables XV, XVI and XVII.

TABLE XV. COMPARISON OF (*b*) AND (*a*) — *Dissimilar* TWINS IN *Similar* ENVIRONMENT WITH *Similar* TWINS IN *Similar* ENVIRONMENT (Hirsch)

	Height, Inches	Weight, Pounds	Head Length, mm.	Head Width, mm.	Cephalic Index	Intelligence Quotient points
(*b*) Average difference of *dissimilar* twins in *similar* environment Number of cases	1.87 54	7 54	5.98 57	3.5 57	2.3 57	13.8 58
(*a*) Average difference of *similar* twins in *similar* environment Number of cases	.4 38	2.6 30	1.2 38	1.6 38	.87 38	2.3 38
Ratio of average differences of (*b*) and (*a*)	1 to 4.7	1 to 2.7	1 to 4.9	1 to 2.2	1 to 2.6	1 to 6.0

Hirsch also found that in his twins —

38 pairs of selected *similar* twins correlated for I.Q. $r = .97 \pm .012$

58 pairs of selected *dissimilar* twins correlated for I.Q. .... $r = .53 \pm .071$

Although some of the differences in Tables XV, XVI and XVII are not statistically significant, the general trend of the findings is in support of the hereditarian argument, although neither the extreme hereditarian nor the extreme environmentalist claim is upheld. Hirsch's data show "that heredity was about five times as significant as environment in determining I.Q. differences between twins, while for weight, heredity was only about twice as potent in its causal effectiveness as environment. . .

"Education and training vary in their influence in proportion to the hereditary type with which they are dealing — the more intelligent the individual the more potent educational and general environmental influence. It may be stated then that the importance of environment increases roughly as we ascend the human scale. In other words, environment becomes more important as heredity becomes higher and more competent, paradoxical as this may seem. This truth again shows that heredity and environment are by no means intrinsically antagonistic." (p. 148)

TABLE XVI. COMPARISON OF (*a*) AND (*c*) — *Similar* TWINS IN *Similar* ENVIRONMENT WITH *Similar* TWINS IN *Dissimilar* ENVIRONMENT (Hirsch)

	Height, Inches	Weight, Pounds	Head Length, mm.	Head Width, mm.	Cephalic Index	Intelligence Quotient points
(a) Average difference of *similar* twins in *similar* environment Number of cases	.4 38	2.6 30	1.2 38	1.6 38	.87 38	2.3 38
(c) Average difference of *similar* twins in *dissimilar* environments Number of cases	.4 5	6 5	3.2 4	1 4	.75 4	3.5 4
Ratio of average differences of (c) and (a)	1 to 1	1 to 2.3	1 to 2.7	1 to .6	1 to .8	1 to 1.5

TABLE XVII. COMPARISON OF (*b*) AND (*c*) — *Dissimilar* TWINS IN *Similar* ENVIRONMENT WITH *Similar* TWINS IN *Dissimilar* ENVIRONMENT (Hirsch)

	Height, Inches	Weight, Pounds	Head Length, mm.	Head Width, mm.	Cephalic Index	Intelligence Quotient points
(*b*) Average difference of *dissimilar* twins in *similar* environment	1.87	7	5.98	3.5	2.3	13.8
Number of cases	54	54	57	57	57	58
(*c*) Average difference of *similar* twins in *dissimilar* environments	.4	6	3.2	1	.75	3.5
Number of cases	5	5	4	4	4	4
Ratio of average differences of (*b*) and (*c*)	1 to 4.7	1 to 1.17	1 to 1.87	1 to 3.5	1 to 3.0	1 to 3.94

Gesell and Thompson[36] instituted a unique and crucial method of twin study. Briefly, the method is this. One member of a pair of identical twins (T) is given specific training, while the other (C) remains without it. At a somewhat later age the program is reversed; C is given the training and T becomes the control. The influence of maturation can be studied. It is also possible to determine how much change in behavior can be made by special training, and, conversely, how similar the general lines of development remain despite the differences in training. The method has been applied to memory (by Josephine R. Hilgard), to language (by L. C. Strayer) and to motor learning and attention (by Gesell and Thompson). The results are discussed under *maturation hypothesis* in Chapter II. Here it may be said that the behavior of identical twins is extraordinarily alike. "Evidences of functional correspondence and similarity of behavior equipment were established by a series of twelve developmental examinations in which 612 comparative ratings were made; 513 of these ratings indicated complete or nearly complete identity of behavior. The degree of correspondence was so great as to justify the use of

[36] Arnold Gesell and Helen Thompson, *Learning and Growth in Identical Infant Twins*, 1929.

one twin (twin C) as a virtually duplicate control for the
experimental study of twin T." (p. 115)

McNemar[37] experimented with twins along the line of
motor skills, and the effects of practice thereon. He wanted
to find out if uni-ovular twins were more alike than multi-
ovular in certain specific skills, and if practice tended to make
the resemblances of multi-ovular twins approximate those of

TABLE XVIII. SUMMARY OF TWIN RESEMBLANCES IN MOTOR
SKILLS COMPARED WITH RESEMBLANCES IN OTHER TRAITS
(McNemar)

	Test or Trait	r Multi-ovular	r Uni-ovular
McNemar's			
46 multi-ovular pairs	Pursuit rotor	.51	.95
47 uni-ovular pairs	Steadiness	.43	.83
	Speed drill	.56	.82
	Spool packing	.44	.71
	Card sorting	.39	.85
Holzinger's			
52 multi-ovular pairs	Tapping ability	.43	.78
50 uni-ovular pairs	Binet mental age	.67	.95
	Height	.65	.93
	Weight	.63	.92
	Head length	.58	.91
	Head breadth	.55	.89
	Cephalic index	.58	.90
Stock's			
50 (?) pairs each	Height	.49	.95
	Weight	.44	.94

the uni-ovular. His tests included pursuit rotor, steadiness,
speed drill, spool packing and card sorting. His subjects
were all boys of junior high school age — 98 pairs. Of
these 48 were multi-ovular, 47 uni-ovular, and 3 were
doubtful.

[37] Quinn McNemar, "Twin Resemblances in Motor Skills, and the Effect of
Practice thereon," *Ped. Sem. and Jour. of Genetic Psychol.*, 1933, XLII, pp. 70-99.

His results are given in Table XVIII, where Holzinger's and Stock's results are given for comparison.

McNemar found "that practice increased fraternal twin resemblances on the pursuit rotor from .45 to .61, and in spool packing from .41 to .59, the increase in each instance being twice its probable error. The fraternal resemblance in card sorting and the identical resemblance for all three performances changed very slightly with practice." (p. 95)

"Summarized briefly, this research has found that 46 fraternal and 47 identical pairs of male twins of junior high school age show the same order of resemblance in the case of five performances requiring skill as in the case of anthropometric measurements, and the writer concludes that the hereditary hypothesis is the most plausible explanation of individual differences in motor skills." (p. 96)

For a number of years a group of Chicago professors, *Newman, Freeman* and *Holzinger*,[38] have been collecting experimental and other data on cases of identical twins reared apart. They themselves have studied 19 pairs. With a pair studied earlier by Müller, the data on twenty cases are now available. Since identical twins offer identical heredities, any differences found must be ascribed to the differences of environments in which the twins were reared. It is of prime importance that the cases studied must be monozygotic. The following criteria of monozygocity were used:

1. They must be so strikingly similar in general appearance that they are likely to be mistaken the one for the other.
2. They must be essentially identical in hair color, hair texture, and hair form.
3. They must have essentially the same eye color and pigment pattern on the iris.
4. They must have the same skin color (complexion), unless one is modified by tanning, and the same amount and distribution of body down, especially on face, neck, and hands.
5. They must have essentially the same facial features, nose, lips, chin, ears.
6. They must have essentially the same types of teeth, the same irregularities in dentition.
7. They must have hands and fingers of the same type and proportions.

[38] H. H. Newman, F. N. Freeman, K. J. Holzinger, *Twins : a Study of Heredity and Environment*, 1937.

8. The general microscopic character of the friction ridges of fingers and palms must be essentially the same.
9. There must be stronger cross resemblance than internal resemblance in most of the details of finger and palm patterns. (One hand of one twin must be more like one hand of the other twin than like own other hand. This fails in only a few of the least-similar twins for the same reason that it fails in Siamese twins.)
10. The presence of reversed asymmetry (mirror-imaging) in handedness, hair whorl, dentition, palm patterns, etc., is confirmatory evidence of monozygocity, but its absence does not deny monozygocity. Neither does the occasional presence of left-handedness or counter-clockwise hair whorl in one of a pair of decidedly unlike twins indicate that they are monozygotic. (p. 35)

The examination, in addition to a careful case-study of each pair, included the following extraordinarily complete set of items:

PHYSICAL OBSERVATIONS AND MEASUREMENTS

Height, standing and sitting.
Weight.
Head length and width.
Cephalic index.
Hair color and texture.
Hair whorl (location and direction of twist).
Eye color and pigment pattern on the iris.
Skin texture and coloration.
Handedness:
    Subject's statement.
    Mother's statement.
Palm prints and fingerprints.
Ears, general contour and peculiarities.
Other facial features.
Birthmarks, moles, etc.

TESTS

Stanford Revision of the Binet-Simon Test of Intelligence.
Otis Self-administering Test of Mental Ability.
Thurstone Psychological Examination (American Council Test).
Stanford Achievement Test.
Woodworth-Mathews Personal Data Sheet.

TABLE XIX. BASIC SCORES AND DIFFERENCES FOR NINETEEN PAIRS OF SEPARATED IDENTICAL TWINS
(Newman, Freeman & Holzinger)

Case	Age	Stanford-Binet Mental Age			Stanford-Binet I.Q.		Otis I.Q.		Stanford Educational Age		Psych. Exam. Thurstone		International Test		Woodworth-Mathews No. of Neurotic Traits	
		Yr.-Mo.	Yr.-Mo.	Diff.	Score	Diff.	Score	Diff.	Months	Diff.	Score	Diff.	Score	Diff.		Diff.
I	19– 1	13– 7	15– 6	23	85 97	12	90 108	18	181 200	19	77 143	66	79 123	44	17 18	1
II	26– 8	10– 6	12– 5	23	66 78	12	69 84	15	131 169	38	omitted		69 98	29	18 26	8
III	23– 0	15–11	16– 2	3	99 101	2	110 100	10	205 189	16	101 74	27	160 147	13	13 15	2
IV	29– 7	14– 2	17– 0	34	89 106	17	97 111	14	173 207	34	45 115	70	96 104	8	3 8	5
V	37– 8	14– 3	14–10	7	89 93	4	86 89	3	176 182	6	20 30	10	59 60	1	18 15	3
VI	59– 2	16– 3	15– 0	15	102 94	8	68 70	2	151 155	4	omitted		75 70	5	17 17	0
VII	13– 6	14– 2	14– 4	2	105 106	1	105 101	4	191 189	2	43 58	15	101 107	6	14 12	2
VIII	15– 5	14– 4	11–10	28	92 77	15	101 86	15	175 162	13	74 35	39	144 114	30	11 19	8
IX	19– 4	16– 3	15– 5	10	102 96	6	104 99	5	210 202	8	139 105	34	154 146	8	12 8	4
X	12– 9	15– 7	16– 3	8	122 127	5	113 121	8	181 200	19	62 67	5	144 144	0	14 11	3
XI	35– 0	14– 8	18– 6	46	92 116	24	94 106	12	157 226	69	5 93	88	143 188	45	30 30	0
XII	29– 8	18– 7	17– 6	13	116 109	7	116 115	1	224 210	14	95 98	3	190 190	0	26 20	6
XIII	19– 0	15– 2	15– 5	1	94 95	1	106 103	3	196 189	7	90 32	58	151 139	12	24 19	5
XIV	39– 9	13– 8	13– 5	3	85 84	1	96 86	10	176 159	17	11 4	7	94 103	9	37 15	22
XV	26– 0	14– 7	14– 3	4	91 90	1	92 84	8	159 161	2	28 30	2	123 95	28	11 7	4
XVI	11– 5	10– 3	10– 0	3	90 88	2	87 90	3	130 131	1	24 29	5	103 106	3	5 2	3
XVII	13–11	16– 0	14– 7	17	115 105	10	119 119	0	176 176	0	33 22	11	153 135	18	18 26	11
XVIII	27– 0	15– 4	12– 4	36	96 77	19	104 84	20	192 157	35	53 35	18	124 89	35	5 11	6
XIX	41–10	14– 0	12– 7	17	88 79	9	89 90	1	177 172	5	40 38	2	95 94	2	13 15	2
Mean scores		14.58±.21 yr.			95.68±1.42		97.16±1.49		178.87±2.57		57.29±4.25		118.66±3.80		15.71±0.84	
S.D. scores		1.96 yr.			13.00		13.58		23.47		36.74		34.71		7.65	
Mean diff.		15.42±1.98 mo.			8.21±1.03		8.00±0.94		16.26±2.61		27.06±4.38		15.53±2.26		5.00±0.75	
S.D. diff.		12.82 mo.			6.65±0.73		6.07±0.66		16.85±1.84		26.80		14.60±1.60		4.88±0.53	

TABLE XIX. BASIC SCORES AND DIFFERENCES FOR NINETEEN PAIRS OF SEPARATED IDENTICAL TWINS (Cont'd)

(Newman, Freeman & Holzinger)

Case	Age	Otis S.-A. Test				Kent-Rosanoff				Pressey Emotions				Downey Will-Temperament		
		No. Right	No. Attempted	Percentage Right	Diff.	No. of Common Reactions	Diff.	Average Frequency of Responses	Diff.	Total No. Crossed Out	Diff.	Total No. of Deviations (Idiosyncrasy Score)	Diff.	Total Score	Diff.	Pattern Difference (Average on Diff. on Parts)
I	19– 1	32 50	x	55.6|81.3	25.7	94 95	1	120|110	10	154|150	4	51 55	4	39 53	14	2.3
II	26– 8	11 26	37|35	29.7|74.3	44.6	79 95	16	105|143	38	159|232	73	58 50	8	56 59	3	2.9
III	23– 0	52 42	x	78.0	3.6	98 100	2	163|133	30	161|257	96	51 45	6	55 61	6	1.7
IV	29– 7	39 53	x	66.7|85.4	18.7	95 96	1	130|121	9	195|231	36	53 50	3	52 76	24	3.0
V	37– 8	28 31	40|49	70.0|63.3	6.7	92 86	6	133|81	52	184|167	17	44 41	3	55 56	1	2.9
VI	59– 2	26 28	44|33	59.1|84.8	25.7	99 81	18	134|101	33	210|179	31	48 46	2	45 41	4	1.3
VII	13– 6	36 31	57|62	63.2|50.0	13.2	33 87	54	61|116	55	200|186	14	59 56	3	52 69	17	2.3
VIII	15– 5	38 23	52|52	73.1|44.2	28.9	93 85	12	170|96	74	221|185	36	43 67	24	72 57	15	2.1
IX	19– 4	46 41	55|44	83.6|93.2	9.6	99 87	12	154|156	2	154|221	67	42 42	0	52 50	1	1.3
X	12– 9	40 48	63|66	63.5|72.7	9.2	87 93	6	148|133	15	221|188	33	54 49	5	52 62	10	2.5
XI	35– 1	36 48	69|55	65.5|69.6	4.1	79 71	8	128|121	7	232|164	68	39 51	12	54 82	28	2.9
XII	29– 8	58 57	68|63	85.3|90.5	5.2	93 93	0	112|170	58	201|115	86	58 58	0	52 68	16	1.9
XIII	19– 0	48 45	75|62	64.0|72.6	8.6	90 97	7	116|167	51	202|181	21	52 47	5	66 65	1	1.9
XIV	39– 9	38 28	48|51	79.2|54.9	24.3	84 87	3	47|155	108	187|148	39	48 53	5	55 53	2	1.2
XV	26– 0	34 26	46|39	73.9|66.7	7.2	97 88	9	155|127	28	170|112	58	44 65	9	70 63	7	2.7
XVI	11– 5	10 13	32|45	31.3|28.9	2.4	60 87	27	40|114	74	179|115	64	68 65	3	53 49	5	0.6
XVII	13–11	40 40	50|50	80.0|80.0	0.0	85 83	2	70|103	33	188|145	43	45 50	5	53 62	9	1.6
XVIII	27– 0	46 26	58|54	79.3|48.1	31.2	85 88	3	145|117	28	117|161	44	53 53	0	58 57	1	1.3
XIX	41–10	31 32	43|47	72.1|68.1	4.0	98 98	0	117|161	44	165|231	66	44 45	1	55 55	10	1.3
Mean scores	.....	36.2±1.28	.....	64.0±3.06		87.8±1.33		120.3±4.47		180.7±3.88		50.7±0.76		57.7±0.97		....
S.D. scores	.....	11.70	.....	27.93		12.14		40.85		35.44		6.91		8.88		
Mean diff	.....	.....	.....	14.36±2.03		9.63±1.93		39.42±4.09		47.16±3.81		4.89±0.85		9.16±1.21		1.98±0.31
S.D. diff	.....	.....	.....	13.10		12.49		26.43		24.61		5.51		7.80		0.695

x Test given for twenty minutes only. The scores are equivalent to thirty-minute scores.

International Test, devised by Stuart C. Dodd.
Kent-Rosanoff Free Association Test.
Pressey Test of the Emotions.
Downey Will-Temperament Test, Individual Form (Complete).

INFORMATION GATHERED BY INTERVIEW WITH PARENTS OR OTHERS

Age	School history	General
Physical history	School and grade	Interests
Birth	Previous progress	Recreation
Diseases	Character of work	Reading (voluntary)
General health	Interest	Talents
Defects	Ambitions	Siblings
Handedness	Disposition	

In Table XIX, the basic scores and differences for nineteen pairs of separated identical twins are given:

A statistical analysis of this data is a complex task. As a result of his analysis, Holzinger finds that separation of identical twins leads to significant changes in weight, intelligence, and school achievement. "From the viewpoint of the educator it is important to note that extreme differences in educational and social environments are accompanied by significant changes in intelligence and educational achievement as measured by our tests." (p. 349) The correlations given in Table XX support this argument, for the correlations of intelligence and achievement of separated twins are very similar to those of fraternal twins. (p. 347)

As a conclusion of their study, the authors state (p. 359):

"In brief, if the environment differs greatly as compared with heredity, the share of environment in determining traits which are susceptible to environmental influence is large. If, on the other hand, there is large genetic difference and small environmental difference, the share of heredity is relatively large. This is what makes the solution of the question as to the relative share of the two sets of factors indeterminate. We would have to specify what degree of genetic difference is to be compared with what degree of environmental difference. We may, however, add this statement that differences in the environment which actually sometimes occur, as exemplified in our separated pairs, are sufficient to produce differences in weight, ability, and behavior large enough to overshadow the genetic differences which occur between siblings."

TABLE XX. CORRELATIONS FOR THREE GROUPS OF TWINS
(Newman, Freeman & Holzinger)

Trait	Identical	Fraternal	Separated
Standing height	.981	.934	.969
Sitting height	.965	.901	.960
Weight	.973	.900	.886
Head length	.910	.691	.917
Head width	.908	.654	.880
Binet mental age	.922	.831	.637
Binet I.Q.	.910	.640	.670
Otis I.Q.	.922	.621	.727
Stanford Achievement	.955	.883	.507
Woodworth-Mathews	.562	.371	.583

Such a conclusion makes it appear at first as if the mountain had labored and produced a mouse. In comparison with the authors of other studies, the Chicago professors tend to place more emphasis upon environment. Indeed they are inclined to accept Jenning's dictum "that what heredity can do environment can also do." What they have proved is what most people have been naïvely inclined to accept, namely, that heredity seems more potent in regard to physical traits — height, weight, head length, head width, fingerprints, etc. — and less potent in regard to mental traits and achievements, such as intelligence and school acquirements. But we should give a wrong idea if we left the reader with the impression that the study was a negligible one. As a matter of fact, it is the most carefully conducted study of twins that has yet been made and will repay the student handsomely who gives it a careful reading.

The Dionne Quintuplets. On May 28th, 1934, near Callander in Ontario, were born the only quintuplets who have ever survived past infancy as an unbroken set. Contrary to general opinion, quintuplet births are not so very uncommon. Dr. MacArthur and Dr. Ford [39] have collected more

---

[39] J. W. MacArthur and N. H. C. Ford, "A Biological Study of the Dionne Quintuplets — an Identical Set," in Blatz's *Collected Studies on the Dionne Quintuplets*, 1937.

than 60 cases which have been reported, mostly during the past two centuries, and for 45 of these considerable information is available. Of the 45, only 3 are believed to be identical sets, although 40 per cent of them contain either all boys or all girls.

Quintuplets of the same sex may be derived in 42 ways as follows:

(1)	monozygotic as (♀ ♀ ♀ ♀ ♀)		in 14 ways
(2)	dizygotic as (♀ ♀ ♀ ♀)(♀)		in 10 ways
	or as (♀ ♀ ♀)(♀ ♀)		in 4 ways
(3)	trizygotic as (♀ ♀ ♀)(♀)(♀)		in 6 ways
	or as (♀ ♀)(♀ ♀)(♀)		in 3 ways
(4)	quadzygotic as (♀ ♀)(♀)(♀)(♀)		in 4 ways
(5)	quintzygotic as (♀)(♀)(♀)(♀)(♀)		in 1 way

——
42

There is evidence to show that in the case of the Dionnes, the splitting was in some such fashion as the following:

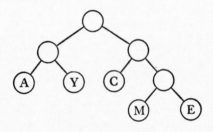

There seem to be closer resemblances between E and M, and between A and Y than between any other possible pairs.

That they are monozygotic in origin is shown by the following lines of evidence:

(1) They are of the same sex.
(2) They had one placenta and one common chorion, and, probably, five amnia (birth membranes were destroyed early).
(3) They are confusingly similar in facial features; only those who remain with them for long periods learn to distinguish among them. However, the quintuplets themselves never mistake each other and are greatly amused at the mistakes of outsiders.
(4) They have the same color of skin, iris and hair.

(5) They all belong to the same blood group, O.

(6) The hand and palm patterns are such that only monozygocity could produce them. Further, the partial syndactyly of the second and third toes is found in all of them, as are certain rare patterns, e.g., whorls on the palms. The right and left hands of any member of the set are less alike than one of her hands and a hand of a sister.

The finger pattern types and sizes are given in Table XXI, together with those of two sisters and a brother.

TABLE XXI. FINGER PATTERN TYPES, AND RIDGE COUNTS READ FROM LEFT TO RIGHT, AND TOTAL QUANTITATIVE VALUES FOR EACH HAND OF THE QUINTUPLETS; EMILIE (E), YVONNE (Y), CECILE (C), MARIE (M), AND ANNETTE (A), AND THREE OLDER SIBS, ERNEST (ER), ROSE (R), AND THERESE (T) (MacArthur & Ford)

	Left Fingers					Quantitative Value		Right Fingers				
	5	4	3	2	1	L total	R	1	2	3	4	5
E	U 0–4	U 0–10	T.A	U 0–12	U 0–18	44	55 99	Wdu 19–11	U 12–0	U 10–0	R 0–8	U 6–0
Y	U 0–7	U 0–12	U 0–11	U 0–11	Wdu 10–17	58	44 102	Wdu 18–10	T.A	U 14–0	U 6–0	U 6–0
C	U 0–6	U 0–4	U 0–12	U 0–7	U 0–18	47	53 100	U 19–0	U 11–0	U 12–0	R 0–6	U 5–0
M	U 0–7	U 0–11	U 0–8	U 0–10	U 0–16	52	49 101	U 18–0	U 7–0	U 12–0	U 7–0	U 5–0
A	U 0–7	U 0–10	U 0–9	U 0–9	U 0–13	51	50 101	U 18–0	Uta 3–0	U 10–0	Rw 0–12	U 7–0
Er	Ua 0–2	Uw 0–7	U 0–5	U 0–4	U 0–13	31	47 78	W 21–14	U 10–0	U 4–0	U 8–0	U 4–0
R	U 0–3	U 0–7	U 0–10	Ra 1–0	U 0–7	28	41 69	U 13–0	U 4–0	U 13–0	U 8–0	U 3–0
T	U 0–8	U 0–14	U 0–6	U 0–12	U 0–20	60	79 139	U 24–0	U 16–0	U 11–0	U 17–0	U 11–0

The pattern form index, computed in two ways (Geipel; and Cummins and Steggerda) together with the genetic for-

mulae determined by the Bonnevie method are given in
Table XXII.

TABLE XXII. A SERIES OF NINE VALUES DETERMINED FROM
THE FINGER PATTERNS IN THE DIONNE FAMILY
(MacArthur & Ford)

Finger Pattern

Type			Shape		Size	
Pattern Index	Pattern Intensity Index		Individual Form Index		Individual Quantitative Value	Genetic Formula Indicated
	L	R	(1)	(2)		
E 10	0	25	76.3	43.8	99	VvRRUU
Y 11	25	33.3	75.6	45.8	102	VvRRUU
C 10	0	0	78.4	49.8	100	VvRRUU
M 10	0	0	79.7	43.1	101	VvRRUU
A 10	0	25	76.4	43.6	101	VvRRUU
Er 11	0	25	125.1	77.1	78	VvRRUU
R 10	0	0	104.9	72.7	69	VVRrUU
T 10	0	0	103.4	70.1	139	vvRRUU

A mere glance at these Tables shows the extraordinarily
close resemblances of the quintuplets in finger patterns;
monozygocity is clearly indicated.

The quintuplets started life with identical heredities.
What changes has environment made? First, as to physique. When born prematurely at 7 months, no member
weighed as much as three pounds. After three years, with
the exception of M, they have reached or exceeded the normal levels for weight and height. (See Figs. 16 and 17.)
In height and weight, therefore, despite their initial handicap, they can be regarded as normal. Their deciduous teeth
erupted at a definitely later time than normal, from 3 to 7
months after the maximum time-limit as shown by Logan
and Kronfeld's chart. Compared with most children, they
have been remarkably free from infectious diseases and gas-
tro-intestinal upsets. This is due, no doubt, to the more than
royal care to which they have been subjected.

In mental development, the tendency to improve is also shown. In Table XXIII, are given the mental test scores (Gesell) showing percentage of possible score passed at four age levels. [40] The scores on the Kuhlmann and the Merrill-Palmer (Stutsman) tests show similar tendencies. All five children are retarded in language development, but as lan-

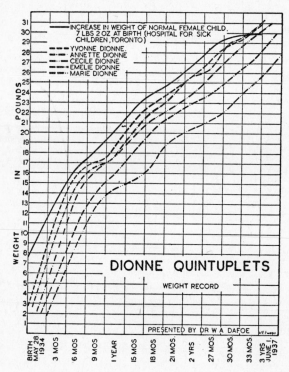

Fig. 16. Weight Record of the Dionne Quintuplets.

guage retardation averaging three months is shown by twins, this phenomenon should occasion no surprise. It has been estimated that their mental development curves will cross the normal around 5 or 6 years of age. In regard to social development, their friendly and happy attitudes towards each other and towards the staff is noticed by all observers.

[40] From W. E. Blatz and D. A. Millichamp, "The Mental Growth of the Dionne Quintuplets" in Blatz, *Collected Studies on the Dionne Quintuplets*, 1937.

From all these studies of closely related individuals, including those on the quintuplets which have so far been made, the inevitable conclusion is reached that heredity is the primary factor in regard to the inheritance of physical characteristics. With intellectual and social (emotional) reactions the factor of environment begins to loom large, especially in regard to the social development. But in all

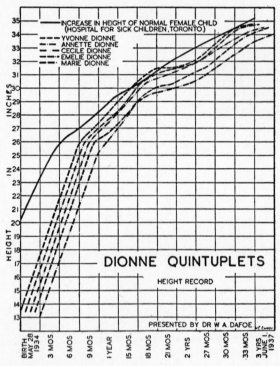

Fig. 17. Height Record of the Dionne Quintuplets.

three types of development, the correlative nature of heredity and environment is strongly shown. Which is the more important, heredity or environment? This question is just about as sensible as the one — which is more important, the engine or gasolene? Nobody in his senses would belittle either. However, personally, if I had to choose between a good engine and good gasolene, I would choose the good engine. There is a slight suspicion that the Chicago

TABLE XXIII. MENTAL TEST SCORES OF QUINTUPLETS
(Gesell) (Blatz & Millichamp)
Percentage of "possible" score passed at four age levels

Chronological Age	Motor					Language					Adaptive				
	A	C	E	M	Y	A	C	E	M	Y	A	C	E	M	Y
17 months	71	64	64	43	79	50	50	50	50	50	26	37	32	26	42
23 months	86	86	86	71	86	53	47	47	42	47	63	63	63	41	74
29 months	88	85	85	77	88	64	64	59	55	68	68	68	68	71	77
35 months	82	79	76	76	86	77	77	77	69	77	72	81	69	89	78

Chronological Age	Personal-Social					Total				
	A	C	E	M	Y	A	C	E	M	Y
17 months	59	59	59	59	59	48	52	48	44	56
23 months	95	87	83	70	87	73	71	70	58	74
29 months	79	79	79	79	79	75	74	73	71	79
35 months	91	91	91	91	91	80	81	78	76	83

professors would choose the gasolene (environment). However, Newman and his colleagues have done the world an important service by pointing out that in some circumstances, at least, the gasolene may be all-important, and that in no case should it be neglected. As far as heredity and environment are concerned, the only thing changeable by teachers is the environment. Working on this factor alone, astonishing improvements in the present generation can be made by improved methods of education. But, unfortunately for the progress of civilization, these acquired characters are not inherited.

(6) *Studies of the inheritance of special traits.* Every trait inherited in mendelian fashion is a tribute to the potency of inheritance, for in such cases the trait appears in any normal environment. However, since an environment is needed, we cannot say unequivocally that the trait is due to heredity. In the case of the scientific bias shown by the Darwins, the factor of environment is undoubtedly an important one. Even a casual study of a dictionary of biography or a Who's Who discloses the fact that intellectualism is apt to run in families. There are some intellectual traits, such as music, which seem to have a marked hereditary basis. Take the following example from the *Bach* family, whose major luminary, of course, was Johann Sebastian. Only the more immediate relatives of this great musician are shown in Table XXIV.

It is conceivable, but very unlikely, that inheritance had nothing to do with the musical talent of the Bach family. On the other hand, it is again conceivable, but very unlikely, that a similar number of persons selected at random from the general population and reared in the musical environment the Bachs provided, would have risen to equal eminence in music.

(7) *Studies of children of cousin marriages.* So far as I am aware, this is a field that has never been investigated. Yet it is a promising one. Cousin marriages are permitted in most states (in Europe they range between one-half and one per cent of the total marriages), and a considerable number of children must be born of such marriages. Their importance for the problem of heredity and environment lies in the fact that the parents are genetically related. By comparing the siblings of cousin marriages with equated siblings of non-related parents, we should get a measure of the potency of heredity. If, for instance, siblings from cousin marriages were more alike than ordinary siblings, a good case would be made out for heredity. If environment was the more potent, then siblings of cousin marriages would be no more alike than siblings of ordinary marriages.

The Egyptian and Aztec rulers were predominantly the children of brother and sister marriages. Unfortunately, we have no data about them which could be used for comparison with children of ordinary Egyptian or Aztec marriages of

TABLE XXIV. THE BACH FAMILY

(Those in italics are known to have been competent musicians. All but two gained their livelihoods with music.)

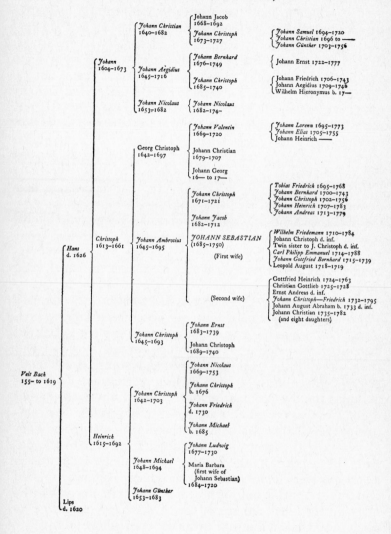

Johann Jacob
1668–1692

Johann Christoph
1673–1727
{ *Johann Samuel* 1694–1720
Johann Christian 1696 to ——
Johann Günther 1703–1756

Johann Bernhard
1676–1749
{ Johann Ernst 1722–1777

Johann Christoph
1685–1740
{ Johann Friedrich 1706–1743
Johann Aegidius 1709–1746
Wilhelm Hieronymus b. 17—

Johann Christian
1640–1682

Johann Aegidius
1645–1716

Johann
1604–1673

Johann Nicolaus
1653–1682
Johann Nicolaus
1682–174–

Georg Christoph
1642–1697
Johann Valentin
1669–1720
{ *Johann Lorenz* 1695–1773
Johann Elias 1705–1755
Johann Heinrich ——

Johann Christian
1679–1707

Johann Georg
16— to 17—

Johann Christoph
1671–1721
{ *Tobias Friedrich* 1695–1768
Johann Bernhard 1700–1743
Johann Christoph 1702–1756
Johann Heinrich 1707–1783
Johann Andreas 1713–1779

Johann Jacob
1682–1712

Christoph
1613–1661
Johann Ambrosius
1645–1695

JOHANN SEBASTIAN
(1685–1750)

(First wife)
{ *Wilhelm Friedemann* 1710–1784
Johann Christoph d. inf.
Twin sister to J. Christoph d. inf.
Carl Philipp Emmanuel 1714–1788
Johann Gottfried Bernhard 1715–1739
Leopold August 1718–1719

(Second wife)
Gottfried Heinrich 1724–1763
Christian Gottlieb 1725–1728
Ernst Andreas d. inf.
Johann Christoph—Friedrich 1732–1795
Johann August Abraham b. 1733 d. inf.
Johann Christian 1735–1782
(and eight daughters)

Hans
d. 1626

Johann Christoph
1645–1693
Johann Ernst
1683–1739

Johann Christoph
1689–1740

Johann Nicolaus
1669–1753

Johann Christoph
1642–1703
Johann Christoph
b. 1676

Johann Friedrich
d. 1730

Heinrich
1615–1692
Johann Michael
b. 1685

Johann Michael
1648–1694
Johann Ludwig
1677–1730

Maria Barbara
(first wife of
Johann Sebastian)
1684–1720

Johann Günther
1653–1683

Veit Bach
155– to 1619

Lips
d. 1620

that period. However, very close inbreeding is practised by stock-breeders, and studies similar to the one suggested above could be made quite easily. A beginning was made by *Burlingame and Stone*,[41] who found the coefficient of correlation for learning ability of sibling white rats born to parents closely inbred over many generations to be .31 ± .04.

Social Heredity.— If the reader has kept an open mind, he will probably agree that "heredity and environment are correlative factors." Heredity or nature provides whatever potentialities we possess; environment or nurture determines whether or not they shall be realized in actuality. If the "Wild Boy of Aveyron" had been a potential genius, instead of the dullard he proved to be, he would never have developed his genius running wild in the forest. A feebleminded person can never be educated into normality, although he can and should be trained to do some of the economically useful things which lie within his capacity. When these limitations of education are widely recognized, we shall refrain from expecting grapes to be grown of thorns and figs of thistles. On the other hand, and this is equally important, we shall see to it that potential ability, wherever found, does not languish for want of educational opportunity. Education can and does perform wonders in one generation as Russia can testify; but its effects are mostly limited to one generation.

Not quite, for social heredity as it has been called, which is a form of educational environment, affects more than one generation. Children are born *with* a biological heritage; they are also born *into* a social heritage. Although parents cannot will their knowledge and learning to children as they will their property, yet in a very real sense their achievements change the environments that their children are reared in. We are to some extent masters of our fate since we can create or at least seek the environment that suits us best. Good environments are generally the deliberate creations of able people, and these good environments stimulate the potentialities of the people who live in them. The whole thing is a circle, but it need not be a vicious circle. Mankind through countless generations has stored his acquisitions of

---

[41] Mildred Burlingame and Calvin P. Stone, "Family Resemblance in Maze-Learning Ability in White Rats," *N.S.S.E.*, *27th Yearbook*, 1928, pp. 89-99.

knowledge in books, pictures, works of art and utility, laws and traditions. These become environmental stimuli of powerful potency to succeeding generations, providing, of course, they have the natural intelligence to profit from them. A parent who surrounds his children with good books, good pictures and good standards of citizenship in a home that is tasteful; who provides them with opportunities for travel, and converses with them intelligently on topics of social importance, is providing them with a social heritage of the highest value. In fact, so important is family life in the home that the family might usefully be added to heredity and environment to make the trio — *heredity, environment* and *family*. If children do not profit from a good home life it is probably because they cannot.

The teacher, likewise, through improved text-books and better methods of teaching, provides a better social heredity for his pupils in that he makes learning and achievement more certain, thorough, and expeditious. This social inheritance, unlike the biological inheritance which is passed from parent to child through each generation, must be acquired anew by each generation. Compared with biological heredity, social inheritance is more easily lost and more easily regained. It is therefore much less stable. To some extent a good social heritage can offset a bad biological inheritance, as when a knowledge of health laws helps to overcome the handicap of a bad physical constitution. In the same way a good system of education offsets a mediocre intellectual inheritance. Even the I.Q. can be improved several points by good training and education. But these environmental effects are comparatively limited and mainly affect but one generation. No social heritage, however good, can offset completely or replace a sound biological inheritance. Yet it is with education as a social heritage that the teacher concerns himself all the time. It is the one factor under his control by means of which he makes the most of the potentialities each pupil brings with him to school. But the teacher, as a citizen, should also be concerned about the biological heritage of the coming generation, for it is the biological factor which, in the long run, determines the future of mankind.

REFERENCES

Bagley, W. C. *Educational Determinism.* Baltimore, Warwick and York, 1925. Pp. 194.

Blatz, W. E. et al. *Collected Studies on the Dionne Quintuplets.* University of Toronto Press, 1937. Each study separately paged.

Burt, C. *Mental and Scholastic Tests.* London, P. S. King and Sons, 1922. Pp. xv + 432.

Cattell, J. M. "A Statistical Study of American Men of Science." *Science*, XVI, 1906, pp. 732ff.

Clark, W. E. L. *Early Forerunners of Man: a Morphological Study of the Evolutionary Origin of the Primates.* Baltimore, Wood and Co., 1934. Pp. xvi + 296.

Conklin, E. G. *Heredity and Environment in the Development of Man.* Princeton University Press, 5th Ed., 1923. Pp. 379.

Davenport, C. B. *Heredity in Relation to Eugenics.* New York, Holt, 1911. Pp. xi + 298.

De Candolle, A. *Histoire des Sciences et des Savants depuis deux Siècles.* Geneva, Georg, 1873; 2nd Ed. 1885. Pp. xvi + 594.

Dodge, R. *Conditions and Consequences of Human Variability.* New Haven, Yale University Press, 1931. Pp. xi + 162.

Dugdale, R. L. *The Jukes.* New York, Putnam, 1877. Pp. viii + 120.

East, E. M. *Heredity and Human Affairs.* New York, Scribner, 1929. Pp. ix + 325.

Ellis, H. *A Study of British Genius.* 1904. Boston, Houghton Mifflin, 1926. Pp. xvi + 396.

Estabrook, A. H. *The Jukes in 1915.* Washington, Carnegie Institution, 1916. Pp. vii + 85.

Fisher, R. A. *The Genetical Theory of Natural Selection.* Oxford University Press, 1931. Pp. xiv + 272.

Fisher, R. A. *Statistical Methods for Research Workers.* Edinburgh, Oliver and Boyd, 1932. Pp. xiii + 307.

Freeman, F. S. *Individual Differences: the Nature and Causes of Variations in Intelligence and Special Abilities.* New York, Holt, 1934. Pp. xi + 355.

Galton, F. *English Men of Science; their Nature and Nurture.* 1874. Reprint, New York, Appleton, 1890. Pp. xiii + 270.

Galton, F. *Inquiries into Human Faculty and its Development.* 1883. Reprint, London, Dent, no date. Pp. xviii + 261.

Galton, F. *Natural Inheritance.* London, Macmillan, 1889. Pp. ix + 259.

Galton, F. "The Average Contribution of each Several Ancestor to the total Heritage of the Offspring." *Proc. Roy. Soc. London*, 1897, 61 B, pp. 401-413.

Galton and Schuster. *Noteworthy Families.* London, Murray, 1906. Pp. xlii + 96.

Gesell, A. "The Developmental Psychology of Twins." *Handbook of Child Psychology* (Ed. Murchison). Worcester, Clark University Press, 1931, pp. 158-203.

Gesell and Thompson. "Learning and Growth in Identical Infant Twins." *Genetic Psychol. Monogs.*, VI, 1, (1929), pp. 5-120.

Goddard, H. H. *The Kallikak Family.* New York, Macmillan, 1914. Pp. xv + 125.

Gordon, H. *Mental and Scholastic Tests among Retarded Children; an Enquiry into the Effects of Schooling on the Various Tests.* London, Board of Education Pamphlet No. 44, 1923. O.P.

Goring, C. *The English Convict; a Statistical Study.* (Abridged edition.) London, His Majesty's Stationery Office, 1919. Pp. xvi + 275.

Hirsch, N. D. M. *Twins: Heredity and Environment.* Cambridge, Harvard University Press, 1934. Pp. 159.

Hogben, L. *Nature and Nurture.* New York, Norton, 1933. Pp. 144.

Holzinger, K. J. "The Relative Effect of Nature and Nurture Influences on Twin Differences," *Jour. Educ. Psychol.*, 1929, XX, pp. 241-248.

Hurst, C. C. *The Mechanism of Creative Evolution.* Cambridge University Press, 1932. Pp. xxi + 365.

Huxley, T. H. *Man's Place in Nature.* 1863. Reprint, London, Dent, 1906. Pp. xviii + 372.

Iltis, H. *Life of Mendel.* London, Allen, 1932. Pp. 336.

Jenkins, R. L. "Twin and Triplet Birth Ratios," *Jour. of Heredity*, XX, 10, 1929, pp. 485-494.

Jennings, H. S. *The Biological Bases of Human Nature.* New York, Norton, 1930. Pp. xviii + 384.

Jennings, H. S. *Genetics.* New York, Norton, 1935. Pp. xiii + 373.

Journal of Heredity. Many excellent articles, especially in Vols. XVII and XXI-XXVII. Washington, D. C., American Genetic Association.

Lauterbach, C. E. "Studies in Twin Resemblances," *Genetics*, X, 6, 1925, pp. 528-568.

McNemar, Q. "Twin Resemblances in Motor Skills, and the Effect of Practice thereon." *Ped. Sem. and Jour. Genetic Psychol.*, 1933, XLII, pp. 70-99.

Merriman, C. "The Intellectual Resemblances of Twins," *Psychol. Monog. Suppl. 33*, Princeton, Psychol. Review Co., 1924. Pp. 58.

Moore, E. *Heredity: mainly Human.* London, Chapman and Hall, 1934. Pp. vii + 343.

Morgan, T. H. *The Theory of the Gene.* New Haven, Yale University Press, 1928. Pp. xviii + 358.

Murchison, C. (Ed.) *A Handbook of General Experimental Psychology.* Worcester, Clark University Press, 1934. Pp. xii + 1125.

National Society for the Study of Education. *Twenty-seventh Yearbook, Part I: Nature and Nurture; their Influence upon Intelligence.* Bloomington, Public School Publishing Co., 1928. Pp. ix + 465.

Newman, H. H. *The Biology of Twins.* Chicago University Press, 1917. Pp. 195.

Newman, H. H. *The Physiology of Twinning.* Chicago University Press, 1923. Pp. 230.

Newman, H. H.   "Studies of Human Twins: I. Methods of Diagnosing Monozygotic and Dizygotic Twins," 1928, *Biol. Bull.*, LV, pp. 283-297.

Newman, H. H., Freeman, F. S. and Holzinger, K. J.   *Twins: a Study of Heredity and Environment.*   Chicago University Press, 1937. Pp. xvi + 369.

Pearson, K.   "On the Inheritance of the Mental and Moral Characters in Man, and its Comparison with the Inheritance of Physical Characters."   (Huxley Lecture 1903.)   *Trans. Anthrop. Instit. Great Britain and Ireland*, pp. 179-237 ; and *Biometrica*, III, pt. 2, 1904, pp. 131-190.

Pearson, K.   "On the Criterion which may serve to test the Various Theories of Inheritance," 1904, *Proc. Roy. Soc. London*, 73 B, pp. 262-280.

Pearson, K.   "On the Influence of Double Selection on the Variation and Correlation of two Characters," 1908, *Biometrica*, VI, pp. 111-112.

Popenoe, P. and Johnson, R. H.   *Applied Eugenics*, (Rev. Ed.).   New York, Macmillan, 1933.   Pp. ix + 429.

Sanders, B. S.   *Environment and Growth.*   Baltimore, Warwick and York, 1934.   Pp. xviii + 375.

Scott, W. B.   *The Theory of Evolution.*   New York, Macmillan, 1917. Pp. ix + 183.

Stockard, C. R.   "Experimental Modification of the Germ-plasm and its Bearing on the Inheritance of Acquired Characters."   1923, *Proc. Amer. Philos. Soc.*, LXII, p. 5.

Stocks, P.   "A Biometric Investigation of Twins and their Brothers and Sisters."   *Annals Eugenics*, IV, 1930, pp. 49-108.

Terman, L. M. et al.   *Genetic Studies of Genius, I.*   Stanford University Press, 1925.   Pp. xv + 648.

Thorndike, E. L. "Measurement of Twins." *Archives of Phil., Psy., and Scientific Methods.*   New York, Science Press, 1905.   Pp. 64.

Ward, L. F.   *Applied Sociology.*   Boston, Ginn, 1906.   Pp. xviii + 384.

Warden, C. J.   *The Evolution of Human Behavior.*   New York, Macmillan, 1932.   Pp. ix + 248.

Wheeler, W. F.   *Inheritance and Evolution.*   London, Methuen, 1936. Pp. xii + 116.

Wiggam, A. E.   *The Fruit of the Family Tree.*   Indianapolis, Bobbs-Merrill, 1924.   Pp. 368.

Wilson, E. B.   *The Cell in Development and Heredity.*   3rd Ed.   New York, Macmillan, 1928.   Pp. 1232.

Wingfield, A. H.   *Twins and Orphans: the Inheritance of Intelligence.* London, Dent, 1928.   Pp. 127.

Winship, A. E.   *Jukes-Edwards: a Study in Education and Heredity.* Harrisburg, Myers, 1900.   Pp. 88.

Woods, F. A.   *Mental and Moral Heredity in Royalty.*   New York, Holt, 1906.   Pp. viii + 312.

Yerkes, R. M. and Yerkes, A. W.   *The Great Apes.*   New Haven, Yale University Press, 1929.   Pp. xix + 652.

Zeleny, C. "The Relative Numbers of Twins and Triplets." *Science,* LIII, p. 262.

Zuckerman, S. *Functional Affinities of Man, Monkeys and Apes.* New York, Harcourt, Brace, 1933. Pp. ix + 203.

CHAPTER II

INDIVIDUAL DIFFERENCES FOUND IN HUMAN NATURE

In Chapter I, we saw that variations were frequently distributed according to the law of chance. This causes a concentration around the central tendency or average; so much so that we declared it fair to say that "mediocrity was the one type found in nature." This clustering of variations around the average is a fortunate feature as far as education is concerned. Since two-thirds of the variants of a normal distribution are found within a range of 1 *sigma* from the mean, these individuals are so similar in talent that group or class methods of instructing them would seem to be justified. The majority of pupils in any class will be so much alike that they can be conveniently taught together. Only the extremes, the very superior and the very inferior in the trait under consideration, will require special attention.

One of our concerns in the previous chapter was to show that pure chance, working impartially among a given set of independent factors, produces a typical normal distribution. We showed that a reconciliation between the biometric methods of the Pearsonian school and the genetic methods of the Morgan school became possible, providing that the genes composing the various chromosomes were really independent factors. If such were the case, these genes, entering into the heritable make-up of a very large and unselected group, would inevitably produce the normal forms of distribution found by the biometricians. The two points of view are therefore supplementary, not antagonistic. The geneticist seeks to discover the hereditary elements which make up the individual; the biometrician, taking large populations of individuals, finds that any given trait is distributed according to the normal surface of frequency — as it must necessarily be if the independence of the genes is fact rather than fiction. However, the importance of individual differences for education is so great that further discussion must be given to it.

Galton's Pioneering Work.— Historians in the field of psychology are generally agreed that Galton (1822–1911) was the chief instigator of research in the field of individual differences. His first and abiding scientific love was the problem of inheritance of genius and his *Hereditary Genius* (1869) is rightfully regarded as a landmark in the subject. Gradually his interests widened, and we soon find him measuring human "faculties" of every kind. *Inquiries into Human Faculty and its Development* (1883) was a product of these further investigations and may be regarded as the first great work on the psychology of individual differences. For the interpretation of individual differences, Galton realized that statistics were needed. He therefore delved into the subject and, although comparatively untrained as a mathematician, had the acumen to formulate the theory of correlation and to devise rough measurements for the calculation of what we now know as a coefficient of correlation. To show how far Galton progressed, the student interested in the problem may consult one of his early tables reproduced by Garrett in *Great Experiments in Psychology*. (p. 172)

It is almost certain that J. McKeen Cattell, regarded as the father of the psychology of individual differences on the North American continent, was influenced by Galton when they became associated at Cambridge University in 1888, during Cattell's tenure of a lectureship in that institution. We can also trace Cattell's strengthened interest in statistics and faith in the probable error to this early friendship. Through Cattell's students — Thorndike, Woodworth, Wissler, Franz, Dearborn, Strong, Brown, Poffenberger, Kelley, Gates and many others — the study of individual differences has become the dominant type of American psychology. Indeed, Europeans think of American psychology mainly in terms of individual differences and "rat running." Fortunately, these branches of psychology are the ones that find their greatest usefulness in the field of education, hence America leads the world today in educational psychology.

Types of Individual Differences.— Since human beings are variable in many directions, there are literally scores of ways in which individual differences may be studied. Many classifications of these differences have been attempted, none of them wholly satisfactory. The time-honored classification into physical, mental and moral traits is too coarse for scientific use. It also suffers from the serious defect, at least from the standpoint of the student of original nature, that moral traits seem to be influenced to a greater extent by environmental agencies than mental and, especially, physical traits. It is known that physical traits, such as height, and mental traits, such as general intelligence, undoubtedly distribute themselves in normal fashion. If we could get reliable measures of moral traits, we should probably find them distributed according to the normal surface of frequency.

Individual differences have been studied from the standpoint of remote ancestry or race, and from that of nearer ancestry or family. This is a promising field from the point of view of original nature. Sex differences are important in education, especially those which attempt to settle the problem of the differential variabilities of male and female. If one sex were found to be inherently more variable than the other, the social and educational implications would be very far reaching. Again, we may study the effects of maturity on individual differences found in human beings. How many of these differences are really due to maturation? We may also study the variations which occur within the individual himself. Does variability increase or decrease with age? Extreme individual differences, such as those that are found in the blind, deaf, genius, mental defective and emotionally unbalanced, have provided a fruitful field of investigation. Individual differences in glandular secretions, in sensitivity of receptors, in muscular reactions and so forth are of great importance in schooling and should normally find a place in any comprehensive treatise on the psychology of education.[1] In the discussion which follows, only those individual differences which seem to have the greatest significance for education and also to be greatly dependent upon heredity, will be dealt with.

Differences Due to Remote Ancestry or Race.— No branch of the subject of individual differences is in such a

---

[1] At the time of writing, two texts bear the title *Individual Differences ;* those of R. S. Ellis (1928) and F. S. Freeman (1934). The subdivisions of Freeman seem to be both logical and practical. His titles for chapters are Introduction, the Extent of Individual Differences, the Influence of Inheritance, the Influence of Environment, the Influence of Race and Nationality, Differences Due to Sex, the Factor of Age : Infancy to Adolescence, the Factor of Age : Maturity and Decline, Special Abilities and Disabilities, the Factors of Physical Development and Personality. Anne Anastasi's *Differential Psychology* has recently appeared, making the third comprehensive discussion of individual differences.

muddle as this one. And the reason is due to the fact that few students have realized that race is a biological concept. Garth, in an Appendix to his *Race Psychology,* entitled "A Description of Experimental and Statistical Studies in Race Psychology," lists the following, among others, under races — whites, negroes, Indians, mulattoes, Japanese, Chinese, Jews, English, Nordic, Alpine, Mediterranean, French-Canadians, Greeks, Poles, Italians, Mexicans, Hindus, Brahmans, and Filipinos. Some of these — English, Greeks, Poles, and Italians — are obviously national groups and may contain a mixture of races. The terms Jew, Hindu and Brahman refer to religious groups and have little to do with race. Whites and negroes, although the respective members belong mainly to the great caucasoid and negroid races, are pigmentation groups. Aryans are not listed by Garth, but in other writings are frequently regarded as a race. The term Aryan refers to community in language and has nothing to do with race. Thus national groupings, religions, languages, pigmentation have been used indiscriminately in describing races. A race, of course, is a biological concept. Any big group of human beings who have a large percentage of common ancestors is liable to be called a race. The common ancestry has been furthered by geographical isolation. Thus, the greater this common ancestral element and the more rigid the geographical segregation, the more distinct the race appears to be.

Geographical isolation, which favors inbreeding, stamps a race with certain characters, or, in genetic terms, the race becomes homozygous. Anthropologists, who are students of race, usually select for study and measurement such features as skin color, hair texture and color, head size and shape, nose size and shape, eye pigmentation and slant, eyelid shape, etc., and use them to define race. Using these categories, anthropologists usually arrive at three great racial divisions — caucasoids, mongoloids and negroids; and have subdivided the caucasoids into three sub-groups, namely, the Mediterraneans, Nordics and Alpines.

The geographer, Griffith Taylor,[2] is somewhat sceptical about the scientific soundness of the anthropologists' classifi-

---

[2] Griffith Taylor, *Environment, Race and Migration,* (Rev. Ed.), 1937.
Griffith Taylor, *Environment and Nation,* 1936.

cation of races. Working on the Matthew theory of "zones and strata," he shows that the races of mankind have evolved in Central Asia — first the negroid types, then the Australoid, followed by the Nordic and Mediterranean, and lastly the Alpines both early and late. The dolicho-cephalic Nordics and Mediterraneans are but two slightly differing branches of the same racial stock.

The rise of a new and superior race at the center of origin forces the more primitive type towards the margin, hence the various races are found in concentric rings (imperfect rings, of course) around the center of dispersion. The most primitive races will be found on the outer margins or in remote mountainous regions; the highest and most recently evolved race in the center. Arguing in this fashion, Taylor claims that the broad-headed Alpine race is the latest to evolve and, with various shades of skin color, stretches across the center of Europe and Asia from the Bay of Biscay to Korea. He thus links the mongoloids with the Alpines of Europe. It is interesting to note that psychologists, using intelligence tests on racial groups, place the Alpines and mongoloids at the same level of intellectual power. Many anthropologists, of course, think that Taylor, in including the yellow stocks among the Alpines, has over-emphasized cephalic index and hair texture, and has not paid sufficient attention to skin color, stature and slant of eye. Whatever be the outcome of the controversy, Taylor is the first man to give a rational interpretation of the dispersions of races and the relationships found among them.

If race is a biological concept, it must be solved by accepted biological procedures. When man is studied by the biologist, he is found to belong to a single species — *Homo sapiens*. And this classification is biologically correct. Human beings everywhere, whatever their color, nationality, religion, blood-grouping or language, form a single biological group. They inter-breed freely, and the offspring is fertile. Their structural anatomy, physiological functioning, blood-grouping — in fact, every biological feature which can be used in classification shows them to have a common biological origin. Biologically, then, we have *one* race — the human race. Differences in skin color, cephalic index, etc., are largely adventitious. They correspond to the various breeds of pigeon which by selective mating have been derived from the rock pigeon, and which, by indiscriminate mating, return to the ancestral form; or they correspond to breeds of dogs and other animals.

With freer communication and social intercourse, miscegenation will increase on the earth and mankind, the world over, will tend to fuse into a mass of closely similar individuals. Language and religion, twin fruits of geographical isolation, will also cease to play the disturbing parts they now play in human affairs. Such statements as these may seem to be fantastic, but a study of the United States, where less than one-tenth of the negroes are now pure-blooded, and of Hawaii, the melting-pot of the Pacific, clearly indicates the trends. The break-down of racial barriers by the rapidity and ease of our transportation systems is apt to be overlooked by the average man.

But what the educator wants to know is whether there are reliable differences among existing races that have significance for education. He wants to know, for instance, whether or not caucasoids are cleverer than mongoloids or negroids, and Alpines cleverer than Nordics and Mediterraneans. Such information would be of great service, but, unfortunately, we do not possess it.

The problem, of course, is an old one. As a scientific problem it was first raised by Gobineau.[3] To him we are indebted for the mythical doctrine of Aryan supremacy, and to its successors in various forms — the Nordic doctrine,[4] for example. The versatile Galton[5] discussed the problem and threw some light on it, but failed to settle the issues he raised. Galton compared the Greeks of the Golden Age with modern Europeans and modern Africans. He placed the negro two grades below the Anglo-Saxon in natural ability, and the Anglo-Saxon two grades below the Greek. (p. 342) The Australian aborigine, lowest of all, was placed one grade below the negro. His scale was, presumably, one of fourteen points, since he declared that, taking negroes on

---

[3] J. A. de Gobineau, *The Inequality of Races*, (tr. A. Collins), 1915.

[4] See C. C. Brigham, *A Study of American Intelligence*, 1922.
T. L. Stoddard, *The Rising Tide of Color against White World-Supremacy*, 1920.
M. Grant, *The Passing of the Great Race*, 1921.

[5] Francis Galton, "The Comparative Worth of Different Races," in *Hereditary Genius*, 1869.

their own intellectual ground, they still are inferior to Europeans by about one-eighth of the difference, say, between Aristotle and the lowest idiot.   Hence we get:

	points
Greeks of Golden Age	14
Modern Europeans	12
Modern Africans	10
Australian aborigines	9

Karl Pearson [6] in his life of Galton criticizes Galton's naïve acceptance of Greek superiority.   He says:

"If we require a fair test of relative fineness of intellect in two ages, surely we may ask this: Would the ablest minds of Age A have grasped the subtlest thought of Age B, and would the genius of B have failed to appreciate the intellectual product of A's most eminent minds?   Judged by this test, I think both Kant and Einstein could fully grasp and duly appreciate what the Platonic Socrates had to say, but I gravely doubt whether the ideas of both Kant and Einstein would not have transcended Socrates' mental capacity, even as the modern geometrician himself fully understands Euclid, but Euclid would have failed to understand him.   And this is not a matter of accumulated *knowledge* of the intervening centuries, it is a result of the ablest intellects being more subtle, more capable of forming generalized conceptions than the most capable of ancient Greeks." (p. 107)

All this, of course, though founded by Galton and Pearson on wide reading and close observation, amounts to little more than futile speculation.   With the development of fairly valid and reliable measures of intelligence, and especially after the publication of the results of group intelligence testing in the American Army,[7] the problem assumed another character.   It actually became possible to compare racial groups rather fairly.   There is, however, the perennial bugaboo of environment that intrudes itself into the problem.   Suppose, for example, we want to discover whether or not the negro children of New York are as clever as the white children of that city.   We take white and colored pupils of the same ages, the same grades, attending the

---

[6] Karl Pearson, *The Life, Letters and Labours of Francis Galton*, Vol. II, 1924.
[7] R. Yerkes (Ed.), *National Academy of Science Memoirs*, Vol. XV, 1921.

same schools, etc., and submit them to a series of standardized intelligence tests. We then compare the results. Generally speaking we find, under such circumstances as these, that white pupils secure higher ratings than colored ones. Are we therefore justified in saying that American whites are cleverer than American negroes? After all, the tests seem eminently fair, as both sets of pupils have been taught the same courses of study by the same teachers. But we must ever remember that every intelligence test is a test of achievement. We try to limit it to those experiences which a common environment provides and every testee has the chance of learning, but we can never get away from the fact that it depends on environmental learning, in-school and out-of-school. It is obvious that for white and colored pupils in New York City, the out-of-school environment cannot possibly be the same, and the in-school environment is probably subtly different for the two groups. The negro pupil probably lives in Harlem in a home in which books and other elements of culture are at a minimum; in any case he has lived all his life in an atmosphere of social ostracism. The white pupil, in comparison, has lived in a much more favorable environment. The differences found may simply be the reflections of the environment and may have nothing at all to do with hereditary or racial differences. Since so few of the studies of racial differences have even tried to take this factor into account, their findings must be cautiously interpreted. Bearing this in mind, we can give some of the results that have been found without laying ourselves open to the charge that they are uncritically accepted.

In Tables XXV and XXVI we give the results of tests of negroes and whites which have been summarized by Pintner.[8] (pp. 433 and 437)

According to Pintner, "all results show the negro decidedly inferior to the white on standard intelligence tests. . . These results are sufficiently numerous and consistent to point to a racial difference in intelligence. The overlapping of the two races is great, and the most liberal estimate seems to be that at most 25 per cent of the colored reach or exceed the median intelligence of the whites." (p. 443)

[8] Rudolph Pintner, *Intelligence Testing : Methods and Results* (New Ed.), 1931.

TABLE XXV. COMPARISON OF NEGRO AND WHITE BY MEANS
OF THE BINET TESTS (Pintner)

Author	Negro		White	
	Median I.Q.	No. of Cases	Median I.Q.	No. of Cases
Schwegler and Winn	89	58	103	58
Arlitt	83	71	106	191
Pintner and Keller	88	71	95	249
Arlitt	86	243	no white group	
Lacy	91	817	103	5,159
Graham	99	105	no white group	
Strachan	93	609	102	14,463
Strachan	92	375	101	6,063

TABLE XXVI. NEGRO AND WHITE SCHOOL CHILDREN TESTED
BY GROUP TESTS (Pintner)

Author	No. of cases		Test used	Negro I.Q.
	Negro	White		
Jordan	247	1,504	N.I.T.	75
Peterson	37-734	71-641	Otis	58-75
			Pressey	
			Haggerty	
			Myers	
Garth and Whatley	1,272		N.I.T.	75
St. Louis Report	1,574	8,998	Pintner-Cunningham	92
Hirsch	449	1,030	Pintner-Cunningham and Dearborn	85
Kempf and Collins	399	677	Various	71
Gray and Bingham	258	219	Not given	76
Garth et al.	2,006		Otis	76 or 78

Of all the other so-called racial tests listed by Pintner,
Garth and others, only those concerned with American Indians, Chinese and Japanese deal even approximately with
true racial groups; the rest are national or religious groups.

In Table XXVII we give a sample of the findings of tests on American Indians, Chinese and Japanese residing on the North American continent.

TABLE XXVII. I.Q.'s OF SAMPLES OF RACIAL GROUPS
(from Various Sources)

Author	*No. of Cases*	*Test Used*	*I.Q.*
A. *American Indians*			
Garth & Garrett (28)	1022 (Full-blood)	N.I.T.	69.6
Garth & Garrett	291 (Full-blood)	N.I.T.	72.5
Garth & Garrett	631 (Mixed-blood)	N.I.T.	78.9
Garth & Garrett	311 (Mixed-blood)	N.I.T.	90.5
Jamieson & Sandiford (28)	275 (Mixed-blood)	N.I.T.	79.8
Jamieson & Sandiford	280 (Mixed-blood)	Pintner Non-Language	96.9
Jamieson & Sandiford	115 (Mixed-blood)	Pintner-Paterson Performance	96.4
Jamieson & Sandiford	59 (Mixed-blood)	Pintner-Cunningham	77.9
B. *Chinese*			
Yeung (21)	109	Binet	97
Symonds (24)	513	Pintner Non-Language	99.3
Sandiford & Kerr (26)	224	Pintner-Paterson Performance	107.2
Graham (26)	62	Binet	87
C. *Japanese*			
Fukuda (25)	43	Binet	98
Darsie (26)	658	Binet	91
Sandiford & Kerr (26)	276	Pintner-Paterson Performance	114

It is difficult to interpret these results. Full-blood Indians make poorer scores on tests than Mixed-bloods. All Indians obtain higher I.Q.'s on the non-language tests than on those which involve language. The language handicap, therefore, is a very real one. With respect to the Chinese and Japanese, it should be noted that these, when tested, were living on the North American continent, not in China and Japan. For these also, there is an obvious linguistic handicap. In non-linguistic tests, such as the Pintner-Paterson Performance Tests, they seem to be consistently superior to white children of corresponding ages. This may be a matter of selection. Their parents are probably of higher intelligence than the average of the group from which they were drawn, since only the enterprising, ambitious and tenacious of purpose would break home ties and migrate. Certain it is, that the feebleminded would be left at home. Since the children tend to inherit the parental intelligence, the good showing they make may thus be explained. On the whole, we can say that the Chinese and Japanese living on the North American continent are equal in intelligence to the native born. They may even show a superiority, but this is not fully proven. This does not mean that the mongoloid race as a whole is superior in intelligence to the caucasoid race, since there are many reasons for believing that the two averages are approximately equal.

Brigham,[9] by some unwarrantable statistical juggling with the results of the American Army tests, arrived at what he considered reliable measures of the three racial groups of Europe. The Nordic group had a Mental Age of 13.28; the Alpine 11.67; and the Mediterranean 11.43. Since he assumed that the Germanic group in the United States had the same proportions of Nordics and Alpines as Germany itself, it is easily seen that he did not prove his case. In fact, he has partially repented of his error,[10] but on grounds of the internal inconsistency of the Army Alpha test, rather than on grounds of the selective character of immigration.

But Brigham's work apparently stimulated Klineberg[11] to make a unique study of racial intelligence. He took a non-linguistic test to Europe and administered it in areas that were inhabited by Nordics, Alpines and Mediterraneans respectively. The idea was a splendid one; it is unfortunate that we have no really good non-linguistic test of intelligence, although the six tests of the Pintner-Paterson Performance Scale, which Klineberg used, were the best available at the time. He studied groups residing in ten centers, namely, Hanover (German Nordic), Flanders (French Nordic), Baden (German Alpine), Auvergne and Velay (French Alpine), Piedmont (Italian Alpine), Eastern Pyrenees (French Mediterranean), Sicily (Italian Mediterranean), and three city groups — Paris, Hamburg and Rome.

Table XXVIII gives the results for the ten groups. (p. 27)

[9] C. C. Brigham, *A Study of American Intelligence*, 1922.

[10] C. C. Brigham, "Intelligence Tests of Immigrant Groups," *Psychol. Rev.*, XXXVII, 1930.

[11] Otto Klineberg, *A Study of Psychological Differences between "Racial" and National Groups in Europe*, 1931.

TABLE XXVIII. COMBINED POINT SCALE SCORES (Pintner and Paterson) FOR KLINEBERG'S TEN EUROPEAN GROUPS

Group	Average	Median	Range	S.D.	S.D.Av.	N
Paris	219.0	218.9	100–302	46.2	4.62	100
Hamburg	216.4	218.3	105–322	45.6	4.56	100
Rome	211.8	213.6	109–313	42.6	4.26	100
German Nordic	198.2	197.6	69–289	49.0	4.90	100
French Mediterranean	197.4	204.4	71–271	45.6	4.56	100
German Alpine	193.6	199.0	80–211	48.0	4.80	100
Italian Alpine	188.8	186.3	69–306	48.4	4.84	100
French Alpine	180.2	185.3	72–296	46.6	4.66	100
French Nordic	178.8	183.3	63–314	56.4	5.64	100
Italian Mediterranean	173.0	172.7	69–308	54.2	5.42	100

Even a cursory examination of Table XXVIII shows that the city pupils make consistently higher scores on the tests than country pupils. This may be due to the fact either that cities tend to attract the abler families or that the education given in cities is superior to that given in the country. Both factors are probably at work. Secondly, the German Alpines resemble the German Nordics far more closely than the German Nordics resemble the French Nordics. Education and environment seem to be better explanations of these resemblances and similarities than race. In fact the average scores of the Nordic, Alpine and Mediterranean are very similar. As Klineberg says: "The results offer no substantiation of a definite 'racial' hierarchy, but they do not thereby rule out 'heredity' as an explanation of the observed differences between [sic] the ten groups. It is suggested, however, that there are a number of cultural and environmental factors which may account for the results."

With this finding Garth is in substantial agreement. He finds that the quantitative results, which indicate the presence of racial differences, are all "open to the criticism that the factor of nurture has not been equalized between the two races compared with as much success as would seem fair to both races." He might, with equal truth, have said that the factor of selection has been neglected. The fact that negroes north of the Mason-Dixon line are more intelligent than those of the Southern States can be explained by saying that the more intelligent negroes have migrated from the region of "Jim-Crow" cars and the indignities that colored people are

subject to in the South.   Equally well, of course, the fact
can be explained by saying that the negroes of the North
receive, on the whole, a better education than is given to
negroes in the South.   Probably both explanations have
some truth; the problem is another beautiful illustration of
the difficulty one finds in unraveling the respective contributions of heredity and environment.   Attention, however,
should be drawn to the considered judgment of Pintner, a
careful student of the problem, who thinks that the facts
justify us in thinking that there is, on the average, an innate
inferiority in the negroid race.

This should, however, not blind us to the obvious fact
that the differences among individuals of any given race are
immensely greater than the differences between the averages
of any two given races.   The best negro, for example, is not
only markedly superior in intelligence to the worst white,
but he is also greatly superior to the average white.   If this
overlapping be remembered, it will prevent us from assuming superiority, or inferiority, simply on account of member-
ship in any racial group.   At bottom it is not the race that
counts, but the individual.   And with this observation, we
may leave the subject for the present.

Differences Due to Nearer Ancestry or Family.— Remote ancestry, as we have seen, determines the shape of our
heads and the color of our skins; nearer ancestry or family
determines the more intimate resemblances between parent
and offspring — the family traits in which the child, to use
old-fashioned terms, favors or takes after its father or
mother.   Thorndike has truly said: "What ancestry does is
to reduce the variability of the offspring and determine the
point about which they do vary." (*Educational Psychology*,
1903, p. 70)   The heights of the father and mother determine the heights of the children, although as Galton found,
there will be a regression towards the normal.   Traits such
as deafness, myopia, etc., which may have a genetic basis, are
obviously influenced by a person's immediate ancestry.   Thus
Fay [12] found that if a person had a congenitally deaf brother
or sister the chances of being deaf were at least 245 times as
great as they would be if the brothers and sisters had normal
hearing.   The percentage of deaf children born to parents

[12] E. A. Fay, *Marriages of the Deaf in America*, 1898.

both of whom were deaf, Fay found to be 25.9. Thus we can say truthfully that deafness tends to run in families. In exactly the same way, intelligence, stupidity, criminality and insanity are influenced by inheritance. As George Bernard Shaw is reputed to have said, "the most important thing a child can do is to choose his parents wisely."

The individual differences due to family are due, of course, to the differences in the genes. If there are six sons in a family, then only by the remotest chance will their genetic inheritances be identical. The greater the age interval, the greater will be the differences (or the less the resemblances) found among them. Thus on the average we know that sibling resemblance is represented in round figures by a co-efficient of correlation of .50; resemblance of fraternal twins by .60; of all twins by .80; and of identical twins by .90. The resemblance of non-related individuals, when the factor of age is eliminated, is zero. We are apt to regard the similarities among offspring as being due to heredity; it is well to remind ourselves that the differences may also be inherited.

Differences Due to Sex.— Schopenhauer said that "woman, far from being a model of physical grace, appears, when set by the side of man, a narrow-chested, large-breasted, short-legged, broad-hipped, fat-thighed, knock-kneed anomaly." Apparently, he did not care much for women. Yet scientific measurements undoubtedly establish the fact that, on the average, women are shorter, lighter and weaker than men; they have broader hips and narrower chests, shorter legs and smaller heads; they are also more thinly covered with muscle and more thickly covered with fat. Some of these differences are inherent, yet with the emancipation of women from the sedentary life of the home and their participation in open-air games, these physical differences tend to decrease, though they never disappear altogether.

Modern life lessens the importance of the physical differences between the sexes. In ancient times the shorter legs of women may have made them into a class apart, but today the advantages are equalized by trams, trains, motor cars and airplanes. Again women have undoubtedly smaller cranial capacities than men, but they have smaller bodies also. In proportion to the bulk of the body, the skulls and brains of men and women show equal ratios; the bigger body of the male demands a bigger brain to move it and to control it.

Formerly the impression was general that woman's intelligence was inferior to man's. When careful measurements are made of the intelligence of boys and girls and of men and women (and thousands of such measurements have been made), the averages for the two sexes are found to be identical. In tests of school achievement, where intelligence undoubtedly plays an important part, the results sometimes favor one sex, sometimes the other. Thus, girls are most frequently found superior in the language studies — oral and silent reading, spelling, composition and language completion tests, freedom from speech defects, handwriting[13] and modern languages. They are also superior in the biological sciences and these have a large element of language in them. Since sheer mechanical retentiveness plays a large part in the acquisition of language, and since girls are undoubtedly superior to boys in this trait, the explanation of the superiority of girls in linguistic achievements may lie in their superior memory powers.

Boys, however, are found to be rather consistently superior in history and geography, and in both these subjects language undoubtedly enters. The other subjects in which a masculine superiority is generally exhibited are reasoning in arithmetic, mathematics, physics, chemistry, engineering and the classical languages. These differences must be regarded only as trends; any study of the summarized findings, such as Lincoln's,[14] shows many discrepancies and reversals.

Defects, such as color-blindness and haemophilia, which involve the sex chromosomes, are invariably found more frequently among males. Color-blindness, as we have seen, occurs in a marked degree in about 4 per cent of males and 0.4 per cent of females; in a lesser degree about 9 per cent of males are affected. Certain disturbances of finer muscular control, such as stuttering, stammering, squinting and left-handedness, occur more frequently among boys than girls.

Common opinion regards the sexes as complementary in

---

[13] Handwriting tends to be masculine or feminine. About two samples out of three can be judged correctly as being written by a male or female. However, some women write a masculine hand and some men a feminine one.

[14] E. A. Lincoln, *Sex Differences in the Growth of American Children*, 1927.

their personalities and emotional lives. Terman and Miles,[15] in presenting a composite picture of this general opinion, write as follows:

"In modern occidental cultures, at least, the typical woman is believed to differ from the typical man in the greater richness of her emotional life and in the extent to which her every-day behavior is emotionally determined. In particular, she is believed to experience in greater degree than the average man the tender emotions, including sympathy, pity and parental love; to be more given to cherishing and protective behavior of all kinds. Compared with man she is more timid and more rapidly overcome by fear. She is more religious and at the same time more prone to jealousy, suspicion, and injured feelings. Sexually she is by nature less promiscuous than man, is coy rather than aggressive, and her sexual feelings are less specifically localized in her body. Submissiveness, docility, inferior steadfastness of purpose, and a general lack of aggressiveness reflect her weaker conative tendencies. Her moral life is shaped less by principles than by personal relationships, but thanks to her lack of adventurousness she is much less subject than man to most types of criminal behavior. Her sentiments are more complex than man's and dispose her personality to refinement, gentility, and pre-occupation with the artistic and cultural." (p. 2)

John Stuart Mill[16] attributed the personality differences of men and women to the kind of lives they lived. Woman stayed at home and lived more or less in seclusion keeping house and tending children. The husband, on the other hand, went forth to battle and business, and acquired a set of specialized habits different from his wife. Given exactly the same kinds of lives, men and women would be exactly alike both in their temperaments and intellects. Darwin believed that these same habits were inherited and became ingrained in the race; and Lombroso, the Italian criminologist, thought that criminal tendencies were inherited. But inheritance of acquired characteristics, as we have seen, has never been definitely proved. Darwin also added sexual selection as a factor in promoting sex differences. The most aggressive man, for example, would secure the coyest woman for wife, and these distinctive traits would gradually be

---

[15] L. M. Terman and Catharine C. Miles, *Sex and Personality*, 1936.
[16] John Stuart Mill, *The Subjection of Women*, Reprint, Oxford Classics, 1912.

stamped into the inheritance. Herbert Spencer thought that woman's development suffered arrest at adolescence and she remained permanently in a stage midway between that of a child and of an adult man. Darwin's man, therefore, is evolved woman; Spencer's woman is arrested man.

Endocrinology comes to our assistance at this stage. The essential sex differences are due to the differences of the hormones secreted by the gonads. Deprive a male of the secretions of his interstitial tissue and his behavior and personality become distinctly less masculine. Indeed, in some animals, fowls for example, sex may even be completely reversed.[17] Sex, then, seems to be basically determined by biology: if this be the case, we should normally expect permanent differentiations between male and female. However, in the case of human beings, another factor enters. The conditioning powers of education and environment are immensely more potent in man than they are in the lower animals, such as fowls, and this fact must never be overlooked.

Man is usually regarded as superior in mechanical ability to woman. Even such domestic appliances as sewing machines, looms, labor-saving utensils of the kitchen and the home are the inventions of men, not of women. This may be due to the differences in training that boys and girls customarily receive. When opportunities are equalized, women seem to make just as good aviators, architects and mechanics as men. Indeed, sex differences, which seem to loom so large, either decrease in amount or disappear altogether under identical systems of training.

Sex differences in sensation are small. In touch, discrimination of sounds and colors women seem to be superior; they are also less sensitive to cold because of their thicker layer of natural fat. Men have a more acute kinaesthetic sense and are sharper in their discriminations of odors and taste; they also suffer less from myopia.

In animals that seem to love fighting for its own sake, the male is bigger and stronger than the female. In this class

[17] F. A. E. Crew, "Abnormal Sexuality in Animals; III Sex Reversal," *Quarterly Review of Biology,* 1927, II, pp. 427–441.
  In this article Crew reports the case of a hen that, after becoming the mother of two broods of chickens, lost her ovaries by tubercular infection. Subsequently she developed male sexual organs and became the father of another brood of chickens.

of fighting animals, man must be included; in fact the difficulty of establishing peace on earth may be attributed to the pugnacious instincts of the human male.

In 1936, Terman and Miles[18] published the results of many years of study of masculinity and femininity. Masculinity and femininity are found admixed in different proportions in male and female. Some men are more feminine than others; some women may even be more masculine than some men. Briefly, they investigated by a series of paper tests devised for the purpose, the degree of masculinity and femininity exhibited by various groups of men and women. The sexes were found to overlap on the trait in question; some men were found to be predominantly feminine and some women predominantly masculine. Seven tests or exercises were devised, validated, and their reliabilities obtained. No assumptions were made; only those tests and items which actually separated males and females from early adolescence to life's extreme into two distinguishable groups were utilized. The tests included —

Type of Test or Exercise	*No. of Items in Form A*	*No. of Items in Form B*
Word Association	60	60
Ink-blot Association	18	18
Information	70	70
Emotional and Ethical Response	105	105
Interests	119	118
Personalities and Opinions	42	41
Introvertive Response	42	42
Totals	456	454

In Tables XXIX and XXX we give some of the main findings. A plus sign indicates masculinity, a minus sign femininity.

[18] L. M. Terman and Catharine C. Miles, *Sex and Personality : Studies in Masculinity and Femininity*, 1936.

TABLE XXIX. M-F SCORES OF MALE GROUPS. MEANS AND STANDARD DEVIATIONS OF MEANS FOR VARIOUS GROUPS ARRANGED IN ORDER OF MASCULINITY OF STANDARD SCORE (Terman & Miles)

Group	No.	Exercises							Total	
		1	2	3	4	5	6	7	M-F Score	S.S.
College athletes	46	− 4.4 / 1.18	− .1 / .14	+ 8.7 / .88	+ 30.7 / 2.57	+ 51.7 / 4.20	+ 5.1 / .84	− .8 / .31	+ 92.54 / 4.92	+ 1.00
Engineers	44	− 1.9 / 1.23	+ .4 / .18	+ 3.5 / .84	+ 33.7 / 2.73	+ 36.6 / 5.18	+ 2.2 / 1.00	− .6 / .25	+ 77.3 / 7.33	+ .75
High-school boys	308	− .8 / .44	+ .0 / .06	+ 5.2 / .46	+ 14.4 / 1.29	+ 56.7 / 1.80	+ .8 / .46	− .7 / .11	+ 77.1 / 2.98	+ .75
College students (four colleges)	278	+ .7 / .46	+ .0 / .00	+ 6.4 / .40	+ 24.4 / 1.13	+ 35.1 / 2.02	+ 2.5 / .36	− 1.3 / .13	+ 69.3 / 3.44	+ .60
Gifted boys	75	− 6.1 / .89	+ .1 / .06	+ 8.4 / .63	+ 22.2 / 2.18	+ 34.2 / 4.16	+ 5.6 / 1.12	+ .3 / .18	+ 66.2 / 5.28	+ .55
Army prisoners (active homosexuals)	44	− .8 / .8	− .1 / .17	+ 1.2 / 1.28	+ 20.6 / 3.12	+ 42.2 / 5.22	+ .4 / 1.28	+ .1 / .31	+ 66.2 / 6.97	+ .55
Adults, 20's	342	− 2.2 / .43	− .03 / .06	+ 3.6 / .39	+ 26.7 / 1.14	+ 30.0 / 1.89	− .5 / .37	− 1.2 / .11	+ 57.9 / 2.76	+ .35
Delinquent boys (older group)	153	− 1.4 / .63	− .3 / .11	+ 3.0 / .82	+ 9.3 / 1.92	+ 42.2 / 2.58	− 1.7 / .68	+ .2 / .23	+ 52.6 / 4.01	+ .30
Adults, 30's	330	− 2.7 / .45	+ .1 / .06	+ 1.8 / .44	+ 23.3 / 1.18	+ 26.3 / 1.87	− .4 / .40	− .6 / .11	+ 49.5 / 3.05	+ .20

TABLE XXIX. M-F SCORES OF MALE GROUPS. MEANS AND STANDARD DEVIATIONS OF MEANS FOR VARIOUS GROUPS ARRANGED IN ORDER OF MASCULINITY OF STANDARD SCORE (Continued)

Group	No.	1	2	3	4	5	6	7	M-F Score	S.S.
Delinquent boys (younger group)	129	− .0	− .1	+ 5.4	− 7.1	+46.9	− 3.1	+ .1	+43.7	+ .10
		.62	.12	.73	1.93	2.71	1.10	.28	4.10	
Adults, 40's	178	− 2.7	+ .1	+ 1.3	+19.5	+22.3	+ 1.2	− .8	+39.7	+ .05
		.62	.08	.55	1.73	2.57	.52	.13	3.64	
Adults, general population	552	− 3.4	− .0	+ .9	+16.8	+24.2	− 1.4	− .6	+36.5	0
		.34	.05	.37	.98	1.45	.33	.08	2.28	
Who's Who men	31	− 8.1	− .1	+ 3.3	+25.8	+ 5.5	+ 3.8	− .3	+31.2	− .10
		1.2	.2	.9	3.1	5.7	1.1	.3	7.6	
Adults, 50's	108	− 4.2	+ .2	+ 1.9	+16.8	+12.4	− .1	− .5	+26.6	− .15
		.80	.11	.71	1.99	2.86	.72	.18	4.46	
Who's Who women's husbands	23	− 9.7	− .6	+ 7.4	+20.7	+ .3	+ 4.8	− .9	+24.4	− .20
		1.53	.24	1.02	4.07	5.39	.85	.41	7.55	
Student priests	46	−11.8	− .2	+ 6.5	+14.1	+ 7.7	+ 2.4	− 1.2	+18.9	− .30
		1.13	.17	.96	2.91	3.64	.87	.31	5.14	
College of Music students	50	− 8.9	+ .0	+ 3.0	+26.1	− 4.3	− .1	− .8	+15.7	− .35
		1.32	.15	1.21	3.34	4.55	1.04	3.60	6.87	
Negro college students	51	− 6.2	+ .1	+ 3.4	+ 8.1	+ 6.6	+ 2.3	− .9	+14.5	− .40
		.87	.14	1.15	2.50	3.95	.57	.22	6.15	

TABLE XXIX. M-F Scores of Male Groups. Means and Standard Deviations of Means for Various Groups Arranged in Order of Masculinity of Standard Score (Continued)

Group	No.	1	2	3	4	5	6	7	Total M-F Score	Total S.S.
Adults, 60's	75	− 3.6 / .71	.0 / .14	+ 1.6 / .88	+10.0 / 2.47	+ 7.8 / 3.15	− 1.9 / .93	.5 / .21	+10.8 / 4.99	.45
Theological students (protestants)	53	− 5.8 / 1.08	.2 / .18	+ 2.7 / .95	+29.8 / 2.39	−14.3 / 4.01	− 1.6 / .90	− 2.1 / .25	+ 9.0 / 5.23	.50
Clergymen	63	− 5.6 / 1.01	.0 / .17	+ 2.6 / .64	+12.8 / 2.69	−11.8 / 3.49	.6 / .66	1.5 / .28	+ 8.0 / 4.52	.50
Adults, 70's and 80's	44	− 4.1 / 1.13	.2 / .22	+ 1.3 / 1.16	+11.2 / 3.57	.8 / 4.16	− 2.8 / 1.33	.1 / .31	+ 3.2 / 7.04	.60
Artists	41	− 9.6 / 1.14	.5 / .15	+ .1 / 1.10	+16.2 / 3.35	− 4.3 / 3.44	− 1.2 / 1.15	1.0 / .28	+ .3 / 6.10	.65
Inverts (passive homosexual prostitutes)	77	− 5.7 / .94	.9 / .15	− .1 / 1.01	+21.3 / 3.11	−36.2 / 3.52	− 2.8 / .64	− 2.7 / .29	−28.0 / 4.81	1.05

TABLE XXX. M-F SCORES OF FEMALE GROUPS. MEANS AND STANDARD DEVIATIONS OF MEANS FOR VARIOUS GROUPS ARRANGED IN ORDER OF MASCULINITY OF STANDARD SCORE (Terman & Miles)

Group	No.	Exercises							Total	
		1	2	3	4	5	6	7	M-F Score	S.S.
College athletes (high intelligence)	37	− 10.7 / 1.22	− 1.0 / .18	− 3.8 / 1.28	+ 26.6 / 3.60	− 25.3 / 4.41	− .6 / 1.08	− 1.6 / .30	− 13.7 / 3.61	+ 1.65
Ph.D.'s & M.D.'s	20	− 11.7 / 2.27	− 1.3 / .28	− 2.8 / 1.37	+ 24.0 / 4.60	− 43.5 / 5.38	− 1.1 / 1.41	− .9 / .52	− 34.5 / 10.85	+ 1.15
College students (high intelligence)	92	− 10.9 / .88	− .6 / .13	− 6.2 / .91	+ 20.2 / 1.79	− 36.7 / 3.02	+ .3 / .61	− 2.9 / .18	− 36.2 / 4.38	+ 1.15
Inverts (active & passive)	18	− 18.2 / 2.57	+ .3 / .28	− 7.5 / 1.74	+ 11.5 / 5.32	− 18.0 / 4.87	− 1.6 / 1.24	− 1.6 / .49	− 36.4 / 9.73	+ 1.15
Who's Who women	25	− 14.5 / 2.08	− 1.4 / .24	− 3.2 / 1.19	+ 12.3 / 3.91	− 36.5 / 5.80	− .1 / 1.06	− 1.49 / .37	− 45.5 / 8.47	+ .90
Student nurses	78	− 16.7 / .80	− 1.2 / .14	− 8.7 / .97	+ 2.6 / 2.12	− 29.9 / 3.04	− 2.9 / .64	− 2.8 / .23	− 63.4 / 4.47	+ .50
Prostitutes	12	− 11.9 / 2.13	− 1.6 / 1.16	− 20.7 / 3.19	+ 7.0 / 4.85	− 15.2 / 10.50	− 11.0 / 2.34	− .9 / .58	− 68.2 / 12.80	+ .40
College of music students	50	− 18.8 / 1.04	− .7 / .16	− 7.7 / 1.13	+ 12.1 / 3.13	− 51.7 / 3.42	− 2.7 / .91	− 2.7 / .25	− 71.1 / 5.60	+ .30
Adults, 20's	604	− 14.2 / .31	− 1.0 / .04	− 8.5 / .38	+ 4.1 / .92	− 45.5 / .77	− 5.6 / .30	− 2.7 / .08	− 74.2 / 1.82	+ .25
Adults, college education	760	− 14.4 / .27	− .9 / .04	− 6.9 / .29	+ 4.6 / .81	− 51.3 / 1.02	− 4.1 / .24	− 2.5 / .07	− 74.7 / 1.60	+ .20
Chinese girls	51	− 14.2 / .92	− 1.3 / .13	− 6.9 / 1.35	− 16.3 / 2.89	− 37.7 / 3.97	− 8.0 / 1.15	− 3.4 / .33	− 75.0 / 6.99	+ .20

TABLE XXX. M-F SCORES OF FEMALE GROUPS. MEANS AND STANDARD DEVIATIONS OF MEANS FOR VARIOUS GROUPS ARRANGED IN ORDER OF MASCULINITY OF STANDARD SCORE (Continued)

Group	No.	Exercises							Total	
		1	2	3	4	5	6	7	M-F Score	S.S.
Adults, 40's	297	—13.1 .45	—1.1 .06	—8.2 .49	—1.0 1.30	—47.5 2.20	—5.8 .41	—2.2 .11	—78.4 2.54	+ .15
High-school girls	245	—14.3 .48	—1.1 .06	—10.7 .58	—12.9 1.55	—32.2 1.85	—6.6 .50	—2.4 .13	—79.3 3.04	+ .10
Adults, 30's	466	—14.2 .38	—1.0 .05	—9.5 .43	—.3 1.09	—52.8 1.27	—5.7 .33	—2.4 .09	—84.5 1.93	0
Adults (general population)	1,107	—14.1 .25	—1.0 .04	—10.3 .29	—5.1 .73	—45.8 .85	—7.0 .24	—2.1 .06	—85.1 1.27	0
Adults, 50's	234	—14.3 .55	—.9 .08	—9.4 .58	—6.6 1.39	—48.6 1.68	—5.6 .51	—2.0 .12	—86.5 2.50	0
Adults, 70's & 80's	119	—14.4 .71	—1.0 .13	—10.7 .82	—11.6 2.09	—43.2 2.18	—6.3 .72	—1.0 .15	—87.2 3.37	0
Adults, 60's	153	—15.2 .63	—.7 .10	—8.5 .76	—9.0 1.74	—47.6 2.16	—6.6 .62	—1.8 .16	—89.1 3.02	.05
Mothers of gifted	78	—19.8 .80	—1.1 .14	—6.4 .99	—5.4 2.60	—59.2 2.66	—1.3 .78	—2.1 .20	—91.6 4.26	.15
Negro college students	25	—15.9 1.52	—.9 .23	—11.6 1.60	—8.5 4.04	—52.9 3.56	—2.1 1.31	—2.7 .49	—94.3 8.3	.20
Grade-school girls	256	—12.4 .47	—1.2 .08	—12.9 .59	—27.0 1.47	—30.2 1.81	—9.4 .62	—2.5 .13	—95.4 2.98	.20
Dressmakers & Domestics	57	—12.5 1.18	—.7 .18	—13.3 1.40	—17.1 2.74	—47.7 2.94	—10.8 1.18	—2.2 .28	—103.9 5.01	.40

From a study of Tables XXIX and XXX, several interesting facts appear. In both sexes femininity increases with age. Theological students, male artists and music students are distinctly feminine in their personality reactions. The most pronounced femininity in males was found in a group of passive homosexual prostitutes. Women who go in for higher education are (or become so because of their studies) pronouncedly masculine. Female college athletes of high intelligence were the most masculine group found among females; and at the other end of the scale, the most feminine women found were dressmakers and domestics.

Ever since Havelock Ellis [19] declared that "of 1030 persons of eminence in British History, but 55 are women," interest in the relative variability of the two sexes has been pronounced. If it could be shown that the male was the more variable, a simple explanation of the predominance of male geniuses would be secured. Cattell found that out of 1000 most eminent persons in the entire history of the whole civilized world, women are represented by only 32. Most of these have become eminent by the accidents of beauty or birth. The only intellectual sphere in which women are well represented is that of fiction and *belles lettres;* here of the 82 most famous, 10 are women and 72 are men. Is this because women are innately inferior? Or is it due, first, to lack of training and opportunity and, second, to the fact that biographies and other records of women are seldom kept? Child bearing among women obviously restricts their activities in many pursuits which might make them famous; and only within the past fifty years have women been given equal chances in the higher realms of education.

At the other end of the scale, we find that men furnish the greater proportion of mental defectives, criminals and insane. Male idiots, for example, are at least twice as numerous as female idiots. This seems to furnish further evidence of the greater variability of the male. But the real test is to examine all the records where the variability of the two sexes can be reliably compared, and abide by the findings.

This task, McNemar and Terman [20] have accomplished.

[19] Havelock Ellis, *A Study of British Genius*, (New Ed.), 1926.
[20] Quinn McNemar and Lewis M. Terman "Sex Differences in Variational Tendency," *Genetic Psychol. Monogs.*, 1936, XVIII, 1.

Dividing the studies of sex differences into three groups —
anthropometric, psychological and educational, they give the
size of the sample, the means and standard deviations, the
difference between the two measures of dispersion, the standard error of this difference, and the ratio of the difference
to its standard error. The valuable tables are, unfortunately, too long to quote, but they should be consulted by
the serious student of the problem. Excerpts from their
conclusions are given below:

"Perhaps some readers would like one super-statistical figure which
would represent a summary of the great mass of differences, more or
less significant when considered alone, which have been brought
together in this review. The authors are unable to satisfy their
natural craving. No meaning can be attached to an average based
upon such diverse elements as, for example, height, intelligence,
musicality, and art ability; even the pooling of results from related
traits cannot be entirely justified. The need for some type of summary, however, would seem to warrant the latter procedure. Perhaps it should be pointed out that if no difference in variation exists,
then one would expect the distribution of ratios of differences to
their standard errors to center about zero with a standard deviation
of unity, and of course where we have only the direction of the difference given, one would expect approximately as many in one as in
the other direction.

"A careful consideration of the anthropometric data reveals that for
ages up to ten the average of 43 ratios (difference to standard error)
is + .19, which is not significantly different from zero, but for ages
10 to 14 inclusive, the mean of 38 ratios is − 2.47 (greater female
variation), a value which differs from zero by 15 times its standard
error. For ages 15 and up, the seven ratios have a mean of + 6.64,
which is highly significant in favor of greater male variation. The
greater variation for the females at ages 10 to 14 can be explained
on the basis of pubertal changes which would not affect the distributions for the males until about ages 14 to 16. It should be noted
that the use of the coefficient of variation would not change the
results at ages 10 to 14, whereas for the older and adult levels such
a measure would tend to reduce the differences between the sexes
with regard to variation in physical characteristics. As stated previously, the authors feel that the significance of the anthropometric
findings for the more important psychological problem is open to
question.

"An examination of the results for psychological and educational
tests fails to indicate any trends with age, except in so far as greater

male variation is revealed for samples of the college population, which cannot be interpreted because of the network of selective factors involved. There appears to be nothing but inconsistencies with regard to differences in variability in educational achievement, a finding which agrees with the conclusion of Lincoln's earlier review.

"The meager data for special abilities would seem to indicate the absence of a sex difference in variation with respect to art ability, whereas for music tests administered to grade school children, the males show greater variability 22 times, the females 7 times, and 7 times the variation is equal. At the college level the respective figures are ten, seven, three. It should be noted that the differences are small, and that none of the samples is based on age groups.

"The large amount of data based on more or less non-standardized psychological tests can perhaps best be summarized by a count of the direction of the differences: 320 times greater male variation, 322 times greater female, and 24 times equal. When the results are considered for a classification of the tests into somewhat narrower groupings, verbal, arithmetic, and performance, no consistent trends are discoverable. It would seem safe, therefore, to conclude that on the basis of the available data it cannot be said that there is a sex difference in variation in the functions measured by these varied tests.

"When we turn to the evidence given by standardized verbal intelligence test batteries, we find a rather significant trend. Of 33 comparisons based on age groupings, 29 show greater male variation. The mean of the ratios of differences to their standard errors is + 1.47, which differs from zero by 8.4 times its standard error, and the median value of 1.18 is 5.4 times its standard error. These data, being consistent from battery to battery and for the several age levels, would seem to be rather conclusive in favor of greater male variation in intelligence as defined by these tests. If one considers the mean ratio of standard deviations for boys to those for girls it will be found that the difference in standard deviations is equivalent to about one point on the I.Q. scale, that is, if the standard deviation for girls is 16 I.Q. points, that for the boys would be 17 points. Such a conclusion was reached by the Scottish survey, which is based on the largest random sample ever used in a psychological study, and is here supported by results from Thorndike's CAVD, the National Intelligence test, the Pressey group test, and the Stanford-Binet. If we can assume that Intelligence (as measured) is distributed in a Gaussian manner, this difference of one I.Q. point in variability would mean that in general about nine boys to six girls would score above 140 or below 60 I.Q., and that twice as many boys as girls would exceed 160 or fall below 40."

Surveys of differences between the sexes have been made by Goodenough, Wellman, Smith, Catharine Miles, Burt [21] and others.

From these surveys the facts shown in Table XXXI have been extracted.

Finally, we may conclude this section by saying that the differences between male and female human beings are slight. The two groups overlap each other greatly. In intelligence, the most important factor for education, the averages of the two groups are substantially the same. Even if we admit a slightly greater variability in the male, this fact alone does not justify different educational treatment of boys and girls. This admission does not rule out of consideration the fact that the different biological functions of male and female may justify different types of education. After all, women must be the mothers of the race and, to a greater extent than men, the trainers of their families. When women get over the idea that they must prove themselves the equal of men in all forms of intellectual pursuits, they may permit a wise differentiation of education for the growing girl — a greater emphasis, for example, on home making and child rearing than they now permit. Every serious student of the problem now admits that the sex differences of mental life are smaller than those of the emotional and physical life. But should we not arrange our education to take care of all sex differences that are socially significant?

Differences Due to Maturation. — Maturation is usually defined as the attainment of the state of complete development. An organism which has completed its development is said to be mature. Thus we speak of mature trees, mature (or ripe) seeds, and mature men and women. Maturation always involves two factors, so curiously interrelated and interwoven that it is sometimes difficult to keep our thoughts

[21] F. L. Goodenough, "The Consistency of Sex Differences in Mental Traits at Various Ages," *Psychol. Rev.* XXXIV, pp. 440-462.

B. L. Wellman, "Sex Differences" in Murchison's *Handbook of Child Psychology*, 1933, pp. 626-649.

V. C. Smith, "Sex Differences in the Study of General Science," *Science*, LXXV, pp. 55-57.

Catharine C. Miles, "Sex in Social Psychology," in Murchison's *Handbook of Social Psychology*, 1935, pp. 683-797.

C. Burt & R. C. Moore, "The Mental Differences Between the Sexes," *Jour. Exper. Pedagogy*, I, pp 273-284, 355-388.

TABLE XXXI. SOME FINDINGS REGARDING SEX DIFFERENCES

Traits	Authority or Investigator	Date	Results
I. EARLY CHILDHOOD			
—Walking	Wellman	1933	Girls walk earlier.
—Talking	Wellman	1933	Girls talk earlier.
II. PRESCHOOL CHILD			
—Preferential use of hands	Wellman	1933	No difference.
—Attention to delayed visual stimulus	Miles	1933	No difference.
—Tapping & tracing board	Miles	1933	No difference.
—Number concepts	Goodenough	1927	No definite superiority of boys.
—Peg boards, form boards, mazes, picture puzzles	Wellman	1933	Boys show better performance.
—Questioning	Smith	1933b	Boys ask more casual questions.
—Color	Wellman	1933	Girls more responsive.
—Cancellation tests	Wellman	1933	Girls excel boys even at very young age.
—Speech and language development	{ Goodenough	1927	{ Girls tend to be in advance of boys in the beginning.
	{ Smith	1933b	{ Boys in general less proficient.
—Memory	{ Goodenough	1927	Girls tend to excel.
	{ Bryan	1934	Girls tend to excel.
—Intelligence	Wellman	1933	Strong evidence that girls exceed boys in tasks involving memory and verbal facility.
III. SCHOOL CHILD			
General Intelligence	Pintner	1927	No real differences—taken for granted in testing at this age by most workers.
—Mental tests	Goodenough	1927	Main impression of studies is the inconsistency of the various findings; high reliability of difference shown; girls appear slightly superior on many of the group tests.
	Pressey	1918	Girls slightly superior, ages 8—16.
	{ Whipple	1927	{ Girls somewhat superior. (N.I.T. scores) (ages 11, 10–11, 7–16).
	Winsor	1927	
	{ St. Louis Report	1925	
	Pintner (Commins' study)	1927	No difference on N.I.T. scale for 5th grade.
	Whipple	1927b	Girls superior (ages 8–13) (Illinois test)

TABLE XXXI. SOME FINDINGS REGARDING SEX DIFFERENCES
(Continued)

Traits	Authority or Investigator	Date	Results
III. (cont'd)	Pintner (Commins' study)	1927	Girls superior (ages 9–14) (McCall Multi-mental)
	Armstrong	1932	No appreciable difference (Otis, Army Alpha, Army Beta); any differences were in favor of boys.
	Marshall	1934	No differences (ages 9–14) (Spearman's "Measure of Intelligence").
	Terman	1916–17	Girls consistently superior (Stanford-Binet).
	Goodenough (Porteus' study)	1927	Boys superior to girls.
	Heilman	1933	Average Stanford-Binet M.A. differed in favor of boys by 2.32. (age 10)
—Test Material	Schiller	1934	Girls relatively better with Goodenough test; Boys relatively better with Otis, Army Beta & Arithmetic Reasoning.
	Lincoln	1927	Danger of weighting test material in favor of one sex or the other.
—Verbal Test Material	Hardie	1928–29	Medians for sexes equal on Spearman's "Measure of Intelligence," P.E.'s 9.0 for boys & 7.5 for girls.
—Less Verbal Test Material	Pintner	1924	Girls superior at age 10, but difference less than its P.E.
	Pintner	1924	Boys superior at age 12, but difference less than its P. E.
	Lincoln	1927	Girls superior at two ages; boys superior at eight ages (range 7–16) but difference very small.
—Correlation of intelligence scores with intelligence of parents height weight dentition carpal-bone area	Wellman	1933	No appreciable differences.
IV. PSYCHOPHYSIOLOGICAL —Muscular coordination	Wellman	1933	Earlier development in girls.

TABLE XXXI. SOME FINDINGS REGARDING SEX DIFFERENCES
(Continued)

Traits	Authority or Investigator	Date	Results
IV. (cont'd)			
—Motor functions	Oseretzky	1929	No appreciable differences for children 4–8 yrs. in 12 motor functions.
	Wellman	1933	Boys markedly superior in motor tasks; but where learning took place girls made greater relative gains
—Delayed visual stimulus	Meltzer	1933	Older preschool girls sustained attention more adequately.
V. EMOTIONAL-PHYSIO-LOGICAL BEHAVIOR			
—Nail biting; thumb-sucking, protrusion of tongue	Wellman	1933	More characteristic of very young girls.
—Overt expressive activity	Wellman	1933	More marked in boys in a mental-test situation.
—Extrovert activity (questioning)	Wellman	1933	More marked in boys.
—Companionships (reactions)	Wellman	1933	More marked in boys.
—Tendency to anger	Wellman	1933	More marked in boys.
—Quarrelsome	Green	1933	Boys more quarrelsome.
—Resistance to mental tests	Caille Wellman	1933 1933	Girls more resistant.
—Resistance to social situations	Caille Wellman	1933	Girls less resistant.
—Social behavior	Wellman	1933	Girls show more "motherliness" at this age. Girls show greater sense of responsibility. Girls not divergent from boys in other traits measured.
—Choice of companionships	Green Koch Fuxloch Parten	1933 1933 1930 1934	Girls tend to prefer girls. Boys tend to prefer boys.
—Popularity	Koch		Girls more popular.
—Social interest	Smith	1933b	Girls show more social interest in their questions.
—Friendships	Green	1933	Girls form slightly more friendships. Boys' friendships deeper.
—Interests	Smith	1933b	Girls more interested in places and things.

TABLE XXXI. SOME FINDINGS REGARDING SEX DIFFERENCES (Continued)

Traits	Authority or Investigator	Date	Results
V. (Cont'd) —Play	Parten	1933–34	59% of "playing house" with dolls engaged in by girls, nearly always being with dolls (53%). 89% train play by boys. 76% Kiddie-Kar play by boys. 71% play with blocks by boys. 86% use of swings by girls. 63% use of paper by girls. 78% use of beads by girls. 59% painting done by girls.
VI. SUB-TESTS OF INTELLIGENCE Problem-solving tests (slot mazes, form board performances, picture puzzles, mechanical).	Wellman	1933	Boys slightly superior.

straight on the problem. These factors are *growth* and *development*. By growth we mean mere increase of size. A crystal, a bank-balance, a child grows. The growth of a child, or of any organism for that matter, is different from that of a crystal. The crystal grows by *accretion*, by the addition of solid material from a solution to the outside of the crystal. The child grows by an increase in the number of cells composing his body and by an increase in the size of these cells. Cells grow by *intussuception*, that is, by the absorption of food material in solution through the cell walls. Owing to the fact that the volume of a cell increases more rapidly than its absorbing surface (cf. the sphere whose volume is $\frac{4}{3}\pi r^3$ and surface is $4\pi r^2$), the growth of a cell cannot go on indefinitely. A stage is reached when the cell begins to starve. Final starvation is prevented by the division of the cell into two daughter cells, each approximately one-half the size of the parent. The growth of an organism, therefore, is chiefly due to the multiplication of cells by this process of *fission*. Cells grow old, lose weight and finally die. Hence growth, measured at any moment, is a very complex affair. Its amount may be said to be the true growth due to multiplication of cells and their increase in size minus an amount due to atrophy of cells. In infancy, the period when the body is maturing, the balance of growth is plus; in senile decay the balance is minus; in middle life a state of general equilibrium is maintained. Growth then is purely a quantitative affair.

If growth is quantitative, development is qualitative in character. Cells not only grow in size, but the constitution of their contents changes also. Exercise a muscle and it grows in size. It also hardens and assumes a better tonus. This hardening is, in part at least, due to development. An immature plant is tender. As it grows it also develops. Certain cells change their character and the plant becomes more sturdy. This sturdiness is mainly due to development. A child, so the neurologists tell us, is born with a full complement of nerve cells. These cells grow in size, so much so, that by the time the child is a year old his brain is two-thirds grown, and by seven years it has reached 93 per cent of its full growth. (See Table XXXII.) But his development may proceed until he becomes adult or even senile. All his various learnings are stored somehow in the cells of his body, and this storage constitutes his development. Just how the storage takes place is still unknown, but a rational hypothesis is that the protoplasms of the cell become altered in some way.

When we speak of differences due to maturation, we may refer either to differences due to growth or to development. In educational psychology, the differentiations due to development usually loom largest, so these will be emphasized.

There is, however, another angle to the problem, which is usually referred to as the *maturation hypothesis*. Animals as they mature seem to grow into more elaborate forms of behavior simply from the inner development and organization of their cells, especially of their nerve cells. This links the problem to that of instinctive and unlearned behavior. A human being, for example, starts life as an undifferentiated zygote. By the time he is born, or soon afterwards, he can suck, grasp, wriggle his limbs and so on. A little later, he stands, walks and climbs, the stimuli being those normally

TABLE XXXII. INCREASE IN BRAIN-WEIGHT WITH AGE. EN-
CEPHALON WEIGHED ENTIRE WITH PIA. (From Vierordt, *Arch.
für Anat. und Physiol.*, 1890. Reproduced by H. H. Donaldson,
Growth of the Brain, p. 104.)

Age in Years	Males		Females	
	No. of Cases	Brain-weight in grams	Brain-weight in grams	No. of Cases
0 (Birth)	36	381	384	38
1	17	945	872	11
2	27	1025	961	28
3	19	1108	1040	23
4	19	1330	1139	13
5	16	1263	1221	19
6	10	1359	1265	10
7	14	1348	1296	8
8	4	1377	1150	9
9	3	1425	1243	1
10	8	1408	1284	4
11	7	1360	1238	1
12	5	1416	1245	2
13	8	1487	1256	3
14	12	1289	1345	5
15	3	1490	1238	8
16	7	1435	1273	15
17	15	1409	1237	18
18	18	1421	1325	21
19	21	1397	1234	15
20	14	1445	1228	33
21	29	1412	1320	31
22	26	1348	1283	16
23	22	1397	1278	26
24	30	1424	1249	33
25	25	1431	1224	33

found in every environment. Inner development of this
type seems to be as much controlled by regulatory agencies
as the growth of arms, legs and eyes. If we place a normal
baby of a few days in age so that the soles of his feet press
on our thighs, no thrusting movements are felt. But if we
place the same baby in the same position three months later,
distinct downward thrusts are perceptible. These thrusts
mark the beginnings of behavior that result later in standing

and walking. Hence we say that standing and walking are either instinctive or have an instinctive basis. At birth, the stimuli that are later adequate to produce the reaction are quite ineffective; the appropriate organs, or the specific innate neural pathways, have not matured. Each species of animal matures in its own special way, and the resultant behavior is special for the species. This seems to lead to the conclusion that certain modes of behavior are as much inherited as the shapes of our bodies. Environmental stimuli are still needed; the organism must be kept alive by air, food and appropriate temperatures; but, given these omnipresent conditions, nature alone is an all-sufficient teacher. It is therefore wrong to maintain that all forms of behavior are the results of learning rather than of inheritance. As Stone[22] pertinently says:

"An excellent foundation for descriptive studies of unlearned behavior was laid by anatomists and embryologists during the past one hundred years through detailed analyses of structural and functional development in diverse forms of animals. Their researches convincingly demonstrated that structural development is orderly, that differentiations of organs and their subsequent mass development goes on with definite temporal intervals, and that schedules of development are highly stereotyped in members of the same species. One healthy individual is found to be the prototype of all members of the species. These early observers, particularly those who were physiologically minded, also observed that behavioral growth followed laws that are remarkably similar to those describing somatic growth. This discovery was one of capital importance for psychology because it suggested the possibility of describing stages of ontogenetic development in terms of the animal's repertoire of responses or in terms of the deftness or precision with which a given response might be executed. In this lies the germ of all subsequent attempts at describing mental, physiological, and developmental ages in terms of behavior." (pp. 353-354)

Guinea pigs, for example, do not orient themselves in regard to space during the intra-uterine period, but if removed from the womb by a Cæsarean operation some four or five days before the time of normal birth and placed upon their sides or back, they roll over and stand upon their feet. In

[22] Calvin P. Stone, "Learning : I. The Factor of Maturation," *Handbook of General Experimental Psychology*, (Ed., Carl Murchison.)

other words the functional development of this behavior was mature at least four or five days before it could normally be exercised. Fetal rats, rabbits and opossums have been intensively studied and the picture they give is unequivocal; structure and behavior are inseparably intertwined. Similar evidence is secured by crossing pacing and trotting horses, different breeds of dogs, etc. The distinctive behaviors as well as the distinctive forms are inherited.

Will the behavior make its appearance when the normal opportunities for its development are withheld? That is, will the inner development or maturation be continued at the normal pace? This question was settled in the affirmative for frogs (*Rana*) and salamanders (*Amblystoma punctatum*) by Carmichael.[23] Dividing the animals in the larval state into two groups, one of which was allowed to develop normally in water and the other anesthetized by a weak chloretone solution which did not inhibit development, he found that the animals that developed to the swimming stage in an anesthetized condition, swam just as well as the control group when they were transferred to water. Inner growth had been going on.

Even more striking are the results obtained by Gesell and Thompson [24] in their co-twin study with T and C as subjects. These twin girls were studied from one month to eighteen months of age. Twin T was practised for 6 weeks (46 weeks to 52 weeks of age) in such activities as climbing steps, building towers with cubical blocks, etc., while twin C was deprived of all specific training in these respects. At the age of 52 weeks, twin T could climb 5 steps in 26 seconds. At 53 weeks twin C's training began and in two weeks she climbed the staircase in 10 seconds. It should be noted that C climbed the staircase without any previous training in 45 seconds at the age of 53 weeks. Thus maturity was an important factor, for three weeks' superiority in maturity enabled C with two weeks' training to excel T with 6 weeks' training at a somewhat earlier age. The authors could only conclude that the time of appearance of activities, such as

[23] L. Carmichael, "The Development of Behavior in Vertebrates Experimentally Removed from the Influence of External Stimulation," *Psychol. Review*, XXXIII, pp. 51-58. And later studies in Vols. XXXIV and XXXV.

[24] Arnold Gesell and Helen Thompson., "Learning and Growth in Identical Infant Twins," *Genetic Psychol. Monogs.*, V, I, 1929, p. 124.

stair climbing, is "fundamentally determined by the ripeness of the neural structures. The effects of experience may well enter into the growth complex in the manner suggested by Coghill's studies of locomotion in *amblystoma*, but maturation plays the primary rôle and preserves the generic aspects of the behavior pattern. For all these reasons learning is profoundly conditioned by the factor of maturity. The infant grows rapidly. Although function enters into the growth, training does not transcend maturation. Maturation, however, constantly tends to supplant or modify the results of training. If it were not so, the infant could scarcely grow." (p. 114)

Myrtle McGraw's [25] study of the twins Johnny and Jimmy leads to somewhat similar conclusions. It was at first thought that they were identical twins, but it is now almost certain that they are dizygotic. Johnny, slightly smaller than Jimmy, was the one selected for special training, while Jimmy served as control. Johnny, under special training, electrified the psychological world by learning, while still a mere baby, to swim, roller-skate, climb an inclined board set at an angle of 70°, and to climb down from tallish pedestals. Thus between the ages of 633 and 652 days he learned to climb the 70° incline. Later the twins were tested together in situations that demanded insight; in fact they were situations similar to those normally used in experiments with chimpanzees. Not much difference was found between them. "Although Johnny had enjoyed earlier and more extensive practice in certain activities, he apparently was not greatly benefited thereby in the acquisition of performances of a different order." (p. 280) Generally speaking when Jimmy, at a later age than Johnny, was practised in Johnny's tricks, he learned them more easily. Here again maturation definitely played an important part.

Intelligence testers, as we shall see later, endeavor to test the factor of maturation that we have termed development. But development never takes place *in vacuo*. If, however, tests are used in which the element of formal schooling is reduced to a minimum, they measure approximately the inner development of the individual. What is it, then, that intelligence tests tell us? In the first place, the results show

[25] Myrtle B. McGraw, *Growth ; a Study of Johnny and Jimmy*, 1935.

that development, like growth, is a fairly steady affair and parallels it pretty closely. Secondly, the rate of development is strictly an individual affair. Some children develop slowly, some quickly, but the rate seems to be fixed by inheritance. In any case, it is very difficult to change the rate. If a child starts developing at the moron-rate, it is practically certain that he cannot be accelerated to the normal-rate, much less to the genius-rate of development. This is usually expressed by the statement that the I.Q. tends to be constant.

These facts are shown graphically in Figs. 18 and 19.

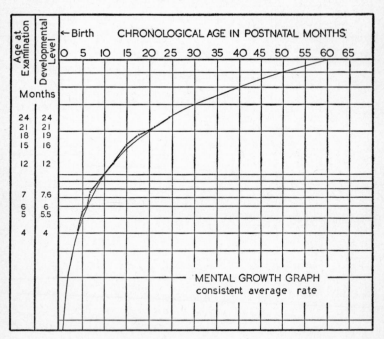

Fig. 18. Mental Growth Curve of Normal Infant from 4 to 24 Months. Infant tested 9 times. (Gesell)

There are differentials between mental and chronological rates of growth. The superior child advances more rapidly in mental than in chronological age; the dull child matures less rapidly in mentality than he does in chronological age. Attempts have been made to correlate mental age with other maturational factors, such as growth of brain in size, ana-

tomical age, physiological age, pedagogical age, etc. All of
these are positive, but the correlations are so low that they
become useless for predictive purposes.

If a child is accelerated in anatomical development, we
should normally expect some reflection of it to be found in
measures of his intellectual development. As measures of
anatomical development, the eruption of teeth and the ossi-

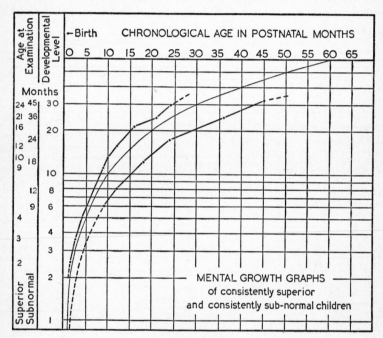

Fig. 19.   Mental Growth Curves of Superior & Sub-normal Children.
(Gesell)

fication of the carpal bones of the wrist have been frequently
used.

The age of eruption of teeth has been studied by Bean,[26]
James and Pitts,[27] Psyche Cattell[28] and others. From the

[26] R. B. Bean, "The Eruption of the Teeth as a Physiological Standard for
Testing Development," *Ped. Sem.*, 1914, XXI, pp. 596-614.

[27] James and Pitts, "Some Notes on the Dates of Eruption of 4850 Children,
Ages under Twelve," *Proc. of the Royal Society of Medicine*, 1912, V.

[28] Psyche Cattell, "Dentition as a Measure of Maturity," *Harvard Monogs.
in Education*, No. 9, 1928.

data obtained from James and Pitts, Woodrow[29] compiled a scale for measuring anatomical age. It is shown as Table XXXIII. If the teeth erupt at the normal ages shown in the second column, the child is of normal anatomical age; if at a later age he is anatomically retarded, and if at an earlier age, anatomically advanced. The measure, however, is too crude, and proof is still lacking that age of eruption of teeth correlates closely with the I.Q.

TABLE XXXIII. THE AGE OF THE ERUPTION OF THE PERMA-
NENT TEETH. A SCALE FOR MEASURING ANATOMICAL AGE.
(Woodrow)

Name of Tooth	Normal Age (Present in 50%)	Present in 25% of Children	Present in 75% of Children
Lower first molar	6 – 0	5 – 6	6 – 6
Upper first molar	6 – 3	5 – 9	7 – 0
Lower central incisors	6 – 6	6 – 0	7 – 0
Upper central incisors	7 – 6	7 – 0	8 – 3
Lower lateral incisors	7 – 6	7 – 0	8 – 6
Upper lateral incisors	8 – 6	8 – 0	9 – 3
Upper first premolars	10 – 0	8 – 9	10 – 9
Lower first premolars	10 – 6	9 – 6	11 – 9
Lower canines	10 – 6	9 – 9	12 – 3
Upper second premolars	11 – 0	9 – 9	12 – 6
Lower second premolars	11 – 6	10 – 3	12 – 6
Upper canines	11 – 9	10 – 9	12 – 9
Lower second molars	11 – 9	10 – 9	14 – 0
Upper second molars	12 – 6	11 – 6	14 – 3
Third molars	17th to 24th year		

The use of radiographs of the wrist bones as a measure of anatomical age is made possible by the fact that the individual carpal bones ossify at different times — one of them as early as the end of the first year of life, another as late as the middle of the eleventh, and the rest at intermediate ages. Although ossification of these bones is highly regarded as a measure of anatomical development, the correlations

[29] Herbert Woodrow, *Brightness and Dullness in Children*, 1923.

between anatomical and mental ages are so low that radiographs are not of much service to education.

Physiological age is a measure of the functional development of the organism. The measure of this age that has been most used with pupils is the age of onset of puberty. The signs of puberty are well-defined and from them the physiological age can be fairly accurately determined. Girls become adolescent between two and three years earlier than boys. If mental age and physiological age were strict concomitants, then the intelligence test records of girls from eleven years of age onwards should be superior to those of boys. Intelligence records for boys and girls at all ages are approximately the same, so it is unlikely that physiological age, determined by the onset of puberty, will prove of much value to education. If, as some educators think, the major changes at puberty are not mental but emotional, then physiological age might correlate positively with the results of personality tests. Unfortunately, we have no information on this point.

It is evident, then, that the anatomical, mental and physiological ages of a child each differ from his chronological age. This means that maturation is a very complex affair and may proceed at different rates in different directions. The pattern of each is well defined, and it is probable that the basic rate of development for each individual is a remarkably constant function.

If all the inter-correlations among mental, anatomical and physiological ages were found to be unity, then educators could justify gradings on the basis of chronological age alone. Unfortunately, the inter-correlations are low, which means that anatomically, physiologically, and mentally the child is developing at different rates. Maturation, then, is the complex resultant of a number of factors. The picture of the maturation in any animal is fairly clear-cut, but the underlying factors are intricate and difficult to unravel. Undoubtedly, rapid progress is being made. The new lines of attack, illustrated by the study of embryos, the swimming stage of salamanders, and co-twin studies of children, are most promising.

However, we should not overlook the pioneering studies of Preyer on infant behavior; of Loeb on tropisms of sea-animals; of Conradi on the songs of birds; of the Peckhams on the behavior of wasps. While these were not strictly studies of individual differences in maturation, they have an important bearing on the problem.

According to Loeb a tropism is the total bodily displacement as a result of an environmental stimulus of a rather simple kind — light, chemicals, gravity and so forth. Thus, moths are positively heliotropic; they move themselves bodily towards the source of light. Loeb thought that maturation of human beings would ultimately be explained in terms of tropisms, but his prophecy is still unfulfilled. Human behavior is much too complex to be explained in any such simple way. The studies of reflexes in babies and instincts in animals show that maturation is a regular and almost preordained affair. Still, by changing the environmental stimuli, even the songs of birds can be changed. Conradi reared sparrows with canaries, and the sparrows learned a hoarse type of canary song. However, on being released and associating with other sparrows, they lost their canary song and gained the natural sparrow chirp. These experiments, then, on tropisms, reflexes and instincts give valuable information on the maturation of behavior. That there are important differences in the development of behavior through intrinsic factors among human beings is no longer open to doubt. Education will sooner or later have to take greater account of them. Maturation provides, as it were, for the basic developments that keep the animal alive and perpetuate the race. Education, in the form of specific learnings, builds on this foundation, changing the maturational direction in some cases, but always extending the number and forms of adaptations and fitting them to individual circumstances. In the schoolroom, the teacher must perforce make allowances for differential rates of maturation, especially in mental development. Otherwise, he might be trying to use the same course of studies for pupils of the same chronological age who differed in mental age by as much as six years.

Variation within the Individual.—While the study of variation within the individual really falls outside the scope of individual differences, it is obviously closely related to this topic. It is a commonplace to say that man may exhibit talent along some lines and be below the average in other pursuits. We speak glibly of intelligent or stupid persons, but when intelligence is analyzed, either by scrutiny of intelligence test scores or by some other means, it is found to be a complex trait; a person may be clever with his fingers yet relatively stupid in bookish tasks. A person may be "a good mixer" yet totally uninterested in intellectual tasks or practical pursuits. If we are to regard the ability of a skilled craftsman as an exhibition of concrete intelligence, what shall we say of the sculptor who conceives a beautiful statue and carves it? There is something more than mere skill exhibited here; there is invention which is usually regarded as one of the highest forms of abstract intelligence. Here we find two sorts of intelligence combined in one and the same person.

Coming to the more prosaic atmosphere of the schoolroom, we are aware that every teacher knows pupils who are notably clever along some lines and incredibly stupid along others. Cases are by no means uncommon where a pupil may be able to add, subtract and multiply but be unable to learn long division. Some pupils may be prodigies of learning yet be unable to carry a tune or sing a scale. On the other hand, we sometimes find pupils who are musical prodigies or lightning calculators who are markedly deficient in general intelligence. A mere glance at any psychograph, a diagram on which are plotted the comparable scores an individual makes on a series of tests, shows that variation within the individual is the rule; the "profile" is never a straight line but always irregular. Take, for example, Fig. 20, which is the profile of D.E.R., a girl aged 8-9, with a mental age 13-7, who was studied by DeVoss as part of the California study of genius. While this pupil makes consistently higher scores than the average for her age, in science information and language-literature information her scores are remarkably high; in computation they are not much above the average.

Even more striking are the psychographs of identical twins. In some traits, palm patterns, for instance, the resemblances between the individuals are frequently greater

than those within either member.   The striking resemblances
of monozygotic twins and the variations within the individual are excellently illustrated in Fig. 21 opposite.

Similar lines of evidence of variation within the individual
are obtained from correlation studies.   If there were no internal variation the correlations between, say, a reading comprehension test and a test of arithmetical reasoning would be

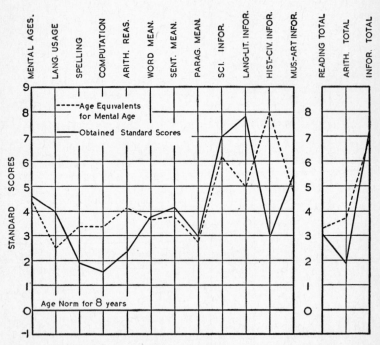

Fig. 20. Psychograph of D.E.R., an Intellectually Superior Pupil. (After
DeVoss, p. 359, in Vol. I of Terman's *Genetic Studies of Genius*.)

high.   As a matter of fact such correlations are generally
found to be low.

All the above facts support the theory of the gene and the
independent inheritance of traits.   The pattern of inheritance
is a complex mosaic which shows up when various traits are
carefully tested.

Extreme Individual Differences in Man.—We have seen
that the clustering of individuals around the average for any
given trait provides a plausible reason for group instruction.

But beyond this somewhat homogeneous central group and extending in both directions to the limits of the distribution, we find individuals so markedly different from the average that they literally force themselves upon the attention of

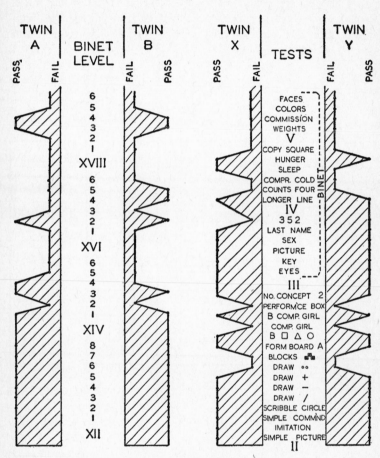

Fig. 21. Comparative Psychograph, showing Intellectual Correspondence and Variations within the Individuals of two sets of Twins (after Gesell).

teachers. At one end of the scale for mentality we find the pupil we designate as a genius; at the other we find the moron, the imbecile and the idiot. In regard to sensory acuities, the range is equally great. Some of these are not so significant for schooling as others. Thus a child who is defective in taste or in smell can be educated with a normal group, since these sensory capacities are of little importance either in modern schooling or in modern life. But it is far otherwise with sight and hearing. Supernormal sight and supernormal hearing call for no comment, but if the child cannot see and hear properly he cannot be taught in ordinary ways. The totally blind and the totally deaf are the extremes at the lower ends of the scale, but between the extremes and the normal are the myopes and the partially deaf who create a very real educational problem. The partially deaf are not easily discovered by the teacher and even the children with defective eyesight may be overlooked.

The *blind* seem to be an easily definable group, but, curiously enough, the laws dealing with them define blindness in different ways. Thus the Blind Persons Act of Great Britain, 1920, defines a blind person as "one so blind as to be unable to perform any work for which eyesight is essential"; and the British Education Act of 1921 defines a blind child as one "too blind to be able to read ordinary school books." These are not very satisfactory definitions from the standpoint of education. As far as schooling is concerned, all children having one-tenth vision $\left(\frac{6}{60}\text{ or }\frac{20}{200}\right)$ or less may, for educational purposes, be considered blind, as they will have to depend on braille for reading. All others with defective vision, about 1 child in 500, can get some good from sight-saving (myopic or conservation of vision) classes, in which oral teaching, music, games and handwork are at a maximum, and reading and writing, if used at all, are used to a minimum extent. If handwriting is permitted it is of the free-arm variety on the blackboard; and any reading books that are necessary are printed in specially large, black type. Pupils, however, are usually taught to typewrite by the touch system. Similarly knitting, if done without the use of the eyes, is encouraged. The object is to give the children as much of a general education as they can encompass, with vocational training as a secondary aim.

The blind are generally segregated in special schools. As more than one child in a thousand is blind, the problem of their education is a considerable one. Moreover, as far as can be ascertained by intelligence tests, the blind have a greater proportion with inferior intelligence than have sighted pupils. Thus Hayes [30] found that 670 blind children tested by means of the Irwin-Binet tests, when compared with 1000 unselected pupils as tested by Terman, gave the following comparative results:

Classification	Percentage	
	Blind	*Sighted*
Genius	0.3	0.5
Very Superior	1.0	2.0
Superior	5.0	9.0
Average	68.0	76.0
Dull	12.0	8.0
Borderline	7.0	2.0
Feebleminded	5.0	0.3

The ordinary citizen, seeing the marvelous things that the blind sometimes accomplish, is apt to think that their blindness is compensated by an acuter sensitivity in other directions, especially of hearing and of touch, and by superior memory powers. Careful tests seem to show that this is not so. The blind make more practical use of such touch and hearing that they possess, but they are fundamentally no more sensitive than sighted persons. Similarly their dependence upon rote memory undoubtedly strengthens this power, but they show no superiority in logical memory.

The instruction in most schools for the blind has a vocational bias. The graduates, however, find difficulty in securing remunerative employment in factories or business houses. Of the adult blind, about two-thirds are (or speedily become) unemployable. Hence many states reduce the pensionable age of the blind from 70 to 50 years. In Canada, the pensionable age of the blind is now 40 years.

From the social standpoint, the reduction in the number of the blind is imperative. Fortunately, more than half the present blindness is preventable (ophthalmia neonatorum or

[30] S. P. Hayes, "Mental and Educational Surveys in Seven Schools for the Blind." *Report of Twenty-fifth Convention of American Association of Instructors of the Blind*, 1920.

gonorrheal ophthalmia of the newborn, 25%; congenital syphilis, 10%; acquired syphilis, 10-15%; injuries, 5-8%), so we may expect a steadily diminishing number of blind people in the future.

The *deaf* are another group of pupils who show wide variation from the normal, and cause serious problems for teachers. They are more numerous than is popularly supposed, since deafness is relatively difficult to detect. The census returns are quite misleading, since they neglect the partially deaf portion of the population. According to these returns, deaf persons on the North American continent constitute about .05 per cent of the total population: U. S. A. .05 and Canada .06 per cent. Over a period of fifty years, the figures for Canada are given in Table XXXIV.

TABLE XXXIV. DEAF-MUTES AND BLIND IN CANADA OVER A PERIOD OF FIFTY YEARS. (Compiled from *Canada Year Book,* 1936, Tables 30, 31, 32.)

Deaf-Mutes		Year	Blind	
No.	Per 10,000 Population		No.	Per 10,000 Population
5368	12.6	1881	3002	7.0
4793	10.1	1891	3350	7.1
6159	11.6	1901	3266	6.1
4567	6.4	1911	3226	4.5
5331	6.1	1921	4388	5.0
6767	6.5	1931*	7343	7.1

* In addition there were 107 blind deaf-mutes.

If a survey in which an audiometer is used, be made among school pupils, the percentage of discoverable deaf pupils rises enormously. Thus Conway[31] of the Department of Educational Research of the University of Toronto found that 6.7 per cent of the ears tested registered a loss of hearing of 10 decibels and over. Even if we take the better ear, since it is the better ear that fixes the limit of hearing,

[31] C. B. Conway, *Hearing Abilities of Children in Toronto Public Schools,* 1937.

2.8 per cent of these have a decibel hearing loss of 10 or more. These facts are shown in Table XXXV.

TABLE XXXV. DISTRIBUTION OF DEAFNESS AMONG TORONTO PUBLIC SCHOOL PUPILS

Decibel Hearing Loss	No. of individual ears per thousand showing given Decibel Hearing Loss	No. of better ears per thousand showing given Decibel Hearing Loss
−5 − 0	42	61
0 − 5	657	702
5 − 10	234	209
10 − 15	40 ⎫	18 ⎫
15 − 20	15 ⎪	7 ⎪
20 − 30	5 ⎬ 67	1 ⎬ 28
30 − 40	3 ⎪	1 ⎪
40 − 50	2 ⎪	1 ⎭
50 − 60	1 ⎪	
60 − 70	1 ⎭	
Totals	1000	1000

Fig. 22 gives some of these facts in graphical form. The White House Conference estimated that there were 3,000,000 children in the United States with some impairment of hearing. Since deafness increases with age we may be reasonably sure that of the people now living in North America, at least 10 per cent will die deaf — so deaf that the defect will be noticed by acquaintances.

The researches carried out in the Bell Telephone Laboratories in recent years show that hearing is not quite such a simple matter as we once thought it. Take, for example, the number of tones which can be distinguished at various frequency and loudness levels. These vary greatly as can be seen by referring to Fig. 23. The area beyond the line marked "Threshold of Feeling" is a region of intense feeling and pain: the tone is so loud that it hurts the ear. If deaf children are tested carefully, the deafness is found to be of different types. Those suffering from otosclerosis (middle-ear deafness) can hear the higher pitches better than the lower. Some children have tonal islands, their deafness being confined to certain definite frequencies. Others hear tones of lower frequencies fairly well but are deaf to the higher ones. The partial deafness of old age is of this type. Still others exhibit "lacunae" or deafness for a short range of frequencies, having better hearing

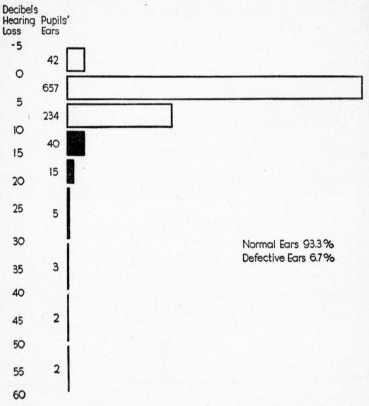

Fig. 22.   Hearing Loss of 1000 Individual Ears of Toronto Public School Pupils, Grades VI to VIII.

for the remainder of the scale. This type is illustrated in Fig. 24.

But educational psychology is concerned with the educability of the deaf. How does deafness affect learning ability? It is generally agreed that children suffering not more than a 30 decibel hearing loss can be educated in classes along with pupils whose hearing is normal. They should, however, be given seats in front of the class. Those with more than 30 decibel hearing loss need special treatment. They should be taught lip-reading in special classes, and every effort should be made to encourage their linguistic development. The extreme cases, at least, should be trained for a vocation in which hearing is relatively unimportant. They may, for example, be trained to become teachers of the deaf, printers, proof-readers, linotype operators, authors, farmers, machine operators, chemists, photographers, drafts-

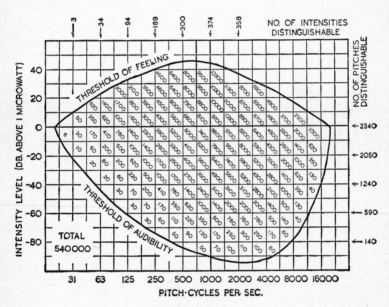

Fig. 23. Chart of the Auditory Sensation Area showing the Number of Distinguishable Tones.

men, librarians, shoemakers, painters, tie builders, seamstresses, cabinet-makers, and janitors. As a matter of fact, deafness is probably advantageous to proof-readers, card cataloguers in libraries, filing clerks, authors, and linotype operators.

Even partial deafness leads to imperfect acquirement of language and through this to loss of normal social intercourse. Since the development of intelligence is conditioned by use of language and contacts with one's fellow men, the deafened, on the whole, prove to be less intelligent (as measured by intelligence tests) than those with normal hearing. Their school work is also inferior, especially in subjects in which language plays an important part. For the totally deaf the best studies show that these have an average I.Q. around 80, and that they tend to be retarded two or three grades in school.[32] (pp. 405-425) Is the deaf child compensated for his deafness by a superiority in motor ability? Long[33] found no pronounced tendencies towards

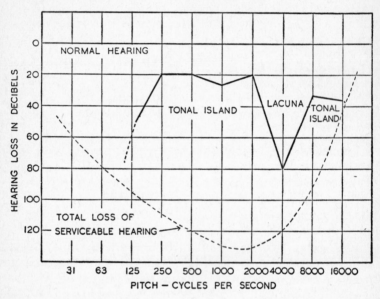

Fig. 24. Audiogram demonstrating Variation in Hearing Loss for Tones of Various Pitches.

compensation and no pronounced inferiorities. His conclusions are as follows:

"As was pointed out in the introductory chapter, motor abilities correlate among themselves so slightly that they cannot properly be spoken of in terms of a general motor ability. In spite of this fact, it is probably justifiable to conclude from the data of the present study that deaf and hearing persons are not widely different in motor abilities in general. If one group or the other were quite significantly inferior, these few tests of rather fundamental abilities should have

[32] Rudolph Pintner, *Intelligence Testing*, 1931.
[33] John A. Long, *The Motor Ability of the Deaf*, 1932.

revealed the fact. Since they have failed to do so, it may be concluded that, with the exception of sense of balance, no significant inferiority exists.

"This conclusion is contrary to what authorities have commonly accepted to be the fact, and it should have important significance vocationally. It appears that we have no right to discriminate against the deaf on the basis of inferiority in motor skills. Such an inferiority probably does not exist. The deaf are as adept in motor skills as their hearing brothers, and there must be many types of work for which they could be fitted, and in which deafness would be no disadvantage. There is need for a thorough survey of the whole field of industry, to the end that the most suitable types of employment may be determined.

"For schools for the deaf the implication of this study is that strong emphasis should be placed on industrial training. Such schools should reap the maximum in returns by stressing education along the line of abilities in which the deaf child seems to have his best chance to compete with the hearing child." (p. 63)

Terman wisely distinguishes between the gifted child, and the one who is specifically talented. In the first class he places those who rate highly in tests of general intelligence. The second includes those whose exceptional gifts are confined to one or more special fields, such as music, art, lightning calculation, chess playing, mechanics, etc.

This section will be confined to the gifted child. The child who exhibits specific talents is usually intelligent, but there are cases on record of morons with prodigious memories and of lightning calculators with average ability or less along other lines.

The *gifted* child may be defined as one who has an I.Q. of 140 or over. In California they form from .4 to .5 per cent of the school population, but for Canada, and perhaps for the North American continent as a whole .25 per cent would be a better figure. About one child in four hundred, therefore, may be regarded as gifted.

With the advent of the movement for intelligence testing, the important discovery was made that schools were really neglecting the education of gifted children. These gifted pupils passed examinations easily and acquired information so readily that they were a pleasure to teach. Why worry about them? Consequently, they were often found in grades lower than those to which they were entitled to belong by right of their intelligence. Fortunately, these pupils had so many interests that the neglect by their teachers did them no serious harm. In some cases, however, they drifted into lazy habits and ultimately became a liability rather than an asset to society. The teachers' attitude can be condoned. They did not want to lose their brilliant pupils by extra promotions; and they were also influenced by the general belief expressed by the proverb "Whom the gods love die young." Not having standardized tests at their command, they were quite unaware of the injury they were doing by their failure to work their pupils at the highest possible levels.

Evidence has been adduced to show that the gifted on the whole are superior in health and physique, precocious in reading, more trustworthy and less boastful than other children. They belong to families that are superior in both social and intellectual status. It is from this gifted group that the leaders, scholars, discoverers and inventors of the next adult generation must be drawn. Their educational neglect is a dereliction of duty that cannot be condoned. Consequently, opinion is rapidly veering round to that which is expressed by the statement "that special classes for gifted children should be formed whenever the number of available children permits it." In these special classes the ordinary academic work of the school can be accomplished in half, even a quarter of the normal time. The rest of the time can be devoted to an enriched curriculum which includes a large amount of individual reading in classical literature, science, history and geography; individual and group projects which test their capabilities in many directions; visits to art galleries, museums, libraries, manufacturing plants, civic institutions, and so forth. To prevent a feeling of social and intellectual superiority from developing among them, opportunities for contact with other children in activities in which all can join, are freely provided. In communities too small for the establishment of separate classes, these gifted children are becoming the special charge of the teachers. They are given opportunities of broadening their horizons of thought, of using their intellectual powers to capacity, and of realizing their social responsibilities. The plan of hurrying them through the grades at top speed has given way to one that permits of a modest acceleration accompanied by an enrichment of the curriculum. Briefly, the attitude that now expresses the teachers' attitude is — since gifted children cannot be produced at will (we have to wait for them to be born), we can at least prevent their waste when nature sends them to us.

At the other end of the scale of intellect we have the *feebleminded*. In terms of the I.Q. all children below 70 are classed among the feebleminded. On the North American continent they constitute about one per cent of the pupils. Generally they are divided into three groups according to their capacity levels, namely, idiots (I.Q. below 20-25) ; imbeciles (I.Q. 20-25 to 50) ; and morons (I.Q. 50 to 70). Practically no work of an intellectual nature can be done with idiots since by definition (British Mental Deficiency Act, 1913) they are "so deeply defective in mind from birth or from an early age as to be unable to guard themselves against common physical dangers." They are obviously cases for institutions, since they will have to be cared for all their lives. Imbeciles, while capable of guarding themselves against common physical dangers, are incapable of managing themselves or their affairs or of being trained to earn their livings. Institutional life, therefore, is also indicated for them. Morons are capable of earning their livings under favorable circumstances, but, because of their defects, are incapable of competition on equal terms with their fellows, or of managing their affairs with ordinary prudence. Since morons are slightly educable, it is customary to separate them from the rest of the pupils, and to educate them in special schools or classes. In these schools or classes the emphasis is placed on hand and craft work of various kinds, with the academic work reduced to a minimum.

Special attention was directed to the training of defectives long before people awoke to the fact that the gifted should receive special treatment. This was, of course, part of the humanitarian movement which began in the eighteenth century and is still with us. Even today an educational administrator finds it far easier to secure funds for the education of the feebleminded than for the intellectually superior. These unfortunates appeal to our compassion since they are so obviously ill-equipped to look after themselves. But another motive is finding its way into the consciousness of the community. The feebleminded, when adult, become the parents of a new crop of feebleminded, and the problem has become so acute in occidental countries that a eugenic conscience has been awakened. We now care for the feebleminded for the protection of society as well as in a compassionate way.

In schools and classes for morons, the work is graded to suit their intelligence. Low morons with a mental age of 8 or 9 years can be taught to run errands, wash windows, hoe crops, scrub floors, wash and iron clothes, polish shoes, and to cook and serve simple meals. Those of slightly higher mental capacity, around 10 years of mental age, can be taught to become routine helpers in trades, to do rough carpentry work, and to do difficult work in basketry, brushmaking, rug-making, and sewing. When opportunity presents itself they can be taught to drive and look after a team of horses, and to do the routine work on farms. Those of still higher intelligence, with a mental age around 11 or 12, can be taught to use machinery and to earn a living as routine workers in a factory. Although they cannot plan successfully, they can be taught to do the work of the hired man on the farm, and in the case of girls to sew but not to design dresses. There is thus a distinct vocational slant to their training. Providing that society keeps guard over them, they can be trained to be an asset to a community instead of a liability.

The blind, deaf, gifted and feebleminded are well-defined groups who exhibit extreme variations from the normal. There is still another group, much less well-defined, who constitute a serious social and educational problem. It is usually termed the *maladjusted*. The maladjustment is of personality or character and may be apparently so innocuous as to be unrecognized as a problem. Take, for instance, the shy retiring pupil who shrinks from contact with his fellows and lives in an inner world of his own. Technically we call him an introvert. He gives the teacher no trouble in regard to discipline; on the contrary he is regarded as a good pupil because he is never involved with the pranks of the others. To the mental hygienist, this shrinking from contact with others is of serious import, since it may mark the beginning of a path that leads to a mental hospital in later life. So far as social adjustments are concerned, the active extravert is the "better bet," regardless of the annoyance he gives his parents and teachers. Teachers and parents are still prone to emphasize submission and discipline, while psychologists and mental hygienists put more stress on freedom.

A physical handicap may lead to aberrations of the personality. Bodily defects have a psychic meaning. A child with harelip and cleft palate, or one who is lame through an attack of infantile paralysis, is obviously going to suffer mentally unless he is treated wisely. But if the handicap is hidden, as in heart disease which prevents him from joining the more boisterous games of his companions, the personality may suffer without anybody trying to prevent it. Impaired vitality due to tuberculosis, malnutrition, anaemia, etc., may be the starting point of personality difficulties which later result in serious behavior problems. Mild cases of truancy may be overlooked and disregarded by the teacher, but he should remember that truancy has a way of starting more serious delinquencies. The scale runs somewhat as follows: truancy, lying, incorrigibility, vagrancy, malicious mischief, stealing. To these, later in life, may be added sex immorality, highway robbery and even murder. The truant, the persistent liar, and the petty thief are socially maladjusted and if not taken in hand during their school days, may become more seriously delinquent as they grow older. By the teacher, the task of training the personalities of pupils should be regarded as seriously as training their minds.

Fortunately, teachers and guidance officers are becoming aware of the great importance of maladjustments of every kind and of the necessity of resolving them early in life. The aim should be to develop well-balanced persons with an objective outlook on life, who blame themselves for their mistakes and deficiencies and seek socially approved remedies for overcoming them, rather than try to avoid and escape such responsibilities. As in so many other aspects of education, starting right is the important thing.

Some of the extreme individual differences in mentality and emotional behavior are undoubtedly due to glandular disturbances, especially disturbances of the *endocrine glands.* These glands of internal secretion control to a great extent both bodily growth and development. Take, for instance, the thyroid gland. It has been known for fifty years that a peculiar type of feeblemindedness coupled with a dwarfing of bodily growth was due to defective secretion of this gland. These dwarfish idiots, known as cretins, could be almost completely restored to normal size and mentality by the administration of thyroxin, the chief product of the thyroid gland. Cannon and his co-workers have demonstrated the close connection between the adrenal secretions and the coarser emotions of anger and fear. The advances in endocrinology have been so marked since 1900 that certain writers are now beginning to describe *endocrine types*. This is a revival of the Hippocratic theory that personality depends on the bodily humors, with modern endocrine secretions substituted for the ancient black and yellow bile, blood and phlegm. While endocrine types, especially the extreme cases, have some scientific basis, the leaders in the movement (Berman especially) have gone far beyond the findings of science in their speculations. This, however, may be said with truth, that the more we learn about the functioning of the endocrine glands, the closer they seem to be related to personality traits. These endocrine types are discussed in a later chapter.

Individual Differences in Sensitivity.— Following the lead given by Dr. Gobineau and Herbert Spencer, common opinion attributed superior sensitivity to the obviously inferior races of mankind. Travelers related marvelous stories of the keenness of senses of savages. The tracking ability of the American Indian was extolled in every "blood and thunder" book. Even modern people who lived in a simple primitive manner were supposed to develop unbelievable sensory acuities. Thus the success of the Boers in the Boer War was attributed to their marvelous eyesight, developed through many generations by gazing towards the far horizons of the veldt. When put to the test, these beliefs are found to be insecurely grounded. Primitive peoples, as Woodworth [34] and others have shown, possess no greater keenness of vision, hearing, smell and touch than sophisticated whites, but they tend to make more use of sensory

[34] R. S. Woodworth, "Racial Differences in Mental Traits," *Science*, N.S., 1910, XXI, pp. 171-186.

cues than civilized people. The Indian may be able to find his way through the bush, but he would probably get lost in a large department store. He pays more attention than we do to wind direction, position of the sun, and the natural features of his environment, but his sensory capacities on the whole are no greater than ours. As Woodworth says: "On the whole, keenness of the senses seems to be about on a par for various races of mankind. Differences exist among the members of any race, and it is not improbable that differences exist between the averages of certain groups, especially when these are small, isolated and much inbred." (p. 177)

While the psychological literature may be searched almost in vain for tables of distribution of sensitivities of the various sense organs, it may be stated that so far as published data are concerned, the individual differences in sensitivity tend to follow the normal curve. The majority of people, in regard to any measurable sensitivity, tend to cluster around the normal. In certain sense organs peculiar gaps are found. Thus, in color vision, the red-green color-blind, who owe their inability to distinguish reds and greens to defective genes, tend to form a definite group. In hearing, we have tonal gaps and tonal islands, by which is meant that deafening is not common to the whole range of frequencies but is more marked at some levels than at others. The general loss of auditory acuity in regard to high frequency tones by the aged has been noted, but this does not detract from the truth of the statement made above, namely, that, in general, individual differences in sensitivity tend to be distributed in normal fashion. However, much research must be done before we can speak with any real assurance on the point.

Individual Differences in Motor Reactions.—When motor reactions in the form of reaction times were first studied by psychologists, their variability was soon established. As a matter of fact, Cattell's early work on the subject in Wundt's laboratory, and his use of the central tendency and probable error in describing them, may be regarded as the beginnings of what has now become the dominant type of American psychology, namely, the psychology of individual differences. The early work on motor reactions, therefore, was concerned with their form of distribution and with the statistical measures (central tendency and probable error), which described this distribution. Later work has been directed to the measurement of improvement of a motor function under the influence of practice. In other words, it now seems more important to know how a pupil improves his typewriting ability through practice than to know the distribution of the number of words typed by a class of students at the first or any other practice. Consequently, modern data on variability of motor reactions is somewhat difficult to find. Pyle,[35] for example, although he states in his preface that he has "tried to state every thing that is known about learning," gives only one example of a distribution of motor learning, namely, marble-sorting by university men and women. (p. 272)

From the data given by Nelson[36] (pp. 61-63) I have constructed Table XXXVI and Fig. 25. They refer to a measurement of steadiness in which a Dunlap plate was used. The object of the test is to insert a stylus into a series of holes of varying size without touching the sides.

TABLE XXXVI. DISTRIBUTION OF SCORES OF GOITROUS AND NON-GOITROUS GIRLS IN A STEADINESS TEST (DUNLAP PLATE) IN WHICH THE DEWEY, CHILD AND RUML METHOD OF SCORING WAS USED. (Nelson.)

Score	No. of Non-goitrous	No. of Goitrous
20 — 29		1
30 — 39	4	2
40 — 49	10	22
50 — 59	14	19
60 — 69	5	27
70 — 79	7	12
80 — 89	4	12
90 — 99	5	7
100 — 109	2	1
Total	51	103

[35] W. H. Pyle, *The Psychology of Learning*, (Rev. Ed.), 1928.
[36] Louise A. Nelson, *Variations in Development and Motor Control in Goiterous and Non-goiterous Adolescent Girls*, 1929.

The distribution is obviously skewed, but even with so few cases the piling up of cases around the central tendency is shown. Fig. 25 shows this graphically.

It would be interesting to learn if there were a general motor ability whose variability could be measured. From work done by Seashore [37] and others, this seems impossible of fulfilment, since the tests show that the assumption of a general motor ability is unjustified. As Seashore says, "The

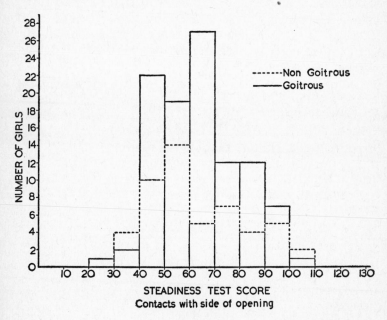

Fig. 25. Graph of Scores of Goitrous and Non-Goitrous Girls in a Steadiness Test.

independence of the skills measured in these tests argues against any theory of general motor ability and in favor of specific skills. The results of related studies have so far presented little evidence that serial performances may be analyzed into speed or accuracy of simple reactions or reflexes.

"The theory by which motor skills are determined by a relatively small number of basic motor capacities is strongly

[37] R. H. Seashore, "Individual Differences in Motor Skills," *Jour. of General Psychol.*, III, 1930.

open to question. The independence of these performances as measured suggests that if there are basic motor capacities, they are more numerous and more specific than previously believed." (p. 62) However, each specific motor ability that Seashore measured exhibited variability, and so it is found by everybody who measures them.

Variability, Training and Age.—As a result of his experiments, Thorndike is inclined to believe that the variability of a group is increased by training. This is also the common sense point of view. A moron and a genius, before they have entered school, are relatively hard to distinguish. As they receive instruction, the bright pupil pulls further and further ahead of the dull one. This makes for greater variability after training. However, when the experiments dealing with this problem are examined, the evidence seems to point the other way. Thus Burns[38] in his review of the question found that of 86 studies made between 1908 and 1936, 46 showed reduced variability, 36 increased variability, while 4 were stationary or gave uncertain results. Some of these discrepancies may be explained by the different ways the results were reported. Reed[39] used the following methods for appraising the results: (1) the ratio of the average of the highest three individuals to the average of the lowest three individuals at the beginning of the practice compared with the ratio of these same individuals at the end of practice; (2) the coefficient of variability; and (3) the correlation between initial performance and per cent of gain. Analyzing the results of others he found that 95 per cent of 59 experiments showed a decrease by use of method (1). Using method (2) on 70 experiments he found 77 per cent showed decreased variability from the coefficients of variability. By method (3), 93 per cent of 58 cases gave negative correlations. These findings point to the conclusion that education as carried on in the public schools reduces the variability of the product, and incidentally, supports the environmentalist against the hereditarian point of view.

Burns has pointed out that motivation was usually uncon-

[38] Zed H. Burns, "Practice, Variability and Motivation," *Jour. of Educational Research*, XXX, 6, pp. 403-420.

[39] H. B. Reed, "The Influence of Practice on Individual Differences," *School and Society*, XXXIV, 1931, pp. 100-102.

trolled in the older experiments reviewed by Reed. In one of his own experiments, however, in which equated groups, one motivated, the other working under ordinary classroom conditions, were practised in addition and in code writing, he found that in each case the variability became reduced during practice.

Probably the conflicting results are due to the manner in which the data are treated. If the gains are measured by an increase in the amount of work per unit time, the results show increased variability with practice. If, however, the gains are measured by time per unit of work then decreased variability is shown by practice. Both results cannot be true. Chapman showed that the discrepancy in time and amount results was due to the fact that performance was measured from an arbitrary zero. When both are measured from an absolute zero, the discrepancy disappears. In measuring from an arbitrary zero, we are really dealing with fractions both with time and amount. However, amount scores are theoretically sounder than time scores when performance is measured from an arbitrary zero point. Anastasi found that when absolute measures of variability are used (Q, A.D. and S.D.), variability increases with practice, but when relative measures are used (V), or some measure making use of relative or percentage gains, or ratio of scores of initially high and low individuals, variability decreases with practice. The better subjects improve somewhat more than the poorer subjects; and the S.D.'s increase with practice, that is, they increase as the scores increase.

One other factor needs consideration. The conflicting results may be due to differing complexities of the task. In general, the harder the task, the greater is the increase of the variability with training. As Hogben has shown, variability in educational achievement is increased when the excellent educational opportunities available for a select few are extended to a bigger group.

When we turn to a similar problem, namely, the effect of age on variability, the results are unequivocal. Age increases variability. This means that babies are more alike than public school pupils, public school pupils than high school pupils, and high school pupils than adults. B.A.'s are more alike than M.A.'s or Ph.D.'s.

In regard to elementary education the most comprehensive study of the problem was made by Burt [40] in London. The variability increased both by age and class and in each subject throughout the elementary school. There was a slight decrease in variability in the upper classes and upper ages, but the numbers investigated were comparatively few. The following quotation from Burt is pertinent not only in regard to the effect of age on variability but also of schooling.

"Inherent capacity is largely the result of inheritance; acquired knowledge, of teaching. If inherited capacity could be assessed quite independently of the results of instruction, the foregoing estimates might (it may be imagined) need considerable correction. It may seem possible that, in certain schools, and still more in certain classes, the apparent backwardness of the children is due merely to ineffective teaching. Such cases should readily be discoverable by an extension of the methods here used. But, from the characteristics of the observed distributions, it seems clear that such cases are not numerous. Again, in other schools and classes, it may seem possible that the particular excellence of the teaching may cause the children to appear unusually advanced. But, in reviewing a large area, the results of exceptional efficiency or inefficiency in teaching will be comparatively small, and probably to a great extent be neutralized by each other in the general averages. The main effect of teaching upon educational ability is, as a rule, to increase the individual differences already present from birth. Children who are naturally bright learn rapidly, and are promoted rapidly to higher classes. Children who are naturally dull learn comparatively little; they tend to remain at the same absolute level so long that their relative backwardness increases year by year. Hence it is, in part, that the "standard deviation"— the measure of the degree to which individuals of a given age-group differ from one another — increases from about half a year at the age of five to a year and a quarter at the age of thirteen. Occasionally, towards the end of his career, a bright boy may be allowed to mark time in an upper standard while others catch up to him. Occasionally, by special coaching, a backward child may be brought up more nearly to the normal level. But, in the main, it is comparatively rare to find original differences lessened in this way by the efforts of teaching, and rarer still to find them reversed. The main effect of teaching, therefore, so far as it affects the validity of our estimates, is to allow the original differences of ability to develop, to increase, and to become more distinct." (p. 45)

[40] Cyril Burt, *The Distribution and Relations of Educational Abilities,* 1917.

We may close the discussion by reminding the reader that Thurstone [41] introduced his method of absolute scaling to provide for the increasing dispersion of ability in successive ages and grades. He [42] showed, for example, that Trabue's scaling of his "Completion-Test Language Scales" assumed that the dispersion was the same at all grades, whereas it increased from 1.00 to 2.12 from Grade II to Grade XII.

Educational Provision for Individual Differences.—The educational psychologist has shown the presence of individual differences among children, but left the duty of providing for them to the philosopher and administrator. The fixed curriculum, which every pupil studied regardless of his capacities, has given place to almost endless devices which cater more or less to the varying gifts of pupils. At one extreme, we have the scheme which provides a separate curriculum for every pupil. This is the plan of the Progressive educators (with a capital P) and they secure it by allowing each child to select his own studies. This statement may be disputed by Progressive educators, but it is the common and distinguishing feature of all their systems. In their writings we find many references to the child-centered school, and to the necessity of allowing the child's individuality to unfold naturally, undisturbed by external disciplinary factors. "What, my dear, would you like to study today?" And what the child chooses is right; it is in line with his native gifts and interests; it unfolds his personality. This is in direct contrast to the fixed curriculum in which the teacher says metaphorically and sometimes in reality: "That's what you've got to learn; get busy, and the Heavens above protect you if you don't do it right!" Like all extreme positions both are wrong. The traditional curriculum makes practically no provision for individual differences; Progressive education throws the burden of selection on the immature pupil who has neither the knowledge nor the experience to select wisely. Adults cannot abrogate their responsibilities in such a care-free manner as the Progressives would have them do. They have the difficult task of providing

---

[41] L. L. Thurstone, "A Method of Scaling Psychological and Educational Tests," *Jour. Educ. Psychol.*, XVI, 7, pp. 433-451.

[42] L. L. Thurstone, "The Unit of Measurement in Educational Scales," *Jour. Educ. Psychol.*, XVIII, 8, p. 521.

common subjects and tasks to secure a community of interests and, at the same time, of making the program sufficiently elastic to take care of individual differences.

The Winnetka and the Dalton Plans, worked out by Carleton Washburne and Helen Parkhurst, respectively, are ultimately derived from the teachings of Jesse D. Burks of the San Francisco Normal School, where Washburne and Parkhurst once held teaching positions. Both of them want to provide for individual differences. In Winnetka, special texts are prepared in each subject and the pupil is allowed to go through them at his own pace. However, before he passes on to a second section, he must show himself to be the master of the first. According to the Dalton Plan, pupils are given assignments which they complete at their own speed. Copious reference material is provided in the library and the pupils are expected to find their way through it. As in the Winnetka Plan, the pupil must complete a project satisfactorily before he passes on to another. In both systems the traditional material of the curriculum is largely accepted, but valiant attempts are made to select up-to-date topics of practical value.

Allied to the above we have the Project Method. Although this method is associated with the name of W. H. Kilpatrick, it was in use in the University School at Columbus, Missouri, when J. L. Meriam was in charge of it. The object is to get away from the tyranny of the fixed lesson period and the bell which often stops a class when they are really warmed to a task. The task, itself, of course, must be one that is largely selected by the pupils (although the teacher can and usually does influence the choice) and must be sufficiently comprehensive to provide for a long-time co-operative solution by the whole of the class. Each member contributes according to his talents and interests. It undoubtedly provides for individual differences, although there may be little continuity in program, and the duller or lazier pupils may escape work altogether.

The plan adopted in the secondary schools of England, France and Germany, is to provide a limited number of fixed offerings. Thus in England a pupil can select the Classical, Mathematical, Modern Language, English, Historical or Science side of the school. There is a basic course in common, running for two or three years, so the pupil usually has an inkling as to where his talents lie before he begins his specialization. But the selection is made in a lump; there is little provision made for individual differences; and it is usually difficult to transfer from one side to the other. In France only four offerings are made. In Germany, by the selection of a school, a pupil chooses also his curriculum — classical; semi-classical; and moderns, including science.

In the United States over a large part of the country, the accepted practice is to demand a foundation of a few fixed subjects of which English is always one. On this foundation a curriculum to suit every need is built, by the offering of a very large number of electives. At first glance this method seems to solve the problem of individual differences satisfactorily. And so it should, but foreign observers note that some of the subjects offered for credit are the "play" subjects, the extra-curricular activities of European schools. Thus credit is given for dramatic art, tap-dancing and similar subjects. To the European this seems to be turning the serious business of education into a farce, but the course has been necessitated by the large numbers of pupils proceeding to secondary schools. Some of the pupils are so poorly equipped mentally that these easy courses have to be provided for them. Curriculum problems, which are, at bottom, problems concerned with individual differences, divide educators into two rather sharply divided camps. On the one hand, we have the conservatives and traditionalists who stress standards of educational achievement; on the other, we have the progressives and radicals who stress individual differences and are more concerned with personality than ability to pass examinations. Although a reconciliation of the two points of view will ultimately be found, the gap between them is still quite wide.

This chapter could be enlarged to several volumes, but enough has been said to show that among human beings any measurable trait exhibits variability. Variability is a universal phenomenon, and consequently the pious hope expressed in the statement that "men are created free and equal" has no foundation in fact.

REFERENCES

Allen, C. N. "Recent Research on Sex Differences." *Psychol. Bulletin.* 1935, XXII, pp. 343-354.

Anastasi, Anne. *Differential Psychology; Individual and Group Differences in Behavior.* New York, Macmillan, 1937. Pp. xvii + 615.

Bean, R. B. "The Eruption of the Teeth as a Physiological Standard for Testing Development." *Ped. Sem.*, 1914, XXI, pp. 596-614.

Boas, F. *Changes in Bodily Form of Descendants of Immigrants.* U. S. Senate Document No. 208, Washington, 1911. Pp. 573.

Boring, E. G. *A History of Experimental Psychology.* New York, Century, 1929. Pp. xviii + 699.

Brigham, C. C. "Intelligence Tests of Immigrant Groups." *Psychol. Review.* 1930, XXXVII, pp. 158-165.

Brigham, C. C. *A Study of American Intelligence.* Princeton University Press, 1922. Pp. 210.

Burns, Z. H. "Practice, Variability and Motivation." *Jour. of Educ. Research.* 1937, XXX, 6, pp. 403-420.

Burt, C. *The Distribution and Relations of Educational Abilities.* London, P. S. King, 1917. Pp. xiii + 93.

Carmichael, L. "The Development of Behavior in Vertebrates Experimentally Removed from the Influence of External Stimulation." *Psychol. Review*, 1926, XXXIII, pp. 51-58; XXXIV, 1927, pp. 34-47; XXXV, 1928, pp. 253-260.

Cattell, Psyche. "Dentition as a Measure of Maturity." *Harvard Monogs. in Education*, No. 9. Cambridge, Harvard University Press, 1928. Pp. viii + 91.

Conway, C. B. *The Hearing Abilities of Children in Toronto Public Schools.* Department of Educational Research, University of Toronto, 1937. Pp. 132.

Crew, F. A. E. "Abnormal Sexuality in Animals; III Sex Reversal." *Quarterly Review of Biology*, 1927, II, pp. 427-441.

Donaldson, H. H. *The Growth of the Brain.* London, Scott, 1895. Pp. 374.

Ellis, R. S. *The Psychology of Individual Differences*, New York, Appleton, 1932. Pp. xxiii + 535.

Fay, E. A. *Marriages of the Deaf in America.* Volta Bureau. Washington, Gibson Brothers, 1898. Pp. vii + 527.

Fletcher, H. *Speech and Hearing.* New York, Van Nostrand, 1929. Pp. xv + 331.

Freeman, F. S. *Individual Differences: the Nature and Causes of Variations in Intelligence and Special Abilities.* New York, Holt, 1934. Pp. xi + 355.

Galton, F. *Hereditary Genius: an Enquiry into its Laws and Consequences.* New York, Appleton, 1880. (Reprint of 1869 edition.) Pp. vi + 390.

Galton, F. *Inquiries into Human Faculty and its Development.* London, Dent, 1883. (Reprint.) Pp. xviii + 261.

Garrett, H. E.   *Great Experiments in Psychology*.   New York, Century, 1930.   Pp. xvii + 337.

Garth, T. R.   *Race Psychology: A Study of Racial Mental Differences*. New York, McGraw-Hill, 1931.   Pp. xiv + 260.

Gesell, A. & Thompson, Helen.   "Learning and Growth in Identical Infant Twins."   *Genetic Psychol. Monogs*. VI, 1, 1929, pp. 1-124.

Gobineau, J. A.   *The Inequality of Races*.   (Tr. A. Collins.)   New York, Putnam, 1915.

Grant, M.   *The Passing of the Great Race*.   New York, Scribner, 1921.

Griffith, C. R.   *An Introduction to Educational Psychology*.   New York, Farrar & Rinehart, 1935.   Pp. xiv + 754.

Hayes, S. P.   "Mental and Educational Surveys in Seven Schools for the Blind."   *Report of the Twenty-fifth Convention of the American Association of Instructors of the Blind*.   1920.

Jamieson, E. & Sandiford, P.   "The Mental Capacity of Southern Ontario Indians."   *Jour. of Educ. Psychol*.   1928.   XIX, 8, pp. 536-551.

Klineberg, O.   *Race Differences*.   New York, Harper, 1935.   Pp. ix + 367.

Klineberg, O.   "A Study of Psychological Differences Between 'Racial' and National Groups in Europe."   *Archives of Psychology*, No. 192, 1931.   Pp. 57.

LaPiere, R. T. & Farnsworth, P. R.   *Social Psychology*.   New York, McGraw-Hill, 1936.   Pp. xii + 504.

Lincoln, E. A.   *Sex Differences in the Growth of American School Children*.   Baltimore, Warwick & York, 1927.   Pp. xii + 189.

Long, J. A.   *The Motor Ability of the Deaf*.   New York, Bureau of Publications, Teachers College, Columbia University, 1932.   Pp. vii + 67.

Macdonald, D. D.   *Sight-saving Classes in the Public Schools*.   Toronto, (privately printed), 1932.   Pp. 88.

McGraw, Myrtle B.   *Growth: A Study of Johnny and Jimmy*.   New York, Century, 1935.   Pp. xxi + 319.

McNemar, Q. & Terman, L. M.   "Sex Differences in Variational Tendency."   *Genetic Psychol. Monogs*.   XVIII, 1, 1936.   Pp. 65.

Miles, W. R.   (Ed.) "Psychological Studies of Human Variability." *Psychol. Monogs*.   1936.   XLVII, 2, pp. x + 415.

Nelson, Louise A.   *Variations in Development and Motor Control in Goiterous and Non-goiterous Adolescent Girls*.   Baltimore, Warwick & York, 1929.   Pp. xii + 193.

Pearson, K.   *The Life, Letters and Labours of Francis Galton*.   Vol. II, Cambridge University Press, 1924.   Pp. xi + 425.

Pintner, R.   *Intelligence Testing; Methods and Results*.   (Rev. Ed.) New York, Holt, 1931.   Pp. xii + 555.

Porteus, S. D.   "Race and Social Differences in Performance Tests." *Genetic Psychol. Monogs*.   VIII, 2, 1930.   Pp. 93-208.

Pyle, W. H.   *The Psychology of Learning*.   (Rev. Ed.)   Baltimore, Warwick & York, 1928.   Pp. ix + 441.

Reed, H. B.   "The Influence of Practice on Individual Differences." *School and Society*, 1931, XXXIV, pp. 100-102.

Sanders, B. S. *Environment and Growth.* Baltimore, Warwick & York, 1934. Pp. xviii + 375.

Sandiford, P. & Kerr, Ruby. "Intelligence of Chinese and Japanese Children." *Jour. of Educ. Psychol.* 1926, XVII, 6, pp. 361-367.

Scheidemann, Norma V. *The Psychology of Exceptional Children.* Boston, Houghton Mifflin, 1931. Pp. xvii + 520.

Seashore, R. H. "Individual Differences in Motor Skills." *Jour. of General Psychology*, 1930, III, pp. 38-65.

Skinner, C. E. (and collaborators). *Readings in Educational Psychology.* New York, Farrar & Rinehart, 1937. Pp. x + 630.

Stoddard, T. L. *The Rising Tide of Color Against White World Supremacy.* New York, Scribner, 1920.

Stone, C. P. "Learning: I. The Factor of Maturation" in *Handbook of General Experimental Psychology.* (Ed. Murchison.) Worcester, Clark University Press, 1934, pp. 352-381.

Taylor, Griffith. *Environment, Race and Migration.* University of Toronto Press, 1937. Pp. xv + 483.

Taylor, Griffith. *Environment and Nation.* University of Toronto Press, 1936. Pp. 571.

Terman, L. M. "The Gifted Child" in *Handbook of Child Psychology.* (Ed. Murchison.) Worcester, Clark University Press, 1931, pp. 568-584.

Terman, L. M. & Miles, Catharine. *Sex and Personality; Studies in Masculinity and Femininity.* New York, McGraw-Hill, 1936.

Thorndike, E. L. *Educational Psychology, Vol. III, Work, Fatigue, and Individual Differences.* New York, Teachers College, Columbia University, 1921. Pp. x + 408.

Thurstone, L. L. "A Method of Scaling Psychological and Educational Tests." *Jour. of Educ. Psychology*, 1925, XVI, 7, pp. 433-451.

Thurstone, L. L. "The Unit of Measurement in Educational Scales." *Jour. of Educ. Psychology*, 1927, XVIII, 8, pp. 505-524.

Wechsler, D. *The Range of Human Capacities.* Baltimore, Williams and Wilkins, 1935. Pp. 150.

Woodrow, H. *Brightness and Dullness in Children.* Philadelphia, Lippincott, 1919. Pp. 322.

Woodworth, R. S. "Racial Differences in Mental Traits." *Science*, N. S., 1910, XXI, pp. 171-186.

Yerkes, R. M. (Ed.) "Psychological Examining in the U. S. Army." *National Academy of Science Memoirs*, XV, 1921. Pp. 890.

CHAPTER III

THE FOUNDATIONS OF BEHAVIOR

The Meaning of Behavior. — Educational Psychology, as we have seen, is concerned with the study of the behavior of human beings as they are subjected to the process of education, that is, as they learn to do and to say. It is mostly concerned with the behavior of the young, but as learning takes place at all ages up to senility, it now includes adult education as well. It is also mostly concerned with the behavior of normal pupils, but since many pupils are abnormal, it now includes the education of the halt, lame and blind, the deaf and dullard, and of those with abnormal personalities or characters. Whatever branch of educational psychology is selected for study, behavior becomes the key word, and there must be no dubiety regarding its meaning and significance. Let us therefore begin by making a number of explicit statements about behavior in general:

(1) In the first place, behavior is the response of an organism to some form of stimulation. Without this stimulation by the energies of the environment — light, heat, pressure, sound, and the like — the organism would be an inert mass incapable of any form of behavior. The response it makes is an adjustment or regulation of some kind; the organism, acting as a system, maintains its integrity, providing the environmental changes are not too pronounced. In other words, if the adjustments made by the organism in response to environmental stimuli are adequate, the organism lives and flourishes; if they are inadequate, it either lives on a lower plane or dies. As Spencer truly said, "life is the continuous adjustment of internal relations to external relations."

In the higher organisms the response is a manifestation of an excitation-conduction phenomenon. Responses are generally movements or changes in movements; and secretions or changes in secretions. The movements may be due either to striped or unstriped muscles, and the secretions either to duct or ductless glands. The responses, therefore, may either be overt or covert; open to direct observation or hidden from it. The movements of the body in writing, drawing, walking and playing games may be directly observed. The movements of the laryngeal muscles during speaking and thinking, and the peristaltic movements of the intestines during digestion cannot be directly observed; they are examples of hidden movements. By the adoption of suitable means, X-rays, for instance, some hidden movements may be made overt. However, with the hidden, intrinsic, physiological, or vital processes of the body, psychology has little concern; they are the special province of physiology.

(2) Behavior always takes place in some environment. Organisms have no meaning except in relation to some environment; in fact, an organism without an environment is inconceivable. This does not mean that the differences in the behavior of organisms are determined solely by the environment. The potentialities of the organism, as we saw in Chapter I, reside in the genes of the chromosomes, but the orderly unfolding and realization of these potentialities is due to environmental stimulation. However, not all the genes and their possibilities are developed by the environment. In the higher organisms at least, and especially in man, each individual represents but a portion, probably a very small portion, of his hereditary possibilities. The selective agency is environment. Thus the genes of man may determine that under the stimulation of food, use and other factors he shall grow arms instead of wings; while the genes of a chicken determine that under similar conditions wings instead of arms shall be grown. And the behavior possibilities of arms and wings are very different. The same stimuli of food and use also determine whether a particular man shall grow big, hard muscles, or small, flabby ones. Human genes give man the power of learning language, but it is environment that determines which language shall be learned. Moreover, although any normal person has the potentiality to learn, perhaps, fifty languages fairly well, yet few languages are ordinarily learned by any of us. One further observation should be made. The genes do not start their own development; the starting agency is environment. Hence we may say with some assurance that an organism is no self-starting mechanism, but is one that requires starting by some agency outside of itself.

There is one more difficulty that confronts us in regard to this stimulation of hereditary potentialities by environment. We have seen that each cell of a multicellular organism must, perforce, contain identical chromosomes and identical genes. Yet some of these cells grow into muscle cells, others into nerve cells and so on. The same food material apparently produces different results from identical potentialities. There must be some agency determining this differentiation. According to Child[1] the differentiating agent is the physiological gradient. Of this more will be said later in the chapter.

(3) The kind of behavior an organism exhibits is dependent upon its structure and constitution, and upon the nature of the exciting stimulus. Differing organisms behave differently even when excited by the same stimulus. If one could imagine a situation in which a partridge, sparrow, deer and man were startled simultaneously by the same noise, the resultant behavior would be very different. The partridge would freeze, the sparrow fly, the deer run, and the man start.

The relationship between these different organic mechanisms and the stimulus which results in behavior is not unlike the relation between the subjective and objective. The same stimulus, a loud sound, results in different behavior because the living mechanisms are different. Even when the mechanisms appear to be the same, as when an artist, a scientist and a rustic each see a primrose, they are really different. According to Wordsworth, the traveling rustic (Peter Bell) sees the primrose and

> "A primrose by a river's brim
> A yellow primrose was to him
> And it was nothing more."

But the same object, the primrose, affects the other human observers very differently. To the artist, it is an object of beauty, arousing deep emotions, which may stimulate him to produce a work of art. To the scientist it is a member of the family *Primulaceae,* genus *Primula,* species *vulgaris,* with characteristics which enable him to distinguish it from every other species of flower in the wide world. These three ob-

[1] Charles M. Child, *Physiological Foundations of Behavior,* 1924.

servers, outwardly alike as members of the human species, are inwardly different, hence the same object produces different subjective experiences in each of them.

(4) The grade or level of behavior is dependent upon the grade or level of biological development of the organism. This is equivalent to saying that behavior is dependent upon the position the animal occupies on the evolutionary scale. The higher the position, the more complex is the behavior.

Behavior runs from low to high, high being defined as the greater capacity for diversified living. Plants undoubtedly behave. They react towards light, heat, winds, and moisture, but such adjustments as they make are necessarily to a narrower environment than those which animals make. Some reactions of plants are so rapid that Bose maintains they have a primitive kind of nervous system. Certainly the reactions of the sensitive plant (*Mimosa sensitiva*) resemble reflexes very closely indeed.

The lowest animal organisms exhibit little more than tropisms — relatively simple, definite responses to external stimulations generally of a physical or chemical character, which lead to the orientation of the body with respect to the stimulus. Both plants and moths react to light; both of them are said to be positively heliotropic.

As the biological scale is ascended, as the biological development becomes more complex, other forms of behavior — reflexes and instincts — make their appearance. Fishes, reptiles and many of the birds and mammals live their lives at this reflexive and instinctive level. In the higher animals, intelligent behavior makes its appearance and in man, and in some gregarious animals, social behavior — behavior within a group — makes its appearance. Certain insects, of course, exhibit social behavior of a kind, but it is different from that of the higher animals, especially that of man, where the social behavior has more behind it than a mere division of labor. Hence bodily structure throughout the whole range of natural forms, is paralleled by appropriate bodily behavior.

The organism's complexity of structure is due to the correlated differentiation of muscles and glands on the one hand, and to the nervous system on the other. Biologists, therefore, are right in maintaining that "what is functionally higher is biologically higher." The lowly earthworm creeping among the roots of a giant tree is biologically higher than the tree. The worm can move away but the tree must stand in the same place. It is the complexity of the behavior patterns that counts; neither the work done nor the energy transformed is a satisfactory criterion. As Herrick[2] says, "The energy expenditure of a single calorie in the brain of an engineer may be of more significance in the construction of a cantilever bridge than of all the muscular work required in its fabrication." (p. 15)

(5) Behavior, in all but the simplest organisms, shows increasing complexity with age. Adult behavior in mankind is more complex and elaborate than infantile behavior. Behavior in childhood resembles more closely than that of adults the behavior of the sub-human animals who live mostly at the level of reflexes and instincts. Behavior at maturity is more intelligent, more diversified, more unpredictable than that of childhood. So true is this that Stanley Hall, following Ernst Haeckel, maintained that the development of behavior in the individual paralleled its development in the race. In technical terms — ontogeny repeats phylogeny. This is obviously far from being universally true. Paddling in water and climbing trees both take place at about the same age in normal children, but living in trees must have occurred millions of years after organisms left the water for land. Sex must have been present in organisms from the earliest beginnings, but in man it is the latest of all instincts to come to full fruition. Nevertheless, it is indubitably true that throughout the span of childhood and far into maturity, behavior in mankind becomes increasingly complex.

If maturity brings increased complexity of behavior, why should there be a rejuvenation, a return to the ignorance of childhood? The whole process seems wasteful. From all points of view it would seem to be far more economical for man to go on developing for ever. Apparently infancy is a "setting back of the clock," for only through painful struggles do children reach the point of development attained by their parents. Decay, which ends in death, seems to begin

[2] C. Judson Herrick, *Neurological Foundations of Animal Behavior*, 1924.

when man, through the complexity of his behavior, has become most useful to society. John Fiske,[3] in his famous essay, emphasized the educational importance of infancy. Animals such as the amoeba, which is literally born grown-up, have no infancy and are ineducable. Those animals with the longest infancy are the most educable, *ergo*, infancy is nature's device for providing for an education.

Age may bring increasing complexity of behavior, but it also brings with it an increasing rigidity of mind and body, which is reflected in decreased physical activity and increased conservatism of thought. Infancy, on the other hand, is the period of plasticity and adaptability *par excellence*. The rigidity of age means a widening gulf between the organism and its environment. Old people are notoriously bad at adapting themselves to the changing world. Hence age, despite its body of experience, makes progress increasingly difficult or impossible. At this point the rejuvenation of the race takes place and saves it from decrepitude and destruction. Infancy is thus a means of exit when age has become a bar to progress. The young alone are able to adapt themselves to the progressive evolution of the race.

If the following ratios are calculated for various species of animals and arranged in order of size, an order of relative intelligence is obtained:

(1) Length of life to length of adolescence.
(2) Weight of body to weight of brain.
(3) Period from birth to death to period from birth to puberty.

In Table XXXVII the first of these ratios is given.

The reason for these ratios seems to be two-fold. Man has been selected because of brain-power and as a result of this selection, life has now become enormously complex. To meet life's complexity satisfactorily, man is now forced to have great mental adaptability. While his physical body has hardly evolved beyond that of a simian, his mental powers are separated by a gap that is immeasurably great. Mental power is dependent upon a slow-developing nerve tissue, hence the period of gestation, long as it is in man, is too short for adequate growth and development. Hence in-

---

[3] John Fiske, *The Meaning of Infancy*, 1883.

TABLE XXXVII. THE RATIO OF LONGEVITY TO ADOLESCENCE.
(Abridged and Adapted from A. F. Chamberlain, *The Child;
A Study in the Evolution of Man*, p. 8.)

Animal	Authority	Length of Adolescence	Length of Life	Ratio of Longevity to Adolescence
Dormouse	Hollis	3 months	4–5 years	16–20
Guinea-pig	Flourens; Hollis	7 months	6–7	10.2–12
Cat	Mivart	1 year	12	12
Cat	Jennings	2 years	15	7.5
Goat	Pegler	1.25 years	12	9.6
English cattle	Hollis	2 years	18	9
Large dogs	Dalziel	2 years	15–20	7.5–10
Hippopotamus	Chambers' Encyclopedia	5 years	30	6
Lion	Mivart	6 years	30–40	5–6.6
English horse (hunter)	Blaine Hollis	6.25 years	35	5.6
Camel	Flourens	8 years	40	5
Elephant	Holder	35 years	120	3.4
Elephant	Darwin	30 years	100	3.3
Man	Buffon	25 years	90–100	3.8–4
Man (Englishman)	Hollis	25 years	75	3

fancy, with plasticity as its dominant feature, has come into being.

Secondly, infancy is a period in which desirable inherited tendencies can be developed, and undesirable ones eliminated. For not all of nature's gifts are unmixed blessings; harmful atavistic and unsocial traits often appear. By this selection during infancy, society fits the child to a changing world and makes him a fitter subject than his parents before him. Infancy has also a moral significance. It was the helplessness of infancy that created the family, and the bond of the family is the one permanent moral basis of society.

Thus we see that although behavior becomes more complex with increasing age, infancy or rejuvenation is needed in order that better adaptations to the changing world may be made.

(6) Organisms show two major groups of behavior activities. The first group, which includes the metabolic processes of nutrition, respiration, circulation, and excretion, has

been variously called *intrinsic, visceral,* or *physiological* behavior. Intrinsic behavior, therefore, is concerned with the life processes of the body — those which maintain it in health and vigor, and secure its reproduction. Psychology, as such, is little concerned with intrinsic behavior, but it is the chief province of the science of physiology.

The second group is known as *integrative* or *somatic* behavior. Integrative behavior is pre-eminently the field of psychology, since it has to do with the way the organism adjusts itself to the changing environment. Locomotion (or movement) is the chief overt form of integrative behavior, but the secretions of glands and internal modifications of the organism are also important. As a matter of fact, it is sometimes very difficult to draw sharp lines of demarcation between intrinsic and integrative forms of behavior. Springing from a common root — the inherent irritability of protoplasm, they simply represent two different lines of development which forever remain mutually dependent and interactive.

(7) Since behavior represents a response to a stimulus, psychologists customarily symbolize it by the formula S-R. Although all schools agree that behavior is a response to a stimulus, there is a sharp division of opinion as to the part that a simple reaction plays in the total behavior. Thorndike and those who believe in the reaction-hypothesis are inclined to believe that complex behavior is the sum total of simple reactions of the reflex type. The gestaltists and the organismic school believe that behavior is relatively undifferentiated and unco-ordinated at first and becomes specialized through maturation and experience. Reflexes and other simple elements in behavior instead of coming first, grow out of the diffuse unco-ordinated behavior of infancy and early childhood. The two points of view are not as far apart as they at first appear to be. In the later stages of development of behavior, the S-R formula becomes increasingly appropriate, for the paths from sense organ to reacting mechanism have been rather definitely traced. Any break in the path destroys the customary response. According to Herrick,[4] this unit of behavior in higher animals includes the following processes:

---

[4] C. Judson Herrick, *Neurological Foundations of Animal Behavior*, 1924.

1. The *stimulus*, a physical agent of some sort which impinges upon excitable protoplasm.
2. The *excitation*, or the direct effect of the stimulus upon the specific protoplasm which is affected. A special receptive apparatus is usually provided for each kind of stimulus to which the body is sensitive, namely, the sense organ or receptor. The sense organ is usually regarded as part of the nervous system, though it may contain a very complex assortment of non-nervous accessory tissues.
3. The *afferent transmission*. The apparatus is a sensory nervous pathway which transmits the excitation from the receptor to a center of correlation.
4. The *central adjustment*. The adjustor is a nerve center in which the afferent impulse is transferred to an efferent pathway, with or without more complex modification of the excitation in the center itself.
5. The *efferent transmission*. The apparatus is a motor nervous pathway which transmits the excitation to the peripheral organ of response.
6. The *response*. The specific apparatus of response is termed the effector, which is usually not a part of the nervous system — muscle, gland, electric organ, etc. (p. 12)

The above classical view of the phenomenon may have to be modified slightly. For example, recent researches have shown that the nervous system is never quiescent; there are surgings in the brain of various nervous currents; the stimulus and conductive processes, it is argued, simply lend direction to the discharge of these impulses.

To the previous seven explicit statements about behavior we may add four descriptive principles:

(*a*) All organisms are active because they are alive, and are being subjected to continual sensory stimulation. Just what life is, still remains a mystery. As far as is known at present, the bases of life are the various protoplasms comprising the bodies of plants and animals. Protoplasms are organic chemical compounds of highly complex molecular structure. They exhibit irritability or excitability, and this is the fundamental fact about life. Touch a piece of chalk and nothing happens; touch an amoeba and it moves away. These reactions of protoplasms to sensory stimulations are the foundations of behavior in living things. Apparently a protoplasm cannot excite itself, but when stimulated by an external factor, changes in some way not yet made out. After such a stimulation it is doubtful if the protoplasm ever returns again to the same condition. Memory and learning are associated with this property of protoplasm.

(*b*) All sensory stimuli exert some effect on the activity of the organism, not necessarily overt. This principle is really an application of the doctrine of the conservation of energy. If heat, light, sound, or other energies of the external world stimulate sense organs and the nervous system, energy is released and something must result. This something in man is usually the movement of a muscle or the secretion of a gland, which can either be directly observed or, if hidden, can be made apparent by means of a suitable apparatus. It is quite possible, of course, that the whole of the energy may be absorbed in the internal structures of cells, but it is very difficult, if not impossible, to demonstrate this. What complicates the problem is that the energy released is greater than the exciting stimulus and bears no direct quantitative relation to it. The cells are magazines of energy which are set off by some form of initial external stimulation. Just as a spark may set off a pound or a ton of gun-powder, so a relatively feeble stimulation may have profound consequences. The response of one cell may also be the stimulus for another and the chain of reactions may become very extended both in space and time.

(*c*) All activity is initiated by some form of sensory stimulus. This principle denies the claim of the vitalist who, in effect, says that protoplasm is fundamentally capable of self-excitation. But it does not imply that the external, objective environment is the only starting point of behavior reactions. Intraorganic states, such as hunger and thirst, may be very effective in starting a whole series of behavior reactions. It does imply that protoplasmic impulses cannot be spontaneously aroused. If we could conceive an organism in a perfectly constant, unchanging environment, it would remain absolutely inert; it would require some change in the environment, that is, some stimulus, before it could begin to function. Not all the physical energies are adequate stimuli for an organism. Because of the limitations of our sense organs, we are insensitive to ether waves of certain lengths, and to sound waves of certain frequencies. Cosmic rays have been passing through us all our lives but we have never been conscious of them. There may be more things in heaven and earth than are dreamt of in our philosophies.

(*d*) Every reaction (movement or secretion or internal change) resulting from a sensory stimulation inevitably modifies the situation, and the subsequent response is to the modified situation. Thus James's "great big blooming buzzing confusion" of a world gradually becomes an orderly and logical one. The movement recorded by the kinaesthetic sense organs of the muscles, tendons and membranes covering the movable joints, modifies the succeeding one. As a matter of fact, it may become the stimulus for a continuing movement. This is certainly true of writing, where the writing of a particular letter becomes the stimulus for the next one; and of walking, where the movement of one leg becomes the stimulus for the other. In speaking, the muscles of the larynx (as well as the sound of the voice) help us to keep the sentence going. People who become stone deaf do not forget how to speak, nor do they muddle their sentences. The balance of the body is partly preserved automatically through the agency of sensory stimulations from muscles that have previously moved. The importance of this principle has long been overlooked because this mechanism, in its working, does not usually evoke consciousness.

Organismic Behavior. — Previous discussion of behavior has emphasized the fact that organisms which behave are coherent unities. Life, in terms of behavior, means essentially that any organism represents an order and unity which can be understood only if we think of specific behaviors as contributing to the maintenance and survival of the organism. This point of view is that which has been called organismic behavior. It emphasizes the total behavior of the organism in contra-distinction to the behavior of its parts. It states that organismic behavior, at bottom, is designed to preserve the integrity of a "living system" in face of a constantly changing environment. If the adjustments are satisfactorily made, the organism survives; if the changes of environment are so profound that the organism cannot adapt itself to them, the organism dies.

Coghill[5] and others have shown conclusively that behavior

---

[5] G. E. Coghill, *Anatomy and the Problem of Behavior*, 1929.

is coarsely organismic from the start, and that differentiation, individuation and refinement of behavior patterns take place later. This view, of course, is in line with an earlier statement from the field of child psychology, namely, that the wave of development proceeds outwards towards the extremities. The child can pound with his arms, using the bigger muscles of the shoulder and upper arm, before he can eat with a spoon, in which the smaller muscles of the wrist are called into play. But the statement needs qualification. The grasping reflex at the extremity of the arm is dependent upon the coordination of the smaller muscles of the fingers and is prior in its development to the coarser use of the larger muscles of the arm. Nevertheless, the generalization is a useful one; it fits the theory of the physiological gradient (see later), and has been confirmed by reports of the developmental history of many organisms. Take Coghill's description of the development of *Amblystoma* (salamander) as an illustration:

"In *Amblystoma* the total pattern first extends through the trunk and tail. As this pattern enlarges, the parts involved are always perfectly integrated. This totally integrated pattern then extends into the gills, next into the fore limbs and finally into the hind limbs. But as the totally integrated pattern expands through the organism, its parts, one after another, in the same order as they were invaded by the total pattern, begin to acquire a measure of individuality of their own; first the gills, then the fore limbs and finally the hind limbs. This means that local reflexes emerge as, in the language of 'Gestalt,' a 'quality upon the ground,' that is to say, they emerge as a special feature within a more diffuse but dominant mechanism of integration of the whole organism. They cannot be regarded as simply the action of a chain of neurons, excepting as every link of the chain is conceived to be welded into the organism as a whole.

"This principle is thoroughly demonstrated for *Amblystoma*, a typical vertebrate, and there is nothing in our knowledge of the development of behavior to indicate that the principle does not prevail universally in vertebrates, including man. There is no direct evidence for the hypothesis that behavior, in so far as the form of the pattern is concerned, is simply a combination or co-ordination of reflexes. On the contrary, there is conclusive evidence of a dominant organic unity from the beginning. That evidence appears not only in the manner in which behavior develops, but particularly in the manner in which the nervous system puts the principle into effect, for, as shown in the first lecture, the nervous system concerns itself first with the maintenance of the integrity of the individual, and only later makes provision for local reflexes. . . . (pp. 88-89)

"If, then, it is conceded that growth is one of the means by which the nervous system performs its function in behavior, it must be granted, contrary to the dogma of certain behaviorists, that man is more than the sum of his reflexes, instincts, and immediate reactions of all sorts. He is all these plus his creative potential for the future. Even the embryo of *Amblystoma* is, mechanistically considered, more than the sum of its reflexes or immediate behavior possibilities. The real measure of the individual, accordingly, whether lower animal or man, must include the element of growth as a creative power. Man is, indeed, a mechanism, but he is a mechanism which within his limitations of life, sensitivity and growth, is creating and operating himself." (pp. 109-110)

This view of behavior correlates nicely with the teachings of the Gestalt psychologists who maintain: (*a*) that the mind works as a whole and gains insight into the patterns of behavior; (*b*) that the whole organism reacts in a completely integrated form from the beginning; (*c*) that the organism reacts as a whole to the total situation; (*d*) that learning proceeds from the whole to parts, from the general to the specific; and (*e*) that the whole is always greater than the sum of its parts.

It is also supported by the cerebral studies of Lashley and by the work of Child on the physiological gradient. It fits in with the view of Bell and Kilpatrick who maintain that the central field of psychological study must be "personality," and even with that of Herrick who looks upon man as a thinking machine. It receives support from Humphrey, Raup, Rignano and Judd and, indeed, from all psychologists who view the learning process in terms of systemic adjustment, the maintenance of equilibrium or complacency, or the generalization of experience.[6]

[6] See K. S. Lashley, *Brain Mechanisms and Intelligence*, 1929. C. M. Child, *Physiological Foundations of Behavior*, 1924. Reginald Bell, "Educational Psychology and its Social Implications," *Progressive Education*, XIII, 7, 1936, pp. 550-555. W. H. Kilpatrick, "Psychological Bases and their Implications for the American Curriculum," *Teachers College Record*, 1937, XXXVIII, 6, pp. 491-502. C. Judson Herrick, *The Thinking Machine*, 1929. George Humphrey, *The Nature of Learning*, 1933. B. R. Raup, *Complacency; the Foundation of Human Behavior*, 1925. Chas. H. Judd, *Education as Cultivation of the Higher Mental Processes*, 1936.

Granted that organismic behavior is a reality, it still remains true to say that the organism, besides acting as a whole, also acts in parts. An observer looking at me at the present moment would be right in saying that I am writing, but what he would chiefly observe would be movements occasioned by the action of muscles in my hand and forearm. Sometimes, as in swimming and rock-climbing, the activity is so diffuse that the whole of the body seems to participate. At other times, as in silent reading, the activity is reduced to a minimum; the only overt movement is the jerky movement of the eyes as the reading progresses. If some educational psychologists have been so concerned with the minute analysis of behavior that they have overlooked the organism, some organismic psychologists have been so blind that they could not see the working of the parts.

As Coghill has shown, the parts grow out of the wholes during the process of maturation. Specific reflexes and other modes of behavior develop from the diffuse but integrated movements of the immature organism. Gestaltists may inveigh against analysis, yet it is by careful analysis of educational situations that Thorndike and his followers have been enabled greatly to improve education (as they have undoubtedly done) during the past three decades. It is by the help of analysis that man has progressed upward in his mental life. So the better point of view is to accept the obvious truth that behavior is both by wholes and by parts (molar and molecular). Improvement can be made only when the specific parts are analyzed. How have the records in running, pole-vaulting, hurdles, etc., been achieved? By careful analysis of the movements made in each activity and by special drills on the elements. In the same way the football coach is forever analyzing plays and drilling his squad on selected elements in them. This, indeed, is the way of progress. But if it be maintained that the sum is the mere total of these elements, then there is ample evidence to show that it is untrue.

The reaction-hypothesis, which stresses elements in behavior, has been scornfully termed "the bundle hypothesis" by the Gestaltists, who refuse to recognize analysis as an essential part of mental life. Without analysis, as Brunswick sagely observes, we get "a mental world of form without content." Gestaltists in claiming the uniqueness of wholes are simply substituting large chunks for small ones.

Both organismic behavior and behavior by parts are realities. Therefore, instead of quarreling about them, we should follow the lead of Dashiell [7] and try to synthesize them, or, at least, try to reconcile the conflicting points of view.

Protoplasmic Behavior. — All students of living things arrive ultimately at the conclusion that in protoplasm lies the unsolved riddle of life. We owe the word protoplasm to Purkinje (1840). Later, Huxley called it the physical basis of life.

Protoplasms are highly complex chemical compounds, frequently containing more than 1000 atoms to the molecule, comprising the contents of living cells. Molecules of protoplasm in the form of a gluey paste (colloid, from *colla* = glue), combine to form cells. Protoplasms are thus the bases of cells, as cells are of organisms. Protoplasms vary in composition from species to species, and from cell to cell within the species. There is every reason for believing that the characteristic differences between species result from the hereditary constitution of their protoplasms. From generation to generation protoplasm is continuous, although it may change slowly in the long course of evolution. In this respect, therefore, protoplasm may be regarded as remarkably stable.

Chemical analyses of protoplasms show that they are composed of water, salts, oxygen and carbon dioxide in solution, carbohydrates, lipins and proteins. They maintain their properties only in the living cell, that is, protoplasms maintain their properties only as they "exist in the form of organized, structural units of microscopic dimensions." Each unit cell possesses all the life properties called nutrition, growth, reproduction, motility and irritability. It is this latter property, irritability, that is of importance to the psychologist. Through irritability, all protoplasms respond or react to appropriate stimulation. Thus we get a hierarchy of behavior. Different sorts of protoplasmic behavior become integrated into the behavior of cells; different forms of cellular behavior become integrated into the behavior of multicellu-

[7] J. F. Dashiell, "A Survey and Synthesis of Learning Theories," *Psychol. Bull.*, XXXII, 1935, pp. 261-275.

lar organisms; and the behavior of multicellular organisms becomes integrated into the behavior of the group. In other words, protoplasmic behavior is colloidal; organismic behavior is cellular; and group behavior is organismic, the whole forming a continuous series. Differences in behavior patterns found among organisms rest upon differences in the stable organization of the protoplasmic substratum of cells.

While protoplasms are stable and, under certain conditions, are immortal, nevertheless they may be destroyed relatively easily by means of chemicals. Thus a comparatively slight change in the chemical environment will break down a protoplasm into a mixture of chemical substances. When this occurs the protoplasm may be said to die, for it is, at present, impossible to reverse the process and build up the protoplasms again from these simpler chemical substances.

All protoplasms, whatever their variety, can form a plasma membrane. The plasma membrane plays a different part in behavior from the rest of the protoplasm of the cell. Thus the amoeba, consisting mainly of a granular protoplasm, forms a plasma membrane which resembles a cell wall whenever the protoplasm comes into contact with water. The protoplasm at the surface is more rigid than the gluey mass in the interior of the cell. Although there is a continual movement of protoplasm from surface to interior, and *vice versa,* the plasma membrane remains intact, being formed the instant the interior protoplasm comes in contact with the water. The plasma membrane exhibits the phenomenon of dominant polarity, the surface of the amoeba being physiologically more active than the interior. This gives rise to a physiological gradient (see below) running from the surface to the interior, which is the beginning of those excitation-transmission gradients out of which nervous systems evolve.

Embryonic protoplasm is characterized by intense metabolic activity. The embryo lives intensely, as may be seen from its rapid rate of growth, and from the relative ease with which chemical agencies can destroy it. As the embryonic protoplasm differentiates progressively to form the protoplasm of bone, muscle, nerve and epithelial tissue, it assumes a more rigid and stable organization. The derived tissues are better adapted structurally for the performance of their particular functions. And of the derived tissues, that which constitutes the nervous system dominates the rest.

It will thus be seen that protoplasms lie at the foundation of behavior. When learning takes place, the protoplasms are changed in some way more or less permanent. They also lie at the foundation of learning. Indeed, a physiological theory of learning would state: Learning means change; when an animal learns it is changed in some way. The change is reflected in changes in the protoplasm of the animal. What the changes are we do not know at present, but so far as is known, protoplasm is the only substance in which the changes can be stored or registered.

The Physiological Gradient.—When protoplasm is stimulated, the excitation aroused is transmitted through it, usually in diminishing degree from the point of application to points more remote. Such lines of decreasing intensity of vital reaction to stimulation are known as physiological gradients. A physiological gradient, therefore, represents a quantitative gradation in physiological condition in a definite direction. This suggests that the gradient may be akin to an electrical or to a chemical gradient. There is a considerable body of evidence supporting the hypothesis that each cell of an organism is a tiny electric cell, the whole organism constituting a battery in which the fluids and saps form the connecting elements. There is also evidence to show that the physiological gradient is due to, or closely associated with, differences in the rates of metabolism. Thus the points of highest metabolism (a chemical phenomenon) become the centers of dominance. In plants, these centers are the apical tips and the ends of the rootlets. In animals with nervous systems, the center of dominance is the brain. Thus, associated with the physiological gradient are the correlative phenomena of dominance and subordination of parts, of polarity and symmetry. The parts exhibiting high metabolic rate exert a wider influence upon the surrounding protoplasm and become centers of dominance; those of low metabolic rate become subordinated; the physiological gradient runs from the high to the low.

We saw that in unicellular animals such as the amoeba, the surface is physiologically dominant, the interior subordinate; therefore, the gradient is of the radiate or surface-interior kind. In plants, the growing tip dominates everything and the gradient is of the apico-basal or antero-posterior kind. Should the growing tip be removed, the tip of the nearest lateral branch becomes the center of dominance and the branch gradually assumes a central position. A third type of gradient occurs in bi-laterally symmetrical organisms such as man. While the main physiological gradient runs from the head downward, subsidiary gradients are found which run from median to lateral and from back to front. The important fact to remember as far as behavior is concerned, is that the physiological gradients determine the rates of cell-division, growth, and differentiation of parts. These in turn determine behavior patterns. Hence behavior can be traced to physiological gradients which are due to the fundamental properties of protoplasm.

That physiological gradients actually exist can be proved in many ways.

(1) Respiration. The oxygen consumed and the carbon dioxide given off at different levels of organisms can be measured. These measurements show graded variations in metabolic rates.

(2) Susceptibility to poisons, narcotics, heat, cold and lack of oxygen. In general, the susceptibility to poisons, narcotics, etc., is greatest at the point of highest metabolic activity. If, for example, an earthworm is poisoned with potassium cyanide of appropriate concentration, the tissues at the head end of the body die first. When the head disintegration has involved several segments, disintegration of the tail end begins. The middle segments of the worm are affected last. This shows that the worm exhibits head dominance with a secondary center of dominance in the tail. This fits in with the evidence we get from the regeneration of parts after severance. It is comparatively easy to get the regeneration of a tail on a head part consisting of not less than thirteen segments, but it is very difficult to grow the anterior half on to the posterior half of a severed worm. From a middle section of an earthworm neither head nor tail can be grown; the middle part invariably dies. It also fits the evidence we obtain from the behavior of the worm under various forms of stimulation. The head is invariably the most active part

of the worm, the tail next, and the middle parts least active under stimulation. In the same way, a plant dies from the growing tips of stem and roots inwards; the main stem is the last part to die. The growing tips of stem and roots are the regions of highest polarity.

(3) Differences of electrical potential along the gradients. In general, the heads of animals are electro-negative to lower levels; in some plants at least the growing tip is electro-positive. In a large douglas fir we get a difference potential of six volts.

(4) Oxidation-reduction reactions. If instead of poisoning the worm by potassium cyanide, we subject it to potassium permanganate we find, first, a darkening of head due to the deposition of manganese dioxide from the reduction of the permanganate. The tail darkens next and the middle parts last of all. The rate of reduction after penetration by stains such as methylene blue tells the same story.

(5) Structure and behavior. Axial gradients are early visible in the protoplasmic structure of the developing embryonic areas of eggs and of early embryos. In axiate plants they can be seen in growing stems and roots at all stages of growth. The dominance of certain parts with respect to behavior is shown in all animals. A "pithed" frog exhibits only the most primitive forms of spinal reflexes. A human being who has lost an arm or a leg still behaves fairly normally, but the same cannot be said if he loses his head.

(6) The evidence from the rate of cell division, growth and differentiation of parts confirms the conclusions drawn from all other lines of experiments.

The foregoing analysis indicates that a physiological gradient may be regarded as a primitive form of nervous system since it exhibits all the physiological characteristics of an excitation-transmission gradient, and may be determined by any persistent local stimulus which changes the rate of metabolism. In fact, we may regard the nervous system as an evolved form of physiological gradient. The following statement from Child,[8] who has worked for so many years on the subject, gives his views:

"First, all living protoplasms are to some extent irritable or excitable and capable of transmission. Second, excitation is a dynamic

[8] C. M. Child, *Physiological Foundations of Behavior*, 1924.

change involving increased energy — liberation in the protoplasmic system. Third, it is initiated by the impact from without of some form of energy upon the protoplasm excited and the relation between the exciting factor and the process of excitation is non-specific; in other words, the same excitatory changes may be induced by different forms of external energy. Fourth, transmission results from the fact that an excited region is capable of inducing in some way excitation in adjoining regions within a certain distance. Fifth, in non-nervous transmission and in nervous transmission under certain conditions a decrement in intensity or energy, in short, of physiological effectiveness, of the excitation very generally, if not always occurs. In other words, the excitatory change loses its effectiveness in the course of its progress, so that finally at a greater or less distance from the point of origin, it is no longer effective in exciting further points and so transmission ceases. And finally, no specialized structure of any kind beyond that of a living protoplasm with limiting surface is necessary for the occurrence of excitation and transmission." (pp. 173-174)

As a matter of fact, the physiological gradient determines the position, structure, and function of the nervous system, for it is out of the physiological gradient that the nervous system evolves. In axiate animals the point of highest metabolism is generally the head. This becomes the center of the nervous system and of the chief sense organs. Nerve tissue, with its higher rate of metabolism, dominates all other tissues with lower rates, such as connective, epithelial and muscular tissues. If, however, a gland secretes an endocrine secretion which can effect reactions, it may secure a temporary ascendancy over the nervous system. With respect to the apparatus of transmission and response, the sense organs are the highest points of the excitation-transmission gradients and dominate the muscles which are immediately activated by them. Within the nervous system itself it is difficult to demonstrate any decrement in transmission (hence the all-or-none law), but it is impossible to conceive of a radius of nerve action that is infinitely great.

All gradients are diminished with advancing age, and as vitality runs low. It is the opposite of the condition found in the embryo, where vitality and growth are greatest. When the gradient finally disappears, death ensues; but, generally speaking, the "tailing off" in the gradient is a very gradual process.

Variable and Non-Variable Behavior. — Strictly speaking, all human behavior is variable. Even the pupillary reflex can be conditioned. But in the behavior reactions of organisms in general, a rough distinction can be made between the variable and non-variable forms. The avoiding reaction of the paramecium may be taken as an example of the non-variable kind. If a paramecium swimming in forward spirals by the lashing of its cilia encounters an obstacle, the following behavior may be observed: First, the paramecium reverses its direction by spiraling backwards. Secondly, it turns through an angle by a side-paddling movement. Thirdly, it forges ahead again on a new course. If it meets with a second obstacle, the series is gone through again and in the same order. This is a form of behavior that is remarkably fixed and definite in character and is sufficiently adaptive for efficient living in such a simple organism. But even this behavior can be modified. If, for example, the paramecium is placed in a length of water in a horizontal capillary tube just wide enough to permit the forward movement, the paramecium will swim to the end of the water by spiraling. The motion will then be reversed for some distance, but finding it impossible to side-paddle, a new movement will be introduced. By a series of rapid contractions, the paramecium will turn a somersault in the narrow tube and then spiral forward in the reverse direction. Thus, a typical series of non-variable reactions may be modified to a slight extent. In the same way, tropic movements of sea animals seeking or avoiding light may be reversed by changes in the concentration of salts in the water.

In all lowly organized animals, the regulative behavior and adjustments are of this simple non-variable kind. They are concerned very directly with keeping the animal alive. In other words, every animal is organized to meet the usual variations found in its normal environment. Should the variations be too great — excessive heat, excessive cold, etc. — these organisms die, because their behavior patterns are too inflexible to meet the new demands. With organisms in the upper level of the biological scale, non-variable behavior, while undoubtedly present, plays a decreasingly important part. A child withdraws its hand from a hot stove, and at the same time becomes conditioned so that hot stoves are avoided in future. A tickling in the nose causes a sneeze, but even this may be modified. In very young children, pressure on the sphincter muscles of the bladder or rectum leads to reflex micturition or defecation. Life in modern society demands that these reflexes become cortically controlled and this is usually accomplished in the period of a few months or years.

What seems to be true is this: The hereditary and maturational behavior patterns in man are mostly of the nonvariable kind. These are sufficient to keep him alive in the lowest terms of life. But upon these basic behavior patterns are built others that are preponderantly intelligent and variable. Man's learning capacity is so great that the nonvariable behavior becomes swamped with the variable. Nevertheless, it should not be overlooked that even man needs to keep himself alive. So nature provides him with a series of unlearned, basically non-variable reactions, which, especially during infancy, are conducive to this end.

The Mechanisms of Behavior.— The human body is an organic machine whose workings are extraordinarily complex. Although the psychologist is supposed to be able to get along without much knowledge of its structure or of the way the machine works, nevertheless, the point of view is a mistaken one. The more we know of the body, the sounder is our knowledge of its behavior. Hence the student of psychology should be urged to study both the anatomy and the physiology of the human body as deeply as time permits. However, in a textbook of psychology such as this, nothing more than a general outline need be attempted.

It is obvious to the layman that in some mysterious way his behavior is dependent upon the integrity of three principal parts of the body. He moves various parts of his body and secretes from many glands. He sees, hears, smells, feels and tastes, and his sensations are dependent upon the integrity and proper functioning of his sense organs. The impairment of eyes and ears leads obviously to loss of sight and hearing. Impairment of the sense of taste or smell, while handicapping him to some extent, is not nearly so distressing as the loss of sight or hearing. He is also generally aware that his brain and his nerves have something to do with his behavior. He may have suffered or seen people who suffer from some form of paralysis or loss of sensation. In such cases he learns, generally correctly, that there is something wrong with the nerves or the brain.

Technically, these three parts of the organic machine, looked at as a behaving organism, are known as *effectors, receptors* and *connectors.*

Effectors. — The *effectors* are the organs of response. In man, the chief sorts of effectors are muscles and glands; in certain animals, electric organs, luminescent organs and so forth, serve as effectors also. They work only when they receive excitations from the nervous system, and, as we have seen, the excitation can usually be traced to some external stimulation of a sense organ. Destroy the connection with the nervous system, and effectors become paralyzed and useless. Further analysis shows that both muscles and glands may be divided into classes and the classification shown in Table XXXVIII is one that can usefully be made:

TABLE XXXVIII. THE EFFECTORS OF THE BODY

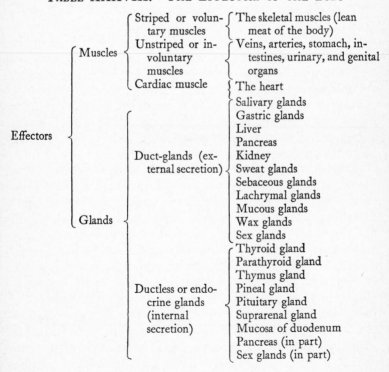

		Striped or voluntary muscles	The skeletal muscles (lean meat of the body)
	Muscles	Unstriped or involuntary muscles	Veins, arteries, stomach, intestines, urinary, and genital organs
		Cardiac muscle	The heart
Effectors		Duct-glands (external secretion)	Salivary glands / Gastric glands / Liver / Pancreas / Kidney / Sweat glands / Sebaceous glands / Lachrymal glands / Mucous glands / Wax glands / Sex glands
	Glands	Ductless or endocrine glands (internal secretion)	Thyroid gland / Parathyroid gland / Thymus gland / Pineal gland / Pituitary gland / Suprarenal gland / Mucosa of duodenum / Pancreas (in part) / Sex glands (in part)

Considerations of space preclude extended mention of each of the sections represented in the preceding classification. However, following our rule of enlarging upon topics on which recent and important research has been done, which has also an important bearing on problems of behavior, we shall devote a few paragraphs to some of the more important of the endocrine glands.

The Endocrine Glands. — The endocrine or ductless glands secrete specific chemical substances called endocrine compounds which diffuse into the circulating fluids of the body, especially into the blood, and produce physiological effects upon other organs. These endocrine compounds are potent, drug-like chemicals of which only two — *thyroxin* and *adrenalin* — have been synthesized in the laboratory. Four others have been prepared in a crystalline state, but as some of the endocrine compounds appear to be very complex proteins, the synthesis of them will be long deferred.

(1) *The Thyroid Gland,* purplish in color, is situated on each side of the larynx and windpipe. It consists of two wing-like lateral lobes which are connected by an isthmus. If the thyroid gland is defective at birth, or becomes atrophied later in life, the following important effects upon development and behavior can be discerned.

(*a*) In youth, *cretinism* appears. The growth of the body as a whole, and especially of the skeleton, is arrested; the development of the generative organs is delayed; the skin remains dry and the hair thin; the pituitary enlarges and the involution of the thymus gland is delayed; the body temperature tends to be subnormal; the abdomen is swollen; the fontanelles of the cranium remain open; and the cells of the cerebral cortex remain undeveloped, causing feeble-mindedness of the imbecilic or idiotic type. A child born with a defective thyroid gland becomes a cretin — a pot-bellied dwarf of low intelligence who can be taught to do only the simplest of things.

(*b*) In adults, *myxedema* appears. Myxedema is characterized by a thickening and drying of the skin, falling out of the hair, low body temperatures, lethargy, diminished metabolism, diminution of sex function, and increased tolerance for sugar. The myxedemic person, while retaining his stature, becomes very lethargic, falling asleep without apparent cause.

Fortunately, however, relief from both these conditions can be secured by the administration of thyroid substance. As the substance is chemically stable it can be administered through the mouth. Formerly, extract of sheep's thyroid was used but now the synthetic product replaces it. Under treatment, the cretin begins to grow and becomes much brighter, although he seldom becomes as intelligent as nature intended him to be. Similarly, the myxedemic person becomes almost normal again and his expectancy of life almost average. Thyroxin, unfortunately, is not a cure; it must be given throughout life. Thyroid substance controls the oxidation and heat production of the body; it acts upon the body very much in the same way as controlling the dampers affects the rate of combustion in the furnace. Thyroid substance fed to tadpoles hastens metamorphosis. If tadpoles are deprived of their glands they never develop into frogs.

Though three substances, iodothyroglobulin, diiodotyrosine and thyroxin can be isolated from thyroid secretion, physiologists agree that thyroxin is the active one. The formula of thyroxin, as determined by Harington and Barger, both by analysis and synthesis (1926–28), is

$$\text{OH-C} \underset{\underset{\text{I}}{\text{C}}\quad\underset{\text{H}}{\text{C}}}{\overset{\overset{\text{I}}{\text{C}}\quad\overset{\text{H}}{\text{C}}}{\bigcirc}} \text{C-O-C} \underset{\underset{\text{I}}{\text{C}}\quad\underset{\text{H}}{\text{C}}}{\overset{\overset{\text{I}}{\text{C}}\quad\overset{\text{H}}{\text{C}}}{\bigcirc}} \text{C-CH}_2\text{- CH (NH}_2)\text{-COOH}$$

or $C_{15}H_{11}O_4NI_4$. It is therefore one of the few bodily compounds into whose composition iodine enters. In fact, thyroxin consists of 65.3 per cent of iodine by weight. It should be noted that thyroxin, either synthesized or prepared from thyroid tissue, is optically inactive. The levo-form possesses far greater physiological activity than the dextro.

Thus iodine is important in human life. Some regions of the earth contain no iodine in the rocks or soil and therefore none in the plants grown in those regions. They are known as goiter belts, since enlargement of the thyroid gland (goiter) is very prevalent among the inhabitants, especially the women, living in the area. Goiter is difficult to cure but easy to prevent. All that needs to be done is to supply the people and animals with the iodine their bodies lack. For animals, a few drops of tincture of iodine is used; for human beings the simplest way is to supply them with iodized salt — common salt to which one part of sodium or potassium iodide has been added to every 200,000 parts of common salt. In Canada, one part of KI to 10,000 parts of NaCl is used or twenty times more than is necessary. As women suffer from goiter twelve times as frequently as men, it is especially important to supply growing girls between ten and sixteen years of age with iodine.

Thyroid secretion is under the control of one of the principles secreted by the anterior lobe of the pituitary. In the thyroid gland, we have a beautiful illustration of the close connection between behavior and an endocrine secretion.

(2) *The Adrenal* or *Suprarenal Glands* are two small, yellowish, flat, somewhat triangular capsules which surmount each kidney like a cocked hat. Their dimensions in man are about $1\frac{1}{2}$ x 1 x $\frac{1}{4}$ inches. In mammals, and only in mammals, each consists of two separate types of tissue — the *cortex* and the *medulla*; in fishes the cortex and medulla are separated. The cortex is essential to life, but the medulla is not. Complete extirpation of both glands is fatal within a few days, but removal of the medulla alone does not particularly discommode the animal.

The active principle of the cortex is *cortin*. There is certainly some connection, either direct or indirect via the pituitary, between cortin and the sex glands. The hyper-function of the cortex leads to precocious puberty in children, and to the growth of beards and deepening of the voice in adult women. Hypo-function of the cortex is associated with the lowering of blood pressure and emaciation, and sometimes with increased pigmentation of the skin.

The active principle of the medulla is known as *adrenalin* or *epinephrin*. Its formula is $C_9H_{13}NO_3$ and its structure, determined conclusively by the synthesis of the substance by Stolz and Dakin, is

$$OH-C \underset{\underset{H}{C}}{\overset{\overset{H}{C}}{\diagdown}} \overset{\overset{H}{C}}{\underset{\underset{H}{C}}{\diagup}} C-CH.OH-CH_2-NH.CH_3$$

As with thyroxin, the synthetic adrenalin is racemic, but the levo-form is the more active in the physiological sense.

Professor Cannon[9] and his co-workers have made a number of studies on the action of adrenalin. They have shown that under strong bodily emotions, the amount of adrenalin in the blood is increased. These secretions are stimulated by discharges through the sympathetic division of the autonomic system and its connections with the adrenal glands. This system in turn, as Bard has shown, is governed by a center in the subthalamus, a part of the diencephalon, an ancient part of the brain.

Using a specially prepared segment of the intestines removed from a rabbit, Cannon showed that blood from a quiet animal had no effect on the contractions of the muscle, but blood drawn from an animal in fear and rage always showed an inhibiting action. So delicate was the reaction that one part of adrenalin in 200,000,000 parts of the solvent produced an effect. He also showed the inhibitory effect of adrenalin on the visceral movements of a living cat. If a cat is fed and the meal made visible by X-rays through an admixture of bismuth, the rhythmical movements of the stomach during the act of digestion can be seen. If now the cat is angered and frightened by the introduction of a barking dog into the room, the digestive processes are inhibited and are not resumed for a considerable time (half an hour to an hour), even though the dog is immediately removed. Similar effects are produced by the injection of adrenalin. Cannon thus provided the scientific basis for the well-known detrimental effects of fear and anger on the process of digestion;

[9] W. B. Cannon, *Bodily Changes in Pain, Hunger, Fear and Rage*, 2nd Ed., 1929.

and for our custom of aiding digestion by means of pleasant music and lively conversation.

Out of these researches, Cannon formulated his emergency theory of emotions. Adrenal activity has enabled man to survive in a hostile environment and has played an important part in evolution. The adrenal gland is, *par excellence*, the gland of the fighting man and the arrant coward. While Cannon's first statement of the action of adrenalin was overly simplified, the following facts regarding the action of adrenalin seem to be fairly well established: (*a*) Adrenalin is able to split up glycogen stored in the liver and set it free in the blood in the form of blood glucose. This blood sugar forms an easily available source of food and energy for striped muscles (muscle glycogen). (*b*) Muscular fatigue is reduced; in other words, the skeletal muscles can work more vigorously and for a longer time. (*c*) The action of the visceral muscles is inhibited; contraction of the blood vessels supplying these muscles renders more blood available for the voluntary muscles. (*d*) The coagulability of the blood increases, and the smaller blood vessels of the skin become constricted. (*e*) Both heart and lungs are stimulated to a more vigorous action. (*f*) The action of the sweat glands is increased, so much so, that the individual often breaks out into a cold sweat. In brief, Cannon maintains, the excess adrenalin during the emotions of fear or rage prepares a man either to fight or run away.

(3) *The Pituitary Body* is a small organ about the size of a pea attached to the brain by a hollow stalk, and lodging in a depression of the flooring of the cranial cavity known as the Turk's saddle (*sella turcica*). It is the best protected part of the whole body. This is as it should be, for evidence accumulates that if any gland should be termed the master gland of the body, the pituitary is the one. It certainly controls the activity of a large number of other glands. It is divided into an anterior and a posterior part and thus, like the adrenal, is a double gland.

The extract of the posterior part of the pituitary has been called *pituitrin*. However, there is almost conclusive evidence that the posterior pituitary secretes at least two endocrine principles. Three important effects are found when extracts of the posterior lobe are injected into the body:

(1) the blood pressure is raised (pressure activity); (2) the uterus and other smooth muscles contract (oxytocic activity); and (3) the secretion of urine is affected (renal activity). The fat metabolism of the body is to some extent controlled by the posterior pituitary, excessive obesity being associated with a hypo-functioning of the gland.

The anterior part is associated with Simmonds' infantilism in the form of pituitary dwarfism, and premature senility (hypo-function); and also with gigantism (a better word would be giantism to correspond with dwarfism), acromegaly, amenorrhoea and disturbances of vision (hyper-function). Many giants, when post-mortemed, are found to have abnormally large pituitary glands. If normal growth be completed before an excess of anterior secretion is produced, then only those projecting parts, such as the nose (cf. Punch), hands, and feet are affected. This condition is known as *acromegaly*.

There is little doubt that the pituitary is the most important gland of the body. It controls other glands — kidneys, sex, and mammary glands. Its effect on the smooth muscles of the body, on physical growth and mental development, on blood pressure and bodily temperature, attest to its importance. If the endocrine glands form an interlocking directorate controlling the various functions of the body, then the pituitary is undoubtedly president of the board of directors.

(4) *The Sex Glands* function both as duct and ductless glands. Many related chemical substances have been isolated from the sex glands and placental tissue. The most important of these are (1) *theelin* ($C_{18}H_{22}O_2$), the so-called female sex hormone; (2) *theelol* ($C_{18}H_{24}O_3$); and (3) the *testicular principle* ($C_{19}H_{30}O_2$). Undoubtedly, the secondary sex characters of males and females are associated with the functioning of the sex glands. In the male, we get the growth of a beard and the deepening of the voice. In the female, we get the development of mammary glands, the broadening of the hips and the deposition of fat beneath the skin, which gives rise to the characteristic roundness of the feminine figure. The work of Steinach (ligation of the *vas deferens*) and of Voronoff (testicular implants) is regarded with suspicion by competent scientists. Certainly no method of permanently preventing senility has been discovered.

(5) *The Pancreas. Insulin,* which was isolated by Banting and Best in Toronto in 1921, is an endocrine substance derived from the pancreas. It is the secretion of the ductless part of the pancreas (the *Islands of Langerhans*), and controls the metabolism of sugar within the body. Hypofunction of the gland causes *diabetes mellitus.* People suffering from this disease are apt to be rather short-tempered and to suffer from other disturbances of behavior.

(6) *The Parathyroid Glands,* associated with the thyroid gland but functionally distinct from it, secrete a substance which controls the calcium metabolism of the body, and through the calcium in the blood, the rate of discharge of the motor neurons. Ossification of bones and calcification of the teeth are associated with the normal functioning of this gland. Gout, arthritis deformans, and marble bone diseases are associated with a hyper-functioning of the parathyroids.

(7) *The Thymus Gland,* situated at the base of the neck, and developing from one of the four pairs of embryonic gill-slits, is concerned with growth and development. It is functionally active at the age of two years, but is antagonized by the hormones of the sex glands and atrophies after puberty.

(8) *The Pineal Gland,* a pinkish sphere about the size of a cherry, situated on the posterior surface of the brain under the cerebral hemisphere, is a transformed third or cyclopean eye. Such a third eye is still functional in certain lizards; in the British slowworm and the New Zealand sphenodon, for instance. It is concerned with growth and development and, like the thymus, atrophies after puberty.

(9) *The mucous membrane of the duodenum* secretes a hormone, *secretin,* the first hormone to be demonstrated (Bayliss and Starling, 1902). When absorbed and circulated, it stimulates the pancreas to greater activity and possibly causes an increased flow of bile at the same time. It is thus intimately concerned with the digestion of fats, sugars and starches.

Endocrinology is a comparatively new science, but one in which enormous strides are being made. While the claims of Berman [10] that they are the chief if not the only regulators of personality, cannot be accepted uncritically, there is un-

---

[10] Louis Berman, *The Glands Regulating Personality,* 1928.

doubted evidence that imbalance of endocrines leads to profound disturbances of personality and behavior. For this reason, psychology cannot afford to neglect the endocrine glands.

Receptors.— The *receptors*, as their name implies, are the receiving mechanisms of the body. They are usually known as sense organs, although sense organs, such as the eye, are mostly auxiliary apparatus which insure the proper stimulation of the true receptors — in this case, the rods and cones of the retina. The function of a receptor is to be stimulated by forces or conditions in the environment or in portions of the body outside of the nervous system. Thus the alimentary canal is supplied with receptors for pain. Structurally, the receptors are either the ending of a sensory neuron, as may be the case with the receptors for pain, or specialized epithelial cells in connection with the ending of a sensory neuron. It is just possible that no free nerve ending acts as a receptor. In the case of pain, the receptors may be epithelial cells in the neighborhood of the nerve ending. These specialized epithelial cells have a low threshold for one sort of stimulus — light waves, sound waves, etc. — and a high threshold for all other kinds of stimuli. Thus taste cells are specialized for stimulation by chemicals in solution and cannot be stimulated by light or sound.

The list of sense organs given on page 236 is one that is accepted by most psychologists. A second classification which provides additional information about the sense organs is given on page 237.

In addition to these senses, some scientists, for example Sherrington and Herrick, would list a large number of visceral senses including those of hunger, thirst, nausea, suffocation, flushing and heart panics, sexual sensations, distension of cavities, visceral pain, and abdominal sensations associated with strong emotions.[11] It is very probable that some of these senses are compounded of simpler ones. In general, it is safer not to admit the existence of a sense unless its sense organ has been discovered.

So far as the maintenance of life is concerned, sense organs exhibit two functions — the protective and the discrimina-

[11] See C. Judson Herrick, *Neurological Foundations of Animal Behavior*, 1924, pp. 22-24.

Sense	Sense organs	Stimulus
Sight (visual sense)	Eye (retina)	Ether waves (400,000 billion to 800,000 billion vibrations per second).
Hearing (auditory sense)	Ear (cochlea)	Sound waves (12-16 to 25,000-30,000 vibrations per second)
Taste (gustatory sense)	Tongue (taste buds)	Sapid fluids (chemical energy in liquid form)
Smell (olfactory sense)	Nose (olfactory cells)	Soluble gaseous particles (chemical energy in gaseous form)
Pressure (pressure sense)	Skin (Pacinian, Meissner, and Krause corpuscles)	Contact with objects (mechanical energy)
Temperature (temperature sense)	Skin (end organs not definitely known)	Ether waves (radiant heat) (3000 billion to 800,000 billion vibrations per second). Also cold objects and warm objects.
Pain (pain sense)	Skin (free branched nerve)	Cutting, burning, pricking, intense chemical (acids) or electrical stimulation
Movement or strain (kinaesthetic or muscle sense)	Muscles, Tendons, and Joints (end brushes in muscle and tendon spindles)	Mechanical energy from change in position of muscle, tendon or joint
Posture and Balance (equilibration sense)	Ear (semi-circular canals)	Mechanical energy from change of position of head

tive. The protective function is the more ancient, and to this has been added the discriminative. Even very lowly animals exhibit a crude awareness, generally through the sense organs of the skin, and this sufficiently protects them against normal changes in their environment. Discrimination by means of tactile examination is quite beyond them. Added to this, we find simple organs of equilibration which record the position of the animal in space. This organ of equilibration is also affected by sound waves in water, hence the later division into sense organs for sound and equilibration. Evolution of the higher senses is closely associated with what has been termed the "arboreal apprenticeship." Sight and "touch" to the animal in the trees are more important than smell. Vision

Physical Phenomena	Range	Greatest Sensitivity	Organs Stimulated	Most Sensitive Region
Ether Vibrations	760 mu to 390 mu	Rods 511 mu Cones 554 mu	Eye (Vision)	Fovea Centralis
Material Media	0~ to 1550~	below 100	Skin (Pressure)	Eyelid, lips, finger tips
Sound waves in air	20~ to 20,000~	3000	Ear (audition)	
Transfer of Heat	0° to 45° C	28° C	Skin (Temperature)	
Energy (Rate of temperature change)	Below 0° and above 45°		Skin (Pain)	Elbow, knee and jugular region
			Tongue (Taste)	tip—sweet back—bitter edge—salt
Chemicals	Vary with character of molecules, molecular weight, solubility and volatility		Nose (Smell)	
Gravity, and Centrifugal Force			Semi-circular canals (Equilibration)	

is necessary to skilled movement; and motor control and sight develop hand in hand. Along with this evolution of sensory apparatus is the concomitant evolution of the brain. As Stopford [12] says, "the essential thing in the transformation of the simian into the human brain, is the greater expansion of the cerebral cortex in the prefrontal, parietal and temporal regions. These expansions have an important influence upon the further development of skilled movements and manual dexterity, and greater and more effective visual, tactile, and auditory powers. The sensory centers are concerned with very high degrees of visual, tactile, and auditory perception and appreciation; but considerable growth of the so-called association areas makes conceptual inference a possibility, and enables man to understand and interpret the true meaning of his sensory experiences." (pp. 3-4)

In 1908, Rivers and Head [13] startled the psychological world by announcing that cutaneous sensations were not as

[12] John S. B. Stopford, Sensation and the Sensory Pathway, 1930.
[13] W. H. R. Rivers and H. Head. "A Human Experiment in Nerve Division," Brain, 1908, XXXI, pp. 323-450.

simple as was formerly supposed. Severing the radial nerve of Dr. Head (operation performed by Sherren) at its origin from the musculo-spiral and the musculo-cutaneous just proximal to its division into the two branches for the supply of the anterior and posterior aspects of the pre-axial half of the forearm, Rivers was able to test the sensory loss and chart its recovery. From their experiment they concluded that the sensory mechanism in peripheral nerves could be divided into three systems, namely:

(1) *protopathic sensibility*. This is the primitive sensitivity which is of vital importance to the life of the organism. This system conveys sensations of a diffuse, low, imperfectly localized kind such as extremes of heat and cold (above 37° C and below 26° C) and pain.

(2) *epicritic sensibility*. This is a more recently evolved sensitivity and is concerned with accurate cutaneous localization and with the discrimination of the finer grades of temperature called cool and warm. The system is probably instrumental in enabling us to recognize the size and shape of objects. Epicritic sensibility is regained after nerve severance much more slowly than protopathic. The *glans penis* possesses only protopathic sensibility, and represents an earlier stage of evolution of sensation.

(3) *deep sensibility*. This system is "capable of answering to pressure and to the movements of parts, and even capable of producing pain under the influence of excessive pressure, or when a joint is injured." "Deep sensibility conveys the power of appreciating the locality of the part pressed upon."

Since the above classical investigation was made, many other workers — Stopford, Trotter, Davies, Boring and Schafer — have also sectioned cutaneous nerves and studied the effects during regeneration. In general, the findings of Head and Rivers have been confirmed, but Stopford has shown that deep sensibility also shows protopathic and epicritic forms. His division of sensation is as follows (p. 29):

I. Cutaneous Sensibility
> (a) *Early recovery (1st stage)*. — Appreciation of the extremes of temperature: Recognition of cutaneous painful stimuli.

(b) *Later and less complete recovery (2nd stage).* — Appreciation of lightest form of touch : Localization of lightest form of touch : Discrimination of the finer differences of temperature : Recognition of two compass points, simultaneously applied, as two.

II. Deep Sensibility

(a) *Early recovery (1st stage).* — Appreciation of the contact of pressure : Recognition of pain from excessive pressure.

(b) *Late and less complete recovery (2nd stage).* — Recognition of position and passive movement of a joint : Localization of a pressure stimulus.

By a brilliant analysis of his own experimental work and of that of other workers, in which he considered the peripheral part of the sensory pathway, the pathway in the nerve trunks and in the spinal cord, the pathways from the spinal cord to the sensory centers, and the sensory cortex and optic thalamus, Stopford was able to show fairly conclusively that the protopathic system was associated with the more primitive thalamus, while the epicritic depended upon later cortical evolution. There is, therefore, for sensation an earlier thalamic system and a later cortical system. Thus (pp. 117-118):

I. Thalamic (Protective and Affective)

Recognition of (a) pain (whether induced by prick or excessive pressure).
Recognition of (b) extremes of temperature.
Recognition of (c) tactile pressure.

II. Cortical (Discriminative)

Power of (a) localization.
Power of (b) discrimination.
Power of (c) recognizing position and passive movement.
Recognition of fine differences of temperature.
Appreciation of lightest form of touch.

One more general aspect of receptors should be noted. The chief sense organs are in the head and surround the mouth. The mouth is important from the standpoint of survival inasmuch as all food must enter the body through this opening. Sight and sound enable the organism to recognize food at a distance. When the food is approached, smell dictates whether or not it should be placed in the mouth. Before it is finally swallowed, taste comes into play to determine its edibility. Unless this aspect of the main sense organs of the body is appreciated, much that is psychologically important regarding the sense organs will be missed. For details of the structure, function, and psychology of the various sense organs, the reader is referred to texts in general psychology.

Connectors.— The *connectors* are the connecting mechanisms of the body and comprise the whole of the nervous system. Nerve cells are distinguished from all other cells of the body by their higher *excitability* and by their greater powers of *conduction*. Structurally, they lie between receptors and effectors; functionally, they expedite and coordinate the responses of organisms.

In the evolution of organisms, the increase in the mass of nerve tissue, both relatively and absolutely, should be noted. In animals with skulls (craniata), the greatest mass of nerve tissue is concentrated in the cranium. The nervous system of man exhibits the following subdivisions:

I. *The Central Nervous System*

A. The Brain

Cerebrum

R. Hemisphere
- Frontal Lobe
- Parietal Lobe
- Occipital Lobe
- Temporal Lobe
- Limbic Lobe

All divided into gyri by fissures or sulci

L. Hemisphere (as above)

Cerebellum
- Two Lateral Lobes (cerebellar hemispheres)
- One Central Lobe (Vermis)

Mid-Brain
Pons
Medulla Oblongata

B. The Spinal Cord

II. *The Peripheral Nervous System*

A. Cerebrospinal Nerves
- 12 Cranial Nerves
- 31 Spinal Nerves

B. The Autonomic Nervous System
- Two Gangliated cords or trunks
- Plexuses
- Nerves

Structurally, the nervous system is made up of nerve cells or *neurons*. It is estimated that there are ten billions of them in a normal person. According to function, neurons may be classified as *sensory, motor,* and *connecting* neurons. Sensory neurons, as their name implies, are connected with sense organs at the periphery, and conduct impulses towards the central nervous system. Motor neurons are connected with muscles and glands and always conduct away from the central nervous system. Connecting neurons connect one part of the nervous system with another and bridge the gaps between sensory and motor neurons. Unlike both sensory

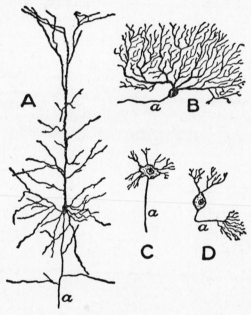

Fig. 26. Typical Forms of Neurons. A is a Pyramidal Cell from the Cortex. B is a Neuron from the Cerebellum. C is a Motor Neuron from the Spinal Cord. D is a Connecting Neuron. The Axon in each case is marked "a."

and motor neurons, connecting neurons lie wholly within the central nervous system. In Figs. 26, 27 and 28 we see representations of (*a*) typical forms of neurons; (*b*) the conduction path from a sense organ to a muscle; and (*c*) a simple reflex arc of three neurons. The picture thus given is so simplified that it gives a false impression, nevertheless it is fairly true regarding the functional use and connections of the three kinds of neurons.

The typical neuron, which is a true genetic unit comprising the cell with all its processes, has three parts — a central *cell-body* which contains the nucleus, and two kinds of fiber-like processes which grow out from the cell-body during development (see Fig. 26). The first of these processes is a relatively smooth, long, relatively unbranched process called

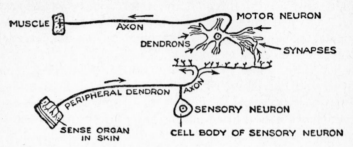

Fig. 27. Path of Conduction from a Sense Organ to a Muscle. Arrows show the direction of conduction. (After Ranson.)

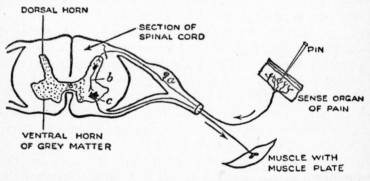

Fig. 28. Simple Reflex Arc of three Neurons — sensory neuron (a), connecting neuron (b), motor neuron (c). The Stimulus from the prick of the pin passes through the Spinal Cord and causes the Muscle to react.

the *axon*. The axon conducts impulses away from the cell-body. The second kind of process is known as a *dendron* or *dendrite*. It is much more branched than the axon, resembling the branching of the twigs of a tree. The dendron is a receiving apparatus and conducts impulses towards the cell body (see Fig. 27). Generally speaking, a neuron has many dendrons; twenty would be a normal number, though neurons with more than a hundred dendrons have been seen.

Axons, though relatively unbranched, are frequently found

connected with other axons by means of fine fibers known as *collaterals*. Only recently has the importance of collaterals been realized. They undoubtedly help to spread the various nerve impulses and to make the action more organismic in nature than the reflex-arc concept would lead us to suppose. In the brain, the ramifications are exceedingly complex. In the cortical region, the connections between pyramidal cells and the Golgi cells, type II, are probably instrumental in helping to cause the phenomenon discovered by Lashley and called by him *mass action*. The Golgi cells are believed to come into synaptic association with incoming fibers and, therefore, to act as receptors and distributors of afferent impressions to the cortex. There is thus a sort of circular action to the nervous discharges of the cortex and this unifies brain action in a way that the older synaptic theory could not conceive possible. This, indeed, may be the explanation of "brain waves" on which important research is now being done. Much work still remains to be done, but it is unwise to introduce unknown X's into the explanation of the complicated process of brain action. The newer researches of Ranson, Hinsey and others in connection with cortical processes are helping to clear up many of the difficulties previously encountered in arriving at a satisfactory explanation.

In all animals with spinal cords, the transmission of a nerve impulse from a receptor to an effector requires at least two neurons, the impulse passing from one to the other along a neuron chain. The place where two neurons come into functional relationships is called a *synapse*. Between the neurons, of course, there is a membranous barrier, which imposes some obstacle to the passage of a nervous impulse. However, it is supposed that the membranes are permeable to ions dissociated during the excitation-conduction process. As the ions can pass in one direction only, the nervous discharge can cross a synapse in one direction only, and hence the synapse acts as a one-way valve, although in the neurons themselves the impulse can freely travel in either direction. The synapse, then, insures that the discharge shall pass always in the direction of receptor towards the effector and never in the reverse way.

The Autonomic Nervous System. — This part of the

nervous system consists of two gangliated cords paralleling the spinal cord from the level of the second cervical vertebra to the coccyx. It is connected on the one side with the spinal cord and brain, and on the other with the glands and unstriped muscles of the body. Although under some form of indirect cortical control, it is relatively independent and autonomous in its action; it is certainly not under the direct control of the cortex (or the will). Like Gaul, it is divided into three parts — the cranial division, the thoracico-lumbar division (sympathetic), and the sacral division. These three divisions are shown in Fig. 29.

The cranial and sacral divisions constitute the *parasympathetic*, which works antagonistically to the *sympathetic*. By this is meant, that which the sympathetic excites, the parasympathetic inhibits and *vice versa*. The parasympathetic during normal functioning is associated with feelings of wellbeing (euphoria), while the sympathetic has close relationship with the emotions of anger and fear, and also with pain and hunger. These relationships are shown in the following summary:

(*a*) *Cranial* (euphoria)

$+$ $-$
    1. Contraction of pupils.
    2. Salivation.
    3. Inhibition of heart.
    4. Increased activity of alimentary canal.

(*b*) *Thoracico-lumbar* (sympathetic, associated with strong emotions; dysphoria)

    1. Dilatation of pupils.
    2. Inhibition of salivation.
    3. Acceleration of heart.
    4. Acceleration of lungs.
    5. Secretion of sweat.
$-$ $+$
    6. Inhibition of alimentary tone.
    7. Inhibition of digestive secretions.
    8. Removal of blood from visceral to striped muscles.
    9. Pilomotor reflex.
   10. Secretion of adrenalin.

(*c*) *Sacral* (euphoria)

$+$ $-$
    1. Excretion.
    2. Micturition.
    3. Reproductive activities (sex glands).

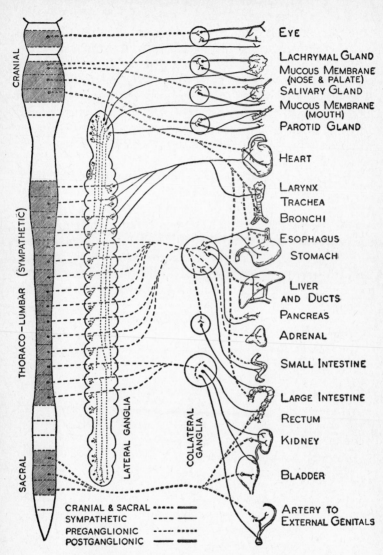

Fig. 29. General Arrangement of the Autonomic Nervous System. The brain and spinal cord are represented at left. The nerves of the somatic system are not shown. (After Philip Bard.)

By referring to Fig. 29, it will be observed that activation of the adrenal medulla is exclusively a function of the sympathetic division, nerve fibers from other divisions not being connected with the gland. In fact, the medulla of the adrenal gland is an integral part of the sympathetic system. Adrenalin produces exactly the same effects on tissues under sympathetic control as an impulse from the sympathetic itself. Sweat glands constitute the only known exception, for while they are innervated by the sympathetic, they do not respond to adrenal stimulation.

Further study of Fig. 29 shows that the sympathetic through its plexuses (solar and others), which are distantly placed from the autonomic cords, has a greater number of connections than the parasympathetic and, therefore, exhibits a greater possibility of widespread or diffuse discharges. The sympathetic works more as a whole than the parasympathetic, and since it is connected with the stronger emotions, these emotions, when aroused, seem to diffuse and possess the whole of the body. The restricted distribution of the parasympathetic connections enables the central nervous system to exert effects upon single organs without disturbing other organs at the same time. This is, perhaps, just as well, for it would be exceedingly uncomfortable to have the emptying movements of the sacral division inevitably stimulated every time the pupils were contracted or the heart inhibited.

The Nervous Impulse. — When an impulse travels along a nerve fiber, which, of course, is a part of a neuron, thermal, chemical and electrical changes occur. The thermal and chemical changes are difficult to record. For example, when a single impulse travels along a medullated nerve there is an immediate rise in temperature of the order of 10^{-7}, one ten-millionth of a degree centigrade. The energy liberation represents about 4 ergs per gram of nerve. The electrical changes are easily demonstrated; in fact, the *action current* or *electric response* is the simplest and most sensitive method known for detecting the passage of an impulse. However, nerve fibers do not conduct with the speed of light as do electric wires. Owing to the fact that nervous transmission is oscillatory in character and involves both building up and discharge, the rate of propagation in human nerve fibers at normal temperatures is around 100 meters per second.

If a sensory or a motor nerve fiber be stimulated by means of a brief electric current, a disturbance is set up which follows the all-or-none law. This means that the discharge does not take place at all unless the stimulus is adequate, but stimulation beyond the minimum threshold does not add to the response. The explanation of this phenomenon is still hypothetical. One theory of conduction maintains that the membrane surrounding the nerve becomes permeable and allows the positive ions on the outside to unite with the negative ions on the inside of the membrane. This sets up a local action current which travels along the nerve fiber. Once the fiber has been excited, it cannot be excited again immediately afterward. This period of non-excitability is called the *absolute refractory period*. It is undoubtedly an electro-chemical phenomenon. In man, this refractory period is of the order of one-thousandth of a second. The return to a condition of excitability and conduction is a gradual affair, usually several times the length of the absolute refractory period. But this fact determines that the nerve fiber shall transmit its excitation in a series of impulses and these in man cannot exceed the rate of a thousand or so per second. Yet we undoubtedly hear sounds of an oscillatory rate of 20,000 cycles per second, and perceive light waves of the order of 10^{15}, both of which are beyond the frequency of the nerve fiber. It is very probable that the nerve responds at some (highest) submultiple of the frequency providing it is not too high, but beyond this limit it fails to respond at all. Auditory vibrations of very high frequency cannot be heard at all.

These two features — the fact that the intensity of the impulse cannot be changed by altering the intensity of the stimulus (all-or-none law) and that the nervous discharge is not continuous as a stream of water, but a series of oscillatory impulses of moderate frequency — are the fundamental facts of nerve conduction.

The action current in a nerve fiber is illustrated in Fig. 30, which shows why it is di-phasic in character.

What is well known to us by introspection is that some sensory stimulations produce profounder or more intense sensations than others. Sounds may be faint or loud, weights may be light or heavy and so forth. The relation existing between stimulus and sensation has been of interest to psychologists since the time of Weber and Fechner. But what we are concerned with here is the problem of how can these things be if the all-or-none law is followed. Why are not all sensations of equal intensity? The factors to bear in mind are the number of fibers which are affected by end organs; the frequency of the waves evoked in each of these fibers; and the state of the nervous system as affected by other simultaneous stimulations, or other factors. Three theories

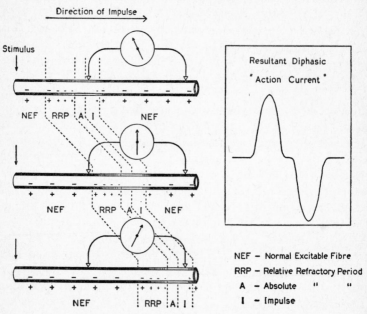

Fig. 30. Production of a di-phasic "Action Current" as the Impulse travels down a Nerve Fiber. (After Adrian.)

have been propounded to account for the intensity of the sensation, which must, of course, be a correlate of the action of nerve fiber. These are the *Multiple Fiber Theory*, the *Frequency Theory*, and the *Volley Theory* respectively.

(1) The *multiple fiber theory* supposes that the stronger the stimulus the greater the irradiation of its effect. In regard to sensory neurons, for example, more receptors are stimulated by strong than by weak stimuli, more neurons are activated, and the intensity of the resultant sensation is directly proportional to the number of fibers excited. A sound

stimulus of great amplitude, according to this theory, would cause a greater displacement of fluid within the cochlea, penetrate farther into the cochlea, and excite a greater number of hair cells, which, in turn, would excite a greater number of auditory nerve fibers. The greater the number of auditory nerve fibers excited, the louder the sound would appear to be.

(2) The *frequency theory* is based on the demonstrable fact that the stronger the stimulus the greater the frequency of the nerve waves it produces. Adrian[14] showed that with the increase of pressure or pain on one of the toe pads of a cat's hind foot the frequency of the impulses was increased. Under constant stimulation the discharge declines in frequency, and this may be regarded as an adaptation of the sense organ rather than a fatiguing of the nerve fiber. The intensity of a sensation, according to this theory, is a function of the frequency of the impulses in the sensory nerve fibers. The sensation due to a stimulus is measured by (or at least is paralleled by) the frequency of the nerve waves which it produces. As far as is known at present, the only way in which the message (sensation) can be made to vary at all is by the variation in the total number of the impulses and in the frequency with which they recur.

(3) The *volley theory* combines in one hypothesis the multiple fiber and the frequency theories. It states that the intensity of a sensation is dependent on both the number of fibers stimulated and on the rate of discharge of each one. The theory is the work of Wever and Bray and was developed to explain the results they obtained from experiments on transmission in the auditory nerve of a cat. If the auditory receptors vary in sensitivity, then some sensory fibers would be discharged more rapidly than others. Combining these differential discharges (or volleys) for different fibers, then summation effects are produced. As Boring[15] says: "The more frequent the discharges, the greater the number of coincidences, and the larger the sums. Hence the amplitude of the current of action would vary with the amplitude of the stimulus, although every single fiber is nevertheless following the all-or-none law. It is both a simple and re-

14 E. D. Adrian, *The Basis of Sensation*, 1934.
15 Edwin G. Boring, *The Physical Dimensions of Consciousness*, 1933.

markable conclusion. Frequency and amplitude could be scrambled in the nerve, and yet an electrode merely hooked about the nerve could pick them out in their original forms because the effect depends upon the sum of all the differences of electrical potential in all the fibers in the nerve. It is thus that the volley theory represents an intelligible combination of the multiple fibre and the frequency theories of intensity. The volley theory also restores plausibility to a frequency theory of pitch, in spite of the fact that frequency in the single fiber means intensity and that the single fiber cannot transmit frequencies as great as those of the higher pitches." (pp. 51-52)

In the Introduction we stated that one of the unsolved riddles of psychology was how nerve action was transmuted in the cortex into sensations and perceptions. Although unsolved, a few words may be added to show the lines that recent researches have opened up. Adrian, as we have seen, has shown that the relation between the sensation and impulse frequency is a clear and simple one. The mental correlate, he says "is a very close copy of the physical events in the sensory nerves. The only kind of distortion which takes place in the transference from body to mind (or in the parallelism of the bodily and mental events) is that the sensations rise and fall smoothly, whereas the nervous message consists of a series of discrete impulses with pauses between." (p. 118) He thinks the explanation lies in the fact that excitatory processes of the brain rise and decline more slowly than they do in the nerve fiber. This explanation is in line with the fact that in some reflex arcs, as Sherrington found, a brief sensory stimulus provokes a motor discharge of much more gradual onset and decline.

Adrian's views are pictured in Fig. 31. The stimulus is supposed to arise suddenly and to continue steadily without impairment. The excitatory process in the receptor declines gradually, and, correspondingly, the nervous discharges in the sensory fiber become less frequent. The integration in the brain leads to a sensation which is a close copy of the rise and decline of the excitatory processes in the receptors. How different qualities of sensation arise is not shown, for, as far as is known, all nervous discharges from all receptors seem

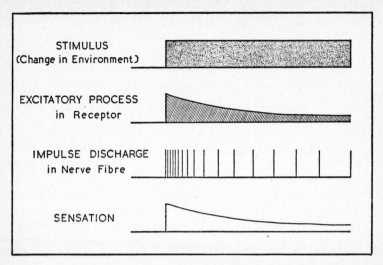

Fig. 31. Relation between Stimulus, Sensory Message and Sensation.
(Adrian)

to be alike in their nature. Adrian thinks the quality must depend on the path which the impulses must travel, but this is, of course, sheer guess work, and we have decided not to admit guesses in this text.

Lashley's Mass Action.— The traditional view of the nervous system held by those who believe in the Reaction Hypothesis is that the neurons are organized into functional arcs (reflex and conditioned) of various degrees of complexity. The arcs of the third or cortical level are concerned with what have been termed the higher thought processes — judgment, reasoning, memory and so forth. The lower arcs are concerned with simpler functions; those of the first or spinal level, for instance, with nothing more elaborate than rather simple reflexes. Learning takes place by the additive elaboration of arc-patterns; retention by changes in the internal structure of neurons, especially of the cell-bodies; and gradualness in learning is explained by the necessity of overcoming the resistance of synapses. A corollary of this theory is that brain functions must be rather definitely localized since the neuronic paths must be definite tracts with definite end-stations in the cortex. This theory of synaptic learning has a great deal of experimental evidence to support it. Anatomists have traced the paths from sense organs to the cortex and from the cortex to the organs of response. Certain areas of the brain have been shown to be concerned with vision, hearing, movement and somaesthetic sensations. But there were always well established observations which did not fit the scheme. Even data concerning learning, which was beautifully and simply explained by decreased resistance of the synapses, failed to fit this over-simplified picture.

To Franz (1902 and 1907) must be given credit for originating the experimental method of teaching an animal (cat and monkey) a specific habit, then extirpating a part of the cortex and noting whether or not the habit was lost, and if it were lost, whether or not it could be as easily relearned. He showed conclusively that destruction of the frontal areas led to loss of certain habits, and that these may be relearned. Lesions in other areas did not lead to the loss of these habits. Long standing habits seemed to be retained better than newly formed ones when frontal lesions were made.

Lashley was a pupil of Franz and has carried on, from 1917, the line of experiments begun by his teacher in 1902. Lashley uses rats as subjects and destroys portions of the cortex by thermo-cautery. After the experiments, the rats are killed and the extent of the brain injury accurately determined from thin parallel sectionings. Most of his researches have been reported in technical journals, but one important series was recorded in the only monograph that Lashley[16] so far has written. He is a careful worker and his experiments are classics in their field.

In the monograph, Lashley reports that ten problems were finally selected for study. To test the influence of the complexity of the problem on the degree of deterioration, three mazes were used; and for the permanence of defect, a fourth. For diversity of sensory components the brightness habit and the incline box were included. Retention tests for two mazes and the brightness habit, and a test for the case of substitution of one habit for another completed the series. The problems, then, were the following:

[16] K. S. Lashley, *Brain Mechanisms and Intelligence*, 1929.

1. Maze III   7. Reversal of Maze I
2. Maze II   8. Retention of Brightness Dis-
3. Maze I   crimination
4. Brightness Discrimination   9. Maze IV
5. Retention on Maze III   10. Incline Box
6. Retention on Maze I

In the mazes, hunger was the incentive; in discrimination, hunger plus electric shocks. Ten successive errorless trials constituted learning. The scores were computed in terms of time, trials and errors, with trials and errors proving superior to time.

His main findings were as follows:

(1) For some problems (mazes) a retardation results from injury to any part of the cortex, and for equal amounts of destruction the retardation is approximately the same. The difficulty of the problem becomes progressively greater as the magnitude of the lesion increases. The magnitude of injury is important; the locus is not.

(2) The more complex the problem to be learned, the greater the retardation produced by any given extent of lesion. The capacity to form simple habits of sensory discrimination is not significantly reduced by cerebral lesions even when the entire sensory field is destroyed. This immunity is probably due to the relative simplicity of such habits.

(3) The capacity to retain is reduced, as is the capacity to learn.

(4) Thalamic injury reduces the learning rate of the brightness habit, while injury to the cortex has practically no effect.

From these facts Lashley draws the following inferences:

1. "The learning process and the retention of habits are not dependent upon any finely localized structural changes within the cerebral cortex. The results are incompatible with theories of learning by changes in synaptic structure, or with any theories which assume that particular neural integrations are dependent upon definite anatomical paths specialized for them. Integration cannot be expressed in terms of connections between specific neurons.

2. "The contribution of the different parts of a specialized area or of the whole cortex, in the case of non-localized functions, is qualitatively the same. There is not a summation of diverse functions, but a non-specialized dynamic function of the tissue as a whole.

3. "Analysis of the maze habit indicates that its formation in-

volves processes which are characteristic of intelligent behavior. Hence the results for the rat are generalized for cerebral functions in intelligence. Data on dementia in man are suggestive of conditions similar to those found after cerebral injury in the rat.

4. "The mechanisms of integration are to be sought in the dynamic relations among the parts of the nervous system rather than in details of structural differentiation." (p. 176)

These conclusions, as Lashley has since admitted, are probably too sweeping. They make the connections of the brain of a radio-like nature rather than telephonic, and there is little evidence except the recently discovered "brain waves" to support this view. The stages in the evolution of the brain have not been given sufficient weight. The cortical area is of later evolution than the mid-brain, and the cortical projections from the mid-brain are comparatively recent. Stopford's analysis, which associates the thalamus with protopathic sensitivity and the cortex with epicritic, should not be overlooked. Lashley himself found that although cortical injuries did not disturb brightness discrimination (a very primitive form of vision), thalamic injuries did. Nor can we press too far the analogies between rats and men. There is a great amount of evidence which shows that brains as they become more specialized in evolution also exhibit more definite localizations. Finally, although recent work on the nervous system seems to show that there are surgings of energy and impulses even when the brain is supposedly at rest, and that stimulation simply directs these energies into co-ordinated channels, we must not overlook the importance of Golgi cells, type II, or the collaterals of neurons, or, in fact, the immense complexity of anatomical structure of the nervous system. The synaptic theory will have to be modified, but we are far from the stage when we can discard it altogether and with impunity. Educationally, the bond theory of learning, which is based on the synaptic theory, is still the most valuable for schoolroom use, and need not be discarded, even if the synaptic theory is finally modified beyond recognition. Lashley, however, must be given credit for adding greatly to our knowledge of the way the brain functions.

REFERENCES

Adrian, E. D. *The Basis of Sensation.* London, Christophers, 1934. Pp. 122.

Bainbridge, F. A. *The Physiology of Muscular Exercise.* London, Longmans, 1919. Pp. ix + 215.

Bard, P. "The Neuro-Humoral Basis of Emotional Reactions," in Carl Murchison (Ed.), *Handbook of General Experimental Psychology.* Worcester, Clark University Press, 1934. Pp. 264-311.

Berman, L. *The Glands Regulating Personality.* New York, Macmillan, 1935. Pp. viii + 341.

Boring, E. G. *The Physical Dimensions of Consciousness.* New York, Century, 1933. Pp. xii + 241.

Cameron, A. T. *Recent Advances in Endocrinology.* Philadelphia, Blakiston, 1934. Pp. vi + 365.

Cannon, W. B. *Bodily Changes in Pain, Hunger, Fear and Rage.* New York, Appleton, 1914. Pp. 311.

Cannon, W. B. "Neural Organization for Emotional Expression," in Reymert's *Feelings and Emotions: the Wittenberg Symposium.* Worcester, Clark University Press, 1928, pp. 257-268.

Chamberlain, A. F. *The Child: a Study in the Evolution of Man.* New York, Scribner, 1911. Pp. xii + 498.

Child, C. M. *Physiological Foundations of Behavior.* New York, Holt, 1924. Pp. xii + 330.

Coghill, G. E. *Anatomy and the Problem of Behavior.* Cambridge University Press, 1928. Pp. xii + 113.

Dashiell, J. F. "A Survey and Synthesis of Learning Theories," *Psychol. Bull.,* XXXII, 1935, pp. 261-275.

Fiske, J. *The Meaning of Infancy.* Boston, Houghton Mifflin, 1909. Pp. x + 43.

Garrett, H. E. *Great Experiments in Psychology.* New York, Century, 1930. Pp. xvii + 337.

Griffith, C. R. *An Introduction to Educational Psychology.* New York, Farrar and Rinehart, 1935. Pp. xiv + 754.

Head, H. *Aphasia and Kindred Disorders of Speech* (2 Vols.). Cambridge University Press, 1926. Pp. 401 and 407.

Herrick, C. J. *Neurological Foundations of Animal Behavior.* New York, Holt, 1924. Pp. xii + 334.

Herrick, C. J. *The Thinking Machine.* University of Chicago Press, 1929. Pp. xii + 374.

Kempf, E. J. *The Autonomic Functions and the Personality.* New York, Nervous and Mental Disease Publishing Co., 1921. Pp. xiv + 156.

Klein, D. B. *General Psychology.* New York, Holt. 1936. Pp. xiv + 560.

Lashley, K. S. *Brain Mechanisms and Intelligence.* University of Chicago Press, 1930. Pp. xiv + 186.

Murphy, G. *General Psychology.* New York, Harper, 1933. Pp. x + 657.

Paterson, D. G. *Physique and Intellect*. New York, Century, 1930. Pp. xxvii + 304.

Ranson, S. W. *The Anatomy of the Nervous System*. Philadelphia, Saunders, 1923. Pp. 421.

Raup, B. R. *Complacency; the Foundation of Behavior*. New York, Macmillan, 1925. Pp. xii + 197.

Rivers and Head. "A Human Experiment in Nerve Division." *Brain*, 1908, XXI, pp. 323-450.

Sandiford, P. *Educational Psychology: an Objective Study*. New York, Longmans, 1928. Pp. xix + 406.

Sherrington, C. S. *The Integrative Action of the Nervous System*. New Haven, Yale University Press, 1923. Pp. xv + 411.

Skinner and Associates. *Readings in Educational Psychology*. New York, Farrar and Rinehart, 1937. Pp. x + 630.

Stopford, J. S. B. *Sensation and the Sensory Pathway*. London, Longmans, 1930. Pp. xii + 148.

Verworn, M. *Irritability: a Physiological Analysis of the General Effect of Stimuli in Living Substance*. New Haven, Yale University Press, 1913. Pp. xii + 264.

CHAPTER IV

NON-VARIABLE OR UNLEARNED BEHAVIOR: REFLEXES, INSTINCTS AND EMOTIONS

The Nature of Unlearned Behavior.— Even the man in the street recognizes that many forms of his behavior are performed without previous teaching or experience. Still more striking are the unlearned performances of the lower animals. To these actions, technically called pattern reactions since they are performed in much the same way every time, he gives the name instincts or, sometimes, emotions. In some vague way, he is aware that these actions are based on innate dispositions (the animal, he thinks, is born or grows that way), but he is usually ignorant of the complex interplay of hereditary and environmental factors which their overt manifestations involve. Sometimes, indeed, he makes no distinction between pattern actions in which learning is involved, such as shaving and skating, and those which are performed more or less perfectly at the first trial, such as blinking and sneezing. He usually thinks that the lower animals have more numerous and more perfected forms of instincts than man, and that, in general, man uses more intelligence.

These somewhat vague but nevertheless plausible notions of instincts which the common man holds today were exactly the kind that even professional psychologists and biologists held a generation ago. But as soon as they began to observe more carefully and to make simple but tentative experiments, the problem acquired new angles. Instincts and emotions were not as simple as they had seemed to be. Indeed, the more they were studied, the less agreement there was regarding both their number and nomenclature. The number of instincts ran from one to over three hundred, and the same name, fear for example, was frequently given to both an instinct and an emotion. Since science demands consistency in the use of technical terms, psychologists, almost in despair over the chaotic state of affairs, advised that instincts be cast out of the vocabulary of psychology and, a little later, that emotions be thrown overboard also. But this is easier said than done. The words are part of the vocabulary of the masses, and, further, they name something that everybody recognizes as having actual existence. When psychologists, such as McDougall, begin to call them propensities, they are simply using another word to describe the same thing. Since instincts and emotions have been in the vocabulary of psychologists for so long, the reasonable thing to do is to retain them if possible and to define them more sharply.

We have insisted, *ad nauseam*, that organisms must adjust themselves to their environments or die. Each one is born into an ecological niche and its behavior is designed to preserve the ecological norm. Since so many survive, there must be a considerable amount of adjustment in nature. With the simpler organisms only the simpler adjustments are possible. Their primitive structures preclude the more complex forms. Hence their reactions to environmental changes must be more or less *stereotyped* and must be *unlearned*. In other words, they must inherit dispositions towards behavior which are biologically adequate; and this behavior must necessarily be at a low "instinctive" level. With increasing complexity, variations in forms of adjustment will be added and the organism will have a seemingly smaller number of instinctive reactions. But even in the highest animals, in man for example, the basic behaviors for the preservation and continuance of life must be the gifts of nature. It is also natural to expect a greater preponderance of unlearned reactions in infancy than in maturity. A newborn infant is nearer the lower animals, as it were, than a mature adult. We should, therefore, look for the purest expression of unlearned forms of behavior among the simpler organisms, and among the infants of higher ones. And if we look, it is, of course, exactly what we find.

Although unlearned reactions tend to be stereotyped and non-variable, not one of them is purely so. Circumstances arise when the stereotyped reaction fails; in these cases, within limits, a variant of the reaction will appear. Nature provides as many behavior patterns as will normally suffice, but, more important, it gives the urge to survival and, also within limits, the plasticity or the modifiability of behavior which will prevent catastrophe from happening. All this may seem to be adding an unknown X (purpose, will, or desire) to our science of psychology, but in reality it is not so. All that the psychologist or biologist can study is the overt and visible behavior of animals; their inner life or experience cannot be known directly, and must always be a matter of inference. But it would be ridiculous to overlook the fact that organisms exhibit behavior which is directed towards their survival — the supreme end of nature.

A paramecium, for example, normally exhibits the back-paddling, turning, and forging-ahead movements whenever it meets an obstacle. But, as Day and Bentley showed, a paramecium in a fine capillary tube partially filled with water will finally turn over and swim in the opposite direction in its efforts to escape. Yet no paramecium in its ordinary habitat ever turns a somersault. Morgan's dog finally hit upon the variant, grasping the stick by the end instead of the middle, which enabled it to drag it through the palings of the fence. A caddis worm will construct a new tube if ejected from an old one and prevented from returning to it; but not before it has made many attempts to return to the old one. Salmon, eels and other fishes return to their spawning places, varying their movements in accordance with the changing features of their environment, but pushing on relentlessly to the appointed goal. Birds vary their nests according to the situation and materials available. Any urban robin's or oriole's nest will have string as part of the structure. Yet string is an unnatural kind of fiber for constructing nests. Generally speaking, in all these cases, the action is relentless and persistent until either a satisfactory biological end is achieved or the animal is exhausted.

The point to be remembered is that organisms of all kinds exhibit behavior which has an inherited basis. This behavior in lower animals and in the young of higher ones normally tends to be stereotyped and non-variable. If, however, circumstances arise which prevent this behavior from fulfilling its normal biological end, variations will arise and be persisted in until the biological end is achieved or fatigue or death occurs. These variations we call *learning*, since they lead to modifications of behavior. They are generally termed variable or learned behaviors. We thus may somewhat arbitrarily divide behavior into two components, non-variable or unlearned on the one hand and variable or learned on the other. Some forms of behavior are obviously less modifiable, less variable than others. Such, for example, are the physiological reactions of the body. Breathing can be modified, as every pearl-diver or teacher of singing knows, but ordinarily it is less open to modification than movements of skeletal muscles. Tropisms are relatively simple and constant reactions, but Loeb modified them by changing the environment. On the other hand, instincts are relatively easy to modify, and habitual and intelligent actions still easier.

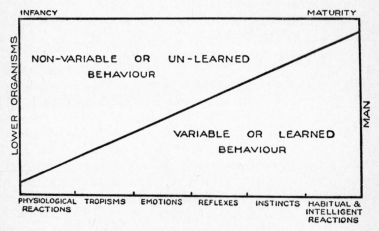

Fig. 32. Diagrammatic representation of the Variable and Non-variable Elements in Behavior, and their Phylogenetic and Ontogenetic Development.

The argument so far may be illustrated by a simple diagram. Fig. 32 is such a one. Too much stress must not be placed on the relative proportions of variable and non-variable behavior at each stage of development. Nor must the order — physiological reactions, tropisms, emotions, reflexes, instincts and intelligent reactions — be taken as scientifically established. All that we wish to show is that the lower organisms and human infants make on the whole more stereotyped reactions than higher organisms and human adults. Also, that physiological actions, being more essential to biological survival than the higher, habitual actions, are essentially less variable and less learned. The fact that the lower organisms mostly live in the relatively unchanging environment of water in contrast with the constantly changing environment of air, explains why their simple inherited dispositions of behavior are adequate for survival. Nor should it be forgotten that insects return to water or the ground for their metamorphoses, and that placental mammals spend the first part of their existence in a fluid environment of constant temperature. In such uniform environments, the stereotyped adjustments provided by nature are entirely adequate; the animal can survive in its special ecological niche.

The Forms of Non-Variable Behavior. — While every form of behavior, as we have seen, is variable to some extent, there are some forms more stable and consistent than others. These will now be discussed.

(*a*) *Physiological Actions.* Few people would dispute the fact that certain tissues of the body respond to excitation. The sense organs with their central connections respond to ether waves, chemical and mechanical stimulation, and certain other energies of the environment. Muscles respond to stimuli originating in motor neurons and, during experimentation in the laboratory, to electrical stimulation also. Such native gifts of excitation, conduction and response, are usually taken for granted. Breathing, digestion, circulation and excretion are physiological actions which are better known. They are also unlearned and usually taken for granted. They are only slightly modifiable. True, we can learn to control our breathing and to determine the time of evacuations, but we are usually less successful in controlling our blushes or learning to digest cucumbers. These physiological processes are basic to existence, and evolutionary nature has provided a competent machinery for their expression. They are more the concern of the physiologist than the psychologist, but recently the psychologist has begun to study them. Disturbances in secretions, as we have pointed out, especially the disturbances of endocrine secretions, lead to marked changes in behavior. The psychologist is also beginning to measure psychogalvanic reflexes, and to record changes in respiration and blood pressure in an effort to unravel emotional and other mental perturbations. On the whole, therefore, physiological actions are neither so stable nor so non-variable as they once appeared to be.

(*b*) *Tropisms.* We owe this term to Jacques Loeb[1] who devoted a goodly portion of his life to their study. In later years his mantle has fallen on Crozier[2] who has introduced the scientific element of mathematical formulae into his presentations. Briefly a tropism is a forced movement or turning of an organism into a definite axial position in reference to the direction of some stimulating agent — chemicals, electricity, gravitation, heat, light, and so forth. Plants, for instance, are usually positively *heliotropic* (phototropic); they turn towards the light. Moths are also positively heliotropic. Some protozoa are known which swim towards a light and others which swim away from it. Loeb, in a number of beautiful experiments, was able to reverse the tropic behavior of a number of sea animals. Normally negatively heliotropic, they were forced to go to the light in two ways: first by lowering the temperature, and second by increasing the concentration of the sea water (whereby the cells of the animals lose water). His explanation of heliotropism in moths is as follows: "If a moth be struck by light on one side, those muscles which turn the head towards the light become more active than those of the opposite side, and correspondingly the head of the animal is turned towards the source of light. As soon as the head of the animal has this orientation and the median plane (or plane of symmetry) comes into the direction of the rays of light, the symmetrical points of the surface of the body are struck by rays of light at the same angle. The intensity of light is the same on both sides, and there is no more reason why the animal should turn to the right or left than away from the direction of rays of light. Thus it is led to the source of the light. Hence the 'instinct' that drives the animal into the light is nothing more than the chemical — and indirectly the mechanical — effect of light, an effect similar to that which forces the stem of the plant at the window to bend toward the source of light."

Many animals are *stereotropic,* usually positive, which re-

---

[1] See Jacques Loeb, *Tropisms, Forced Movement, and Animal Conduct,* 1918.

[2] For a reasonably elementary summary see: W. J. Crozier and Hudson Hoagland, "The Study of Living Organisms," in Murchison's *Handbook of General Experimental Psychology,* 1934, pp. 3-108.

sults in a tendency to crawl into corners, crevices, or holes. Young rats and mice, for instance, move so that the body is in contact with a solid object. The earthworm is negatively heliotropic and positively stereotropic. In general, the stereotropism of the worm is stronger than its heliotropism. The illustrations in Fig. 33, from Crozier and Hoagland's article previously mentioned, clearly show this stereotropism in young rodents. But the important contribution of Crozier, Hoagland and other workers is that they can devise mathematical formulae and draw curves which will predict, within the limits of experimental error, the actual tropic movements of snails, caterpillars, water scorpions, guinea-pigs, goldfish, crickets, catfish, *Daphnia*, ants and other creatures. Their work on Weber's law and other psychological problems is very impressive. When they can make accurate predictions of behavior, they are well within the circle of science.

It should be noted, however, that Jennings' experiments in regard to the *thermotropic* reactions of the protozoon *Oxtricha fallax*, which swims from hot or cold water to water of a moderate temperature, showed no such simple turning movements as the tropistic theory would lead us to expect. Instead, these creatures on reaching the hot or cold water made rapid movements, reversed their direction by backing, and turned to the right. They were thus rapidly scattered, and continued their activity until they reached the part of the water which was of a moderate temperature. Vigorous action now ceased and they began to swim forward in a normal manner. According to Jennings, their behavior seemed to be of a simple "trial and error" variety. More careful experimentation shows that these movements are truly tropic, although Jennings has done well to remind us that the internal physiological state of the animal must be taken into account.

Other important tropisms which have been studied experimentally are *geotropisms* (responses to gravity), *galvanotropisms* (responses to electrical stimulation), *rheotropisms* (responses to currents of water), *hydrotropisms* (responses to water or moisture), *barotropisms* (responses to pressures), *chromotropisms* (responses to colors and hues), *anemotropisms* (responses to air currents), and *magnetotropisms* (responses to magnetic stimulation).

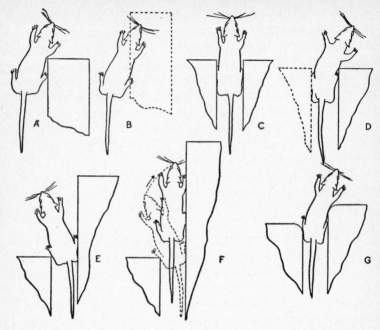

Fig. 33. Stereotropic Orientations of Young Rat or Mouse.

A. Stereotropic orientation of young rat or mouse at the corner of a box along one side of which it has been creeping.

B. A young rat or mouse has been creeping in contact with the side of a box (dashed outline) ; the removal of the box results in partial orientation toward that side.

C. A young rat or mouse creeping in a passage-way between two boxes, just wide enough to permit gentle contact on either side during the animal's swaying progression, is found to emerge from the passage-way without orientation. Equivalent bilateral stimulations prevent stereotropic turning.

D. An individual emerging from equal bilateral contacts with two boxes proceeds in a straight path, without orientation ; but if one of the boxes be removed (dashed outline), it promptly orients toward the remaining one.

E. Contact at one side with the corner of a box may lead to orientation toward that side, apparently due, in part at least, to more intense tactile excitation than is provided by a continuous flat surface (or by smoothly rounded corners).

F. When such a corner is passed, orientation persists toward a continuing contact on the opposite side.

G. When blocks providing lateral contacts are of unequal extent, the young rat or mouse orients toward the side of more extensive contacts but does not completely turn the corner unless the difference in extent of the two blocks is more than half the length of the animal. This, the expected result from a tropistic standpoint, is obtained when the corners of the contact blocks are smoothly rounded. (Crozier and Hoagland)

While Loeb's prophecy — that instincts and even the higher behaviors of man would ultimately be proved to be merely elaborations of tropic responses — has not been fulfilled, modern research has shown that our volitional actions are not as "free" as we formerly supposed them to be.

(*c*) *Reflexes.* Reflexes, according to Sherrington, are reactions in which there follows on an initiating reaction an end-effect reached through the mediation of a conductor, a nerve itself incapable either of the end-effect or, under natural conditions, of the inception of the reaction. In other words, for a reflex act we require a receptor, a conductor and an effector. Such a combination is known as a *simple reflex arc* or *sensori-motor arc.* It is probably nothing more than a convenient and useful abstraction, since most actions demand the functioning of many arcs for their execution. The path of conduction from a receptor (sense organ) to a conductor (muscle) is shown in Fig. 27.

However, as Fearing[3] points out, confusion in regard to the term reflex "is found in the failure to distinguish between its application to (1) the neural structures involved in responses to stimulation, and (2) functionally uniform types of response dependent, presumably, upon certain neural connections." (p. 4) The first usage leads to the view that all responses involving sensory and motor neurons are reflexes and that they depend upon reflex arcs. The second usage leads to the view that certain functionally similar reactions possessing certain characteristics are given the same name, even if the mechanisms of arousal are different. Thus the salivary reflex may be aroused by chemical stimulation or, conditionally, by sight, sound, temperature and so forth. Fearing lists the criteria or characteristics of the reflex given by various writers in roughly the following order of frequency : (1) *involuntary;* (2) *unlearned;* (3) *based on inherited neural mechanisms;* (4) *predictable* and *uniform;* (5) *not conditioned by consciousness;* (6) *rapidity of action;* (7) serves a *protective purpose;* (8) involves a *synaptic nervous system* with, at least, sensory and motor neurons; and (9) *does not usually involve the cerebral cortex.* (p. 5) Unfortunately these criteria are not mutually exclusive. (cf. 2

[3] Franklin Fearing, *Reflex Action : a Study in the History of Physiological Psychology,* 1930.

and 3) What is more serious for psychology, since it is the second usage that psychology has adopted, is to discover the manner in which the cortex (will or consciousness) may modify the trigger-like action of the simpler spinal reflexes. For instance, in babies, both defecation and micturition are of a simple reflex nature aroused by pressure, but, later, both are to a considerable extent cortically controlled. It is easy enough to say that additional, longer loops extending to the cortex are now involved, but we are densely ignorant of the way in which cortical control is exercised.

Two excellent lists of human reflexes are available for the student of the subject. The first is to be found as Table X of Warren's *Dictionary of Psychology* (pp. 311-314), where 76 separate reflexes are listed. The second one, reproduced below, is taken from Warren and Carmichael's *Elements of Human Psychology*. (pp. 395-396)

The difficulties about the above list and other similar ones are that (*a*) the effective stimuli and the mechanisms involved are indeterminate. For instance, sneezing, yawning, weeping, etc. are listed. Each of them may be aroused in many ways but the end action alone is considered; (*b*) the distinction between reflexes and instincts is arbitrarily drawn, although it is readily admitted that the simpler ones are called reflexes. It is usual to regard the earlier, less complex, less modifiable and more easily aroused native reactions as reflexes, and those which appear later, are more complex, etc., as instincts. Thus sucking and swallowing are listed by Warren and Carmichael as reflexes, but feeding, which may involve both, is listed as an instinct. The distinction between instinct and reflex is, however, an arbitrary one; and (*c*) the fact that co-ordinated reactions of organisms as Coghill and others have pointed out are not due to combinations of initial reflexes. In the evolution of behavior diffuse patterns of behavior appear before the true reflexes; in fact, the sensori-motor arcs on which the reflexes depend, develop later than certain afferent systems which are effective in stimulating reactions. Behavior cannot be expressed solely in terms of reflex arcs, nor can the sensori-motor response be regarded as the whole function of the nervous system. The walking posture, for example, appears before it is possible to excite the local exteroceptive reflexes of the

TABLE XXXIX. TABLE OF HUMAN REFLEXES.
(Warren & Carmichael)

A. *Seldom modified in adult:*

'Pupillary' or iris reflex	Shuddering
Ear twitching (controlled in some individuals)	Starting (to sudden noises, etc.)
	Shivering
Hand withdrawal (to heat and pain)	Trembling
Digestive reflexes (autonomic)	Rhythmic contractions (in epilepsy, paralysis agitans, etc.)

B. *Inhibited and reinforced in adult:*

Winking	Hand twitching (to dermal pain)
Accommodation, ciliary reflex	Plantar reflex (to stimulus on sole of foot)
Eye-fixation and convergence	
Hiccoughing	Great toe reflex
Sneezing	Vasomotor changes (blushing, paling)
Patellar reflex (knee-jerk)	Breathing changes (to specific stimuli
Dizziness reflexes	and to onset of sleep)
Yawning	Sudorific reflexes
Vomiting	Groaning
Facial reflexes (to bitter taste, etc.)	Laughing
Salivation	Cramp movements
Tickle reflexes	Squirming

C. *Often modified in adult:*

Coughing	Smiling
Swallowing and gulping	Wincing, etc.
Visceral discharge, etc.	Scowling
Generative reflexes	Stretching
Reflexes to odors	Convulsive contractions (to deep pressure and heat, to pricking and other dermal pains, and to visceral pain)
Gasping	
Weeping	
Sobbing	

D. *Always modified in adult:*

Sucking	Tugging (wrist reflexes)
Biting and grinding	Clasping (elbow reflexes)
Spitting	Reaching (shoulder reflexes)
Hunger and thirst reflexes	Kicking (knee reflexes)
Lip and tongue reflexes	Stepping (gluteal reflexes)
Vocal reflexes	Jumping (ankle reflexes)
Turning the head	Sitting up
Tossing with hand	Bending forward
Grasping (finger reflexes)	Rising

E. *Posture reflexes:*

Holding head erect	Standing
Sitting	Equilibration

legs, and the plantar reflex (elicited by stroking the sole of the foot) begins as an action of the leg as a whole. There is a wealth of evidence to support the contention that instead of combinations of reflexes making elaborate behavior possible, developing behavior is the stimulus which causes the separation, growth and development of the reflex mechanisms.

Probably the solution of the difficulty lies in better and fuller observation and experiment. The work of Minkowski and others on the behavior of the human fetus and of McGraw, Shirley, Gesell and a host of others on neonatal behavior (the first 10-14 days of life) is most promising. An excellent summary of this work is found in Evelyn Dewey's *Behavior Development in Infants*. The behavior during infancy tends more and more to be on what is generally known as the instinctive level, but it should be clearly understood that the process of development is a continuous one. In general, it takes the form of increasing elaboration, a growing co-ordination in movement, and an increasing specificity in responses to external stimulation. Maturation is also an important factor; the young human being, by an inner organization which is part of its inheritance, literally "grows into things."

(*d*) *Instincts*. The distinction between reflex and instinct is an arbitrary one and rather difficult to draw. Lloyd Morgan[4] defined instinct as follows:

"From the biological point of view, instincts are congenital, adaptive, and co-ordinated activities of relative complexity, and involving the behavior of the organism as a whole. They are not characteristic of individuals as such, but are similarly performed by all like members of the same more or less restricted group, under circumstances which are either of frequent recurrence or are vitally essential to the continuance of the race. While they are, broadly-speaking, constant in character, they are subject to variation analogous to that found in organic structures. They are often periodic in development and serial in character. They are to be distinguished from habits which owe their definiteness to individual acquisition and the repetition of individual performance." (pp. 27-28)

The definition is an adequate one. The relative complex-

[4] C. Lloyd Morgan, *Habit and Instinct*, 1896.

ity, the serial character, the involvement of the whole organism are the chief characters which distinguish an instinct from a reflex. While both are concerned with adjustments necessary for self-maintenance and with the exercise of muscles rather than the activity of glands, instincts are more protracted in time, and use a greater number of response mechanisms than reflexes. The serial character of instinctive actions, beautifully illustrated by the nest-building, egg-laying, incubation and feeding of the young of birds, has been noted by every careful observer.

To watch a cycle of instinctive behavior is both illuminating and fascinating. In the summer of 1937, I drew the attention of my family to a dragon-fly nymph which was climbing out of the water preparatory to the emergence of the fly. We watched the whole process of transformation and timed the sectional parts. From the time the nymph left the water to the first flight of the mature dragon-fly the interval was a few seconds over half an hour. The nymph having found a convenient perch on the rock above the highest lappings of the waves, split across and slightly along the back of the neck. Through this rather small, cross-like hole, the head of the dragon-fly, bulging eyes and all, was thrust. A period of rest followed. With a series of lunging movements the body, legs and wings of the fly were dragged out through the same hole, each lunge being followed by a period of quiescence. The final heave brought out the hind parts. The wings, wet and stuck together, were shorter than the body at first, but soon became longer. Pumping movements followed; the body lost water at the rear end and gradually enlarged until it projected beyond the closed wings. Meanwhile, during the pumping of air and blood, the wings had been drying. Unfolding took place and the dragon-fly, a female, took on the adult form. In half an hour the transformation was complete. The dragon-fly then took to its wings and flew away. In less than thirty yards of its first flight, it encountered a fly which was promptly snapped up and eaten. The adult life of the dragon-fly had begun. The whole process from a water-dwelling nymph to an air-breathing insect was definite and pre-determined. Each action fitted in perfectly with the others until the whole circle was completed. The only variation in behavior that we noticed was a partial turning to face the breeze which was blowing the insect over to one side.

Such a description of an instinctive action over-simplifies what really happens. Moreover, this particular one is less variable than many others that could have been cited. Young herring gulls, for example, visited the same week, exhibited much more variable, though indubitably instinctive, behavior. Some were just hatched, some a few days old. Their speckled plumage made them difficult to find. They had left the nests and were generally found in some corner or crevice, the head alone being hidden from sight. Wanting to photograph a baby 3 or 4 days old, I took it up and placed it on a flat portion of a rock in the sun. It was so distressed that it regurgitated food. But it would not stay put. Off it waddled towards a crack and did not stop until its body was protected by a rock and its head was once more tucked out of sight. The reaction was stereotropic; the moment the creature could put its head out of sight and its body against solid rock, locomotion ceased. This hiding response seemed curiously ineffective, but the parents, circling and crying overhead, probably kept off all marauders but human beings. A still younger gull, discovered in a comparatively open place, "feigned death," but on being pushed slightly, went through the customary hiding motions. The actions of the young gulls were far more variable than those of the dragon-fly, but they were obviously instinctive and unlearned.

There are, however, obvious difficulties in regard to instincts. Most people would say that cats have a rat-killing instinct. But if cats are reared with rats as cage companions, as Kuo reared them, the rat-killing instinct never appears. At least Kuo's cats never killed a rat of the same species as those with which they had been reared. But kittens reared with rat-killing mothers, themselves became rat-killers around the age of four months. Kuo argued that there were either no instincts, or, if there were, we must include rat-loving as well as rat-killing among the instincts of cats. What really emerges from this experiment is that instincts are quite variable, and in certain situations extremely so. In Havre, France, they rid the docks of rats by breeding cats of a proven rat-killing strain. These cats attacked rats at every opportunity, while other cats were either indifferent to, or

TABLE XL. GENERAL GROUPING OF ANIMAL ACTIVITIES.
(Holmes)

Behavior
- Non-adaptive
  - Useless tropistic reactions
  - Misdirected instinct
  - Abnormal sex behavior
  - Pathological activity; fits
  - Useless social activity
  - Superfluous random movements
- Adaptive
  - Self maintaining
    - Sustentative
      - Devouring food
      - Discrimination of food
      - Capture of food
      - Activities preparatory to capture as making snares, pitfalls, hunting, stalking
      - Collection of food, digging, boring, gnawing
      - Migration
      - Caring for food for future use, hiding, burying, storing
      - Preparation of food
    - Protective
      - Against enemies (See Table XLI)
      - Against inanimate forces, reactions to heat, light, gravity, chemicals, etc.
      - Against inanimate objects, i.e., avoidance of moving objects, cleaning movements, etc.
    - Ameliorative
      - Rest, sleep, exercise, play, basking
  - Race maintaining
    - Sexual behavior
      - Of male toward female:
        - Copulation
        - Sex discrimination, seeking the female
        - Courtship, sex calls
        - Battling for female
      - Of female toward male:
        - Resisting, accepting, alluring, coyness
    - Parental behavior (see Table XLII)
      - Parents toward offspring
      - Offspring toward parents
    - Social behavior (see Table XLIII)
      - Sustentative
      - Protective
      - Ameliorative

afraid of them. Kuo's experiment ought to be repeated with some of the kittens from the Havre strain.

While instincts are facts, they do not explain behavior. Zebras feed in herds. Why? Because they have a gregarious instinct. But why do they have a gregarious instinct? Because they feed together. The reasoning is circular. As Holt[5] says: "Man is impelled to action, it is said, by his instincts. If he goes with his fellows, it is the 'herd instinct' which actuates him; if he walks alone it is the anti-social instinct; if he fights, it is the instinct of 'pugnacity'; if he defers to another it is the instinct of 'self-abasement'; if he twiddles his thumbs, it is the thumb-twiddling instinct ; if he does not twiddle his thumbs, it is the thumb-not-twiddling instinct. Thus everything is explained with the facility of magic — word magic." (p. 4) While the situation is not as bad as Holt would make out, we find instincts as explanations of behavior far too frequently in psychological literature.

We pointed out that the number of instincts listed, ranged from one to over three hundred. It all depends on the classifier and the purpose of the classification. In general, the old-fashioned view that all unlearned forms of behavior are concerned with self-maintenance and perpetuation of the race, is a sound one. Instinctive actions are directed to these ends. When we take away from our lists all those which have to do with such activities as feeding, escape, reproduction and a few others there is practically nothing left. However, if Thorndike and others want to analyze each one into constituent elements and call these instincts there is really no objection; additional knowledge from analysis is always welcome.

Several excellent lists of instincts have been prepared. The attention of the reader has been drawn to that of Thorndike, which is to be found in Volume I of his *Educational Psychology*. The list was prepared in the following way. Thorndike noted and described an unlearned form of behavior and then defined the stimulus or situation to which the response was made. The difficulty which confronted Thorndike, as it confronts every observer, is to be sure that the behavior exhibited was really independent of learning and experience. But Thorndike's list is a standard one. Warren

[5] Edwin B. Holt, *Animal Drive and the Learning Process*, 1931.

and Carmichael's list (Table XVI of their *Elements of Human Psychology*) is also an excellent one. However, instead of reproducing these lists, I shall give a far more exhaustive analysis of behavior. It is not concerned with unlearned behavior as such, but includes all animal activities. Many of these activities, of course, are instinctive forms of behavior as may be seen from even a cursory examination of the Tables. I refer to Holmes'[6] excellent work from which Tables XL, XLI, XLII, and XLIII are taken. They are self-explanatory and need no further comment.

TABLE XLI. FORMS OF SELF-MAINTAINING PROTECTIVE BEHAVIOR TOWARD ENEMIES. (Holmes)

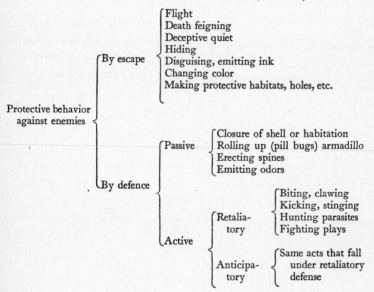

(*e*) *Emotions.* Emotions are difficult to distinguish from instincts; indeed the terms are sometimes used interchangeably. However, there are some characteristics which may be used in distinguishing between them. In emotions, the responses are accompanied by a marked *feeling-tone*, while the term instincts refers to bodily reactions of a serial kind in which the affective quality is not an essential constituent.

[6] S. J. Holmes, "A Tentative Classification of the Forms of Animal Behavior," *J. Comp. Psychol.*, II, 1922.

TABLE XLII. FORMS OF PARENTAL BEHAVIOR. (Holmes)

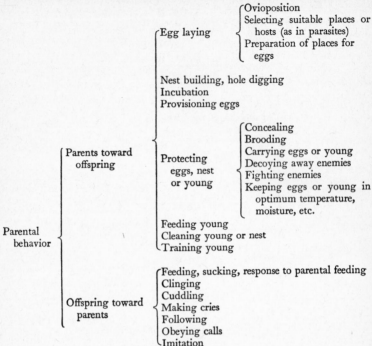

Secondly, the glandular and visceral systems of the body are concerned with emotions; in instincts the skeletal muscular system is chiefly involved. We may therefore define an emotion as an innate response involving the thalamic region of the brain in its display, which is accompanied by a marked feeling-tone, essentially chaotic in its nature and involving the whole body in its characteristic expression, but particularly the glandular and visceral systems and their nervous connections, and having intimate relationship with the preservation of the individual or the species. Although instincts are also intimately connected with self-maintenance, emotions are evoked most easily in those situations which are characterized by emergency and danger. The changes in the constitution of the blood are more pronounced in emotional than in instinctive reactions. However, the relationship between emotions and instincts is undoubtedly a close one, so close indeed that McDougall regards an emotion as the con-

TABLE XLIII. FORMS OF SOCIAL BEHAVIOR. (Holmes)

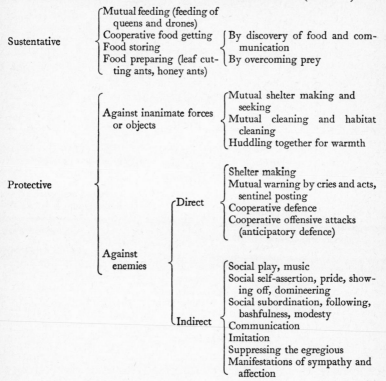

Sustentative
- Mutual feeding (feeding of queens and drones)
- Cooperative food getting — By discovery of food and communication
- Food storing
- Food preparing (leaf cutting ants, honey ants) — By overcoming prey

Protective
- Against inanimate forces or objects
  - Mutual shelter making and seeking
  - Mutual cleaning and habitat cleaning
  - Huddling together for warmth
- Against enemies
  - Direct
    - Shelter making
    - Mutual warning by cries and acts, sentinel posting
    - Cooperative defence
    - Cooperative offensive attacks (anticipatory defence)
  - Indirect
    - Social play, music
    - Social self-assertion, pride, showing off, domineering
    - Social subordination, following, bashfulness, modesty
    - Communication
    - Imitation
    - Suppressing the egregious
    - Manifestations of sympathy and affection

Ameliorative
- Many social plays and amusements
- Music
- Aesthetic activity

scious concomitant of the expression of an instinct. "A specific emotion is the affective phase of specific instincts."

The main characteristics of an emotion would seem to be the following:

(1) *A Characteristic Bodily Expression.* We *see* when a man is angry, sorrowful, or full of fear. We become red with anger, bent with grief, and rigid with fear. The success of the moving picture is a testimony to this feature of the emotions. Illiterate and half-savage peoples can interpret correctly the characteristic bodily signs of emotion as depicted by the movie actor or actress. However, we should not overlook the fact that some of these signs may be quite

conventional, and if the conventions are unknown, the signs may be misinterpreted. Further, the actor or actress may use the same conventions or "bag of tricks" for different emotions. Photographs of persons expressing emotions, posed or real, are interpreted differently by different observers (see later) and students, as Sherman[7] showed, viewing moving pictures of infants, were at a loss in naming the emotion unless they were also shown the stimulus-situation which caused it. In other words, the situation is always important in defining the emotion.

Despite these difficulties, man normally responds correctly to the expression of emotions both in animals and in other people. He may sometimes be at a loss to know whether to respond to the growling of a dog or to the wagging of its tail when both reactions occur simultaneously, but, generally speaking, misinterpretation is unlikely. The teacher may learn to control his emotional expression, yet the pupils generally know when he is pleased or angry with them. Consequently Darwin's[8] early work in the field of emotional expression is still of value. He at least attacked the problem in an objective manner. His technique is illustrated by the following abridgement of his account of *rage* or intense anger:

"Rage exhibits itself in the most diversified manner. The heart and circulation are always affected; the face reddens or becomes purple, with the veins on the forehead and neck distended... With one of my infants, under four months old, I repeatedly observed that the first symptom of an approaching passion was the rushing of the blood into his bare scalp. On the other hand, the action of the heart is sometimes so much impeded by great rage, that the countenance becomes pallid or livid, and not a few with heart-disease have dropped down dead under this powerful emotion.

"The respiration is likewise affected; the chest heaves and the dilated nostrils quiver...

"The excited brain gives strength to the muscles, and at the same time energy to the will. The body is commonly held erect for instant action, but sometimes it is bent towards the offending person, with the limbs more or less rigid. The mouth is generally closed

[7] Mandel Sherman, "The Differentiation of Emotional Responses in Infants. I and II," *J. Comp. Psychol.*, VII, 1928, pp. 265-284; 335-351.

[8] Charles Darwin, *On the Expression of Emotions in Man and Animals*, 1872.

with firmness, showing fixed determination, and the teeth are clenched or ground together. Such gestures as the raising of the arms, with the fists clenched, as if to strike the offender are common. Few men in a great passion, and telling some one to be gone, can resist acting as if they intended to strike or push the man violently away. The desire, indeed, to strike often becomes so intolerably strong, that inanimate objects are struck or dashed to the ground; but the gestures frequently become altogether purposeless or frantic. Young children, when in a violent rage, roll on the ground on their backs or bellies, screaming, kicking, scratching, biting everything within reach. . .

"But the muscular system is often affected in a wholly different way; for trembling is a frequent consequence of extreme rage. The paralysed lips then refuse to obey the will, 'and the voice sticks in the throat'; or it is rendered loud, harsh, and discordant. If there be much and rapid speaking, the mouth froths. The hair sometimes bristles. . . There is in most cases a strongly marked frown on the forehead, for this follows from the sense of anything displeasing or difficult, together with concentration of mind. But sometimes the brow, instead of being much contracted and lowered, remains smooth, with the glaring eyes kept widely open. The eyes are always bright or may, as Homer expresses it, glisten with fire. They are sometimes bloodshot, and are said to protrude from their sockets — the result, no doubt, of the head being gorged with blood, as shown by the veins being distended.

"The lips are sometimes protruded. . . The lips, however, are much more commonly retracted, the grinning or clenched teeth being thus exposed.

"Under moderate anger the action of the heart is a little increased, the colour heightened and the eyes become bright. The respiration is likewise a little hurried; and as all the muscles serving for this function act in association, the wings of the nostrils are somewhat raised to allow of a free indraught of air."

As a result of his study Darwin concluded that the gestures involuntarily used by man and the lower animals under the influence of various emotions could be accounted for by three principles, namely,

(*a*) *The principle of serviceable associated habits.* Habits having proved valuable are inherited (acquired characteristics!) Many forms of emotional expression are inherited vestiges of acts which were previously of value, but no longer have any direct use. Such, for example, are the baring of the teeth and the clenching of the fist during anger.

(*b*) *The principle of antithesis.* "Certain states of the mind lead to certain habitual actions, which are of service, as under our first principle. Now when a directly opposite state of mind is induced, there is a strong and involuntary tendency to the performance of movements of a directly opposite nature, though these are of no use." (p. 28) Though this principle may be questioned, through it Darwin directed attention to an undoubted fact about emotions, namely, their tendency to occur in antithetical pairs, one member of the pair being usually associated with agreeable or pleasurable feelings, the other with unpleasant or even painful feelings. Thus we get joy and sorrow, amusement and boredom, love and hate, pride and shame, tenderness and cruelty, gratitude and envy, elation and depression, hope and despair, anger and fear, confidence and anxiety, and generally, euphoria (feeling of well-being) contrasted with dysphoria. In fact, as Katharine Banham Bridges maintains, the whole gamut of adult emotions may simply be acquired refinements of the primitive *distress* and *delight* (the pain and pleasure) of infancy. Nor should it be forgotten that Darwin's study was primarily an attempt to show that man's emotional life, equally with his bodily form, was evolutionary in its nature, that is, man's emotional equipment lay on the same line as that of animals and displayed an evolutionary development. Watson extends the list to three — *fear, rage* and *love* — and explains all others as consolidations of emotion with instincts and habits.

(*c*) *The principle of the direct action of the nervous system.* A better name for this principle is that of *overflow* or *excess action*. Perspiring during pain, trembling during terror and sheer *joie de vivre* of childhood are illustrations of this principle. We now know from the researches of Cannon and others how widespread emotional effects are, owing to the circulation of endocrine hormones and the diffuse action of the autonomic nervous system. We can assume that a facial expression, such as we find in blushing, is a vasomotor phenomenon due to a widespread autonomic disturbance.

(2) *Appearance at all ages.* Fear and anger responses appear very early in life and persist until death. A baby can be made angry by restraining his movements, and fearful by subjecting him to a sudden noise. A grown man, hemmed

in by a crowd, pushes vigorously and tends to become angry. And though naturally brave, he can be made afraid. An octogenarian may give way to fits of anger and fear, though by this time, it must be confessed, the emotional life is neither so rich nor so varied as it was earlier, say in adolescence.

(3) *Wide range and easy arousal.* Fear is normally aroused in a young child by sudden loud sounds and by insecurity of posture (falling). This emotion, however, is so easily conditioned that practically anything may excite fear in a somewhat older child. There is not just one thing that makes him afraid, but several; and the ease of arousal from various sources is often a sore trial to parents and other adults. These conditioned fears — of the dark, of animals, and the like — may be experienced at every stage of development. A child of three months may be afraid of falling, and a man of forty may be afraid of losing his job, his savings, or his loved ones. We may grow out of some fears, but we grow into many more, even if most of them are merely imaginary. But fears are ever with us. If we could imagine a brave new world in which fear of want, dependency and the like could be banished from the lives of its citizens, we should have a veritable Utopia.

(4) *Persistency.* Another characteristic of emotions is their persistence when once aroused. An angry man is usually angry for a long time; he refuses to cool down and vents his anger right and left on both the innocent and the guilty. A child sobs on his mother's breast long after he has discovered that the fearful ogre is only his older brother disguised with a mask. Cannon showed that the peristaltic movements of the intestines of a cat, frightened after eating a meal, were not resumed until the lapse of almost an hour. Even when our emotions have apparently passed, a mood usually supervenes, which we designate by the same name as the emotion. Thus an emotion of anger may subside into an angry mood which may persist for hours.

(5) *Interference with judgment.* Mark Twain, among his aphorisms in *Pudd'nhead Wilson,* included the following: "When angry count four, when very angry, swear." The first part of his dictum is certainly good advice, though difficult to put into practice. As for the second, there are obvious drawbacks to it, although a good many people un-

doubtedly use swearing as an emotional outlet. Emotions master us; they refuse to be used either for intellectual or practical ends. We do and say things under the influence of emotion, which sober reflection later declares to have been stupid and unwise. "Sleep on it" before making an important decision is wise advice, since sleep will tend to dissipate any emotion that interferes with judgment. Similarly my advice to students (which they never by any chance follow) not to get engaged under the gay lights at the ball but to wait for the cold grey dawn of the next morning, is equally sound for a similar reason. And how many motor accidents are due to the fact that the driver became emotionally flustered and could not use his habits or judgment! Yet in a calmer state he could have met the situation easily and successfully.

(6) *Easily conditioned.* Pavlov and his school have shown how easily certain reflexes can be conditioned. Watson and his school have shown that emotions can be conditioned with equal ease. As we shall deal with this and other topics relating to emotions later in the chapter, nothing further need be said at this point.

Criteria of Native Responses. — Assuming, as we have every right to assume, that native responses, whether physiological, tropic, reflex, instinctive or emotional, are built on an inherited structure and organization, what criteria can be applied to discover which of the many responses of an organism are truly unlearned? Among the criteria which have been proposed, the following occur most frequently:

(1) Appearance at birth or soon after birth without opportunity of learning.
(2) Universality — wide distribution in the animal kingdom.
(3) Related to a definite structure and a definite or determinate sensory stimulus.
(4) Stereotyped and unconscious performance.
(5) Biological utility.
(6) Full-fledged at their first appearance.
(7) Similarity within a given species.
(8) Inevitability of occurrence.
(9) Not amenable to control.

(10) Capable of becoming abnormally exaggerated without any general mental abnormality.

(11) Frequency of occurrence.

(12) Biological inheritance, especially of a mendelian nature.

While each of the above criteria has some reasonable foundation, most of them fail when put to a crucial test. Take universality, for example, which has frequently been assumed to be a valid criterion. Universality of behavior may be the result of common social contacts. Religion for Arabs and Thibetans may be such a social contact, and sufficient to account for a universality of behavior which would appear to be instinctive. Applying this criterion, a visitor from Mars might rightfully assume that newspaper reading was innate among Britishers and Americans. Universal fear of the dark is probably a conditioned reaction. Human beings are so universally apt to stumble in the dark, to experience thunderstorms at night and so forth, that fear of darkness takes on the character of an innate response. Since, however, this conditioning takes place so easily, there may be an innate maturation factor connected with it. Pugnacity seems to be lacking in negroes from the South, but is present in negroes in Harlem. The submissiveness of the southern negro may be socially conditioned and not truly innate. If the criterion be guarded by certain restrictive clauses its validity is increased. Thus Gates says: "When a trait is found universally among members of the same species, whatever their environment and training, the assumption is that it is native unless evidence to the contrary is produced." But even in this form it must still be used with caution.

A stereotyped and unconscious performance may simply be a perfected habit. Thus writing or typewriting among literate people is both stereotyped and unconscious for the most part. Oral speech is learned but is indistinguishable from an innate response if this criterion be applied. Speech and writing have hereditary bases, but so has every habit.

If the action is full-fledged at its first appearance it is regarded as instinctive. Unfortunately, no instinctive reaction is full-fledged on its first appearance. Even reflexes are subject to maturation. Pecking in chicks is instinctive, but the action gains precision and accuracy with maturation and practice.

If the action is not amenable to control it is regarded as innate. While it is difficult to run counter to nature, there is practically no innate reaction which cannot be controlled. The control of fear, caused by insecurity of position or by loud noises, is difficult to secure, but not impossible. Soldiers at the front have been known to sleep peacefully during bombardments, and rock-climbers get hardened to exposed climbing on precipitous cliffs. Man is an adaptable animal and can apparently adjust himself to most unnatural situations.

Miserliness such as that pictured in the classic *Silas Marner* or in *Riceyman Steps* may occur without any general mental abnormality, but it usually does not. Acquisitiveness is therefore regarded as instinctive. However, it would be absurd to say that any innate response could become abnormally exaggerated and the individual remain normal in other ways. Life is a unitary whole and the repercussions of an abnormal development are shown in the total personality. As a criterion, then, this one proposed by McDougall must be regarded with suspicion.

Even appearance at birth or soon after is not an infallible criterion. The reflexes at birth matured during fetal life. There is a learned element as well as an unlearned one about them. Minkowski's [9] researches seem to be conclusive on this point. He reports that certain movements which become reflex later, such as the dorsal flexion of the big toe, were observed in two fetuses in the fourth month (160-180 mm.), although there was no response to touch on the sole of the foot. Maturation undoubtedly played its part, although the innate disposition was the basic element of the reaction. Grasping is a reflex in normal, young babies, but Watson found that three or four per cent proved exceptions. This grasping reflex tended to disappear around the age of 120 days, but the grasping habit which supersedes it, is mainly a learned reaction. However, if maturation and possible pre-natal learning be taken into consideration, early appearance is an excellent criterion of an unlearned reaction.

[9] The best summary of Minkowski's work is to be found in Evelyn Dewey, *Behavior Development in Infants*, 1935.

Indeed, early appearance is the best practical criterion to use if we wish to make a list of the unlearned reactions of human beings.

Frequency of occurrence is a criterion that should receive further study. Undoubtedly, the more non-variable a form of behavior is, the more frequently it tends to recur. Physiological actions occur more frequently than reflexes, reflexes than instincts and so on, and we have seen that this is in line with the argument we used, namely, that physiological actions are less modifiable, more purely native than reflexes and instincts. We breathe more often than we blink, blink more often than we swallow, swallow more often than we eat, etc. However, we have no scientific records of the frequency of occurrence of the various responses, so, for the present this criterion must be regarded as unusable. The comparison of the frequency of responses in fraternal and identical twins would prove a useful criterion of innateness. Those in which the frequency rate tended to coincide in both types of twins, would be the unlearned responses. However, we have no studies on this subject.

What criteria, then, are valid? The following are, like Caesar's wife, above suspicion:

(1) If there is a true biological inheritance which expresses itself in the mendelian ratio, irrespective of environment, the trait may be regarded as truly innate. If, for example, as Wile maintains, left-handedness is a mendelian recessive, then handedness is instinctive. However, handedness is so socially conditioned that it is difficult to establish its mendelian inheritance. Transmission from generation to generation, when the factor of social conditioning is excluded, is a characteristic of all non-variable behavior.

(2) Allied to the above is the fact that if a response or trait can be assigned to a structural character, and to a determinate sensory stimulus, the response is either innate or has an innate basis. Birds possess wings and this structural character of birds makes it certain that flying is innate. Learned elements enter into it later, but flying as flying, is basically unlearned. If the mouth when food is placed in it, salivation is innate because we possess salivary glands. If, however, the mouth waters when we see or smell food, this act of salivation is learned. The act is con-

ditioned because the sensory stimulus is not now the natural and determinate one.

(3) If a response appears when all possible opportunities of learning have been excluded, it is innate. This is a valid criterion, providing we are sure the opportunities of learning have been excluded. But the difficulty is to be sure that they have been excluded. Generally speaking, the younger the organism, the less the opportunity for learning. Hence the criterion of appearance at birth or soon after is usually accepted. Most of us would regard the songs of birds as purely innate. These songs are similar within the species and are used by naturalists as classificatory factors. But Conradi [10] showed, as we have previously mentioned, that sparrows reared with canaries learned, somewhat hoarsely and imperfectly it is true, the canary song. That they lost it when freed to mix with other sparrows and learned the sparrow chirp, only goes to show that the inherited structure of the syrinx was sparrow-like rather than canary-like. To that extent, and to that extent only, may the sparrow be said to inherit its song.

Methods Used in Securing Lists of Unlearned Reactions. — From the foregoing discussion it will be clear that there are only two practical methods of securing lists of unlearned reactions. These are: the observation of young animals both in the fetal and early infancy stages, especially the neo-natal stage; and the study of biological structures, and their inheritance. Other methods may be useful but they are apt to lead one astray. Ball games of one form or another may be so universal that they appear to be innate. But what appears to be the truth about them is that play is innate and rounded objects are convenient to play with, hence their universal use.

The most useful place for studying innate behavior is the nursery. This genetic method was the one introduced by Darwin [11] and Preyer [12] and followed by Perez, Shinn, Watson, Blanton, Jones, Gesell and many others. At first, children were merely observed and their actions faithfully

---

[10] E. Conradi, "Song and Call-notes of English Sparrows when reared by Canaries," *Amer. Jour. Psychol.*, XVI, p. 190.

[11] Charles Darwin, "A Biographical Sketch of an Infant," *Mind*, II, 1877.

[12] Wilhelm Preyer, *The Mind of the Child* (tr. by H. W. Brown), 1890.

recorded. Later, experimental procedures or situations were introduced. Mrs. Blanton,[13] for instance, under the direction of John B. Watson, made an extensive study of infant behavior under laboratory conditions in 1917. Of the responses made within the first few weeks by all or nearly all of the infants, without opportunity for learning and therefore considered unlearned, the following are the most important:

(1) Sneezing. Full-fledged from birth.

(2) Hiccoughing. Not present at birth, but observable from seven days of age on with great ease.

(3) Crying. Present at birth and soon conditioned because it leads to the control of nurse, parents and attendants.

(4) Erection of penis. This can occur at birth and from that time on throughout life.

(5) Voiding of urine. This occurs from birth. The unconditioned stimulus is unquestionably intra-organic, due to the pressure of the fluid in the bladder. Conditioning of the act of urination can begin as early as the second week. Usually, however, conditioning at this age requires almost infinite patience. Anywhere from the third month on, the infant can be conditioned easily by a little care.

(6) Defecation. This mechanism seems to be perfect from birth; it can be conditioned from a very early age.

(7) Early eye movements. Infants from birth will slowly turn their eyes towards a faint light, but the movement is not so well co-ordinated for some time.

(8) Smiling. Appears as early as the fourth day, most often after a full feeding. It can be conditioned by the thirtieth day.

(9) Turning the head. From birth.

(10) Holding up head when the infant is held in upright position. Some new-born infants can support their heads for a few seconds. The head can be held up in most infants from the sixth month on.

(11) Hand movements. Such movements as closing and opening the hand, stretching and spreading the fingers can be observed at birth.

(12) Grasping. With few exceptions infants at birth can support their full weight with either right or left hands. It begins to disappear around the 120th day.

[13] Margaret Gray Blanton, "The Behavior of the Human Infant During the First Thirty Days of Life," *Psychol. Rev.*, XXIV, 1917.

(13) Arm movements. Arm, wrist, hand, and shoulder responses can be aroused from birth by stimulating the skin slightly anywhere, but the most pronounced reactions are brought about by holding the nose of the infant.

(14) Leg and foot movements. Kicking is one of the most pronounced movements to be seen at birth. It can be brought out by touching the soles of the feet, by stimulating with hot and cold air, but best of all by pinching the knee.

(15) Trunk, leg, foot, and toe movements. When an infant is suspending itself with either right or left hand, marked climbing movements in the trunk and hips are noticeable. Tickling the foot produces movements in the foot and toes. Stroking the sole with a match stick produces the Babinski reflex (extension of big toe, flexion of others, but toes may simply be fanned). Many infants almost from birth can turn over from face to back when placed naked, face downward, on an unyielding surface.

(16) Feeding responses. Touching the face of a hungry baby causes movement of the mouth towards sources of stimulation. Sucking and swallowing can be demonstrated within an hour of birth.

(17) Crawling. This is an indeterminate response. Mostly a habit, since many babies never crawl at all.

(18) Standing and walking. These, though of slow development, are probably innate and develop from the extensor thrust of the legs. A great deal of the act of walking, balancing, and the like is learned. It may be positively conditioned by coaching and negatively conditioned by injuries from falling.

(19) Vocal behavior. Begins with crying and babbling. These native cries become conditioned and organized into word habits.

(20) Blinking when the eye is touched is unconditioned at birth; the blink when a shadow crosses the eye is learned between 40 and 80 days. (pp. 458-483)

More recently valuable work on the unlearned reactions of fetuses has been done. In human fetuses, the observations are necessarily limited to the behavior of those born prematurely, including many too young to survive more than a few minutes or, at most, hours. The observations of mothers on the movements of their unborn children are usually too unreliable for scientific purposes. With animals, such as rats, guinea pigs and the like, the young can be artificially delivered and observed at various stages of development. This work has shown that reflexes and instincts are not born full blown, but each has a traceable history of development. An excellent account of the developmental schedules of fetal guinea pigs, rats and rabbits is given by Stone.[14] For similar material relating to the fetal development of human beings, consult an excellent summary made by Evelyn Dewey.[15]

To John B. Watson and his school we are indebted for the experimental study of unlearned behavior of human beings. The reactions singled out for study comprised: Nursing; Grasping Reflex; Right- and Left-Handedness; Defence Movements; Swimming Movement; Orientation to Light; Blinking; the Babinski Reflex; Crawling; and Positive and Negative Reaction Tendencies. The best summaries of this work are to be found in his *Psychology from the Standpoint of a Behaviorist* and in Murchison's *Psychologies of 1925.* While the earlier reactions could be regarded as pure and unlearned, the later reactions, such as blinking, reaching, handling, handedness, crawling, standing, sitting up, walking, running and jumping were so overlaid with training and conditioning (combined with maturation), that Watson concluded the concept of instincts had become unusable in psychology, and suggested the term "Activity Stream" should be substituted for James's "Stream of Consciousness." (see later)

To Watson must be given the credit of introducing experiment into the study of emotional reactions. The work has been extended by Mary C. Jones,[16] her husband, and by many others. A more careful study of emotional development has been made possible by the foundation of nursery schools, and the work of Mrs. Bridges[17] indicates the value of this method of carefully recorded observation.

The following description of the first experimental conditioning of an emotion, the famous case of Albert, is taken

---

[14] Calvin P. Stone, "Learning : I. The Factor of Maturation" in Murchison's *Handbook of General Experimental Psychology,* pp. 352-381.

[15] Evelyn Dewey, *Behavior Development in Infants,* 1935.

[16] See Mary Cover Jones, "The Conditioning of Children's Emotions," in Murchison's *Handbook of Child Psychology,* 71-93.

[17] Katharine M. Banham Bridges, *The Social and Emotional Development of the Pre-school Child,* 1931.

from Watson's account as given in the *Psychologies of 1925.* (pp. 51-54)   The original account is to be found in the *Scientific Monthly* for 1921.[18]

"We chose as our first subject Albert B, an infant weighing twenty-one pounds, at eleven months of age.   Albert was the son of one of the wet nurses in the Harriet Lane Hospital.   He had lived his whole life in the hospital.   He was a wonderfully 'good' baby. In all the months we worked with him we never saw him cry until after our experiments were made! . . .

"Our first experiment with Albert had for its object the conditioning of a fear response to a white rat.   We first showed by repeated tests that nothing but loud sounds and removal of support would bring out fear response in this child.   Everything coming within twelve inches of him was reached for and manipulated.   His reaction, however, to a loud sound was characteristic of what occurs with most children.   A steel bar about one inch in diameter and three feet long, when struck with a carpenter's hammer produced the most marked kind of reaction.

"Our laboratory notes showing the progress in establishing a conditioned emotional response are given here in full :

"*Eleven months, three days old.* — (1) White rat which he played with for weeks was suddenly taken from the basket (the usual routine) and presented to Albert.   He began to reach for the rat with left hand.   Just as his hand touched the animal the bar was struck immediately behind his head.   The infant jumped violently and fell forward burying his face in the mattress.   He did not cry, however.

"(2) Just as his right hand touched the rat the bar was again struck.   Again the infant jumped violently, fell forward and began to whimper.

"On account of his disturbed condition no further tests were made for one week.

"*Eleven months, ten days old.* — (1) Rat presented suddenly without sound.   There was steady fixation but no tendency at first to reach for it.   The rat was then placed nearer, whereupon tentative reaching movements began with the right hand.   When the rat nosed the infant's left hand, the hand was immediately withdrawn. He started to reach for the head of the animal with the forefinger of his left hand, but withdrew it suddenly before contact.   It is thus seen that the two joint stimulations given last week were not without effect.   He was tested with his blocks immediately afterwards to see

---

[18] Rosalie Rayner Watson, and John B. Watson, "Studies in Infant Psychology," *Scientific Monthly*, XIII, December, 1921, 493-513.

if they shared in the process of conditioning. He began immediately to pick them up, dropping them and pounding them, etc. In the remainder of the test the blocks were given frequently to quiet him and to test his general emotional state. They were always removed from sight when the process of conditioning was under way.

(2) Combined stimulation with rat and sound. Started, then fell over immediately to right side. No crying.

(3) Combined stimulation. Fell to right side and rested on hands with head turned from rat. No crying.

(4) Combined stimulation. Same reaction.

(5) Rat suddenly presented alone. Puckered face, whimpered, and withdrew body sharply to left.

(6) Combined stimulation. Fell over immediately to right side and began to whimper.

(7) Combined stimulation. Started violently and cried, but did not fall over.

(8) Rat alone. The instant the rat was shown the baby began to cry. Almost immediately he turned sharply to the left, fell over, raised himself on all fours and began to crawl away so rapidly that he was caught with difficulty before he reached the edge of the mattress.

"Surely this proof of the conditioned origin of a fear response puts us on a natural science ground in our study of emotional behavior."

Not only was Albert conditioned emotionally to white rats but the reaction had also spread to other objects of a furry kind as the following evidence shows:

"Before the above experiment on the rat was made, Albert had been playing for weeks with rabbits, pigeons, fur muffs, the hair of the attendants and false faces. What effect will conditioning him upon the rat have upon his response to these animals and other objects when next he sees them? To test this we made no further experiments upon him for five days. That is, during this five-day period he was not allowed to see any of these objects. At the end of the sixth day we again tested him first with the rat to see if the conditioned fear response to it had carried over. Our notes are as follows:

"*Eleven months, fifteen days old.* — (1) Tested first with blocks. He reached readily for them, playing with them as usual. This shows that there has been no general transfer to the room, table, blocks, etc.

(2) Rat alone. Whimpered immediately, withdrew right hand and turned head and trunk away.

(3) Blocks again offered. Played readily with them, smiling and gurgling.

(4) Rat alone. Leaned over to the left side as far away from the rat as possible, then fell over, getting up on all fours and scurrying away as rapidly as possible.

(5) Blocks again offered. Reached immediately for them, smiling and laughing as before.

"This shows that the conditioned response was carried over for a five-day period. Next we presented in order a rabbit, a dog, a seal-skin coat, cotton wool, human hair, and false face.

(6) Rabbit alone. A rabbit was suddenly placed on the mattress in front of him. The reaction was pronounced. Negative responses began at once. He leaned as far away from the animal as possible, whimpered, then burst into tears. When the rabbit was placed in contact with him he buried his face in the mattress, then got up on all fours and crawled away, crying as he went. This was a most convincing test.

(7) The blocks were next given to him, after an interval. He played with them as before. It was observed by four people that he played far more energetically with them than ever before. The blocks were raised high over his head and slammed down with a great deal of force.

(8) Dog alone. The dog did not produce as violent a reaction as the rabbit. The moment fixation of the eyes occurred the child shrank back and as the animal came nearer he attempted to get on all fours, but did not cry at first. As soon as the dog passed out of his range of vision he became quiet. The dog was then made to approach the infant's head (he was lying down at the moment). Albert straightened up immediately, fell over to the opposite side, and turned his head away. He then began to cry.

(9) Blocks were again presented. He began immediately to play with them.

(10) Fur coat (seal). Withdrew immediately to the left side and began to fret. Coat put close to him on the left side, he turned immediately, began to cry, and tried to crawl away on all fours.

(11) Cotton wool. The wool was presented in a paper package. At the ends the cotton was not covered by the paper. It was placed first on his feet. He kicked it away but did not touch it with his hands. When his hand was laid on the wool he immediately withdrew it, but did not show the shock that the animals or fur coat produced in him. He then began to play with the paper, avoiding contact with the wool itself. Before the hour was up, however, he had lost some of his negativism to the wool.

(12) Just in play W., who had made the experiments, put his head down to see if Albert would play with his hair. Albert was completely negative. The other two observers did the same thing. He began immediately to play with their hair. A Santa Claus mask was then brought and presented to Albert. He was again pronouncedly negative, although on all previous occasions he had played with it.

Our notes thus give a convincing proof of spread or transfer."

And so we leave Albert. He was conditioned for fear in the case of furry things at the end of the experiment and probably will be for the rest of his life unless some one unconditions him.

Equally suggestive is the first experimental unconditioning of an emotion by M. C. Jones.[19] Peter was a boy of approximately three years of age. Like Albert, he feared furry things, but these were "home grown," not produced experimentally as were Albert's. His reactions were positive towards toys, strongly negative towards furry things as the following notes on his reactions at the beginning of the experiment will indicate:

Play room and crib	Selected toys, got into crib without protest.
White ball rolled in	Picked it up and held it.
Fur rug hung over crib	Cried until it was removed.
Fur coat hung over crib	Cried until it was removed.
Cotton	Whimpered, withdrew, cried.
Hat with feathers	Cried.
Blue woolly sweater	Looked, turned away, no fear.
White toy rabbit of rough cloth	No interest, no fear.
Wooden doll	No interest, no fear.

Using a rabbit for the reconditioning experiment, since Peter's fear reactions to a rabbit were even more pronounced than to a white rat, the method first tried was social imitation to bring out an approach response by Peter. Gradually Peter's fears disappeared in the presence of non-fearful children and he became nonchalant in the presence of a rabbit. Unfortunately, at this stage of the experiment, he took scarlet fever and was sent away to a hospital. On the return

[19] Mary Cover Jones, "A Laboratory Study of Fear; the Case of Peter," *Ped. Sem.*, XXXI, 1924, pp. 308-315.

journey from the hospital, a large barking dog attacked Peter and his nurse as they were getting into a taxi-cab. Naturally, all fears of animals and furry things returned in an exaggerated form. Mrs. Jones had to adopt a new method with him. She hit upon the plan of direct unconditioning as her procedure, and of using eating as a positive stimulus and as a sign that fear was either absent or in such a mild form that it was not seriously disturbing to Peter.

"We did not have control over his meals, but we secured permission to give him his mid-afternoon lunch consisting of crackers and a glass of milk. We seated him at a small table in a high chair. The lunch was served in a room about forty feet long. Just as he began to eat his lunch, the rabbit was displayed in a wire cage of wide mesh. We displayed it on the first day *just far enough away not to disturb his eating*. This point was then marked. The next day the rabbit was brought closer and closer until disturbance was first barely noticed. This place was marked. The third and succeeding days the same routine was maintained. Finally the rabbit could be placed upon the table — then in Peter's lap. Next tolerance changed to positive reaction. Finally he would eat with one hand and play with the rabbit with the other, a proof that his *viscera were retrained along with his hands*."

The success of the method may be judged from Peter's behavior on the last day of the training period.

"Peter standing in high chair, looking out of the window. He inquired, 'Where is the rabbit?' The rabbit was put down on the chair at Peter's feet. Peter patted him, tried to pick him up, but finding the rabbit too heavy asked the experimenter to help in lifting him to the window sill, where he played with him for several minutes."

· When Peter was tested to see if his unconditioning to the rabbit had transferred to other situations, it was found that such was the case. His fear responses to cotton, the fur coat, fur rug and feathers had entirely disappeared, and he was sufficiently tolerant of the rat to carry it around the room in a tin box. But he never displayed the interest or the fondness for these things that he showed for the rabbit. To a litter of white mice and a collection of earthworms (a new stimulus for Peter), an initial hesitancy was shown followed by quick adjustment and acceptance. Undoubtedly this successful outcome should lead all who have to do with fears and personality difficulties of young children to eliminate them by using a technique similar to the one Mrs. Jones used with Peter.

The second method of securing lists of unlearned reactions — by the study of biological structures — is used only by the biologist. However (since the biologist is acquainted with the fact that function correlates with structure), on the discovery of a new structure, he immediately asks himself, "What is its function?" In this way he discovers new physiological reactions and sometimes even reflexes and instincts.

Watson's Activity Stream.— This contribution of Watson is nothing more nor less than an illustration of the fact that all unlearned reactions tend to be conditioned by the environment and to change their character. It does not refute the fact that they were originally unlearned.

Fig. 34 is a rough diagram of the activity stream. Only a few of the activities are included, and the chart is inadequate because we have not complete information about the genetic changes. As Watson says:

"In spite of these handicaps, though, try to think of a complete life chart — of the ceaseless stream of activity beginning when the egg is fertilized and ever becoming more complex as age increases. Some of the unlearned acts we perform are shortlived — they stay in the stream only a little time — such, for example, as suckling, unlearned grasping (as opposed to learned grasping and manipulation), extension of the great toe (Babinski), etc., then disappear for ever from the stream. Try to think of others beginning later in life, e.g. blinking, menstruation, ejaculation, etc., and remaining in the stream — blinking until death; menstruation until, say, 45-55 years, then disappearing; the act of ejaculation remaining on the chart of the male until the 70th-80th years or even longer.

"But try hardest of all to think of each unlearned act as becoming conditioned shortly after birth — even our respiration and circulation. Try to remember, too, that the unlearned movements of arms, hands, trunks, legs, feet and toes become organized quickly into our stabilized habits, some of which remain in the stream throughout life, others staying in only a short time and then disappearing forever." (pp. 33-34)

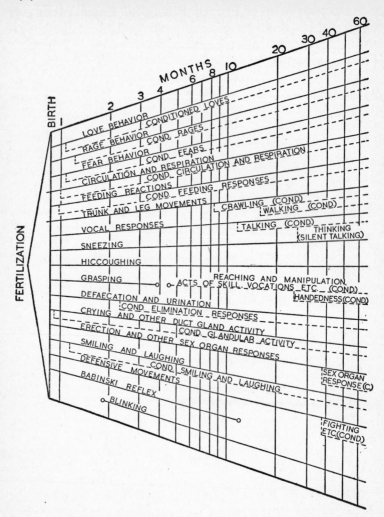

Fig. 34. The Activity Stream. Rough diagram showing increasing complexity of certain human action systems. The black solid line shows the *unlearned beginning* of each system. The dotted line shows how each system is made complex by conditioning it. (From *Psychologies of 1935,* p. 35.)

Responses with a Proven Biological Foundation.— If unlearned responses have significance for biological survival then, conversely, those responses with a known biological foundation should prove to be unlearned. The following is a list of responses with a proven foundation in biology which so far are known:

(1) Hunger
(2) Thirst
(3) Nausea
(4) Aversion from Pain; Pain Avoidance or Avoidance to Noxious Stimulation to Skin
(5) Responses to Temperature — heat and cold
(6) Excretory and Secretory Reactions
    (*a*) response to distended condition of bladder
    (*b*) response to distended condition of colon
    (*c*) maternal response of suckling young
(7) Responses of Striped Musculature
    (*a*) Activity and exercise of rested muscles
    (*b*) Fatigue: Rest or cessation of activity of exercised muscles
(8) Sleep
(9) Respiratory Responses. Desire for air as in suffocation
(10) Responses due to Sex (Sex urges or appetites)
(11) Emergency Reactions
    (*a*) Fear or Fright
    (*b*) Anger or Pugnacity
(12) Reactions to General Bodily Condition
    (*a*) Euphoric reactions (joy, elation, play)
    (*b*) Dysphoric reactions (depression, decreased bodily activity)

Each one, at least, is physiologically distinct and can be differentiated on the basis of organic tissue conditions. For this reason, they make a sound list of man's unlearned responses.

Instinct and Emotion.—When McDougall wrote his *Social Psychology* in 1908 he built upon the foundation laid a generation earlier by James and Lange. These men had pointed out the close relationship of emotions to organic and visceral changes caused by instinctive responses. The emotion, as it were, was the "back-kick" of the instinctive reaction. McDougall worked out in masterly fashion the correspondence of certain specific emotions with certain specific instincts. In his *Outline of Psychology*, the original list of eight explicitly paired instincts and emotions had expanded to fourteen as shown below:

Name of Instincts (Synonyms in Parentheses)	*Names of Emotional Qualities Accompanying the Instinctive Activities*
1. Instinct of escape (of self-preservation, of avoidance, danger instinct).	Fear (terror, fright, alarm, trepidation).
2. Instinct of combat (aggression, pugnacity).	Anger (rage, fury, annoyance, irritation, displeasure).
3. Repulsion (repugnance).	Disgust (nausea, loathing, repugnance)
4. Parental (protective).	Tender emotion (love, tenderness, tender feeling).
5. Appeal	Distress (feeling of helplessness).
6. Pairing (mating, reproduction, sexual).	Lust (sexual emotion or excitement, sometimes called love — an unfortunate and confusing usage).
7. Curiosity (inquiry, discovery, investigation).	Curiosity (feeling of mystery, of strangeness, of the unknown, wonder).
8. Submission (self-abasement).	Feeling of subjection (of inferiority, of devotion, of humility, of attachment, of submission, negative self-feeling).
9. Assertion (self-display).	Elation (feeling of superiority, of masterfulness, of pride, of domination, positive self-feeling).
10. Social or gregarious instinct.	Feeling of loneliness, of isolation, nostalgia.
11. Food-seeking (hunting).	Appetite or craving in the narrower sense (gusto).
12. Acquisition (hoarding instinct).	Feeling of ownership, of possession (protective feeling).
13. Construction.	Feeling of creativeness, of making, of productivity.
14. Laughter.	Amusement (jollity, carelessness, relaxation).

If we follow McDougall's argument blindly we are led into the impasse that the number of emotions must equal the number of instincts, which is demonstrably false. Further, careful scrutiny of the list shows that there is no proven physiological or bodily basis for some of them, and that, in any case, some have such a preponderance of learned elements in them that their instinctive origins are difficult to trace. McDougall, apparently, has sensed these objections and has substituted a list of *innate propensities* to take their place. His latest list is as follows:[20]

1. To seek (and perhaps to store) food (food-seeking propensity).
2. To reject and avoid certain noxious substances (disgust propensity).
3. To court and mate (sex propensity).
4. To flee to cover in response to violent impressions that inflict or threaten pain or injury (fear propensity).
5. To explore strange places and things (curiosity propensity).
6. To feed, protect and shelter the young (protective or parental propensity).
7. To remain in company with fellows, and, if isolated, to seek that company (gregarious propensity).
8. To domineer, to lead, to assert oneself over, or display oneself before one's fellows (self-assertive propensity).
9. To defer, to obey, to follow, to submit in the presence of others who display superior powers (submissive propensity).
10. To resent and forcibly to break down any thwarting or resistance offered to the free exercise of any other tendency (anger propensity).
11. To cry aloud for assistance when our efforts are utterly baffled (appeal propensity).
12. To construct shelters and implements (constructive propensity).
13. To acquire, possess, and defend whatever is found useful or otherwise attractive (acquisitive propensity).
14. To laugh at the defects and failures of our fellow-creatures (laughter propensity).
15. To remove, or to remove oneself from, whatever produces discomfort, as by scratching or by change of position and location (comfort propensity).
16. To lie down, rest and sleep when tired (rest or sleep propensity).
17. To wander to new scenes (migratory propensity).
18. A group of very simple propensities subserving bodily needs, such as coughing, sneezing, breathing, evacuation. (pp. 97-98)

However, it is well to remember, that even such a pronounced instinct as sex may be conditioned by the environ-

[20] William McDougall, *The Energies of Men*, 1932.

ment to an extraordinary degree. The studies of Mead,[21] Malinowski [22] and many others offer convincing evidence on this point.

The Conditioning of Reflexes. —We are indebted to the Russian school of physiologists, led by Pavlov,[23] for the inauguration of a vast amount of experimental work on the conditioning of reflexes. Pavlov's own work grew out of his studies of digestion. During these studies he noticed the "psychic" secretion of saliva and gastric juice by some of the dogs used in his experiments and determined to investigate the subject further by strictly objective methods. His final selection of the salivary reflex was a happy one, since, unlike many others such as the sex reflexes, they were available for experimentation at all times, and the strength of the reaction could be accurately measured by the amount of saliva secreted. The method finally adopted was to place the dog, suitably restrained in one chamber, while the experimenter retained control of the situation in another. By means of a slight operation on the dog, the salivary secretion was conducted to the outside of the cheek and measured. Since disturbances of any kind proved fatal to the experiments, the laboratory was specially built to isolate the animals from chance noises, sights, and other disturbing elements.

Before Pavlov's work can be judged, his technical terms must be understood. Let us take one of his simple experiments as an illustration. If a dog is given a piece of meat to eat, one of the natural responses is an increased flow of saliva from the salivary glands. If now a bell is rung every time the dog is fed, or preferably, a short time before the feeding takes place, the ringing of the bell will eventually become an adequate stimulus for salivation, so that the sound of the bell in the absence of meat will induce a flow of saliva. This connection between the receptors for sound and the effectors for salivation is not a natural one — it is a learned reaction which may be represented by the following outline:

[21] Margaret Mead, *Sex and Temperament*, 1935.
Margaret Mead, *Coming of Age in Samoa*, 1928.
[22] Bronislaw Malinowski, *Sexual Life of Savages in North Western Melanesia*, 1934.
[23] Ivan P. Pavlov (tr. by G. V. Anrep), *Conditioned Reflexes ; an Investigation of the Physiological Activity of the Cerebral Cortex*, 1927.

S$_1$ (meat)_____R$_1$ (salivation, an
                                                           original tendency).

S$_2$ (sound of bell)_____R$_2$ (investigatory response
                                                         to sound, an origi-
                                                          nal tendency).

S$_1$ + S$_2$ (presented simultaneously;____R$_3$ (salivary response).
               several trials)

S$_2$ (bell without meat)_____R$_1$ (salivation).

Diagrammatically it may be represented as follows:

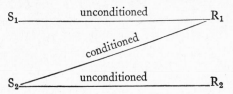

S$_1$ is called by Pavlov the *unconditioned stimulus* for R$_1$;
and R$_1$ is the *unconditioned response* for S$_1$. Similarly for
S$_2$ and R$_2$. S$_2$ is *conditioned stimulus* for R$_1$; and R$_1$ is the
conditioned response for S$_2$.

In a classic series of experiments Pavlov and his hundreds
of assistants showed:

(1) That the restraint to which the animal was subjected sometimes prevented the salivary reflex from becoming conditioned. Pavlov called it an expression of a special *freedom
reflex.*

(2) The slightest disturbance set in motion what Pavlov called
the *investigatory* or *What-is-it?* reflex, hence the necessity
for complete isolation of the animal from distracting
stimuli.

(3) Responses to sight and smell of food are conditioned, not
original.

(4) If the dog was fed before the bell was rung (or other conditioned stimulus) no conditioned reflex was formed. Hence
the rule — *If the unconditioned stimulus precedes the conditioned stimulus no new reflex is found.* This statement
was revised in his Croonian lecture. He thought, however,
that *backward* conditioning gave rise to evanescent conditioned reflexes which were easily inhibited.

(5) The stronger reflex is always conditioned, never the weaker.
That is, giving meat to a dog cannot be made into a signal
for an investigatory cocking of the ears. In the diagram R$_2$
never becomes connected with S$_1$; it is always R$_1$ with S$_2$.

(6) If the bell is rung continuously and the feeding of the dog *delayed* for some time after the commencement of the ringing of the bell, a conditioned response is established but of a peculiar kind. Suppose the dog is fed two minutes after the bell is first rung, then the conditioned salivation (without food) will start exactly two minutes after the bell begins to ring. This is called a *delayed conditioned reflex* to distinguish it from the *simultaneous conditioned reflex.* Duration in time, therefore, acts as a real physiological stimulus.

(7) Similar to the above is the *conditioned trace* or *memory* reflex. This is secured by ringing the bell and then, *after a pause,* feeding the dog. The conditioned salivation begins after an interval of time about equal to the length of the pause between the signal and the feeding.

(8) The conditioned response is anticipatory in character; it tends to precede or anticipate the situation originally giving rise to it. If feeding, say, is regularly eight seconds after bell, conditioned salivation begins after awhile at one or two seconds after the bell.

(9) If a neutral signal (say a black square) is used in conjunction with a well-established conditioned response (say to a bell), a *secondary conditioned reflex* can be established, although the black square by itself has no power to evoke salivation. In some cases a tertiary reflex can be formed, but three is the limit for dogs.

(10) Injection of morphine produces nausea and salivation in a dog. Even the approach of an experimenter with a hypodermic needle may be the conditioned stimulus for these reactions. This shows that the experimenter may prove to be a conditioning stimulus.

(11) The sudden *stoppage* of the sounding of a tuning fork may be used as a signal for a conditioned reflex. The gradual stoppage produces no conditioned reaction. Hence sudden differences in the stimulus are essential to the formation of conditioned reactions.

(12) *In general, any response which is under the control of the central nervous system can be conditioned by any stimulus which acts on an adequate receptor apparatus of an organism.* However, each stimulus is specific for the special conditioned reflex. A conditioned reflex aroused by one stimulus (sound) is not aroused by another (thermal). Even the pitch of a sound is specific since the reaction is not produced by a markedly lower or higher tone.

(13) Conditioned reflexes may be inhibited. Thus if a distracting stimulus is given either during or just before the exhibition of a conditioned reflex, the conditioned response becomes weaker or disappears. The stronger this extra stimulus, the greater is its inhibitory effect, but the effect is usually only temporary and on repetition of the extra stimulus its inhibitory effect becomes smaller. In other words, accommodation occurs; the organism "gets used to" the stimulus.

(14) Conditioned reflexes may be extinguished by applying a conditioned stimulus several times in succession without the accompaniment of the unconditioned stimulus (bell without meat). The shorter the interval between the abortive ringings of the bell, the quicker the extinction.

(15) Such an extinguished reflex regenerates spontaneously but slowly by a rest of a few hours. If the unconditioned stimulus is applied (meat), the conditioned reflex returns to normal almost immediately.

(16) The conditioned reflex resulting from two simultaneous conditioned stimuli is more powerful than when one is used. Thus bell (sound) *plus* ice to chest (thermal) results in a greater amount of conditioned salivation. This *summation of stimuli* also leads to a quicker experimental extinction than either one of them. (Bell *plus* ice, without meat). The extinction is specific, that is, the extinction of a conditioned reaction for a particular stimulus has no effect upon the strength of other conditioned reflexes.

(17) The rate of learning and the strength of conditioned reflexes of a dog are dependent upon its internal organic state — hunger, thirst, state of fatigue, glandular secretions, etc.

(18) Strong emotional reactions which delay the formation of conditioned responses are called out by very strong conditioned stimuli (e.g. by extremely loud sounds). Similarly, a general excitability or neurotic state is produced by trying to establish very fine discriminations to conditioned stimuli, e.g. to sounds of nearly equal pitch. Other reactions and inhibitions become seriously disturbed.

Pavlov's explanation of these phenomena is a fairly simple one. According to him there are relatively few native reflexes — self-defence, investigatory reactions and the like, which are necessary for the self-maintenance of the animal in its normal environment. These become conditioned in literally thousands of ways by various *signalling stimuli* (conditioned). In the process of conditioning, the cortex and the mid-brain play an important part. *Unnatural* or *learned* connections, such as we find in conditioning, are formed in the brain, some of them fairly permanently, so that it is literally true to say that, through integrations in the brain, any receptor may become connected to any effector.

There is thus the temptation to link up conditioning with associative shifting as a theory of learning. However, Thorndike [24] points out that conditioning doesn't quite fit into the reaction-hypothesis theory as developed by him and his assistants. According to him, the chief differences between associative shifting and conditioned (Thorndike thinks conditional is a better translation of the Russian term) reflexes are the following:

1. In associative shifting R_1 belongs to S_2; in a conditioned reflex R_1 does not necessarily belong to S_2.
2. In associative learnings, the time relations of R_1 and R_2 are not so important; in the formation of conditioned reflexes time relations are imperative.
3. In associative shifting, the attachment of S_2 and R_1 is slow unless rewarded; in conditioned learning very few presentations are necessary.
4. In associative learning, the change from S_1 and S_2 is a gradual affair (a bit of S_2, as it were, is added at a time); in conditioned reflexes the change is made abruptly.
5. The one essential condition of associative learning is the rewarding of correct responses; in conditioning, reward is used inadvertently, if at all. Punishment is frequent.
6. Associative connections can be formed in any reasonably undistracting environment; not so in conditioning; special sound-proof rooms and the absence of the experimenter are necessary.
7. In associative shifting different R's can be connected with different S's; in conditioned reflexes the connection S_2—R_1 is specific.
8. Associative learnings are strengthened by repetition and reward; in conditioned learnings, repetition at short intervals kills it off.
9. Lapse of time causes associative shiftings to weaken; conditioned reflexes regain their original strength.

[24] Edward Lee Thorndike, *Fundamentals of Learning*, 1932.

10. Loss of one associative connection does not necessarily weaken others; extinction of one conditioned reflex tends to extinguish others. (pp. 401-412)

From his experiments on the conditioning of human subjects as well as dogs, Hilgard [25] is inclined to discount conditioning as a theory of learning and to think of it as a substitute stimulus. He says:

"Conditioned response facts derive from conditioning experiments. A conditioning experiment is one in which there occurs an alteration in response tendencies in respect to a (conditioned) stimulus by virtue of its repeated presentation in a controlled relationship with another (unconditioned) stimulus which with relative regularity evokes a response from the beginning of the experiment.

"Theories revolving about conditioning fall into two types: (1) those which attempt to explain conditioning facts, and (2) those which attempt to deduce other types of behavior, such as familiar forms of learning, from the facts of conditioning. The first type may be called theories of conditioning, the second, theories of learning (or of other behavior) based on conditioning.

"Systemization of the facts within experiments presupposes a logical procedure. Some writers have utilized as a guiding principle the notion of stimulus-substitution, while others, especially critics, have attempted to view the facts organismically. This paper is concerned with the attempt to organize the facts around the stimulus-substitution formula.

"The substitute-stimulus conception of conditioning is given support by many of the descriptive facts of conditioning, some of which have been supposed to contradict it. On the other hand, conditioned responses possessing a configuration differing widely from the unconditioned responses on which they are based, are not predictable in terms of stimulus substitution. The dynamics of the conditioning process require either the abandonment of the simple formula, or its supplementation with other concepts which will account for descriptive differences in the responses; for the fact that succession of stimuli is more favorable than simultaneity; and for the tendency towards extinction of conditioned responses when not reinforced." (pp. 383-384)

Hilgard, Campbell, Marquis and others, are gradually accumulating a mass of facts which show that conditioned

[25] E. R. Hilgard, "The Nature of the Conditioned Response: I. The Case for and against Stimulus Substitution," *Psychol. Rev.*, XLIII, 4, 1936.

learnings obey the same laws as other forms of somatic learning with respect to such factors as acquisition, extinction, retention and so forth. However, somatic conditioning and visceral conditioning seem to follow different lines in their development, and it may be that the acquisition of motor skills is a form of somatic conditioning. The conditioned reflex, when viewed as a new response which develops in the particular situation in which double stimulations are presented, mostly follows the line of ordinary learning and forgetting.

Hull's [26] masterly summary of the subject shows the progress that has been made since Pavlov first broke new ground. He outlines the work in the following fields: conditioning of (1) reflex wink in dogs and men; (2) knee-jerk; (3) plantar reflex; (4) abdominal reflex; (5) Achilles reflex; (6) reflex withdrawal from painful stimulus in dogs and men; (7) pupillary reflex; (8) pulse; (9) galvanic skin reactions; (10) pitch of voice; (11) breathing; (12) food-taking reactions of newborn infants; (13) fetal kicking reaction; (14) food-taking reactions of children from 3 to 6 years of age; (15) gastric secretion; (16) salivation in human beings; (17) vomiting; (18) defecation and urination; and (19) diuresis. The stimuli which have been conditioned include sounds, visual stimuli, tactual stimuli, thermal stimuli, etc.

One of the most remarkable conditioning experiments was carried out by Hudgins [27] in 1933. "By an ingenious experimental arrangement," says Hull (p. 417), "Hudgins was able to condition the proprioceptive stimuli arising from the subject's own vocal apparatus in such a way as to evoke the hitherto non-voluntary constriction of the iris when the subject whispered certain words, and even when he merely spoke them to himself subvocally, or 'thought' them. This experiment is of considerable significance because it probably lays bare the essential mechanism of what has been known to the classical psychologists as voluntary action, or will. This latter interpretation is perhaps strengthened by the fact that,

[26] Clark L. Hull, "Learning. II. The Factor of the Conditioned Reflex," in Murchison's *Handbook of General Experimental Psychology*, 1934.

[27] C. V. Hudgins, "Conditioning and the Voluntary Control of the Pupillary Light Reflex." *Jour. Gen. Psychol.*, VIII, 1, 1933.

according to Hudgins, reactions conditioned to such stimuli appear to be relatively immune to experimental extinction, one of the most conspicuous characteristics differentiating voluntary reactions from ordinary conditioned reflexes." Perhaps we should withhold judgment, since the work has been criticized adversely by Steckle and Renshaw.[28] It should, however, be repeated under varied conditions.

Razran [29] (1933) published a summary of Russian studies from laboratories other than Pavlov's: — Krasnogorski's, Chuchmarev's, Lenz's, Ivanov-Smolensky's and Bekterev's. Yet, notwithstanding this wide range of studies, the part that conditioning plays in human development is still uncertain.   Hull thinks conditioning is nothing more than a special case of association by contiguity, which principle has been recognized since the time of Plato and Aristotle. (p. 382) The chief thing to bear in mind is the anticipatory nature of the conditioned response. Animals which fled *before* they were injured would have a greater chance of survival than those which responded *after* they were hurt. The anticipatory nature of man's higher life reactions is regarded as a sign of his intelligence. For immediate practical purposes, the possibility of conditioning and unconditioning emotions seems to be the most important application of results from studies in this field.

For those who are interested in the subject the summaries listed in the footnote,[30] in addition to those of Pavlov, Hull and Razran mentioned above, may be consulted.

The History of the Study of Emotions. — In comparatively recent times the elucidation of the problem of the emotions has been attempted from many angles.   Charles Darwin, in characteristic fashion as we have seen, attacked the problem from the strictly objective point of view. His treatise entitled *On the Expression of Emotions in Man and*

---

[28] L. C. Steckle and S. Renshaw, "An Investigation of the Conditioned Iridic Reflex," *J. Gen. Psychol.*, XI, 1934.

[29] Gregory H. S. Razran, "Conditioned Responses in Children ; a Behavioral and Quantitative Critical Review of Experimental Studies," *Archives of Psychol.*, 148, 1933.

[30] H. Cason, "The Conditioned Reflex or Conditioned Response as a Common Activity of Living Organisms," *Psychol. Bull.*, XXII, 1925.   H. S. Liddell, "The Conditioned Reflex," in Moss's *Comparative Psychology*, 1934.   Ernest R. Hilgard, "The Relationship between the Conditioned Response and Conventional Learning Experiments," *Psychol. Bull.*, XXXIV, 1937.

Animals (1872) was the successor of numerous previous studies[31] on physiognomy and emotions, but it differed from all earlier work on the subject in that the emotional expressions of man and animals were linked together on an evolutionary scale.

A *second* line of inquiry was opened up by the observations of James and Lange in 1884 and 1885 respectively. From their speculations, which were very similar in character (except that James emphasized the rôle of viscera, while Lange was impressed by the vaso-motor reactions), grew up a theory of emotions to which both their names are attached — the *James-Lange Theory of Emotions.* This theory (and the modifications introduced by Sergi) consists essentially of the claim that the stimulus which is the exciting cause of the emotion acts first on the nervous center ruling the viscera (or the blood vessels), and their reactions then generate visceral (or vaso-motor) sensations which, in turn, induce the psychical state known as the emotion. The matter will become clearer if we introduce a few excerpts from the explanation given by James.[32]

"Our natural way of thinking about these coarser emotions is that the mental perception of some fact excites the mental affection called the emotion, and that this latter state of mind gives rise to the bodily expression. My theory, on the contrary, is that *the bodily changes follow directly the perception of the existing fact, and that our feeling of the same changes as they occur* is the emotion. Common sense says, we lose our fortune, are sorry and weep; we meet a bear, are frightened and run; we are insulted by a rival, are angry and strike. The hypothesis here to be defended says that this order of sequence is incorrect, that the one mental state is not immediately induced by the other, that the bodily manifestations must first be interposed between, and that the more rational statement is that we feel sorry because we cry, angry because we strike, afraid because we tremble, and not that we cry, strike, or tremble, because we are sorry, angry, or fearful, as the case may be. . . . *Every one of the bodily changes, whatsoever it be, is* felt, *acutely or obscurely, the moment it occurs.* If the reader has never paid any attention to this

---

[31] J. K. Lavater, *Physiognomische Fragmente zur Beförderung der Menschenkenntniss und Menschenliebe,* 3 vols., 1783–87.   Charles Bell, *Anatomy and Philosophy of Expression,* 1806.   Herbert Spencer, "Physiology of Laughter," in *Essays, Scientific, Political, and Speculative,* Second Series, 1863.

[32] William James, *Principles of Psychology,* Vol. II, 1890.

matter, he will be both interested and astonished to learn how many different local bodily feelings he can detect in himself as characteristic of his various emotional moods. . . . *If we fancy some strong emotion, and then try to abstract from our consciousness of it all the feelings of its bodily symptoms, we find we have nothing left behind,* no 'mind-stuff' out of which the emotion can be constituted, and that a cold and neutral state of intellectual perception is all that remains. . . . If I were to become corporeally anaesthetic I should be excluded from the life of the affections, harsh and tender alike, and drag out an existence of merely cognitive or intellectual form." (pp. 449ff)

According to this theory the order of events is: (1) perception of object; (2) instinctive action leading to organic disturbances; (3) the experience of the emotion. Ordinary common sense reverses the order of (2) and (3) and says, for instance, that we feel fear and then jump out of the way of a large oncoming object.

The arguments for and against the theory are as follows:

For the theory. (1) The well-known close connection between certain instincts and emotions (*vide* McDougall).

(2) Every bodily change arising out of instinctive or other unlearned movements "is felt, acutely or obscurely, the moment it occurs."

(3) If the organic sensations or instinctive movements are taken away from an emotion nothing is left. "If we fancy some strong emotion, and then try to abstract from our consciousness of it all the feelings of its bodily symptoms, we find we have nothing left behind, no 'mind stuff' out of which the emotion can be constituted, and that a cold and neutral state of intellectual perception is all that remains." (James)

(4) If we put ourselves in certain bodily attitudes, says James, we tend to experience corresponding emotions. If we bare our teeth, clench our fists, open wide our eyes and throw the body forward, it is almost impossible not to feel angry. In the same way, if we kneel with clasped hands, bowed head and closed eyes, it is practically impossible not to experience "religious" emotions.

(5) A questionnaire sent around by William Archer to various famous actors, elicited the information that about half of them experienced real emotions while acting on the stage. Henry Irving's tears were real, not crocodile tears

and the same could be said for Ellen Terry. Coquelin maintained that acting was fooling the audience and he fooled them by simulated emotions. Sarah Bernhardt's emotions while on the stage were also of the pseudo-kind. Is this difference a national characteristic?

Against the theory. (1) The time factor is a serious one, for the length of the nerve tract to be covered is great in the case of the James-Lange theory. The emotion is the "backstroke" of the action. When we experience fear we do not appear to "start" before we feel the emotion. The two things seem to occur simultaneously. On the other hand, if we can remain calm and refrain from starting we do not feel fear.

(2) It is not every organic sensation that excites an emotion. The feeling-tone of a hot bath is great and delicious, but one would hardly call it an emotion. The emotion is aroused when we interfere with the bodily desires and welfare of organisms.

(3) The theory does not take into account the previous disposition of the subject. In some states, the least disturbance makes us angry or annoyed; in joyous moods nothing that happens can upset our equanimity.

(4) The theory does not account for what Thorndike has called pseudo-emotions. While in the "movie" we may weep at the sorrows of the heroine on the screen, our sorrow is different from the overwhelming grief caused by a real happening; we know the thing is make-believe and rather enjoy our surreptitious tears.

(5) Sherrington[33] made combined spinal and vago-sympathetic nerve sections in dogs in such a manner as to remove completely and immediately the sensation of the viscera and of all the skin and muscles behind the shoulder. At the same time the procedure cuts from connection with the organs of consciousness the whole of the circulatory apparatus of the body. Reporting the case of a bitch of markedly emotional temperament he states:

"The reduction of the field of sensation in this animal by the procedure above mentioned produced no obvious diminution of her emotional character. Her anger, her joy, her disgust, and when provocation arose, her fear, remained as evident as ever. Her joy at the

[33] Charles S. Sherrington, *The Integrative Action of the Nervous System,* 1906.

approach or notice of the attendant, her rage at the intrusion of a cat with which she was unfriendly remained as active and thorough. But among the signs expressive of rage the bristling of the coat along the back no longer occurred." (p. 261)

While the experiment is not a crucial one it does seem to point to the fact "that the visceral expression of the emotion is secondary to the cerebral action occurring with the psychical state."

(6) Cannon[34] removed the entire sympathetic nervous system of cats and kept them in a healthy state for many months afterwards. During this time the emotional responses of the animals were but slightly, if at all, affected.

(7) The viscera are both insensitive and sluggish and the changes in them are too slow to be a source of emotional feeling as the James-Lange theory implies.

(8) Artificial induction of visceral changes, by injection of adrenalin, does not produce emotions, although, in some case, it seems to change the affective state of the individual.

(9) The proof by Bard, Bekterev and others that the seat of the emotions is subcortical, lying in a restricted area of the posterior diencephalon and in the ventral part of this region, is seemingly crucial. This places emotions beyond cortical control, although the somatic manifestations of emotions may be so controlled. We may keep a poker-face while we are boiling inside.

From the above we may gather that the James-Lange theory, to say the least, is somewhat discredited. Its fatal weakness is that it regards emotions as a complex of bodily sensations. Emotion always involves the expression of feeling; it is never merely the reception of impressions, but is always a response to them. These responses, controlled in the sub-cortical thalamic region, consist in the alteration of respiration, secretion, and circulation on the one hand, and the bracing or relaxation of various voluntary muscles on the other. These voluntary muscles may with training be brought under control, but it is practically impossible to condition the visceral and other reactions which are controlled by the autonomic nervous system.

[34] Cannon, Lewis and Britton, *Boston Medical and Surgical Journal*, CXCVII, 1927.

The *third* line of investigation of the emotions is from the side of endocrinology. In Chapter III we reviewed briefly Cannon's work on adrenalin and its connection with the emotions of fear and anger, so we need not go into it again. The endocrinologists tell us that our bodies (in the blood stream) contain a delicate balance of hormones, some of which incite muscles and glands to action while others inhibit them. Functionally, they have, therefore, the same action as the autonomic nervous system, and hence the glands and viscera are under both a secretion and nervous control. If the endocrine balance of the body is disturbed then the intellectual and especially the emotional life is upset.

The *fourth* type of work developed out of Cannon's work on adrenalin. Cannon, Bard and the Harvard school of physiologists sought to discover the center in the brain which controlled the autonomic nervous system and, therefore, the emotions. As we shall see later, they finally discovered it in the *hypothalamus* of the inter-brain.

A *fifth* line of investigation centers in psychoanalysis and psychotherapy. Prior to the World War, Freud, Jung, Adler and others of the psychoanalytic school, had shown that emotional disturbances were not so hopelessly irrational as they seemed, and that with proper methods and infinite patience the problems they presented could be unraveled. Freud undoubtedly over-emphasized the part that sex plays in emotional disturbances. Similarly Jung's introversion and extraversion and Adler's superiority and inferiority have been pushed beyond the limits of scientific justification. As far as Freud was concerned, the War redressed the balance, for it was found that fear rather than sex was the more potent in creating psychoneurosis.

The *sixth* method, as we have seen, centers in Watson and his school. They use a combined genetic and experimental approach. Watson, by genetic observation of infants, especially during the first months of life, could discover only three emotional reactions which indubitably were innate. These were fear, rage, love (using love in approximately the same sense that Freud uses sex). Fear was aroused by removal of support, by sudden loud sounds, and occasionally, when the infant was just falling asleep or was just ready to waken, by a sudden push or slight shake, or by suddenly pulling the blanket upon which the baby was lying. Rage was evoked by hampering the child's movements in any way whatsoever. Love responses were stimulated by stroking or manipulation of some erogenous zone, or by tickling, shaking, gentle rocking, patting, and turning the infant upon its stomach across the attendant's knee. All other experiments — with rabbits, darkness, cats, dogs, animals at the zoo — failed to elicit emotional responses.

The experimental conditioning and unconditioning of emotions has been mentioned. The process of unconditioning inaugurated by Mrs. Jones is exceedingly promising.

In the *seventh* line of study must be grouped a somewhat heterogeneous collection of recent experimental methods of studying emotions. In it must be included (*a*) the attempts to measure emotions and personality factors by means of paper tests. Unfortunately most of these tests have little validity or reliability, but progress is being made; (*b*) the study of emotions by means of facial expression; (*c*) the changes of the psychogalvanic reflex during emotions, as well as the changes in the rate of breathing, heart-beat, blood-volume in various parts of the body, and so forth. These are the bodily concomitants or accompaniments of emotion and are very difficult to hide, hence their use as "lie-detectors" in cases of crime. Some of these methods are described in greater detail in a subsequent section of this chapter.

The Nervous System and Emotions. — In previous discussions we have indicated: (*a*) the close association of the autonomic nervous system and emotional responses; and (*b*) the similarity between the responses due to adrenalin and those initiated by the sympathetic branch of the autonomic nervous system. The question can now be asked — has the central nervous system any direct control of emotional responses? The answer to this has been secured by extirpation of various parts of the brain of dogs and cats, and by the study of the emotional reactions of human beings who had suffered injuries to the brain. Since the evidence cannot be understood without a knowledge of the technical terms used to describe the various parts of the brain, these will now be given.

The brains of the higher vertebrates are invariably composed of the following five parts:

(1) the *myelencephalon* or *medulla oblongata.*

(2) the *metencephalon* or hind-brain, the part from which the medulla oblongata is developed. It is roofed over by the cerebellum. The *cerebellum* is supported by pillars which thicken ventrally forming a protuberance known as the *pons varolii.*

(3) the *mesencephalon* or mid-brain. The dorsal wall of the mid-brain is divided longitudinally by a furrow into two *optic lobes,* and again transversely, thus making four bodies which are known as the *corpora quadrigemina.*

(4) the *diencephalon* or inter-brain, the lateral walls of which form the *optic thalami.* The optic tracts as they enter the inter-brain form a cross known as the optic chiasma. Technically the diencephalon is divided into the *thalamus, epithalamus* and *hypothalamus.*

(5) the *telencephalon* or fore-brain or end-brain. In the higher animals this part is greatly enlarged and constitutes the bulk of the brain. It consists chiefly of the cerebral hemispheres, which are connected with the rest of the brain (*via* the thalamus) by the *corpus striatum.* The hemispheres are connected laterally by bands of commissural fibers, the chief of which is the *corpus callosum.* The cerebrum is usually regarded as consisting genetically of two parts — the *archipallium* which is concerned with olfactory and possibly, gustatory functions; and the *neo-pallium,* that part of the brain which is concerned with visual, auditory and general body sensations, with voluntary actions and with all the complex mental life. The neo-pallium divides its labor and we get a certain amount of localization of function.

What is the result of extirpation of various parts of the brain, in serial order, on the behavior, emotional or otherwise, of the animal? The following are the facts:

(*a*) If the whole of the five parts are excised, the experimental animal, if it lives at all, will be capable of a few protective reactions to pain, of digestive and excretory reflexes and of little else. Nothing in the way of emotional response can be elicited. A spinal animal cannot exhibit emotion.

(*b*) If the brain is cut above the medulla leaving the myelencephalon intact, the animal can breathe rhythmically, walk haltingly, vomit, cough, etc., but its reactions, although more intense than those of the spinal animal, are still insufficiently coordinated or intensely executed to be regarded as emotional.

(*c*) Remove the upper three parts leaving the myelencephalon and metencephalon intact and we get an animal that can respond to food, maintain a bodily posture, and, in general, exhibit fairly extensive integrations.

(*d*) Remove the diencephalon and telencephalon by sectioning the brain above mid-brain and many responses survive. The experimental animal can co-ordinate its eye-movements, vocalize (bark, mew), etc. Such an animal, a decerebrate cat for instance, is more given to mewing, clawing, violent kicking, but the behavior patterns are only pseudo-emotional. They never rise to the level of effective action of attack or escape.

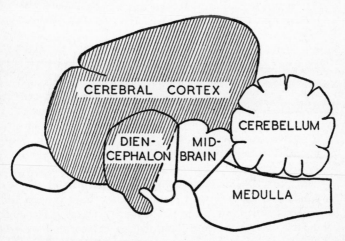

CEREBRAL CORTEX

CEREBELLUM

DIEN-CEPHALON

MID-BRAIN

MEDULLA

Fig. 35. Diagram of the Mid-section of the Cat Brain. The parts distinguished by slanting lines can be wholly removed without destroying the rage-response. (Bard.)

(*e*) Remove the telencephalon, leaving all the diencephalon and all lower structures intact, and we get the characteristic emotional responses of sham rage. A cat, minus its cerebral hemispheres, growls, spits, erects its tail hairs, and profusely sweats through its toe-pads. The pupils dilate and the adrenalin content of the blood is increased. The blood sugar, in consequence of the adrenalin, may be increased to five times the normal amount. The experiment points to the diencephalon or inter-brain as the seat of the emotions. Bard carried the experiment a little further. He carefully removed the whole of the fore-brain (telencephalon) and then successively removed various sections of the diencephalon (see Fig. 35). So long as he left the hypothalamus intact, rage-responses could be evoked, but if this part were removed, they disappeared. Therefore, if any part of the brain can be regarded as "the seat of the emotions," it is the hypothalamus. It should be noted that the emotional responses in these experimental animals are exaggerated; the cortex, when present, obviously exerts a restraining influence. It should also be noted that Bekterev found that if he gently stroked the hypothalamus of such an experimental animal he could get purring (from a cat) and friendly responses (from a dog), but if he were rough in his stimulations he got growlings from both animals.

This evidence, which is fairly conclusive for animals, is supplemented by evidence from human beings whose cortex has been injured in some way or other. The insane, for instance, are given to violent display of emotions. The injuries to the cells of the cortex in the insane prevent them from inhibiting or restraining the actions of the lower and older centers. The insane, therefore, exhibit the phenomenon of "released" behavior. Secondly, under the partial influence of anaesthetics, such as ether, chloroform, nitrous oxide (laughing gas), and alcohol, the subject frequently displays a secondary stage of excitement in which the emotional reactions are pronounced. The subject may weep, groan, sing, babble, laugh or show signs of violent anger. This again may be explained by the fact that the anaesthetic first puts the cortex out of commission and frees the lower emotional centers from its control. Later its action spreads to all parts of the brain. The anaesthetic, therefore, functionally decorticates the subject for a while. Thirdly, some injuries to the brain paralyze the muscles on one side of the face, but when an emotional situation arises the whole face may express sadness or gaiety. This can only be explained on the supposition that the paralyzed muscles are under the non-voluntary control of a lower (emotional) center, although voluntary control from the cortex has been lost. Emotional paralysis cannot be caused by a cortical lesion. Fourthly, a few cases have been recorded of the destruction of the thalamus by disease without any injury to the cortex. Such patients retain voluntary control of the muscles of the face but remain "poker-faced" as they laugh in fun or weep in sorrow. This can best be explained by the hypothesis of a subthalamic center which controls the emotions.

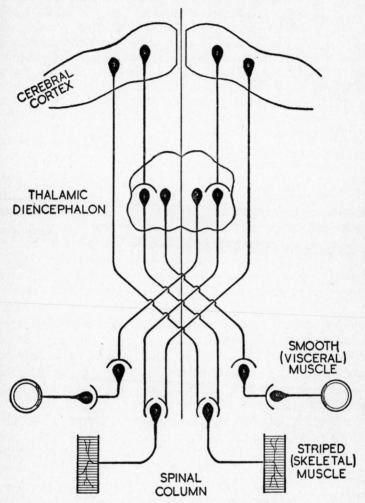

Fig. 36. Diagram showing the Phylogenetic Relations of the Thalamus and Cortex. The cortex can control muscular movements during emotion, but not visceral reactions. (After Cannon.)

If the above evidence is sound, then an emotion is the series of reactions and feeling-tones which operate whenever the thalamic processes are aroused. These reactions are partly under the control of the cortex. The voluntary muscles, for example, may be controlled during emotion, but the reactions controlled by the autonomic system can still take place since this system is controlled by the thalamus, not by the cortex. This partial control of emotional expression by the cortex is shown in Fig. 36.

Theories of Emotion. — From the foregoing discussion it will be seen that there are many theories of emotion, but all of them fall within one or other of four categories, namely :

(1) The classical theory of emotions.
(2) The peripheral theory associated with the names of James, Lange and Sergi.
(3) The central theory, propounded by Ladd and Woodworth.
(4) The phylogenetic theory built up by such workers as Crile, Allport, Cannon, Bard, and given its fullest expression by Ruckmick.

Of the *classical theory* or common-sense view of emotions little need be said. Emotions were the gifts of the gods or of nature to man. The natural view was that we see a large oncoming animal or vehicle, are frightened and jump out of the way ; we lose a loved one and are sorry and weep ; we are insulted by a rival and are angry and strike. The emotion arises out of a perception, and because of this emotion we do things.

The *James-Lange-Sergi theory* reversed the order of the action and the emotion. We first jump out of the way and then feel the emotion ; we are sorry because we cry ; we are angry because we strike. And even if nobody quite believes in the theory, its ghost will not be laid. And chiefly because it brings the viscera and circulatory system into the picture. Anybody who is even half-observant can see that the viscera and the circulatory system are intimately involved in emotion.

The *central theory* of emotion as enunciated by Ladd and Woodworth [35] attributes emotion, not to any particular happening in the external environment, but to a semi-chaotic surplus of energy within the nervous system itself. The following extract gives their point of view:

[35] George Trumbull Ladd and Robert Sessions Woodworth, *Elements of Physiological Psychology*, 1911.

"A not unreasonable conjecture as to the central conditions on which the excitement of the more complex forms of emotion are dependent, would state the case in somewhat the following way: It is a well-known fact that different individuals differ more widely and incalculably as to the particular feelings evoked, on different particular occasions, than as to the sensations and ideas occasioned by changes in the amounts, kinds, and time-rates of the stimuli which act upon the peripheral nervous system. This fact suggests that our feelings are determined by the changeable relations of the neural processes to the constitution, previous habits and temporary mood of the nervous system, and by the relations of each neural process to all the others within the central system, in a more irregular way than are our sensations and our knowledge. Those conditions of the nervous processes which depend immediately upon the quality, intensity, and time-rate of the stimuli that act upon the end-organs of sense, are in general conformable to law; they are regular and — as it were — to be depended upon. In correspondence with them are the regularity and the dependableness of our sensations and of our knowledge by the senses. But over and above the more uniformly recurrent similar elements in all the peripherally originated nervous processes, there is more or less of a 'semi-chaotic surplus' of nervous action occasioned in the brain centers. In this semi-chaotic surplus — the general character of which depends upon what the whole nervous system was, and is, and has recently been doing, and upon how the various new stimulations, running in to the brain centers, fit in with all this and with one another — may we find the physiological conditions of the emotions. No wonder, then, that these conditions are so indeterminate for different individuals, and so changeable in the same individual. At any particular moment the kind and amount of feeling experienced has for its physiological condition the total complex relation in which all the subordinate neural processes, set up by the stimuli of that moment, stand to one another and to the set, or direction of pre-existing related neural processes." (pp 522-523)

The theory that increasingly holds the allegiance of psychologists is the *phylogenetic theory of emotions*. It is one that has gradually grown out of experimentation, and although its clearest statement has been made by Ruckmick,[36] it owes its development to many workers. Crile[37] emphasized the fact that man's chief activities must center in (1) self-defence against enemies or escape from them, that is, man must either fight or run away; (2) the acquisition of

---

[36] Christian A. Ruckmick, *The Psychology of Feeling and Emotion*, 1936.
[37] George W. Crile, *The Origin and Nature of the Emotions*, 1915.

food; and (3) procreation. These groups of activities have gradually evolved through the process of natural selection. If an animal is well protected against attack, flight with its intense emotional accompaniments seldom occurs. It is difficult to scare a skunk, porcupine, armadillo or lion into precipitate flight. But rabbits, deer and mice are ever ready for flight; their continued existence depends on their quick response to danger signals. In man, emotions result from a thwarting of these primitive responses to stimulations. As Crile states:

"When our progenitors came in contact with any exciting element in their environment, action ensued then and there. There was much action — little restraint or emotion. Civilized man is really in auto-captivity. He is subjected to innumerable stimulations, but custom and convention frequently prevent physical action. When these stimulations are sufficiently strong but no action ensues, the reaction constitutes an emotion. A phylogenetic fight is anger; a phylogenetic flight is fear; a phylogenetic copulation is sexual love, and so one finds in this conception an underlying principle which may be the key to an understanding of the emotions and of certain diseases." (p. 76)

Cannon carried the argument still further. He showed experimentally that an animal in a state of fear or anger increased its output of adrenalin and glycogen and transferred blood from visceral to skeletal muscles; its circulation and respiration were accelerated, its blood became more coagulable; and its body temperature tended to rise with the altered metabolism. Hence, during strong emotion, the body was made ready for violent action — either for fighting or for running away. These actions are designed to meet emergencies, hence his emergency theory of emotions.

Allport[38] suggested that emotions can be distinguished on the basis of their pleasantness and unpleasantness, the parasympathetic innervations producing the conscious qualities of pleasantness; the sympathetic producing visceral responses represented in consciousness by unpleasantness. (pp. 90-92) There is a great deal of evidence, neurological and otherwise, in support of this view, but it has never been definitely established by experiment.

[38] F. H. Allport, *Social Psychology*, 1924.

Bard's work, outlined previously, shows that the earlier and lower centers of the brain are concerned with the basic responses which keep the animal alive in an elemental manner. One of these centers, the hypothalamus of the diencephalon, is definitely concerned with primitive emotional responses. With the evolution of the cortex, some control over the lower centers was established. Just as the governor of the engine prevents it from running away by shutting off the steam, so the cortex controls all the lower parts of the nervous system. If the integrity of the cortex be destroyed these lower centers run amuck. Hence the continuous exhibition of sham rage in a decorticate cat or dog, and the intense emotional reactions of an individual whose cortex has been put out of commission by drugs or injury. Further, in the evolution of the brain, the higher centers evolved after the lower ones were established. Latest to evolve was the cortex and this part of the brain is not only concerned with consciousness and the control of the voluntary muscles but also acts as a warden to all the lower centers. To do this, it must know what is happening, hence each lower center is not only connected to the periphery below, but also to the cortex above. In anger, for instance, the action of the thalamus not only affects the autonomic nervous system, and through this system the muscles and glands, but also the cortex. The cortex, in turn, partially controls the action of muscles, and, what is more important, *makes us aware of the emotion.* To the observer, the *action* is the emotion; to the subject the *cortical awareness* is the emotion. In this sense, then, the decorticate cat which exhibits sham rage is "unaware" that it is angry and, therefore, isn't angry at all. A human being in such a condition certainly would be unaware of his emotions, but to the outside observer, he would be violently angry.

The above is, therefore, a brief summary of the phylogenetic view of emotion. Objectively, the emotion is the reaction occasioned by action within the thalamus; subjectively, it is the feeling-tone aroused by the projection of the thalamic disturbance upwards to the cortex. Those who emphasize the feeling-tone of emotions think of them subjectively; those who stress the importance of the bodily reactions have the objective point of view. Both are right, but it is only the bodily reactions of emotions that can be built up into a science of emotions.

Experimental Studies of Emotional Expression.— Since it is impossible to experiment with the feeling-tones of emotion, the scientific work on emotion has been concentrated in five types of study. These are:

(1) Studies of facial expression and vocalization.
(2) Studies of changes in blood pressure, blood volume, and rate of heart beat.
(3) Studies of changes in respiration.
(4) Studies of secretions of glands, chiefly the endocrine glands.
(5) Studies of electrical changes of the skin, the psychogalvanic reflex.
(6) Studies of spontaneous movements.

Curiously enough, the *facial expression* of emotion is a very unreliable index of emotions. Darwin's elaborate treatise boils down to the simple fact that his descriptions are generalized and may be sadly inaccurate for individual cases. The same holds true for physiognomy, which is a pseudo-science, despite our reliance upon it in the selection of employees. Miss Feleky [39] posed for several hundred photographs registering emotions and affective states. From these, 86 photographs with a list of emotions were submitted to 100 judges. No reliability could be placed on the judgments, although surprise, wonder and astonishment, laughter, disgust, and contempt received votes ranging from about 30 to 50 per cent.

Langfeld,[40] in his first study, used 105 of the best portrait drawings in Rudolph's *Der Ausdruck des Menschen* and submitted them to four men and two women, who were afterwards told the original names given to the depicted emotions. Of a total of 525 judgments, only one-third were correct. Hate was frequently misjudged as anger, and anger as distress. The percentages of right responses were — for laughter, 64; pain, 50; disgust, 36; fear, 36; anger, 30.

In a second study, Langfeld [41] proved that part of the dif-

[39] A. M. Feleky, "The Expression of the Emotions," *Psychol. Rev.*, XXI, 1914.
[40] H. S. Langfeld, "The Judgment of Emotions from Facial Expressions," *Jour. Abnorm. Psychol.*, XIII, 1918–19.
[41] H. S. Langfeld, "Judgments of Facial Expression and Suggestion," *Psychol. Rev.*, XXV, 1918.

ficulty was due to the suggestibility of the observers. The poorest observer, for example, accepted 65 per cent of the wrong titles to the portraits which were shown to him.

Ruckmick[42] used 31 photographs of a talented amateur actress and submitted them to observers. As in previous studies, joyful laughter and bodily pain were rather consistently reported; the secondary emotions of repulsiveness, surprise, distrust and defiance, weren't. The fluidity of the vocabulary of emotions led to many inconsistencies in the naming of the pictured emotion.

Landis[43] has carried out a series of experimental studies, in two of which the subject was subjected to a controlled situation likely to arouse emotion. Photographs (still and moving) of the subjects were taken as (*a*) they decapitated a live rat; (*b*) saw colored pictures of loathsome diseases; (*c*) listened to jazz; (*d*) touched a live frog unexpectedly; and so forth. On analyzing the photographs it was seen that all the subjects (twelve men and twelve women) tended to use one set of muscles for the expression of all forms of emotion and to exclude others; that is, to have a characteristic expression for all emotional situations. Where the men tended to show anger and profanity, the women cried and pleaded, but the reactions of the men were distinctly more violent than those of the women.

Using 77 photographs from his collection, Landis found that observers could not judge what emotions they were supposed to represent by greater accuracy than chance would give.

Similar results are obtained from the use of demonstrational models of the human face, such as Boring and Titchener devised, and from the Frois-Wittman group of 46 photographs. Sherman[44] also showed that doctors and nurses could not judge correctly the pictures of babies obtained in the following situations — hunger, dropping, restraint and pain, unless they knew the situation which created the ex-

[42] C. A. Ruckmick, "A Preliminary Study of the Emotions," *Psychol. Monogs.*, XXX, 3, 1921.

[43] Carney Landis, "Studies of Emotional Reactions. II. General Behavior and Facial Expression," *Jour. Comp. Psychol.*, IV, 1924. Carney Landis, "The Interpretation of Facial Expression in Emotion," *Jour. Gen. Psychol.*, II, 1929.

[44] Mandel Sherman, "The Differentiation of Emotional Responses in Infants," I and II, *J. Comp. Psychol.*, VII, 1928.

pression. From all of which we may conclude that naming emotions from photographs is very much of a guessing game; that the vocabulary of emotional terms is far too rich; that we have conventional ideas regarding the way that emotions are expressed; that judging emotions is an acquired power and increases in accuracy with age and experience; and that the situation is always important in helping us to judge the emotion. In other words we judge a baby to be crying from pain if we see it pricked, but not otherwise with any degree of certainty.

With regard to vocalization during emotion, few studies have been made. Philologists tell us that language itself probably developed out of emotional cries, which may be older, phylogenetically, than facial expressions. It is impossible for most people to distinguish between an infant's cry of pain and of hunger. Seashore has shown somewhat conclusively that the *vibrato* of the voice is the chief emotional element in song.

Blood Volume, Blood Pressure, and Rate of Heart Beat. Changes in blood volume are recorded by a *plethysmograph.* The finger, hand or other bodily member is immersed in a rigid vessel filled with water from which leads a small tube connected with a recording instrument. Records of the subject during a normal state are first taken. The subject is then aroused emotionally and the changes in blood volume recorded. Blood pressure is measured by a *sphygmomanometer.* This consists of an air-tight cuff which is fastened around the upper arm and a pump for increasing air pressure within the cuff. This air pressure is recorded either by a mercury column or a dial gauge. Air is pumped into the cuff well above the point where oscillations of the dial gauge are discernible, and then slowly released until the regular fluctuations definitely reappear. This reading gives the systolic blood-pressure (maximum). Air is released until these regular fluctuations disappear and at this stage the reading of the gauge gives the diastolic or pulse pressure. The *rate of the heart-beat* is best obtained from automatic tracings of the fluctuations of the pulse.

The type of experiment in this field is well illustrated by

Blatz's [45] research on fear. The subjects were placed in a collapsible chair. After their normal records were taken, the chair was suddenly tilted backwards. The reactions of the subjects were extremely vigorous. Blatz found (1) an immediate acceleration of the heart-beat (from 88 to 102 per minute for 5 seconds), followed by a marked retardation with a more prolonged but less marked acceleration leading later to a gradual retardation over a final long period; (2) an increase in the ventricular contraction which, though very gradually diminishing, lasted in some cases for as long as six minutes; (3) an irregularity in the cardiac periodicity. After repeated performance, some of the subjects (twelve out of eighteen) began to show an adaptive effect, but when unexpected repetition occurred no adaptive effect was noticed. In these situations the systolic blood pressure showed a sharp rise but soon fell to its original level.

The lie-detector is essentially an instrument (sphygmomanometer, pneumograph, galvanometer) for recording changes during the course of an examination in which awkward and leading questions are asked, in the emotional tensions of a subject suspected of lying or deceit. The theory underlying the device is that, although the voluntary muscles can be controlled by the cortex, the viscera and circulatory system governed by the autonomic nervous system can not.

Marston [46] claims that a subject who is lying, or trying to shield friends, or deceive the experimenter, increases his systolic blood pressure by 8 mm. to 12 mm. While other workers have not confirmed Marston's findings, Larson [47] thought the method could be used successfully as a mild variety of the "third degree" in prisons and police courts.

Respiratory Changes undoubtedly take place during emotional disturbance, but the amount of change is not proportional to the strength of the emotion. Moreover, there are no patterns of change which can be used to differentiate one emotion from another. Blatz found that if his subjects were "tipped" during expiration, the wave was changed to inspira-

[45] William E. Blatz, "The Cardiac, Respiratory, and Electrical Phenomena Involved in the Emotion of Fear," *Jour. Exper. Psychol.*, VIII, 1925.

[46] W. M. Marston, "Systolic Blood Pressure Symptoms of Deception," *Jour. Exper. Psychol.*, II, 1917.

[47] J. A. Larson, "The Cardio-Pneumo-Psychogram in Deception," *Jour. Exper. Psychol.*, VI, 1923.

tion, but if it occurred during inspiration no change could be noted.

The connection of *emotion disturbances with glandular secretions* is well known. The tears of the young, the inhibition of salivary secretion during emotional upset (the tongue cleaves to the roof of the mouth), the secretion of sweat glands during anger, fear and pain, etc., are so well known that they only need passing mention. But Cannon's discovery of the increased activity of the adrenal gland and the resultant effects on the organism during anger and fear, placed the subject on another plane. Some of the best work on changes in personality has developed out of Cannon's pioneering work.

The *psychogalvanic reflex* is a phenomenon connected with the electrical resistance of the skin. It is probably associated with the amount of sweat on the surface of the body and, therefore, with thermal control exercised by the autonomic nervous system. During emotional disturbance the amount of sweat secreted varies and this leads to an increase or decrease of resistance which may be recorded by a galvanometer. Since, however, other mental and bodily states may change the electrical resistance of the skin, the method is not a reliable measure of emotional change. However, thalamic and autonomic changes are undoubtedly the most potent in changing this so-called reflex, and to this extent, it may be regarded as an expression of emotion that is non-specific in character.

A new field of study has been opened up by Luria[48] through his method of investigating *spontaneous movements* of subjects laboring under emotional stress. He combined language response with motor reactions of the hand. The description of his method is as follows:

"The subject is seated in a comfortable arm chair in front of a table. . . The right hand lies on the table so that the finger tips can be used to compress the pneumatic bulb; the left hand during the experiment holds also an analogous apparatus.

"In our routine experiment there is given a word stimulus, to which the subject must answer by another word, and simultaneously

[48] A. R. Luria, *The Nature of Human Conflicts: or Emotion, Conflict and Will; an Objective Study of Disorganization and Control of Human Behavior*, 1932.

he presses with the fingers of the right hand the pneumatic bulb, connected with a recording drum, while the left hand remains passive,
holding the weight without producing any movement. The moment
of stimulation is registered by closing an electrical key by the experimenter, and the instant of the response, by means of a sensitive membrane which is operated by the subject's voice. . .

"The (active) hand rests on the bulb, the left (passive) remains
on the weight. The latter is thus held, in order to make its position
less stable; hence it can be used as a sensitive indicator of the neurodynamic excitation by a general overflow of tremor. This is registered on the drum at the same time as the pressure of the right
hand. . . In the usual experiment, the kymograph ordinarily
turns with the speed of one centimeter per second. We obtained in
this way, a record simultaneously of three very important lines as
shown in Fig. 37 overleaf.

"Besides these three curves, representing the intellectual process,
and the active and passive motor response, there is sometimes added
a fourth curve to record the respiration and pulse, as part of the
cycle of symptoms which arises from the vegetative system. In this
manner we are able to see the reciprocal evidences of the entire system, the changes in which enable us to investigate the structure induced by our neurodynamic disturbance."

The arrangement is thus a lie-detector, which combines
Jung's word-association technique with involuntary tremors
of the (left) hand, and changes in rate of respiration or pulse.
Used with murderers, it seems to have had a fair measure of
success; used with psychopathic and other abnormal cases, it
seems to have shed light upon some of their troubles. As a
corollary of his findings Luria (discussing the problem of
will) states the fundamental law: "direct attempts to control
behavior always lead to negative results; its mastery is
achieved only by indirect means." (p. 403) The method
is sufficiently interesting to merit further experiments with it.

Emotional Levels and Outlets. — It is somewhat unfortunate that Cannon [49] has used the term "emotional level" to
describe the thalamic region in which emotions are controlled.
The more usual use of the term is in describing the more or
less permanent emotional levels or attitudes of individuals
in contrast to their more or less temporary or evanescent

[49] Walter B. Cannon, "The Significance of the Emotional Level," *Scientific
Monthly*, February, 1934.

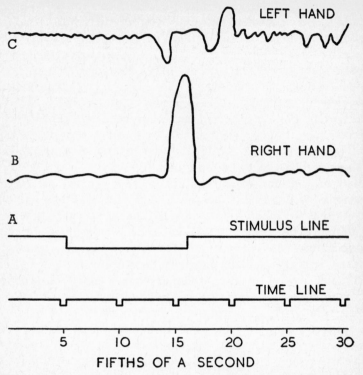

Fig. 37. Luria's Method of combining Jung's Word-association Technique with Voluntary and Non-voluntary Movements of the Hands.

A = the line of speech reaction, the time being in fifths of a second.

B = the curve of the active right hand, which in most experiments is smooth in the latent period, giving a regular rise associated with the speech reaction.

C = the curve of the passive left hand fluctuating with the tremor. (Luria)

moods. We speak of persons being high-strung or stolid. The high-strung seem to be highly emotional, in the sense that their emotions are easily and quickly aroused. Persons of artistic temperament seem to live on a higher emotional plane than ordinary and more bucolic mortals. In the young, also, tears and laughter seem ever to lie just beneath the surface; they certainly have not secured cortical control of their voluntary muscles. Those people, whom we describe as full of energy (pep), likewise seem to live at higher emotional levels than others. The stolid, on the other hand, are unemotional and placid; it almost needs an earthquake to upset them. Between these extremes we recognize the normal — those who can be roused, but whose emotional responses are usually under fair control. These emotional attitudes, these permanent emotional sets of individuals, are probably dependent upon the endocrine balances of the body, but little is known about them that has scientific validity.

Society does not permit an indiscriminate expression of emotions. Young children are permitted a certain amount of quarreling and fighting, but if a grown man allows his pugnacity free play, he soon finds himself in a court of law. But this does not mean that the emotion is never present in adults, or if present, finds no outlet. On the contrary, we condition our emotions in a host of ways. We sublimate our pugnacity by "fighting for peace," for reformers are frequently the most pugnacious of persons. We also find outlets. If a man is made angry by his employer, his wife and children are apt to suffer when he returns home. The coffin containing a loved one may be smothered with flowers to assuage the grief. Swearing is a common emotional outlet for an angry man. In fact, some emotional outlet seems to be necessary for everyone. Certainly those in whom emotions are too tightly bottled tend to become psychopathic.

If emotional outlets are necessary and desirable, society should provide socially acceptable ones. In school, the fields of art, music and literature are desirable outlets, since each of these has an emotional basis. "Cheering the team" is also of profound sociological significance beside providing a safety valve for emotions. Athletics which tire the body are also useful, since there is no further energy left for the expression of emotions. And Crile [50] is right, when he emphasizes the fact that emotions entail a stupendous expenditure of energy, comparable with the expenditure of energy in intense muscular activity. Raup,[51] reviewing Crile's contribution, states:

"The development of civilization has removed the need for these muscular expressions of fear, flight, fighting, etc., in a large measure, yet they persist. Moreover, when the brain, the thyroid, the adrenals, and the liver are activated by the distance stimulus which gives rise to the emotion, and then the action is inhibited, the presence of

[50] G. W. Crile, *Man, an Adaptive Mechanism,* 1916.
[51] R. B. Raup, *Complacency : the Foundation of Human Behavior,* 1925.

these impulses and secretions in the relatively inactive system is practically certain to prove injurious. In other words, the activation provided for does not take place adequately for the relieving of the created tensions. . .

"The fact then that emotions are great spenders of energy, that they throw the organism into strains that must be released through some kind of action, and that the release and the return to equilibrium are the satisfying elements in all such behavior, would tend to put it beyond doubt that the strong annoyances are off-equilibrium conditions and that strong satisfactions are toward-and-on conditions." (pp. 85-86)

While the topic "emotions, their arousal and control," is one of the least known in the psychological field, genetic psychologists and mental hygienists are making great strides in its scientific elucidation. Take, for example, such a study as Jersild and Holmes's *Children's Fears* (1935) and compare it with Hall's *A Study of Fears* published in 1897 (a classic in the field) and the progress shown is enormous. We may not agree altogether with the authors' conclusions, but we cannot refrain from admiring the care they exercised in controlling the experimental situation. Such studies as this, which is symptomatic of the wide interest in the development of children of pre-school age, will, in course of time, undoubtedly change many current methods of child management, not only in the home, but in the school as well.

REFERENCES

Allport, F. H. *Social Psychology.* New York, Houghton Mifflin Co., 1924. Pp. xiv + 453.

Angell, J. R. "A Reconsideration of James's Theory of Emotions in the Light of Recent Criticisms." *Psychol. Rev.*, XXIII, 1916, pp. 259-261.

Baldwin & Stecher. *The Psychology of the Pre-School Child.* New York, Appleton, 1925. Pp. 305.

Bernard, L. L. *Instinct: a Study in Social Psychology.* New York, Holt, 1924. Pp. ix + 550.

Bills, A. G. *General Experimental Psychology.* New York, Longmans Green, 1934. Pp. x + 620.

Blanton, Margaret C. "The Behavior of the Human Infant During the First Thirty Days of Life." *Psychol. Rev.*, XXIV, 1917, pp. 458-483.

Blatz, W. E. "The Cardiac, Respiratory and Electrical Phenomena Involved in the Emotion of Fear." *Jour. Exper. Psychol.*, VIII, 1925, pp. 109-132.

Bridges, J. W. *Psychology: Normal and Abnormal.* New York, Appleton-Century, 1930. Pp. xxii + 552.

Bridges, Katherine M. B. *The Social and Emotional Development of the Pre-School Child.* London, Kegan Paul, 1931. Pp. x + 277.

Cannon, W. B. *Bodily Changes in Pain, Hunger, Fear and Rage.* (Rev. Ed.) New York, Appleton-Century, 1936. Pp. xvi + 404.

Cannon, W. B. "The Significance of the Emotional Level," *Scientific Monthly*, 1934, pp. 101-110.

Cason, H. "The Conditioned Reflex or Conditioned Response as a Common Activity of Living Organisms." *Psychol. Bull.* XXII, 1925, pp. 445-472.

Child, C. M. *Physiological Foundations of Behavior.* New York, Holt, 1924. Pp. xii + 330.

Creed, Denny-Brown, Eccles, Liddell & Sherrington. *Reflex Activity of the Spinal Cord.* Oxford, Clarendon Press, 1932. Pp. vi + 183.

Crile, G. W. *Man, an Adaptive Mechanism.* New York, Macmillan, 1916. Pp. xvi + 387.

Crile, G. W. *The Origin and Nature of the Emotions.* Philadelphia, Saunders, 1915. Pp. vii + 240.

Curti, Margaret W. *Child Psychology.* New York, Longmans Green, 1933. Pp. ix + 527.

Darwin, C. "A Biographical Sketch of an Infant." *Mind*, II, 1877, pp. 285-294.

Darwin, C. *The Expression of the Emotions in Man and Animals.* London, Murray, 1872. Pp. vi + 374.

Dewey, Evelyn. *Behavior Development in Infants; a Survey of the Literature on Prenatal and Postnatal Activity, 1920–34.* New York, Columbia University Press, 1935. Pp. viii + 321.

Dorcus & Shaffer. *Textbook of Abnormal Psychology.* Baltimore, Williams & Wilkins, 1935. Pp. xiii + 389.

Dunlap, K. *Elements of Psychology.* St. Louis, Mosby, 1936. Pp. 499.

Fearing, F. *Reflex Action: a Study in the History of Physiological Psychology.* Baltimore, Williams & Wilkins, 1930. Pp. xiii + 350.

Feleky, Anne M. "The Expression of the Emotions." *Psychol. Rev.* XXI, 1914, pp. 33-41.

Garrett, H. E. *Great Experiments in Psychology.* New York, Century, 1930. Pp. xvii + 337.

Gates, A. I. *Psychology for Students of Education* (Rev. Ed.). New York, Macmillan, 1930. Pp. xv + 612.

Gesell, A. *The Mental Growth of the Pre-School Child.* New York, Macmillan, 1925. Pp. x + 447.

Goodenough, Florence L. *Developmental Psychology: an Introduction to the Study of Human Behavior.* New York, Appleton-Century, 1934. Pp. xvii + 619.

Herrick, C. J. *Neurological Foundations of Animal Behavior.* New York, Holt, 1924. Pp. xii + 334.

Hilgard, E. R. "The Nature of the Conditioned Response: I. The Case for and against Stimulus Substitution." *Psychol. Rev.*, XLIII, 4, 1936, pp. 366-385.

Hilgard, E. R. "The Relationship between the Conditioned Response and Conventional Learning Experiments." *Psychol. Bull.*, XXXIV, 2, 1937, pp. 61-102.

Hilgard & Campbell. "The Course of Acquisition and Retention of Conditioned Eyelid Responses in Man." *Jour. Exper. Psychol.*, XIX, 2, 1936, pp. 227-247.

Hilgard & Marquis. "Acquisition, Extinction and Retention of Conditioned Lid Responses to Light in Dogs." *Jour. Comp. Psychol.*, XIX, 1935, pp. 29-57.

Holmes, S. J. "Forms of Animal Behavior" in Robinson and Robinson, *Readings in General Psychology*. Chicago University Press, 1923, pp. 79-87.

Holmes, S. J. "A Tentative Classification of the Forms of Animal Behavior." *Jour. Comp. Psychol.*, II, 1922, pp. 173-186.

Holt, E. B. *Animal Drive and the Learning Process*. New York, Holt, 1931. Pp. vii + 307.

Hudgins, C. V. "Conditioning and the Voluntary Control of the Pupillary Light Reflex." *Jour. Gen. Psychol.*, VIII, 1, 1933, pp. 3-51.

Jersild and Holmes. *Children's Fears*. New York, Teachers College, Bureau of Publications, 1935. Pp. xv + 356.

Jones, Mary C. "A Laboratory Study of Fear: the Case of Peter." *Ped. Sem.*, XXXI, 1924, pp. 308-315.

Jordan, A. M. *Educational Psychology* (Rev. Ed.). New York, Holt, 1933. Pp. xvii + 522.

Klein, D. B. *General Psychology*. New York, Holt, 1936. Pp. xiv + 560.

Ladd & Woodworth. *Elements of Physiological Psychology*. New York, Scribners, 1911. Pp. xix + 704.

Landis, C. "Studies of Emotional Reactions. II. General Behavior and Facial Expression." *Jour. Comp. Psychol.*, IV, 1924, pp. 447-509.

Landis, C. "The Interpretation of Facial Expression in Emotion." *Jour. Gen. Psychol.*, II, 1929, pp. 59-71.

Lange and James. *The Emotions. (Vol. I, Psychol. Classics.)* Baltimore, Williams and Wilkins, 1922. Pp. 135.

Langfeld, H. S. "The Judgment of Emotions from Facial Expression." *Jour. Abnorm. Psychol.*, XIII, 1918-19, pp. 172-184.

Langfeld, H. S. "Judgments of Facial Expression and Suggestion." *Psychol. Rev.*, XXV, 1918, pp. 488-494.

LaPiere and Farnsworth. *Social Psychology*. New York, McGraw-Hill, 1936. Pp. xii + 504.

Larson, J. A. "The Cardio-Pneumo-Psychogram in Deception." *Jour. Exper. Psychol.*, VI, 1934, pp. 420-454.

Liddell, H. S. "The Conditioned Reflex" in Moss's *Comparative Psychology*, 1934, pp. 247-296.

Loeb, J. *Tropisms, Forced Movement, and Animal Conduct*. Philadelphia, Lippincott, 1918.

Luria, A. R. *The Nature of Human Conflicts: or Emotions, Conflict and Will*. New York, Liveright, 1932. Pp. xvii + 431.

McDougall, W. *The Energies of Men; Fundamentals of Dynamic Psychology.* London, Methuen, 1932. Pp. ix + 395.

McDougall, W. *An Introduction to Social Psychology.* London, Methuen, 1922. Pp. xxiv + 459.

McDougall, W. *Outline of Psychology.* New York, Scribners, 1923. Pp. xvi + 456.

Malinowski, B. *Crime and Custom in Savage Society.* New York, Harcourt Brace, 1926.

Marston, W. M. "Systolic Blood Pressure Symptoms of Deception." *Jour. Exper. Psychol.,* II, 1917, pp. 117-163.

Mead, Margaret. *Sex and Temperament.* New York, Morrow, 1935. Pp. 335.

Mead, Margaret. *Coming of Age in Samoa.* New York, Morrow, 1928. Pp. xv + 297.

Morgan, C. L. *Habit and Instinct.* London, Arnold, 1896. Pp. 351.

Murchison, C. (Ed.) *A Handbook of Child Psychology.* Worcester, Clark University Press, 1931. Pp. xii + 711.

Murchison, C. (Ed.) *A Handbook of General Experimental Psychology.* Worcester, Clark University Press, 1934. Pp. xii + 1125.

Murchison, C. (Ed.) *A Handbook of Social Psychology.* Worcester, Clark University Press, 1935. Pp. xii + 1195.

Murchison, C. (Ed.) *Psychologies of 1925.* Worcester, Clark University Press, 1928. Pp. xiii + 412.

Murphy, G. *General Psychology.* New York, Harper, 1933. Pp. x + 657.

Pavlov, I. P. *Conditioned Reflexes: an Investigation of the Physiological Activity of the Cerebral Cortex.* Oxford University Press, 1927. Pp. xv + 427.

Preyer, W. *The Mind of the Child.* 2 vols. New York, Appleton, 1888 and 1889. Pp. xxv + 346; xli + 317.

Razran, G. H. S. "Conditioned Responses in Children; a Behavioral and Quantitative Critical Review of Experimental Studies." *Archives of Psychol.,* 148, 1933, pp. 120.

Reymert, M. L. (Ed.) *Feelings and Emotions: the Wittenberg Symposium.* Worcester, Clark University Press, 1928. Pp. xvi + 446.

Ruckmick, C. A. "A Preliminary Study of the Emotions." *Psychol. Monogs.,* XXX, 3, 1921, pp. 30-35.

Ruckmick, C. A. *The Psychology of Feeling and Emotion.* New York, McGraw-Hill, 1936. Pp. xii + 529.

Russell, E. S. *The Behavior of Animals: an Introduction to its Study.* London, Arnold, 1934. Pp. vii + 184.

Sherman, M. "The Differentiation of Emotional Responses in Infants; I. Judgments of Emotional Responses from Motion Picture Views and from Actual Observations." *Jour. Comp. Psychol.,* VII, 1927, pp. 265-284.

Sherrington, C. S. *The Integrative Action of the Nervous System.* New Haven, Yale University Press, 1923. Pp. xvi + 411.

Skinner, C. E. *Readings in Educational Psychology.* New York, Farrar & Rinehart, 1937. Pp. 630.

Smith and Guthrie. *General Psychology in Terms of Behavior.* New York, Appleton, 1930. Pp. xii + 270.

Steckle and Renshaw. "An Investigation of the Conditioned Iridic Reflex." *Jour. Gen. Psychol.*, XI, 1934, pp. 3-23.

Stone, C. P. "Learning: I. The Factor of Maturation" in Murchison's *Handbook of General Experimental Psychology*, pp. 352-381.

Stratton, G. M. *Anger: its Religious and Moral Significance.* London, Allen and Unwin, 1924. Pp. x + 277.

Thorndike, E. L. *Educational Psychology, Vol. I. The Original Nature of Man.* New York, Teachers College, Bureau of Publications, 1921. Pp. xii + 327.

Thouless, R. H. *Social Psychology.* London, University Tutorial Press, 1932. Pp. vii + 376.

Troland, L. T. *The Fundamentals of Human Motivation.* New York, Van Nostrand, 1928. Pp. xiv + 521.

Trow, W. C. *Educational Psychology.* Boston, Houghton Mifflin, 1931. Pp. xv + 504.

Warren & Carmichael. *Elements of Human Psychology.* Boston, Houghton Mifflin, 1930. Pp. viii + 462.

Warren, H. C. (Ed.) *Dictionary of Psychology.* Boston, Houghton Mifflin, 1934. Pp. x + 372.

Watson & Rayner. "Studies in Infant Psychology." *Scientific Monthly*, XIII, 1921, pp. 493-515.

Watson, J. B. *Behaviorism.* (Rev. Ed.) New York, Norton, 1930. Pp. xi + 308.

Watson, J. B. *Psychology from the Standpoint of a Behaviorist.* (Rev. Ed.) Philadelphia, Lippincott, 1929. Pp. xvii + 458.

Young, K. *Social Psychology: An Analysis of Social Behavior.* New York, Crofts, 1935. Pp. xvii + xxi + 680.

Young, P. T. *Motivation of Behavior: the Fundamental Determinants of Human and Animal Activity.* New York, Wiley, 1936. Pp. xviii + 562.

CHAPTER V

INTELLIGENCE: ITS NATURE AND MEASUREMENT

Intelligence is Innate. — Studies of heredity show that intelligence is innate, that it actually has its basis in the genes. A baby, however, is not as intelligent as an adult. Maturity and learning play their parts in the development of intelligence. There is thus the customary tangle of hereditary and environmental factors in any exhibition of intelligence. Some workers tend to emphasize the hereditary element; some to stress the influence of the marvelously fluid environment. But that some people are born potentially stupid, some potentially clever, no serious student of the subject now doubts. That men in general are more intelligent than chimpanzees, chimpanzees than dogs, dogs than rats, rats than frogs, and frogs than fishes is also universally conceded. That some children are literally born idiots, and nothing that we can do in the way of education and training will raise them to normal mentality, is no longer open to question. That others are born geniuses and that these, given half a chance, will inevitably reach higher mental levels than their fellows is generally recognized. Even the fact that some animals, such as chimpanzees, rats and dogs are born cleverer than others of the same species is common knowledge. What is not generally known is that the matings from an intelligent strain of rats conserve the intelligence, whereas crossings from a stupid strain conserve the stupidity. Intelligence, apparently, is an heritable factor in all animals, including man.

But what has confused the issue and has resulted in such spirited controversies as that between Bagley and Lippmann on the one hand and Terman and Whipple on the other, is the fact that intelligence must be manifested in behavior before it can be judged.[1] An intelligent person does intelligent things; a stupid person stupid things. Unless we saw them behaving, we could not tell a genius from a moron. Matu-

---

[1] See especially W. C. Bagley, *Determinism in Education*, 1925, and the articles in *School and Society*, XVI, 1922, on April 8, June 3, and August 5.

ration and training must first play their parts with native talents before they can be recognized. Hence the paradox that *achievement is the test of potentiality;* that the capacity to learn is judged, and can only be judged, from the amount that one has actually learned and from the ease with which the learning was assimilated. Intelligence undoubtedly has its origins in hereditary equipment, but it needs a proper environment to bring it to fruition. The final levels of attainment of individuals differ even when the opportunities of training have been made as nearly equal as possible, and these differences must be attributed to variations in native equipment. If this view is not held, then we are forced to conclude that given sufficient time and favorable opportunity everybody could rise to the heights of a Newton, Darwin or Shakespeare, which, as Euclid says, is absurd. If environment alone is sufficient to create intelligence, then teachers are greatly to blame for failing to add to the intelligence of the majority of their pupils. There are literally thousands of people in institutions for the care of the feebleminded in Canada. If environments can be created which will make these children normal, then, in the name of charity, tell us how it is done. These children are a burden to the community. If the burden can be lifted, then let us, by all means, lift it immediately. What is true, of course, is that the most rabid environmentalist will not guarantee to turn a feebleminded person into a normal one. It simply can't be done. The only view of the subject that fits the facts is that intelligence is a native trait. By a favorable environment the highest developments of native talents may be approached; a less favorable one will result in lower levels being reached. In no sphere is the correlative nature of heredity and environment seen so clearly as in that of intelligence.

Intelligence Develops Precociously. — The world is full of stories of the precocity of genius. So invariable is this early budding of intelligence that we may be sure that if a child has not shown marked evidences of intelligence before he is ten years of age, he will never show it. This belief has been put to the test. Catherine Cox[2] collected the early writings and other materials of three hundred of the world's greatest

[2] Catherine M. Cox, *Genetic Studies of Genius, Vol. II: The Early Mental Traits of Three Hundred Geniuses,* 1926.

geniuses. These "records alone, inadequate as they are, warrant an average I.Q. rating between 135 and 145 for the entire group, while a correction of the error in the estimates results in scores that indicate a true average for the group at a point not lower than 155 to 165 I.Q." In the selected list which follows, AI I.Q. represents a rating of behavior and performance in childhood; AII I.Q. a rating in the first period of young manhood.

Name	AI I.Q.	AII I.Q.
Jean de La Fontaine	100	125
John Bunyan	105	120
Miguel de Cervantes	105	110
Nicholas Copernicus	105	130
Michael Faraday	105	150
Robert Lord Clive	110	120
Oliver Cromwell	110	115
George Fox	110	120
John Hunter	110	130
Raphael Sanzio	110	150
Rembrandt H. Van Rijn	110	135
Hernando Cortez	115	120
Oliver Goldsmith	115	115
Martin Luther	115	145
John Adams	120	145
Giuseppe Garibaldi	120	125
William Harvey	120	120
Franz Joseph Haydn	120	140
Ben Jonson	120	145
Antoine Laurent Lavoisier	120	150
John Churchill, first Duke of Marlborough	120	125
Joseph Addison	125	140
Johann Sebastian Bach	125	140
Simon Bolivar	125	135
John Dryden	125	130
Justus Liebig	125	165
Abraham Lincoln	125	140
Carolus Linnaeus	125	145
John Locke	125	135
John Napier	125	125
Horatio Nelson	125	145
Diego Rodriguez de Silva y Velasquez	125	140

Name	AI I.Q.	AII I.Q.
George Washington	125	135
Honoré de Balzac	130	145
Robert Burns	130	130
Christian Huygens	130	150
Sir Isaac Newton	130	170
Jean Jacques Rousseau	130	125
Ludwig van Beethoven	135	140
Edmund Burke	135	150
Charles Robert Darwin	135	140
Desiderius Erasmus	135	140
Giuseppe Mazzini	135	145
Napoleon Bonaparte	135	140
Adam Smith	135	145
Leonardo da Vinci	135	150
Wilhelm Richard Wagner	135	150
Louis Agassiz	140	160
Robert Boyle	140	160
Thomas Carlyle	140	155
Johann Kepler	140	160
Joseph Priestley	140	150
Francis Bacon	145	155
Charles Dickens	145	155
Ralph Waldo Emerson	145	145
Benjamin Franklin	145	145
Galileo Galilei	145	165
George Frederick Handel	145	155
Michaelangelo Buonarroti	145	160
John Milton	145	170
George Berkeley	150	175
George Gordon, Lord Byron	150	170
Humphry Davy	150	175
Henry Wadsworth Longfellow	150	160
Wolfgang Amadeus Mozart	155	155
Walter Scott	150	155
Samuel Johnson	155	155
Alfred Tennyson	155	160
William Pitt	160	180
John Quincy Adams	165	165
François Marie Arouet (Voltaire)	170	180
Samuel Taylor Coleridge	175	165
Thomas Babington Macaulay	180	165
Johann Wolfgang Goethe	185	200
Gottfried Wilhelm Leibnitz	185	190
John Stuart Mill	190	170

We may not agree with the ratings assigned, but collectively they make out a good case for the precocious development of genius. In some cases, Galton for instance, where a late flowering of genius was apparently not associated with precocity in childhood, further research has disclosed the error. Galton was a genius from birth. If intelligence is simply a persistent differential rate of mental growth, then all geniuses must have shown their outstanding characteristics during childhood.

The Nature of Intelligence. — Considering that intelligence is such a widely used word, it is extraordinarily difficult to get a satisfactory definition of it. In a general way, most persons know that it comes from the same root as intellect, and that it has to do with brightness of intellect. But ask a dozen psychologists for a definition of the word and one gets a dozen different answers. That this is so was shown in the Symposium [3] on intelligence in 1921. Despite a general likeness among the answers, the lack of real agreement was obvious. Thorndike defined it as the power of good responses from the point of view of truth or fact; Terman as the ability to carry on abstract thinking; Colvin as the ability to adjust to environment; Pintner as the ability to adapt to relatively new situations in life; Henmon as intellect *plus* knowledge; Woodrow as an acquiring capacity; Dearborn as the capacity to learn or to profit from experience; and so forth. From an examination of scores of definitions in my collection, the following seem to be the commonest features: (1) the ability to adapt oneself to novel situations; (2) the ability to carry on the higher processes of thought, especially abstract thinking; and (3) the ability to learn.

Spearman thinks this muddle a scandalous state of affairs. He has worked out an analysis of mind, which shows the place of intelligence in the process of cognition. Inquiring readers are referred to his *three noegenetic principles* — Apprehension of Experience, Eduction of Relations, and Eduction of Correlates; to his *five quantitative laws* — Mental Energy, Retentivity, Fatigue, Conative Control, and Primordial Potencies; and to his *three anoegenetic principles* — Reproduction, Disparition, and Clearness-Variation, as

[3] *Jour. Educ. Psychol.*, XII, 3 and 4, 1921, pp. 123-147; 195-216.

described in his scholastic work, *The Nature of Intelligence and the Principles of Cognition.* All that need be said here is that to secure successful tests of intelligence, items which demand the eduction of relations and eduction of correlates should receive special emphasis. Hitherto intelligence testers have hit upon types of tests in which these principles are paramount but more by a hit-and-miss, empirical method than by rational thinking.

The Multi-focal and Bi-focal Theories of Intelligence. These theories, held by Thorndike and Spearman respectively, are sufficiently important to merit a detailed description. Fundamentally, they are differing views of mind. *Thorndike,*[4] for instance, states that "the mind must be regarded not as a functional unit, nor even as a collection of a few general faculties which work irrespective of particular material, but rather as a multitude of functions each of which involves content as well as form, and so is related closely to only a few of its fellows, to others with greater and greater degrees of remoteness." (p. 366) In other words, the mind is made up of a large number of independent powers or traits which may exhibit greater or lesser degrees of correlation. In a later work[5] he asserts:

"The hypothesis (that quality of intellect depends upon quantity of connections) which we present and shall defend admits the distinction in respect of surface behavior, but asserts that in their deeper nature the higher forms of intellectual operation are identical with mere association or connection forming, depending upon the same sort of physiological connections but requiring many more of them. By the same argument the person whose intellect is greater or higher or better than that of another person differs from him in the last analysis in having, not a new sort of physiological process, but simply a larger number of connections of the ordinary sort." (p. 415)

"What is essential to the hypothesis is that by original nature, men differ in respect of the number of connections or associations with ideas which they can form, so that despite identical outside environments, some of them would have many more than others." (p. 421)

"The bearing of the hypothesis upon the problem of measurement lies in the fact that we may be able for many purposes to re-

4 E. L. Thorndike, *Educational Psychology,* Vol. 3, 1921.
5 E. L. Thorndike, *The Measurement of Intelligence,* Chap. XV.

place our measurement via a simple inventory of tasks, by a more or less direct measurement of C" (the anatomical cause or correspondent of the original possibility of having such connections). (p. 420)

Thorndike puts his trust not merely in the appreciation and management of relations, but also in analysis, selection and organizing. He places much more confidence in a battery of tests than in a single test, however good that test may be.

Spearman's theory of two factors dates back to a paper published in 1904.[6] Spearman was interested in the correlations between abilities. If abilities correlated they had a common factor. Moreover, "all branches of intellectual activity have in common one fundamental function (or group of functions), whereas the remaining or specific elements seem in every case to be wholly different from that in all the others." This first statement of the now famous "two factor" theory of intelligence was arrived at from a study of intercorrelations. If a battery of tests be used, a table of intercorrelations (that is, the correlation of every test with every other test) can be calculated. If now the high correlations are placed at the head of the table and the low ones at the bottom, a hierarchical order is seen. The table of correlations shows a consistency which Spearman regards as significant. Those tests which have high average correlations have also relatively high correlation with each of the individual tests. From these facts he arrived at the first statement of the two-factor theory quoted above. The central factor common to all abilities tested he first called "general intelligence," but later changed it to *g* so as not to confuse it with other conceptions of intelligence. Every ability has or demands *g* which is a common factor in all. Each ability has also a specific factor, *s*, which, unlike *g*, is unique for that particular ability. Factors *g* and *s* are, however, unrelated. Any given ability, therefore, can be divided into two parts — a common *g* and a specific *s*. The ratio of *g* to *s* differs for different abilities. For classics it was found that the ratio was 15 to 1; for music 1 to 4.

It will thus be seen that the *g* factor probably represents

[6] C. Spearman, "General Intelligence Objectively Determined and Measured," *Amer. Jour. Psychol.*, XV, 1904.

general ability or general intelligence, the thing which intelligence tests measure with some degree of success. It is relatively constant for the same individual, but varies greatly from individual to individual. It is the common element, g, which makes the measures of an individual in a number of traits exhibit positive correlation. The second factor, s, represents the specific factor inherent in the act or performance under consideration. It may represent musical capacity in musical performance and mathematical capacity in mathematical performance, and these two s's may be markedly different in amount in the same individual. It is the variations of these independent s factors which occasion the variety of performance in different tasks when undertaken by the same individual. But a person's success in any form of response or performance is the joint product of his g and s, his ability in general, and his specific ability for the task in question.

In the first paper of Spearman's mentioned above, the hierarchical nature of the correlations was noted and the theory of two factors first promulgated. Later it was shown that these intercorrelations showed an arrangement which could be expressed as a mathematical formula. This was given in the form

$$\frac{r_{ap}}{r_{aq}} = \frac{r_{bp}}{r_{bq}}$$

and later changed to the famous *tetrad equation*

$$r_{ap} \times r_{bq} - r_{aq} \times r_{bp} = 0$$

with the value on the left constituting the tetrad difference. For a discussion of its history and derivation see the Appendix to Spearman's *Abilities of Man*.[7]

---

[7] The tetrad equation can be derived from and perhaps best explained by Yule's formula for partial correlation.

Suppose we have four tests a, b, p and q whose correlations, by theory, are due to a common factor g. Partialling out g, we get

$$r_{ab \cdot g} = \frac{r_{ab} - r_{ag}\, r_{bg}}{\left(\sqrt{1 - r^2_{ag}}\right)\left(\sqrt{1 - r^2_{bg}}\right)}$$

Since $\sqrt{1 - r^2} = k$, we may write

$$r_{ab \cdot g} = \frac{r_{ab} - r_{ag}\, r_{bg}}{k_{ag} \cdot k_{bg}}$$

A quotation from Spearman[8] will make the use of the tetrad equation clear.

"An illustration may be afforded by the following imaginary correlations between mental tests (actually observed correlations will be given in abundance later on):

		Opposites	Completion	Memory	Discrim-ination	Can-cellation
Opposites	1	—	0.80	0.60	0.30	0.30
Completion	2	0.80	—	0.48	0.24	0.24
Memory	3	0.60	0.48	—	0.18	0.18
Discrimination	4	0.30	0.24	0.18	—	0.09
Cancellation	5	0.30	0.24	0.18	0.09	—

For instance, let us try the effect of making —

a denote Opposites
b " Discrimination
p " Completion
q " Cancellation

From the table of correlations above, we see that r_{ap} will mean the correlation between opposites and completion, which is 0.80. Ob-

Since the correlation found is, by definition, due to g, then any partial correlation between two tests over and above that which is due to g is zero. Hence

$$r_{ab \cdot g} = 0$$

$$\text{Since } 0 = \frac{r_{ab} - r_{ag} \cdot r_{bg}}{k_{ag} \cdot k_{bg}}$$

$$\therefore \quad r_{ab} = r_{ag} \cdot r_{bg}$$
$$\text{Similarly } r_{ap} = r_{ag} \cdot r_{pg}$$
$$r_{aq} = r_{ag} \cdot r_{qg}$$
$$r_{bp} = r_{bg} \cdot r_{pg}$$
$$r_{bq} = r_{bg} \cdot r_{qg}$$
$$r_{pq} = r_{pg} \cdot r_{qg}$$

$$\text{hence } \frac{r_{ap}}{r_{aq}} = \frac{r_{ag} \cdot r_{pg}}{r_{ag} \cdot r_{qg}} \text{ and } \frac{r_{bp}}{r_{bq}} = \frac{r_{bg} \cdot r_{pg}}{r_{bg} \cdot r_{qg}}$$

$$\therefore \quad \frac{r_{ap}}{r_{aq}} = \frac{r_{bp}}{r_{bq}}, \text{ since both are equal to } \frac{r_{pg}}{r_{qg}}$$

or $r_{ap} \times r_{bq} - r_{aq} \times r_{bp} = 0$

which is the required tetrad equation. And so for the other two tetrads."

[8] C. Spearman, *The Abilities of Man : their Nature and Measurement*, 1927.

taining in a similar fashion the other three correlations needed, the whole tetrad equation becomes

$$0.80 \times 0.09 - 0.30 \times 0.24 = 0$$

which is obviously correct. And so will be found any other application whatever of the tetrad equation to this table.

"So far, the business is confined to matters of observation; we simply try out the tetrad equation on any table of actually observed correlations and examine whether it fits. . . Whenever the tetrad equation holds throughout any table of correlations, and *only* when it does so, then every individual measurement of every ability (or of any other variable that enters into the table) can be divided into two independent parts which possess the following momentous properties. The one part has been called the 'general factor' and denoted by the letter 'g'; it is so named because, although varying freely from individual to individual, it remains the same for any one individual in respect of all the correlated abilities. The second part has been called the 'specific factor' and denoted by the letter 's.' It not only varies from individual to individual, but even for any one individual from each ability to another. The proof of this all-important mathematical theorem has gradually evolved through successive stages of completeness, and may now be regarded as complete." (pp. 73-75)

The factor *g* is a value or magnitude; it is the constituent "which is common to all the abilities inter-connected by the tetrad equation." It is a universal factor, holding good for the intercorrelations of all sorts of abilities. The success of the Binet tests, group tests, and all others discovered by empirical methods is due to the fact that the constituent elements are saturated more or less with *g*, and that the various *s*'s tend to cancel out.

What is the character of *g*? Psychologically it may be interpreted as intelligence or mental energy. Physiologically, it may be explained by energy, plasticity of the nervous system, the condition of the blood, endocrine balance, oxygenation, and by many other factors. It may be due to chance, providing the *g*'s are equal in every individual. Spearman leans to the view that *g* is analogous to energy, "that is to say, it is some force capable of being transferred from one mental operation to another different one. Even on the physiological side, there are some grounds for hoping that some such energy will sooner or later be discovered in the nervous system, especially the cerebral cortex." The factor g "measures something in the nature of an 'energy' derived from the whole cortex or wider area of the brain."[9] The various s's measure the respective efficiencies of the parts of the brain in which this energy can be concentrated; they are so to speak its "engines." "Whenever the mind turns from one operation to another, the energy is switched off from one engine to another, much as the power supply of a factory can be directed, at one moment to turning a wheel, at the next to heating a furnace, and then to blowing a whistle." The engine also needs an engineer. This is supplied by W, a general factor discovered by Webb, which is to be understood to mean consistency of action resulting from volition or will.

For this two-factor theory, the evidence supplied by Spearman and his students over a period of two decades seems to be overwhelming. E. B. Wilson in reviewing *The Abilities of Man* for *Science*, stated that the mathematics of the two-factor theory was sound, but confessed that he was at a loss to know what the theory really meant. The theory has been attacked in a number of papers by Thomson,[10] who proposes in its stead a sampling theory of intelligence. Kelley[11] concluded that his analysis of the problem pointed to a multiple-factor hypothesis rather than to a single g factor. It should also be noted that the new techniques of factor analysis, instituted by Thurstone, Hotelling and others, lead to the discovery of factors such as language ability, motor ability, etc., when intelligence and other forms of tests are investigated. It is also known that the tetrad equation does not always hold. If two tests resemble each other to a marked degree, that is, if the s factors are much alike, the tetrad equation is not fulfilled. The s's become overlapping or group factors discoverable, presumably, by methods of factor analysis. Intercorrelations of physical measurements cannot be explained by means of a two-factor theory. Yet after examining the evidence, the balance is

[9] C. Spearman, "Some Issues in the Theory of G," *Proceedings, British Association*, Section J, Southampton, 1925.

[10] See especially Brown and Thomson, *The Essentials of Mental Measurement*, 1921.

[11] T. L. Kelley, *Crossroads in the Mind of Man*, 1928.

undoubtedly on the side of a unitary conception of intelligence. There is, as Spearman first surmised, such a thing as general intelligence. And it is this general intelligence which intelligence tests measure rather successfully. The theory will probably have to be modified to include group as well as specific factors, but the theory of a general or unitary intelligence stands up fairly well. Finally, it may be said that Thorndike's and Spearman's views are not so widely separated as was once thought. The fact that Thorndike has, from the first, recognized correlation among his numerous powers and capacities, is now becoming appreciated.

Other Theories of Intelligence. — Other theories have been propounded by Thurstone[12] and Thomson.[13] *Thurstone* starts with the assumption (easily proven false) that conduct originates in the organism itself and is only secondarily determined by the environment. The rôle of the stimulus is that of a modifier of intended conduct, or of a medium through which self-expression takes place. Intelligence is one aspect of self-expression. According to Thurstone, each reflex circuit has a focal point — the stage in the expression of an impulse at which the impulse becomes conscious. If this focal point is reached when the psychological act is almost completed, there is the typical restriction of behavior that we find in a reflex act. On the other hand, the earlier the focal point is reached in the act, the greater the number of possible choices. "The intelligence of any particular psychological act is a function of the incomplete stage of the act at which it is the subject of trial-and-error choice. Intelligence, considered as a mental trait, is the capacity to make impulses focal at their early, unfinished stage of formation. Intelligence is therefore the capacity for abstraction, which is an inhibitory process. In the intelligent moment the impulse is inhibited while it is still only partially specified, while it is still only loosely organized. It is then known as a universal or a concept." (p. 159)

While this analysis is interesting and has much to commend it, its starting point is false. Organisms are never self-starting mechanisms; an organism in a static changeless world of energy would never be able to move. What Thur-

---

12 L. L. Thurstone, *The Nature of Intelligence*, 1927.
13 Brown and Thomson, *The Essentials of Mental Measurement*, 1921.

stone's theory amounts to is nothing more nor less than this. If the nervous discharge reaches the cerebral cortex, intelligent action as opposed to involuntary action may result. But this is part of the older neuron theory.

Thomson's theory is generally known as the *sampling theory of ability* (intelligence). Its nature is shown in the following quotation:

"In place therefore of the two factors of that theory (Spearman's), one General and the other Specific, Thomson prefers to think of a number of factors at play in the carrying out of any activity such as a mental test, these factors being a sample of all those which the individual has at his command.

"The first reason for preferring this theory is that of Occam's razor. It makes fewer assumptions than does the more special form of theory. It does not deny General Ability, for if the samples are large there will of course be factors common to all activities. On the other hand it does not assert General Ability, for the samples may not be so large as this, and no single factor may occur in every activity. If moreover a number of factors do run through the whole gamut of activities, forming a General Factor, this group need not be the same in every individual. In other words General Ability, if possessed by any individual, need not be psychologically of the same nature as any General Ability possessed by another individual. Everyone has probably known men who were good all round, but Jones may be a good all round man for different reasons from those which make Smith good all round.

"The Sampling Theory, then, neither denies nor asserts General Ability, though it says it is unproven. Nor does it deny Specific Factors. On the other hand it does deny the absence of Group Factors. It is this absence of Group Factors which is in truth the crux of Professor Spearman's theory, which is not so much a theory of general ability, or a theory of two factors, as a Theory of the Absence of Group Factors. And inasmuch as its own disciples have begun to require Group Factors to explain their data, its distinguishing mark would appear in any case to be disappearing." (pp. 188-189)

Thomson's theory seems to be strengthened by the findings of those who have developed factor analysis. The steadiness with which a verbal factor analyses out of the results of verbal tests is striking. Nor should it be overlooked that Spearman himself now recognizes group factors as well as special abilities.

The Kinds of Intelligence. — If intelligence is innate; if it is something that a Darwin or an Aristotle has in abundance and an idiot has scarcely at all, how can there possibly be varieties of it? The answer to this question depends on the way we regard intelligence. Intelligence is undoubtedly a native gift, but it can only be seen when it is put to work, as it were. It can only be observed through behavior. It is difficult to conceive of any act which has no intelligence behind it. Certain reflexes, such as the pupillary reflex, seem to be unconcerned with intelligence. Other forms of behavior, such as that which is concerned with the solution of an abstract problem, seem to be saturated with it. The behavior of a normal-minded person is more intelligent than that of an idiot or imbecile. But when we study the actions of a skilled artisan or a skilled statesman and compare them with the behavior of a skilled scientist, we are not certain that one kind should be ranked higher than the rest. All the actions seem highly intelligent, and this has led Thorndike to posit three kinds of intelligence — *abstract, concrete* and *social*. There are as many kinds of intelligence as there are forms of behavior, but by calling some forms abstract while others are designated concrete and social, Thorndike is subscribing to the theory of general factors and to the belief that certain forms of intelligence cluster around nodal points.

By *abstract intelligence* is meant the kind that manifests itself in the management of abstract symbols. It is the kind that is possessed in high degree by the mathematician and the scientist and, in general, by the bookish individual. Such people are generally regarded as impractical and rather self-centered and there may be some degree of truth in it. But university professors are far from being as forgetful and childish as the humorous papers make them out to be.

Concrete intelligence is exhibited in the management of concrete things. In its lower forms, it is exhibited by the unskilled laborer; in intermediate degree by the skilled craftsman; but only in its highest forms by the creative artists of the world. If invention and design are combined with skilled craftsmanship we get a form of intelligence that is regarded highly by everybody. Probably a *Venus de Milo* or a *Night Watch* are truer mileposts on the road of civilization than a *Pyramid* or a *Washington Bridge*. There is, however, a general impression, which is well founded, that the level of intelligence necessary for the successful manipulation of concrete materials is lower than that needed for competence with abstract symbols. One needs more intelligence even to understand relativity than to be a good jack carpenter.

Social intelligence is exhibited by those who either manage, or manage to get on with, people. In this regard we think of statesmen, the business executive, the president of a university and even the humble teacher. These have to manage people in order to be successful. This ability to get along with people is regarded so highly that a Dale Carnegie can sell hundreds of thousands of copies of a book which shows us how to do it in terms a common man can understand. According to the experts on personality, social intelligence is possessed by the extravert rather than the introvert.

If there are varieties of intelligence — scholastic, verbal, abstract, social, concrete, mechanical and the like — then to measure intelligence fairly we must provide a variety of tests in order to sample it properly. This, of course, is what is usually done, but there are special kinds of intelligence tests which presumably measure special kinds of intelligence. Performance and non-verbal tests will measure concrete intelligence rather than social or abstract intelligence. Certain tests of personality are undoubtedly good measures of social intelligence. But the fact remains that verbal tests, designed to measure abstract intelligence, are still the best tests of intelligence invented so far.

The Attributes of Intelligence. — According to Thorndike there are four major attributes of intelligence — (1) difficulty or level; (2) range or width; (3) speed of performance; and (4) area. In measuring intelligence, wide use is made of level, range and speed, in addition to wide sampling involving those operations we term comparison, judgment, skills of various sorts, attention, abstraction, retention, recall, thinking and so forth.

By *level* or *altitude* of intellect we mean the degree of difficulty of the task a person can perform. How hard a task can an individual do? How far can he ascend the ladder representing a developmental scale? This was Binet's basic task when he constructed his tests; he wanted to find the highest level of performance (intelligence) a person could reach. Unfortunately, we do not reach the same levels in every performance. We may, for instance, perform our music at the level of an imbecile, while we do our mathematics at the level of a professor of the subject. We, therefore, regard the average of the highest levels attained in a wide sampling of tasks as a satisfactory measure of intellectual level. The more difficult the tasks a person can perform, the greater is his intelligence. Since the very difficult tasks can be performed only by a select few, this principle of altitude employs the touchstone of rarity. Fewer people can use the calculus than can use the multiplication table, therefore the intelligence needed for the calculus is of a higher level than that needed for multiplication. On a diagram, altitude or level of intelligence or intellect would be represented by a vertical scale ranging from that of the lowest idiot to that of an Aristotle, a Shakespeare or a Newton. It is, however, not certain that the behavior of the lowest idiot is representative of zero intelligence on this vertical scale. Thorndike made a test which he calls intellect CAVD, because it refers to that segment of intellect measured by CAVD, a composite of tests of completion, arithmetic, vocabulary and directions. This scale has a true zero. Discussing the zero problem he stated,[14] "The difficulty of the task which the earthworm's intellect can master is so near zero difficulty that a level slightly below it may safely be accepted as an approximate absolute zero of intellectual difficulty, sufficiently close for all purposes, theoretical and practical." (p. 342) The upper limit of the scale is unknown but it is practically certain that the greatest geniuses of history habitually worked around it, so we may define it in terms of the behavior of a Newton or an Aristotle.

The attribute *range* or *width*, as the term implies, has to do with the number of tasks of a given degree of difficulty (level or altitude) that a person can do. He who can do more tasks of a given degree of difficulty than another is

[14] E. L. Thorndike, *The Measurement of Intelligence*, 1927.

regarded as the more intelligent. At first glance, it would seem as if a person with a mental age level, say, of fifteen years would be able to perform all possible tasks at this level of difficulty. In practice this is not found to be the case. The fifteen mental age level, we must remember, is an average performance level. Some tasks at this level will therefore be beyond the compass of the subject, and some well within it. He may fail at some because of a faulty native equipment (e.g. lack of pitch-discrimination in music); at others because he has failed to master facts or techniques at a lower level (e.g. simple equations or factoring when quadratics are being dealt with) which are essential to the solution of problems at this higher level. Differences of training, of opportunities for learning, of experience, and of native equipment all enter into the picture and cause people to fail in some tasks of a difficulty level representing their general average.

There is also the question of time at the disposal of the examiner. For any given level an almost infinite number of tasks could be devised. In practice, a large sampling of these tasks is provided, and the proportion of them that a person can solve represents his range of intelligence at this level.

Thorndike [15] found that width of intellect correlated with level of intellect around .90, which is very high. This means that if we could get an adequate measure of range or width it would be a fair measure of altitude as well and, generally speaking, of intelligence also. Further, it means that the higher the level, the greater the width of intellect. Persons at a mental age level, say, of 24 years can actually do more tasks at this high level than another whose general level may be much lower. It is a beautiful illustration of the statement "to him that hath shall be given." The poor feebleminded creature with only one talent cannot even put his single talent to useful work. He can do only a few things at his humble level of ability. An imbecile could not be taught to do many more tasks than he can do now, even by an environment as favorable as that which surrounds the Dionne quintuplets.

[15] See E. L. Thorndike, *Measurement of Intelligence*, Chap. XIII.

By combining width and altitude we get a kind of *area* of intellect. Multiply the height by the number of tasks done at that altitude and we get a measure that may fairly be called area.

The relationships among levels, widths and areas are shown in Fig. 38.

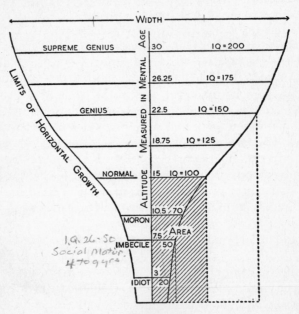

Fig. 38. Diagram showing the Relationships existing among Levels, Widths and Areas of Intellect.

Speed as a factor in intellect is generally recognized. However, it is still under some suspicion as a measure of ability. The slow but patient thinker seems to give the lie to the statement that it is the quick thinker who gets results. When tested, speed is found to correlate with altitude around .40, which is too low to permit speed alone to be used as a measure of intelligence. Level, width and area are closely correlated. Speed does not belong to this group, though it is a factor which cannot be neglected. In commerce and industry, the principle of speed of performance (payment by results) is widely applied. And, generally speaking, we can truthfully say that he who can accomplish more tasks than another in a given time is the more intelligent.

How Intelligence Came to be Measured.— In crude, unreliable ways, intelligence has been measured from the earliest times. Whenever differences in intelligence have been noticed, intelligence has been judged and measured. Probably Eve said to Adam that Abel seemed to be a smarter lad than Cain. Mankind has had a penchant for riddles as tasks of intelligence from the time of earliest recorded history, and Samson's riddle (Out of the eater came forth meat and out of the strong came forth sweetness), and the riddle of the Sphinx (What is it that goes on four legs in the morning, two legs at noon, and three legs in the evening?) are well-known examples. These riddles, however, were unsolvable by unaided intelligence and differed in this respect from the puzzles we were given to solve when young. If we had possessed sufficient reasoning ability in arithmetic we could have solved such problems as the following — "If a herring and a half cost three half-pence, how much would a dozen cost?" And, curiously enough, when the problem of measuring intelligence was eventually mastered, it was through the standardization of just such puzzles and problems as these.

In the meantime, many attempts to evaluate intelligence had been made. Among physical methods of diagnosis, Lavater's physiognomy, Gall's phrenology, Lombroso's stigmata of criminality, and the more modern attempts to use facial expressions as an index of mentality should be mentioned. All these failed. Gall's phrenology failed because the cranial protuberances do not correspond to enlargements of the brain underneath, and the functions assigned by Gall to various parts of the brain were found to be inaccurate by later researches. Cesare Lombroso and his school claimed that it was possible to recognize defective intelligence and degenerate or criminal character from physical stigmata connected principally with the size and shape of the head. The "human anomalies" to which Lombroso pinned his faith were various forms of cranial asymmetry, size of head, shape of forehead, facial asymmetry, development of lower jaw, projecting cheek bones, projecting ears, ferocious physiognomies, defective teeth, shape of nose, hairiness, wrinkles and saddle-shaped palates. Unfortunately for Lombroso, persons of undoubted intelligence and high moral character may exhibit a large number, even a majority, of these anomalies. Goring's [16] study of the English Convict gave the death blow to Lombroso's claims. He found that "the physical and mental constitution of both criminal and law-abiding persons, of the same age, stature, class, and intelligence, are identical. There is no such thing as an anthropological criminal type." (p. 269) Nevertheless, Goring was constrained to say: "On statistical evidence, one assertion can be dogmatically made: it is, that the criminal is differentiated by inferior stature, by defective intelligence and, to some extent, by his anti-social proclivities; but that, apart from these broad differences, there are no physical, mental, or moral characteristics peculiar to the inmates of English prisons." Regarding size of skull, Pearson,[17] from measurements made on 5,000 school children and 1000 undergraduates, concluded that the correlations between intelligence and the dimensions of the skull, though positive, are far too small for trustworthy predictions. In a later review of the evidence, Paterson[18] states — "It appears that variation in head size is a function of race, sex, and family stock. It does not vary between individuals in correspondence with intellect. Not only is head size shown to be of minor importance as a physical correlate or sign of intellect, but the same may be said of head shape. Head shape also varies as a racial characteristic irrespective of the intellectual qualities exhibited by the several racial groups. Within a given racial strain, head shape appears to be indifferently related to intellect." (p. 123)

Another line of endeavor is illustrated by simple sensory and motor tests. Are the more intelligent among us endowed with acuter senses and better motor reactions? When the aesthesiometer was employed, it was at first believed that pressure discrimination could be used as a measure of intelligence. This view has now been abandoned, although the correlation between pressure discrimination and intelligence

---

[16] Charles Goring, *The English Convict* (abridged edition), 1919.

[17] Karl Pearson, "On the Relationship of Intelligence to Size and Shape of the Head," *Biometrika*, V. 1906.

[18] D. G. Paterson, *Physique and Intellect*, 1930.

is positive, but slight. In much the same way, the ability to discriminate between almost equal weights was found to correlate positively with intelligence, but so low as to be useless as a practical measure of it. Similarly, reaction-times and tests of visual and auditory acuity have been tried, but the correlations, though positive, are too low to make the tests dependable. The person of normal or superior intelligence differs from the feebleminded not so much in his eyesight and hearing as in his superior use of his higher mental processes — judgment, comparison, reasoning and the seeing of relationships.

If intelligence is to be measured, we must discard these tests of the simpler mental processes and concentrate upon those which deal with the more complex processes. The first person to do this successfully was a Frenchman named Alfred Binet. He constructed the first usable intelligence test.

Binet was trained in law and medicine, but found his *métier* in experimental psychology, especially in problems concerned with individual differences.[19] The work for which he is most famous, his test of intelligence, developed out of his work as a member of a commission appointed by the Minister of Public Instruction in 1904. The "reference" of the commission was to formulate recommendations for the administration of special classes in public schools and to find a method of distinguishing subnormal children from the normal. The physicians on the commission opposed him, but his biting sarcasm at their distinctions and definitions soon silenced them. The medical men said that in idiocy "the attention is fugitive," while in imbecility "the attention is fleeting." Binet confessed himself unable to grasp the distinctive shade of meaning. In idiocy "there is a gleam of intelligence"; in imbecility "the intellectual faculties exist in a very incomplete degree." Binet stated that this may be so, but the difference between idiots and imbeciles had not been defined. He saw that he must attempt to measure intelligence, and with Dr. Simon as collaborator started, somewhat hesitatingly and with no clear-cut program, to construct a scale for the purpose.

The scale, published in 1905, consisted of thirty items or

[19] See Edith H. Varon, "The Development of Alfred Binet's Psychology," *Psychol. Review Monogs.*, No. 207, 1935.

short tests. Some of them had been used by Binet in previous researches, some were new, and some were borrowed from Blin and Damaye's test of twenty items. They were simple, varied, easily administered, and were more or less independent of schooling. They were scored full credit, half credit or no credit, but were not arranged according to age. However, as they were arranged in some rough order of difficulty, Binet could say that three-year-olds should do up to Test 9; five-year-olds to Test 14 and so on. In 1908, he grouped his 59 tests into years and so provided the first age-scale. At age three, a normal child should be able to point to nose, eyes and mouth; to repeat short sentences; to repeat two digits; to make objects in pictures; and to tell his last name. At age XIII, the highest year in the scale, the tests included the paper cutting test, the reversed triangle test, and the distinction between pairs of abstract terms. The last revision that Binet made (the 1911 scale) consisted of 54 tests, five for each year up to the adult level (XVI) with the following exceptions: there were only four for year IV, and none for XI or XIII. This last scale is a tolerably reliable instrument, and as revised by other workers, notably Terman, Herring, and Kuhlmann, has proved of inestimable value.

During these years his ideas on intelligence were crystallizing, and his measurements becoming more and more objective in character. In *Les idées modernes sur les enfants,* published in 1909, he states: "In our opinion, intelligence, considered independently of phenomena of sensibility, emotion, and will, is above all a faculty of knowing, which is directed toward the external world, and which labors to reconstruct it as a whole, by means of the small fragments of it which are given to us. . . Comprehension, invention, direction and censorship, intelligence is contained in these four words." (pp. 117-118)

Summing up Binet's contributions to the measurement of intelligence we may say that:

(1) Binet first saw that we must have a variety of test problems, that these must be simple, heterogeneous and non-pedagogical, and they must test the higher rather than the lower thought processes. Intelligence was to be measured along whatever lines it was exhibited. The problems were

of such a nature that the answers to them were dictated by a general training in a common environment, and not by any special training which might be given to some and not to others. His final average result may be compared with the grading of a car of grain from which samples have been taken, or, better still, with the valuation of a mine from the average of its sample borings. Previous to this time, psychologists had been employing a single test, or, at most, only a few. Binet was the first to see that intelligence was a highly complex thing, exhibited in many directions, and, therefore, to sample it thoroughly an extensive and diverse series of tests must be employed in its diagnosis.

Spearman is inclined to think that Binet got his idea of testing general intelligence by a variety of tests from his paper of 1904 on general intelligence, or, at least, was profoundly influenced by it. It is likely that Binet knew of Spearman's paper, but if his development in psychology is traced, it will be seen that his scale was a natural development of ideas first expressed in 1890.

(2) He was impressed with the necessity of securing standardized methods of administering and scoring the tests. He strove to make his tests as objective as possible so that they would give strictly comparable results when employed by other workers. As his test was really a standardized interview, complete objectivity was never obtained.

(3) He used the concept of mental age for the expression of intelligence ratings. This simple, but valuable concept has had an important influence on the development of mental tests. Previous to Binet, and in fact, in Binet's first scale, the tests were lumped together in a rough order of increasing difficulty. It was difficult to discover just what a child of five or eight should score on the tests, and still more difficult to interpret the findings. Binet said a child of five is normal if he can do the things that five-year-olds normally do. A child of eight has a mental age of eight providing he can do the tasks which, on the average, a large and unselected group of eight-year-olds can do. In other words, a person's intelligence should be rated directly against that of persons of the same age. If he can perform tasks better than his equals in age, he is of superior intelligence; if he cannot do them as well, then he is of inferior intelligence. The Binet

tests, then, are standardized on an age scale, and the mental age obtained is the score on the test. Mental ages grade persons in order of rank.

One valuable feature about a score given in terms of mental age is that it is easily understood by laymen. If a person is told that his child of eight has a mental age of ten years, the parent knows at once that his child is as intelligent as ordinary ten-year-olds. Even in the derived form of the intelligence quotient (in our illustration the I.Q. is 125) it is understood and used correctly by millions of people. But as a scientific measure it has serious drawbacks. Its zero is unknown; one year of mental age between 5 and 6 years of age is not the same as one year between 15 and 16; and owing to the fact that intelligence normally matures around 15 or 16, it naturally follows that all normal adults have the same mental age. The term is only really significant for children. Consequently other methods of expressing intelligence ratings have been evolved, chief of which are median mental ages, percentile ratings, and age-variability measures.

Binet was inconsistent in regard to the placing of a test in a given year. He used the percentage of pupils of the given age who passed the test as a measure, but his placements varied between 60 per cent and 90 per cent of pupils passing. America usually adopts 75 per cent as a standard, but Burt[20] states that the correct procedure is to assign a test to a given year when it is passed by 50 per cent of the children who are one year younger. Thus a test is a five-year test when it is passed by 50 per cent of four-year-olds. (p. 140)

(4) Binet saw from his results that human mentality was exhibited on a continuous scale ranging from that of the lowest idiot to that of the brightest genius. Any classification we make, for instance into idiots, imbeciles, morons and so on, is merely for convenience; one group shades insensibly into the other.

(5) He saw that intelligence was a unitary function of many psychic powers. This is essentially Spearman's view and may have been borrowed from him.

(6) Binet attempted to ascertain the general level of ability instead of measuring separate "mental faculties" as most

---

[20] Cyril Burt, *Mental and Scholastic Tests*, 1922.

of his forerunners had done. It was Binet's solid horse-sense which brought him through to success, and he is right-fully regarded as the Father of Mental Testing.

Important Contributions to Mental Testing, by Countries.— Although it was a Frenchman, Binet, who constructed the first workable test of intelligence, it must not be supposed that other countries had been, or now were, idle. The history of almost any discovery shows that it is the culmination of ideas that were wide-spread. So it was with mental testing. Many workers in many countries contributed to Binet's ultimate success, and carried his work later to higher levels.

In *England*, for instance, Francis Galton studied individual differences and his work *Inquiries into Human Faculty* is an important contribution to the science of mental measurement. Although an untrained mathematician, he developed many important statistical methods for dealing with mass data. Karl Pearson also contributed many basic mathematical formulae which became valuable tools in the hands of the test makers. Pearson's r is known to every educator today, although it was somewhat of a mystery at the time it was given to the world. Cyril Burt's *Tests of the Higher Thought Processes* (1909) anticipated the group tests of Otis. Burt almost discovered the group test of intelligence. He also made a London revision of the Binet tests which added enormously to our knowledge of test making and of the nature of intelligence. Spearman's work on g and s has been noted. He anticipated the work of Binet and has also made valuable contributions to mathematical theory and practice. Thomson and Garnett, by their work on the validity of g, have extended our ideas of the problem of intelligence. Lastly, Porteus, although an Australian by birth, might be classed with other Britishers. His *Maze Test* (1915) is ingenious and apparently works satisfactorily.

Even in *France*, many workers antedated Binet in researches into the nature of feeblemindedness. The story of *The Wild Boy of Aveyron* by Itard (1797) recently translated by Humphrey of Canada (1932) is the beginning of a continuous line of investigation of the feebleminded by French workers. A pupil of Itard's, Seguin, invented the form-board in 1846, and this still finds wide application in performance tests of intelligence.

In *Italy*, De Sanctis devised some ingenious tests of intelligence in 1906, but, unlike Binet, he did not persist with their development and improvement. Treves and Saffioti developed Binet's tests and made them applicable to Italian children.

In *Germany*, we cannot overlook Wundt's establishment of the first Psychological Laboratory at Leipzig in 1879 and all that it has meant to experimental psychology. His experiments dealt too exclusively with the simpler reactions and thought processes to work well as intelligence tests, but the influence of his laboratory spread to every corner of the civilized world. Stern and Bobertag gave us the intelligence quotient (I.Q.) which was adopted by Terman when he standardized the Binet tests for America, and immediately became popular. Bobertag also produced a German revision of the Binet tests. Ebbinghaus, who is chiefly known to psychologists for his work on memory, should also be gratefully remembered for his completion test, a form of test that is still widely used both in intelligence and achievement testing.

It was, however, in *America* that intelligence testing found its highest development and widest application. Americans surpass all other people in their applications of science. It is within comparatively recent times that they have begun to make fundamental discoveries themselves. Intelligence testing, therefore, suited their particular genius as well as their type of psychology, which had been largely moulded by Cattell, who, first and last, emphasized individual differences. It was Cattell who, in his researches on individual differences, developed the first battery of psychological tests. Unfortunately, they dealt with the simpler reactions and sensory processes and so did not develop into workable intelligence tests. Thorndike, the *doyen* of educational psychologists and the most prolific worker in the field, has contributed largely to the testing movement. He has developed statistical methods; he has made many tests for pupils of various ages; he has developed his CAVD, the first test of intelligence with a true zero and accurately scaled units; and, although it lies outside of the field of mental testing, mention should be made of the first scale for measuring achievement, namely, his scale for measuring handwriting (1910). Goddard, when at Vineland, was the first to translate and use the Binet tests in America, although he did not trouble to standardize them for American conditions. Terman made the best American revision and extension of the Binet tests, the Stanford revision of 1916. More recently (1937), he and Maud A. Merrill have again revised and extended the tests. There are now two equivalent forms, L and M, which range roughly from 2 to 24 years of mental age. This latest revision will probably prove of greater value as a clinical instrument than the first revision, but it is doubtful if it will find such universal application in the schoolroom. Knox devised non-language (chiefly pictorial) tests for use with immigrants at Ellis Island. Yerkes invented a point-scale system of scoring Binet tests, but in connection with intelligence testing he will be chiefly remembered for his testing of Army recruits and for his monumental report on the Army tests published as *Academy of Science Memoirs XV* in 1921. Otis produced the first workable group test of intelligence. Many of his ideas and devices were embodied in the Army tests. Pintner has done valuable work on non-language and performance tests and occupies a unique position in the field of intelligence testing. Miss Engels made the first group test for use with young children. The original Detroit test was really her invention, although the fact is not as widely known as it deserves to be. Thurstone has contributed to statistical methods and to the theory of intelligence. His more recent work on rating scales and factor analysis is extremely important. Kelley is famous in many fields — statistics, factor analysis and the interpretation of the results of intelligence testing. McCall gave us the T-score and also some ingenious tests. All in all, the Americans have done important work in intelligence testing and now dominate the field.

Development of Intelligence Tests after Binet. — Mention has been made of the spread of Binet testing from 1909 on. Binet's tests could not simply be translated from the French and used in a foreign country as Goddard tried to use them in America. Translation altered their norms and there was the further difficulty of securing an environment for them commensurate with the French but appropriate to the country concerned. They needed adaptation as well as translation. Practically every civilized country has its special form of the Binet tests. Mention has been made of Terman's revisions of 1916 and 1937 for America, Bobertag's revision for Germany, Treves and Saffioti's for Italy, and Burt's revision for Great Britain in 1921. Other important American revisions were the Kuhlmann revision of 1922, and the Yerkes-Foster revision of the point-scale in 1923.

But individual tests, such as the Binet in all its revisions, consume a great deal of time in their administration. It is no unusual thing for a bright boy of ten to take an hour or more with the Stanford Binet before the examiner can be certain that he has done all the tests he is capable of doing. The latest Stanford revision is even more time-consuming. Nor could this type of test be used with deaf persons, with foreigners who did not understand the language, with illiterate adults and with very young pupils.

When Americans wanted to test the intelligence of almost 2,000,000 recruits during the Great War, other means of testing had to be devised. A group of American psychologists evolved the Army Alpha tests for the literate recruits and the Army Beta for the illiterate ones. As previously mentioned, the foundation for the Army Alpha was laid by Otis, since it embodied principles that he was mainly instrumental in discovering. It was a group test, that is, a paper and pencil test that could be given to as many as 500 people at a time.

A *group test* usually consists of several sub-tests called a battery (the name reflects the War), five to ten in number, printed in the form of a booklet. Each test of the battery consists of short questions or problems printed on a single page and requiring a minimum amount of writing on the part of a pupil to answer them. Sometimes there are forty or fifty items on a page which have to be answered in a few minutes. By arranging the problems so that only a number or a letter has to be written in parentheses printed opposite each question in column form in the right hand margin of the page, rapid answering as well as easy scoring is made possible. The testees work as rapidly as possible, but only one in four hundred or thereabouts completes all the items before time is called and they have to turn to another test. Precise instructions are given about each test and usually samples or a practice exercise introduce the testee to the type of test he is about to answer. The timing is also very precise, and each candidate has exactly the same working time as another for each of the sub-tests. The items of each test are worded so that the answers given are either right or wrong, thus obviating the necessity of giving partial credits. Favorite types of sub-tests are problems in arithmetic, opposites, number series, general information, analogies, best reasons, sentence completion, proverbs and directions. A great deal of ingenuity has been shown in making these tests. They have been selected in empirical fashion from a great number that have been tried, because they correlate highly with a criterion (usually a teacher's estimate of the intelligence of his pupils) and correlate poorly with each other. This second condition is hard to satisfy since intelligence in practice does seem to behave as a unitary thing, but it must be attempted in order to secure an adequate sampling of all forms of intelligence that a pupil may exhibit. The linguistic form of group test, owing to the ease and economy of its administration, may now be regarded as the normal type of intelligence test for subjects who can read and write. If, however, any pupil is discovered who has trouble with a group test, it is advisable to test him further with a more intimate individual test.

The group test in which *pictures of objects* are used instead of printed problems, is suitable for young children as they enter school. Even a kindergarten child can "mark the thing you put on your foot" when confronted with pictures of a hat, a shoe and a glove. But he must understand the oral instructions which are used or he cannot do the test at all. However, he need not be able to write; all that he has to do is to mark a picture.

With deaf pupils and children of foreign extraction, oral instructions cannot be given as they would either not be heard or would not be understood. For such pupils two forms of tests are available: (1) group tests of a *pencil-and-paper, non-linguistic character* that can be introduced to the pupils by means of pantomime; and (2) *performance tests* in which the response is some motor or manual manipulation. The former is of great value in testing groups of foreign children; the latter for testing, one at a time, individuals who use a foreign language or are deaf or are of limited verbal intelligence. In performance tests, form-boards of many kinds play an important part.

Tests for pre-school children have received attention in recent years, chiefly because of the development of experimental schools for child study. Testing in the accepted sense is impossible with very young children, nevertheless Gesell and Thompson have perfected a developmental schedule of behavior for infants beginning at the low level of one month of age. Obviously, the only thing that can be done with young babies is to watch them and list the things that they càn do. A little later, simple apparatus can be introduced as stimulants of behavior, but on the whole Gesell and Thompson's schedule depends upon accurate observation of children's responses in somewhat carefully defined behavior situations. They have refused to give their schedule numerical scores which could be treated statistically.

The Merrill-Palmer scale of mental tests for pre-school children, devised by Rachel Stutsman, is composed of tests to which numerical scores are attached. It is thus possible to secure a mental age and I.Q. from the tests. The tests cannot be used successfully with normal children younger than a year and a half. The tests are varied and consist of a mixture of linguistic and performance items.

We thus see that in less than three decades from the construction of Binet's first scale, the major problems connected with intelligence testing have been solved. Literally scores of quite good tests have been prepared. Practically all of them fall within the five main classes listed below, where samples of each are mentioned by name:

    I — *Individual Tests involving Language.*— Binet tests in all revisions.

    II — *Group Tests involving Language.*— The National Intelligence Test; Terman Group Test of Mental Ability; Haggerty Delta Tests; Dearborn Tests; Dominion Group Test of Intelligence; Otis Self-Administering Examinations; Army Alpha; and Thorndike Intelligence Examinations for High School Graduates.

III — *Individual Tests not involving Language.* — Pintner and Paterson Scale of Performance Tests; Porteus Maze Tests; Dearborn Form Boards; and Kohs Block Design Scale.

IV — *Group Tests not involving Language.* — Detroit First-Grade Intelligence Test; and Pintner-Cunningham Primary Mental Tests.

V — *Tests for Pre-school Children.* — The Gesell-Thompson Developmental Schedules; and the Merrill-Palmer Test for Pre-school Children.

Intelligence tests can be usefully classified according to the grades for which they are suitable. Books dealing with tests usually print lists of tests arranged according to level, and bibliographies [21] of tests always list the grades for which the test is suitable.

The Standardization of Tests. — Every standardized test is provided with norms. A norm is the average performance (score) of the random sample of the population on which the test was standardized. The securing of norms is a difficult task. The technique used can, perhaps, be best illustrated by a practical example. Suppose we wish to secure age norms for a group test. We select at random a large group of pupils of each age for which the test was deemed suitable, test them and find the average score for each age. Selection at random is not what it first seems to be; it is not random at all but a very careful selection of a small group which is truly representative of the whole. It is the whole in miniature as it were, containing within itself a just proportion of all elements which enter into the total population of which the sample is a part. On the North American continent, we tend to think of samples in terms of sex, socio-economic status, geographical distribution, nationality, skin pigmentation and school grades. The neglect of any of these factors will lead to imperfect sampling.

Suppose that 500 ten-year-old pupils were included in our sample and the average score they made had been calculated. How can we be sure that the selection was a random one, and

[21] See H. L. Smith and W. W. Wright, "Second Revision of the Bibliography of Educational Measurements," *Indiana Bulletins in Field of Education,* IV, 2, 1927.
Also Oscar K. Buros, *Educational, Psychological, Personality Tests,* annually since 1934.

was truly representative of the thousands of ten-year-olds to whom it may possibly be given in future? Two crucial tests are usually applied. The first is to test an additional random group of pupils, say 200, and re-calculate the average score for the new total, 700. If the average remains approximately the same as for the original 500, the test may be regarded as standardized for ten-year-olds. And so also for other ages. If, however, it is widely different, then additional samples must be taken until the average attains a constancy. The second test is to make a graph of the averages for successive ages, including, of course, the one for our ten-year-olds. If the graph is either a straight line or a smooth curve without sudden jogs in it, then the norms for each age are probably reliable. If a jog occurs at any given age, then the sample for that age was an improper one. Further samples must be taken until the graph is smoothed.

When Terman made his 1916 revision of the Binet test he used only Californian children in his sample. He naturally thought that a large Californian sample would be representative of American pupils in general. When the test was used in other parts of the country, the averages were found to be below those of the Californian sample. This meant that the Californian children were more intelligent than those in other parts of the country and hence the norms from a Californian sample were unfair for the country as a whole.

In the Terman and Merrill new revision of 1937, this defect has been overcome by taking random samples of white pupils in every section of the country and by enlarging the sample greatly (from approximately 2000 to 7000). The authors[22] state: "We have devoted more than ordinary effort to secure a representative sampling of the white child population in the United States between the ages of two and eighteen years. Besides increasing the number of subjects tested to 100 at each half-year level below six, to 200 at each age between six and fourteen, and to 100 at each age from fifteen to eighteen, we have made a stubborn attempt to avoid sampling errors inherent in age, grade location, nationality, and geographical distribution." (p. 6) Their account of the

---

[22] L. M. Terman and Maud A. Merrill, *Measuring Intelligence*, 1937.

way the various samples were selected is instructive regarding the difficulty in securing truly random samples.

The *norms* usually calculated are those for *age* and *grade*. British tests usually give age norms, American tests grade norms. Of the two, the British practice is superior for the simple reason that ten-year-olds in all parts of a country resemble each other more closely than, say, Grade IV pupils. The variability in standards of grading is greater than the variabilities in ages. It is better, of course, to use both age and grade norms.

Will norms obtained in such a way be fair for all classes of pupils? In Toronto, as in every large city, we have schools filled with the sons and daughters of unskilled workers, others filled with children of professional people and business executives. Is it fair to use any present nation-wide standardization on these groups? An intelligence test is supposed to be based on equal educational opportunities for all. But, obviously, the children of unskilled workers have fewer opportunities for learning things in their home environment than children of the professional classes. Should not the children of the unskilled be compared with children of the same socio-economic status? Should there not be several standardizations for different socio-economic levels? Carrying the argument still further, should we not use separate standardizations for male and female, rich and poor, urban and rural, white and colored, and so on? The answer to this is that while it seems fair to compare a child's intelligence with the average of those of his own sex, color, language and economic status, it would necessitate such a welter of standardizations that confusion would result. If there is a single standardization of a wide sample, we are able to compare the levels of intelligence of any of these various groups fairly and without bias. This is what the tests do, and, in fact, are constructed to do.

A few problems still remain. It will be remembered that Binet used French children for his standardization, while Terman used American. Does this mean that the two standardizations are equivalent? Not at all. They will be equivalent only if, age for age, French and American pupils are equal in intelligence. But nobody knows whether or not this is the case. We cannot say at present that on the average an American child is either duller, or brighter, or of the same intelligence as a French child. Standardizations made on children of a given nationality are valid only within the group on which the standardizations were originally made. We may be in error in Canada in using the Stanford Binet on English-speaking Canadians, since no sample of this group was included in the original standardization. However, the racial stocks and the environments for whites of the United States and for English-speaking Canadians are sufficiently similar to make serious errors of interpretation unlikely.

The Stanford Binet cannot be used with French-speaking Canadians, unless it is translated and re-standardized on French-speaking pupils. Nor could we use the original French version of the Binet test, since we cannot assume, without proof, that the intelligence of French-speaking Canadians is equal to that of French pupils in France. If, however, we compared the results of a third test on English-speaking and French-speaking Canadians with the results of an English and a French version of the Binet scale on these same pupils, we should be able to evaluate fairly the relative levels of the two major linguistic groups in Canada. The catch is — what third test shall we use? A performance test or some other non-linguistic test is indicated, but performance tests, in general, are inferior instruments for measuring intelligence.

If it is impossible at present to compare the intelligence of English-speaking and French-speaking Canadians, it is still more impossible to compare the intelligence of North Americans, say, with native Africans. One cannot transfer a test holus-bolus, standardizations and all, from one country to another. Yet many workers, undaunted by the difficulty of the task, have endeavored to construct truly international tests of intelligence. They have used only those items which are common to all human environments and are thus roughly fair for all. So far, their efforts have not been crowned with success, although the idea underlying the test is sound in principle.

From what has been said it will be seen that standardizing a test is not a job for intellectual babes and sucklings. And even when norms have been established for a very wide area, they may be inapplicable to large groups within the area (e.g. the Stanford sample did not include negroes and Indians); and it is certain that they cannot be used outside the area unless the group tested is similar to one on which the standardization was made. Thus the Stanford Binet cannot be used with French-speaking Canadians, but its use with English-speaking Canadians is justified on the grounds of similarity of background and stock of Americans and English-speaking Canadians.

The Evaluation of Test Scores. — Suppose a group intelligence test has been administered and a pupil is reported to have made a score of 57 on it. Such a score is meaningless without further interpretation. If the test has age norms we may consult the norms and find that 57 is the average score of ten-year-old pupils. We can then say that our pupil has an intelligence equal to that of average ten-year-olds. But we cannot as yet say that the pupil is bright or dull. If, however, we know his age then we can interpret his score. If the pupil is fourteen then he is dull; he only makes a score equal to that of ten-year-olds. If, however, he is only eight then he is bright; at eight he has the intelligence of a ten-year-old.

It will be remembered that Binet and all others who have made tests of the standardized interview variety, expressed their scores as *mental ages*. Mental age is simple, and readily comprehended by everybody. If a boy of chronological age eight has a mental age of ten then he is brighter than the average. But how much brighter? The answer is two years brighter. Is this two years between eight and ten the equal of the two years between four and six or fourteen and sixteen? We do not know, but the chances are that it is different from both. There is, however, a way in which an evaluation can be made. We owe the idea to Stern and Bobertag, but it is Terman who has made it popular. This is the *intelligence quotient* (I.Q.), the ratio of the mental age to the chronological age. Thus the pupil in question whose chronological age was 8 and mental age 10, has an I.Q. of 1.25. To get rid of the decimal point the ratio is multiplied by 100 and the I.Q. is stated as 125. The average I.Q. is 100 and the range is from zero to something over 200.

The I.Q. is thus a measure of brightness. It shows whether a pupil has inferior, average or superior intelligence for his age. Repeated tests of the same individuals indicate that the I.Q. is relatively stable. If this be so, then the I.Q. indicates the rapidity of the growth of intelligence. Those with high I.Q.'s have grown rapidly in intellectual development and will probably continue to do so; those with low I.Q.'s have grown slowly.

Owing to the fact that we do not know when intelligence ceases to grow, M.A.'s and I.Q.'s for adults are more or less fictitious. In his first revision, Terman assumed that it ceased, on the average, at sixteen, that is, he assumed that all persons sixteen and above would make the same average scores. He therefore used 16 as the divisor in the calculation of I.Q.'s for all persons sixteen and over. In his new revision, he has taken into account the gradual tapering of intellectual growth and has begun his taperings of the chronological age at 13 years and 1 month and completed it at 15. (p. 31) His highest chronological age divisor in the calculation of I.Q. is thus 15. For young pupils, M.A.'s and I.Q.'s are intelligible concepts, but they begin to break down with adolescents and are more or less useless for adults.

Another ratio, somewhat similar to the I.Q., is the *coefficient of intelligence*, C.I. This ratio was used by Yerkes, Hardwick and Bridges in evaluating scores made on their point scale. It is the ratio of the point score of the individual and the point score which is the norm for his age. Thus if he makes a score of 50 when the norm for his age is 40, his C.I. is 1.25. Unlike the I.Q. whose variability increases with age, the variability of the C.I. decreases with age. This is due to the fact that the variation in scores with age is not proportional to the increase in the scores. The C.I. has not been widely used.

Otis introduced the *index to brightness*, I.B. This index is found by calculating the difference between the individual's score and the norm for his age, and summing it algebraically with 100. Thus if a person's score is 90 and the norm is 80, his I.B. is 100 + 10, or 110. If his score is 70 and norm 80, his I.B. is 100 — 10, or 90.

The *percentile rank* (more properly centile rank) has also been used as a method of evaluating scores. A percentile rank means the rank of a given score among 100, assuming that 100 individuals have been tested and ranked. A person

with a percentile ranking for intelligence of 75 is better than
25 in 100 and poorer than 25. If 160 persons are ranked,
the 80th individual has a percentile rank of 50.

Perhaps the best treatment of scores for interpretive purposes is to turn raw scores into *standard or variability scores*.
This makes use of the fact that the commonest element in
human traits is their tendency to be distributed according to
the normal surface of frequency. The usual method is to use
the standard deviation as the unit of variability. The general
formula for translating a raw score into a standard score is

$$z = \frac{X - M}{SD}$$

where z = standard score
X = individual's score on the test
M = mean of scores made by group
SD = standard deviation of scores

It will be seen that z scores may be plus or minus and may
range roughly from —5 to +5.

A modification of the above which gets rid of minus quantities and has a range of 100 units instead of 10, is McCall's
T score. The formula for its calculation is

$$T = 50 + \frac{10(X - M)}{SD}$$

The T unit, as used by McCall, is one-tenth of the standard
deviation of a random 12-year-old group used for standardization purposes. All forms of standard scores secured from
different tests may be summed arithmetically without statistical impropriety.

The Growth of Intelligence. — Intelligence tests confirm
the common-sense view that intelligence goes on growing
from birth to maturity. Yet, because we have lacked tests
which were scaled in equal units, and have had little opportunity of testing the same individuals from year to year, there
is some dispute as to the shape of the curve of growth of intelligence. Excepting CAVD, we have no absolute scale for
the measurement of mental growth. To plot mental age
against chronological age, as Baldwin and Stecher [23] have
done, is futile, since the only possible result which can be got

[23] Baldwin and Stecher, *Mental Growth Curve of Normal and Superior Children*,
University of Iowa Studies 2, No. 1.

with unselected subjects in such cases is a straight I.Q. line. The definitions of mental age and I.Q. preclude any other result. The Stanford Binet, from the method used in its construction, must necessarily give a linear relationship when M.A.'s are plotted against C.A.'s. The graphs representing age-progress of inferior and superior pupils when tested by the Stanford Binet are diverging straight lines. It should be obvious that the straight-line growth curve of intelligence cannot go on indefinitely. Somewhere during adolescence, it is believed, a slackening takes place. The mental age increments do not correspond to the chronological age increments and the linear relationship breaks down. Terman has recognized this, of course, both in his decreasing C.A. divisors in the calculation of I.Q. on his new scale, and in his experimental results. With his first 1916 scale, he found that the mean M.A. of thirty-two high school students, with a mean C.A. of eighteen years was $16 \pm .67$ years.

If the linear relationship breaks down, what is the shape of the mental growth curve? From analogy with physical growth, from results of group testing, and from the work of Thorndike and Thurstone, we can say with a good deal of assurance that the curve of growth of intelligence is either somewhat logarithmic or parabolic in shape. If it is logarith-

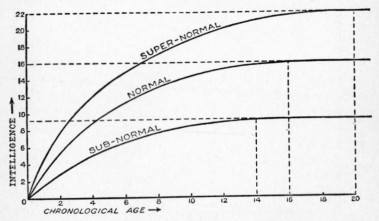

Fig. 39. Curves showing the Growth of Intelligence from Birth to Maturity. Note that the subnormals reach mental maturity at an earlier age than the others.

mic, then Fig. 39 is a faithful representation of the growth curves of supernormal, normal and subnormal individuals.

However, we need not guess its shape, we can appeal to experiment. Using CAVD, which is scaled in equal and absolute units, Thorndike found that "the curve altitudes of Intellect CAVD with age is of the general parabolic form shown in Fig. 40. There is a rise from 0 to about 30 at 6½, to about 34½ at 10½, and to about 36½ for adults 21 years old." (p. 463) A similarly shaped curve is obtained from the results of any tests such as the National A, Otis Advanced, and Haggerty Delta 2, providing the scores are first transmuted into equal-unit-scale scores.

Thurstone took Burt's data, consisting of records of the London-Binet on more than 3000 normal and defective London school children, and first determined mathematically the absolute zero of the scale. The successive increments of mental growth from year to year were measured in terms of a constant achievement unit. The absolute zero of this scale proved to be 13.9. The curve from birth to 15 years is shown in Fig. 41. It is parabolic in shape, rising rapidly to four years and then more slowly to 15 or 16 years. Gesell's curves of

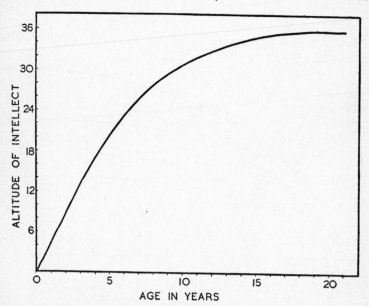

Fig. 40. Curve of Growth of Intelligence when measured by CAVD.

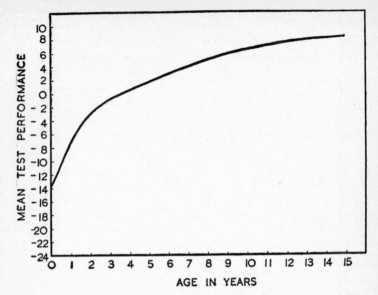

Fig. 41. Mental Growth on the Binet Tests measured in equal Units. (From Thurstone, "The Absolute Zero in Intelligence Measurement," *Psychol. Review*, XXXV, 1928, 175-197.)

mental growth in infants are logarithmic in character; in fact he plots them on a logarithmic chart.

Burt,[24] however, after analysing his data in many ways, came to the conclusion that "generalized logistic curves" best fitted them. His results in graphical form are shown in Fig. 42. "There seem to be two main phases. During the pre-school period, and particularly during the first year of life, there is a good deal of evidence to show that, both quantitatively and qualitatively, the child's mind develops at a more rapid pace than at any subsequent time — a pace which is not continuously maintained. About the third or fourth year of life a process of more steady if slower, advance sets in, which lasts until puberty, when, as has been amply demonstrated by all who have applied tests of intelligence, there is a marked and speedy retardation. Thus, at the two extremes, during the pre-school period and again at puberty and afterwards, the assumption of a constancy in the mental ratio may lead us widely astray." (p. 656)

[24] Cyril Burt, *The Backward Child*, Appendix II.

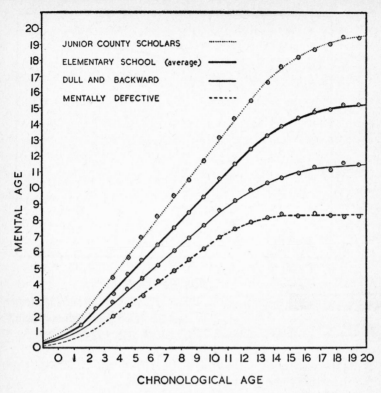

Fig. 42. Curves of Mental Growth for Normal, Subnormal, and Supernormal Children.

Note to Figure. — The centers of the small circles represent the averages in mental
years obtained at each chronological age with tests of intelligence. The curves are
"generalized logistic curves" drawn according to formulae which Burt developed.

The *age of maturity of intelligence* is still unknown. Binet,
from his results, considered that intelligence reached its maturity at fifteen. Terman, using bright Californians, fixed it
at sixteen, but has reduced it to fifteen in his new all-Amer-
ican revision. Otis and Monroe both regard eighteen as the
age of maturity of intelligence. Thorndike found that mental growth with high school pupils continued practically un-
diminished to the end of the high school period. Doll collected evidence which seemed to indicate that it should be
reduced to thirteen years. This latter figure agrees closely
with the results of mental testing in the United States Army,

where it was found that the average recruit made a score equal to that of a mental age of 13.08 on the Stanford Binet. In connection with this figure, it must be remembered that no person can secure a higher mental age than nineteen and a half years on the old Stanford Binet. Pintner placed maturity at 14, Kuhlmann at 15, Dearborn at 14½. This does not mean that intelligence never improves beyond these years; all that is implied is that in the scale employed, the average person fails to record progress beyond these age levels. The reason for some of these very low ages may lie in the lack of discriminative power of the tests at the higher ages. The scale used may be so coarse that it fails to record any progress at the upper levels.

Many studies show that mental maturity, at least with superior pupils, parallels rather closely physical maturity and continues at least to 20 or 21 years. We have referred to Thorndike's CAVD, where increases in scores continue to about 20 years of age, and to his study of 8000 high school students in grades 9 to 11 whose scores on an extensive battery of mental tests increased to eighteen years of age. Miss Teagarden,[25] who tested 408 children ranging from 12½ to 20 years old with the Stanford Binet and several group tests, found increases on all tests beyond sixteen years; and with the Stanford Binet up to eighteen years. Jones[26] tested a cross-section of a rural New England population consisting of 1,151 individuals from 11 to 54 years of age. The test used was the Army Alpha and the results are given in Table XLIV. From the Table it will be seen that the highest scores are made in the age group 19-21.

From the evidence we may conclude that the intelligence of normal individuals reaches maturity somewhere around twenty years of age. The summit of the curve, which is reached at this age, is the result of a negative acceleration of growth which begins in the pre-school period. However, increases in average intelligence will not show beyond fifteen or sixteen years with the coarse and somewhat inadequate intelligence tests now in use. For subnormal individuals, mental maturity may be reached at a much earlier age than fifteen

---

[25] F. M. Teagarden, *A Study of the Upper Limits of the Development of Intelligence*, 1924.

[26] H. B. Jones, reported by Thorndike in *Adult Learning*, pp. 157–159.

TABLE XLIV. SCORES IN *Army Alpha* MADE BY THE POPULATION OF A COMMUNITY, CLASSIFIED BY AGE. (From Data of Harold B. Jones)

Alpha Score	Frequencies at Ages											
	11 and 12	13 and 14	15 and 16	17 and 18	19 to 21	22 to 24	25 to 29	30 to 34	35 to 39	40 to 44	45 to 49	50 to 54
0– 9	4	1					1	1		1		
10– 19	2	5	2			1	3	4	3	6	4	1
20– 29	16	6	5	1	1	1	1	5	7	3	2	4
30– 39	25	8	8	4	6	3	2	6	9	3	5	6
40– 49	14	14	6	8	1	4	3	7	6	5	4	4
50– 59	21	21	7	5	11	2	9	7	10	9	10	6
60– 69	17	15	11	12	7	3	7	8	4	6	8	6
70– 79	9	12	13	6	9	6	13	11	5	4	5	4
80– 89	10	21	18	10	5	2	10	11	11	10	7	2
90– 99	2	8	15	9	9	3	12	2	7	9	5	2
100–109	3	8	8	3	4	3	6	5	5	5	3	3
110–119	2	6	10	11	6	4	8	7	6	6	5	3
120–129		2	9	9	7	4	1	7	8	4	1	7
130–139		2	11	4	1	3	1	9	7	7	2	2
140–149			7	4	6		5	4	4	6	5	1
150–159			5	6	2	3	3	3	1	4	1	2
160–169			2	2	2	1	2	2		3	2	2
170–179				2	6		2	4	2	3		1
180–189				1	3					1	1	
190–199						1	1	1				
200–209					2							

or sixteen, as early as eight in some cases, while super-normal persons may go on growing in mental stature until the middle twenties are reached.

A problem closely related to the growth of intelligence is the *constancy of the I.Q.* Theoretically, constant I.Q.'s can be secured by growth which is represented by straight lines or by logarithmic and parabolic curves. In non-straight line curves, it is necessary to assume that the annual increments of mental age decrease in amount with age and are so represented on the chart. To test the constancy theory, it is necessary to measure pupils for intelligence several times over a given period of years. The constancy or not of the I.Q. of a single individual can be seen from an examination of his growth chart. For groups of individuals the constancy is shown by finding the correlation of later scores with earlier ones. This has now been done by a host of workers. Sample results for Binet tests are given below:

Investigator	r	No. of Cases
Stenquist	.72	(274 cases)
Rugg and Colloton	.84	(137 cases)
Terman	.93	(435 cases)
Baldwin	.72 — .93	(various groups)
Jordan	.84	(44 cases)
Gray and Marsden	.85	(616 cases)
Hildreth	.81	(1112 cases)
	.85	(31 cases)
Cuneo and Terman	.94	(21 cases)
	.95	(25 cases)
Garrison	.88	(298 cases, 1 year's interval)
	.91	(127 cases, 2 years' interval)
	.83	(42 cases, 3 years' interval)
Lincoln	.95	(30 cases, tested same day)
Brown	.88	(707 cases of problem children)

The surprising fact is that the variability does not depend on the time interval between the tests. There is as much fluctuation in scores when the retest is given immediately as when the interval extends over several years. This indicates, of course, that the fluctuations are due to variations in the performances of the individual rather than to a change in the pupil's capacity. We may regard the I.Q., then, as fairly constant during the elementary school period, say, up to fourteen years of age. Absence of data for older ages precludes any statement about high school pupils and adults. A great change in environment, such as adoption into a family of different socio-economic status, or special tuition, or a change in endocrine balance, may lead to improvement or retrogression in I.Q. It should be noted that Barbara Burks concluded that the theoretical limit in the improvement of I.Q. was about 30 points, the practical limit about 20 points, and the actual change less than 10 points. All in all, then, considering the unreliability of the measuring instruments, the personal equations of the examiners, and the variability of the subjects due to practice, illness or fatigue, we may expect a person in late adolescence and as an adult to exhibit the same level of intelligence he showed as a child. Growth in intelligence proceeds fairly steadily from year to year without any marked fluctuations.

In Terman's investigation (435 cases) the following salient facts were found:

(1) The central tendency of the I.Q. on the retest was 1.7 points higher than on the first test.

(2) The middle 50 per cent of changes lay between the limits of 3.3 decrease and 5.7 increase.

(3) The probable error of a prediction based on the first test was 4.5 in terms of I.Q.[27]

The Distribution of Intelligence. — Since intelligence is a native trait we should expect it to be distributed according to the curve of chance as other natural variants are. There is a vast accumulation of evidence to show that this is the form of distribution actually followed. Terman[28] reported the distribution of I.Q.'s of 1000 unselected American children as follows (p. 66):

I.Q.	Percentage falling within group
55–65	0.33
66–75	2.3
76–85	8.6
86–95	20.1
96–105	33.9
106–115	23.1
116–125	9.0
126–135	2.3
136–145	0.55
	Total 100.18

If this distribution be plotted it will be found to follow the curve of chance somewhat closely. More recently,[29] he has

[27] L. M. Terman, *The Intelligence of School Children*, 1919, p. 142.
[28] L. M. Terman, *Measurement of Intelligence*, 1916.
[29] L. M. Terman and M. A. Merrill, *Measuring Intelligence*, 1937.

given the distribution of I.Q.'s of 1964 urban and 940 rural children. The urban child is defined as one who lives in an area having a density population of 1000 or more per square mile, and the rural group all others. These distributions are shown in Fig. 43. They also follow the normal curve closely.

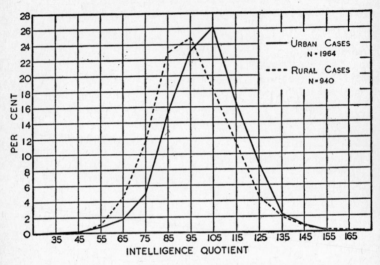

Fig. 43. Distributions of I.Q.'s of Rural and Urban Groups.
(Terman & Merrill)

Any division of intelligence into groups such as genius, normal, feebleminded and so forth, is an arbitrary proceeding since no sharp lines can be drawn at any point. Nevertheless, the divisions drawn in Table XLV have been found useful in practice, although they have encouraged the belief among the unthinking that they represented a sharply defined and immutable classification. The percentages falling within the various groups will also vary with different populations. Thus one child in 200-250 in California reaches an I.Q. of 140, compared with 1 in 400 given in Table XLV. Fig. 44 presents the facts of Table XLV in graphical form, the curve being smoothed to show its close approximation to the curve of chance.

Terman, in the first standardization of the Binet Tests upon 905 Californian children, found a standard deviation of 13 points. In his *Genetic Studies of Genius* (Vol. III, p.

TABLE XLV. DISTRIBUTION OF I.Q.'s IN A NORMAL
POPULATION

Classification	I.Q.	Percentages of all children included
"Near" genius or genius	140 and above	0.25
Very superior	120–139	6.75
Superior	110–119	13.00
Normal or average	90–109	60.00
Dull, rarely feebleminded	80– 89	13.00
Borderline, sometimes dull, often feebleminded	70– 79	6.00
Feebleminded	below 70	1.00
Total		100.00
Subdivisions of the Feebleminded		
(a) Moron	50– 69	0.75
(b) Imbecile	20 or 25 to 49	0.19
(c) Idiot	below 20 or 25	0.06
Total		1.00

29), he speaks of 15 as the usual number. In the famous Scottish Survey,[30] the S.D. on the Binet was 17 for boys and 16 for girls. Assuming a Gaussian distribution, the theoretical percentages showing a given I.Q. for S.D.'s 13, 16, and 17 respectively would be:

I.Q.	Standard Deviation %		
	13	16	17
above 130	1%	3%	4%
110–130	21	24	24
90–110	56	46	44
70– 90	21	24	24
below 70	1	3	4
	100	100	100

[30] Hepburn, Thomson and Kennedy-Fraser, *The Intelligence of Scottish Children; a National Survey of an Age-Group*, 1936.

Two thirds of the boys would range from 83 to 117 I.Q.; two-thirds of the girls from 84 to 116 I.Q. Obviously the percentage of children falling within the normal 90 — 110 I.Q. range usually given (60%) is too high. Forty-five per cent is nearer the mark. This means, of course, that more than one-quarter of pupils fall below 90 I.Q. Moreover, boys are more variable than girls and supply greater numbers both of the feebleminded and genius types.

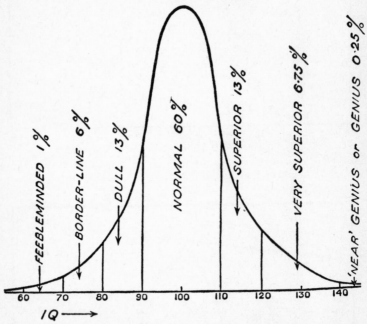

Fig. 44. Diagram showing the Distribution of I.Q.'s in a Normal Population.

Thorndike[31] has carried on a large number of researches to determine the form of distribution of intelligence as measured by group tests. Taking the results of eleven well-known intelligence tests, the distribution of each of which tended to approximate a Gaussian Curve, he combined them into a single composite distribution for grades 6 and 9, by averaging the frequencies for each successive one-tenth sigma and plotting the resultant curves. These are shown in Figs. 45 and 46.

31 E. L. Thorndike, *The Measurement of Intelligence*, 1927.

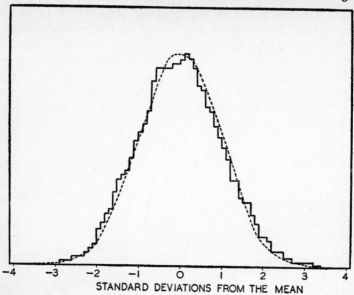

Fig. 45. Composite Curve for the Sixth Grade, based upon Eleven Single Curves. The broken line indicates the theoretical normal curve. (Thorndike)

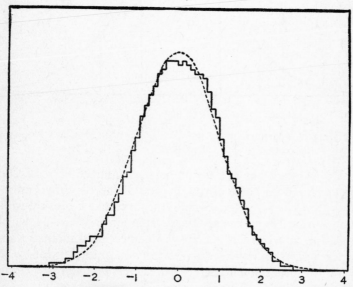

Fig. 46. Composite Curve for the Ninth Grade, based upon Eleven Single Curves. (Thorndike)

Both curves are seen to correspond closely to the Gaussian form. Similar results were obtained by averaging the results of ten tests to obtain a twelfth grade distribution and of eleven others to get a college freshmen distribution. These curves are shown in Figs. 47 and 48.

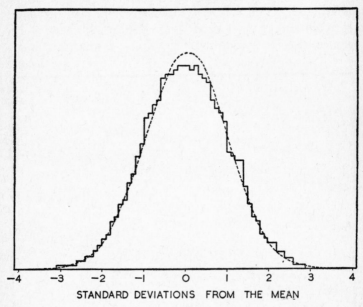

STANDARD DEVIATIONS FROM THE MEAN

Fig. 47. Composite Curve for the Twelfth Grade, based upon Ten Single Scores. (Thorndike)

Testing each of these composite curves by Pearson's Goodness of Fit Method P, Thorndike obtained the following results:

Grade	P (Goodness of Fit)
Sixth	0.999999
Ninth	1.000000
Twelfth	.999911
College Freshmen	.999988

Since 1.0 represents a perfect fit, each one of the curves approximates the Gaussian Curve so closely that it is almost indistinguishable from it. These four curves, therefore, present an impressive verification of the normal distribution of

intelligence. So much so, that if we obtained results from a test which were not distributed in Gaussian fashion, we should be justified in thinking either that the test had its limitations, or that our sample was not a random selection.

Regarding the limitations of the test, they may lie within the test itself. The test may be imperfectly constructed and standardized. The cure for this is to improve the test or start again and make a better one. The discordant results, however, may be due to practice effects, to coaching and to

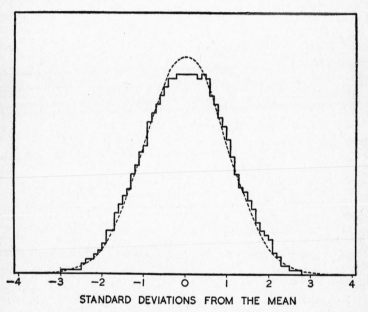

STANDARD DEVIATIONS FROM THE MEAN

Fig. 48. Composite Curve for College Freshmen, derived from Eleven Single Examination Scores. (Thorndike)

special environmental factors. Great care, therefore, must be exercised in the administration of intelligence tests and in the interpretation of results. Skewness of the curve when results are plotted, should arouse suspicion.

The Uses of Intelligence Tests. — Up to the present, intelligence tests have found their greatest usefulness in the *selection and classification of pupils* in terms of mental ability. In Ontario and other provinces of Canada, the pupils in "auxiliary" classes are selected by means of intelligence tests, and this course is universally followed wherever the segregation of the feebleminded is desired. In many cities, with Detroit as an outstanding example, the children are tentatively classified by means of intelligence tests as soon as they begin their schooling. Three classifications are employed — X, Y and Z. The X section consists of the highest 20 per cent in intelligence; the Y section is composed of the middle 60 per cent; while the lowest 20 per cent comprise the Z section. These three groups, the bright, average and dull, are given respectively an enriched course of study, the regular course, and a simplified course in which handwork, singing and games predominate. Although the classifications are considered provisional only, and the shifting of pupils from one group to another is permitted, very little shifting in practice has been found necessary.

As a device for re-grading pupils in a school so that more homogeneous groups may be obtained, intelligence tests have proved of greatest value. Pupils of approximately the same mental age are placed in the same grade. According to Terman,[32] the following may be regarded as the mental age standards for the different school grades of the United States. (pp. 13-14)

Grade	No. of Cases	Actual median mental age	Proposed standard mental age	Standard mental age at mid-grade
I	341	6–10	6–6 to 7–5	7 years
II	189	7–11	7–6 to 8–5	8 years
III	181	9–0	8–6 to 9–5	9 years
IV	253	9–11	9–6 to 10–5	10 years
V	226	11–0	10–6 to 11–5	11 years
VI	236	12–1	11–6 to 12–5	12 years
VII	193	13–1	12–6 to 13–5	13 years
VIII	180	14–2	13–6 to 14–5	14 years
IX	137	15–4	14–6 to 15–5	15 years

Obviously it is a desirable thing for the teacher to secure a group of pupils who are about equal in their learning ability, and for pupils to compete with their intellectual equals. It prevents the bright pupils from becoming bored with the

[32] L. M. Terman, *Intelligence Tests and School Reorganization*, 1923.

ceaseless repetition necessary for the dull pupils and, at the same time, it prevents the dull pupils from becoming discouraged through competition with pupils out of their intellectual class, as always happens when heterogeneous pupils are taught together. But this procedure throws the young, socially-immature pupils into the same grade as the older and bigger pupils. If there are very large numbers within a school, this disadvantage of homogeneous grouping may be overcome to some extent by further sectioning of the pupils. To section pupils of the same mental age, the I.Q.'s or what amounts to the same thing, the chronological ages may be used. Thus three groups for the same school grade can be selected — a dull, older group of low I.Q.; a medium age group of average I.Q.; and a bright, younger group of high I.Q. This device has been elevated by Pintner into a rule — for grading use M.A.; for sectioning use I.Q. (or C.A.). Corning calls the procedure "classifying vertically by M.A. and horizontally by I.Q." For small schools, the wisdom of homogeneous grouping has been questioned, because both the very bright and the very dull may have social difficulties, the former because he is the youngest in the class; the latter because he is the oldest. However, homogeneous grouping has, in general, proved so valuable, that every administrator should take steps to secure it. It is certainly superior to grouping by size or chronological age.

In some high schools and in all colleges and universities, the chief problem is not merely to classify pupils, but to select those who can benefit from the courses of study provided. In Canada, achievement tests, generally called matriculation examinations, are used to determine fitness for a university career. Intelligence tests, if used at all, are given to students in universities for purposes of research and are never used in the selection or guidance of the student body. In the United States, a different state of affairs is found. Over 60 per cent of colleges and universities make official use of mental tests either to select, classify, or to guide students. In fact, MacPhail [33] lists thirteen uses to which mental tests have been put by college and university authorities in the United States. They are as follows:

[33] H. A. MacPhail, *The Intelligence of College Students*, 1924.

1. To predict the probable quality of academic work that each student will do.
2. To select and refuse entrance to those applicants who are not sufficiently gifted in intelligence to do college work.
3. To serve as a regular means of entrance supplementary to or taking the place of certain customary entrance examinations.
4. To determine admission of special cases who cannot fulfil the usual entrance requirements.
5. To classify students for instructional purposes into groups of approximately equal ability.
6. To determine the amount of work a student should be permitted to carry.
7. To select students who should receive scholarship aid.
8. To aid in handling probationary and morally delinquent students.
9. To discover and deal with those who are wilfully slighting college work — "loafers."
10. To dismiss students for poor work.
11. To reinstate students.
12. To recommend students for positions.
13. To constitute a part of a general scheme of educational and vocational advice and direction for freshmen and others.

(p. 27)

Despite selection, university students exhibit wide variations in regard to intelligence. This is shown by examination of the results of the same test given in different institutions. According to Pintner,[34] college students should be able to score between 130 and 140 points on Army Alpha, but one group actually scored 160, and another as low as 80. (p. 296) Similar trends are shown by the results of the Thorndike Intelligence Examination, the means ranging from 64 to 79 in the various institutions which have used it. Even more striking are the findings of Learned[35] in the Pennsylvania Survey. On an Otis Intelligence Test, the engineering students of the state made a median score of 61.4, while students studying for degrees in education made a median score of 51.9. (Chart IV) If Chart I be examined, the remarkable discovery is made that the worst student in one college made a higher score on a comprehensive examination, which had

[34] Rudolph Pintner, *Intelligence Testing*, 1931.
[35] W. S. Learned, *Studies in Measurement in Higher Education*, Carnegie Foundation, 1934. Charts.

some attributes of an intelligence test, than the best student in another. Such diversity of standards of entrance calls for extended use of intelligence tests as a selecting agency.

The objection may be raised that if intelligence tests do not predict school achievement accurately, they should not be used as qualifying tests for entrance into educational institutions. Unfortunately, there are some grounds for this criticism. When the correlations between intelligence and academic tests of achievement are computed, they are found to fall mainly between .35 and .65. A few may run as high as .75 and some as low as .20. Perhaps Wood's and Thurstone's [36] findings are as representative as any. Wood found correlations ranging from .45 to .65 between the Thorndike Intelligence Test and freshman work in Columbia College. Thurstone found that the correlations between the American Council Psychological Examination and college freshmen achievement ranged from .40 to .60.

Disappointing as these correlations undoubtedly are, it should be remembered that they are considerably higher than the reported correlations between grades made in secondary school and those made in college. The intelligence test is a useful instrument in the selection of college students, but not an infallible one. Success in college not only depends upon native ability, but on habits of industry, health, tenacity of purpose and other features of one's personality.

Another important use to which intelligence tests have been put is in *vocational guidance and selection*. The publication of the results of the American Army tests [37] first drew attention to the variability of intelligence within different occupational levels. In general, unskilled laborers, teamsters and barbers made the lowest scores, while accountants, doctors and engineers made the highest. It would, therefore, be unwise to encourage a person of low intelligence to train for a profession. Rugg found that high school algebra demanded a minimum I.Q. of 110 if it were to be pursued with success. Dull pupils, therefore, should be discouraged from entering the academic high school; they are more likely

---

[36] Ben D. Wood, *Measurement in Higher Education*, 1923.
Thurstone and Thurstone, "The 1930 Psychological Examination," *Educational Record*, April, 1931.
[37] *Memoirs of the National Academy of Sciences*, Vol. XV, 1921.

to be successful in less bookish courses. It would be a mistake to suppose that intelligence tests alone will determine vocational fitness. While it is an important one, the factors of proficiency (knowledge or skill), personality and character, and interest in the work have also to be taken into account before vocational guidance and selection can be undertaken.

In the *discovery* and *diagnosis* of feeblemindedness, superior intelligence, special abilities and disabilities of children, and maladjustments of an educational or social nature wherever found, intelligence tests have proved of value. Whenever a "problem child" makes his appearance in a community, one of the first things done is to find his I.Q. Children who are guilty of minor infractions of the law and land in children's courts are almost invariably tested for intelligence. Criminals serving prison terms are also tested. The trouble may not lie in defective intelligence, but it is astonishing how frequently defective intelligence is a contributory factor in delinquency. For diagnostic purposes individual tests must be employed, since a close contact with the individual is necessary in such cases.

In *prognosis*, in forecasting the intellectual or even the vocational future of young persons, intelligence tests have played an important part. While intelligence, as we have seen, is not the only factor determining success, it is an important element in it. Intelligence tests will not tell us which pupils will succeed in school, but only which pupils will succeed providing they work hard, and remain reasonably free from disease, and from mental and moral degeneration. Consequently the forecasts from intelligence tests may be quite wide of the mark, but so may forecasts made on any other basis. All in all, intelligence tests have proved valuable and will be retained until they become obsolescent through the discovery of superior measuring instruments. At the moment, their use is on the increase rather than on the decrease, though more cautious interpretations are now made than was the case a decade ago.

The Results of Intelligence Testing. — Pintner[38] has made such an excellent survey of the results of intelligence testing that to make another would be a work of supererogation. In his comprehensive treatise he collects the results of

[38] Rudolph Pintner, *Intelligence Testing : Methods and Results,* 1931.

tests on pre-school children, elementary school pupils, high school pupils, college students, soldiers, the feebleminded, the superior, delinquents, dependents, the deaf, the blind, negroes, the foreign-born, employees, and the sexes. The reader is directed to this summary of findings. Suffice it to say that, in general, the incidence of feeblemindedness among delinquents has been found to be higher than among the general population — from 15 to 30 per cent in contrast with 1 or 2 per cent.[39]

Any group in the population suffering from a serious sensory defect, such as blindness or deafness, is certain to contain a greater percentage of mentally dull children than the rest of the community. The retardation in mental age of the deaf may be expected to be about 2 years at 12 years of age, 2½ years at 13, 3 years at 14 and 15. Since these retardations represent I.Q. deficiencies of 17, 19, 21 and 20 respectively, the task of educating deaf pupils is a formidable one. Among the blind, the proportion securing high I.Q.'s is less and the proportion with low I.Q.'s is greater than among the sighted group.

Certain racial groups, the negroes of the United States for example, have invariably tested below others. On the Binet tests, the inferiority runs from 1 to 17 points I.Q., with 10 points as the average. The more abstract the test, the greater the inferiority shown. Whether or not this is a real racial difference or merely the reflection of an inferior environment is not known. The negroes who have migrated north beyond the Mason-Dixon line show higher intelligence, as measured by tests, than those who remain in the South. Students in Fisk University almost approach white norms. According to Graham, who used many tests, 36 to 37 per cent of these colored college students reach the median of the whites, but they are, of course, a highly selected group. The mongoloids, represented mainly by Japanese and Chinese groups on the North American continent, seem to be as intelligent as the whites. In some tests, chiefly non-linguistic, they surpass the whites, but whether or not this is due to a

[39] It should be noted that the *White House Conference* report estimated that the lowest five per cent of the population of the United States (6,140,351) is mentally defective and that two per cent (2,456,140) is definitely feebleminded. In England, the best estimate (*Tredgold's*) places the number of feebleminded in the population at 10 per thousand or one per cent.

higher degree of selection, is not known. As stated in a previous section, there is a considerable body of evidence indicating that the caucasoids and mongoloids are about equal in intelligence. For negroids, the evidence so far accumulated indicates a lower level of intelligence in comparison with caucasoids and mongoloids. It is wise, however, to interpret findings about racial groups, immigrant groups, and groups with sensory defects very cautiously, since we usually do not know what selective factors have been at work, and certainly we are grossly ignorant about the proportionate parts that heredity and environment have played in determining the scores made in a test.

With regard to sex differences disclosed by intelligence tests, the evidence clearly points to an equality in average intelligence of the sexes; the central tendencies of scores of boys and girls exactly coincide. Boys, however, seem to be more variable than girls. If this finding is substantiated later, then it will have important social and educational repercussions. Since the very highest and very lowest intellects will be preponderantly male, it will be useless for women to expect to occupy with men the highest positions in invention, discovery, art and government.

Finally, the results from vocational groups show that occupational status correlates positively with intelligence; professional people test high, unskilled laborers test low. The environmental factor influences the scores, but not to the extent that environmentalists claim. Further, whenever the children of these people in different occupations have been tested, those from professional homes have invariably tested higher than those from homes of manual laborers. This means that intelligence sufficiently great to achieve success in a profession tends to be passed on to the next generation. Yet the fact remains that of a given selected population of school children with I.Q.'s 140 and above, the skilled labor group will contribute more members than the professional group. The reason is that there are so many more manual than professional workers; the professional group always contributes many times its quota if the size of the professional group is taken into consideration.

REFERENCES

Baldwin & Stecher. *Mental Growth Curves of Normal and Superior Children.* University of Iowa Studies 2, No. 1.

Binet & Simon. *Mentally Defective Children* (tr. W. B. Drummond). New York, Longmans, 1914. Pp. xi + 180.

Boynton, P. L. *Intelligence: its Manifestations and Measurement.* New York, Appleton, 1933. Pp. xi + 466.

Brown & Thomson. *The Essentials of Mental Measurement.* Cambridge University Press, 1921. Pp. x + 216.

Buros, Oscar K. *Educational, Psychological and Personality Tests.* Annual Bibliography since 1934: New Brunswick, N. J.: School of Education, Rutgers University.

Burt, C. *The Distribution and Relations of Educational Abilities.* London, P. S. King & Son, 1917. Pp. xiii + 93.

Burt, C. *Mental and Scholastic Tests.* London, P. S. King & Son, 1922. Pp. xv + 432.

Cox, Catherine M. *The Early Mental Traits of Three Hundred Geniuses.* Vol. II of Terman's "Genetic Studies of Genius." Stanford University Press, 1926. Pp. xxiii + 842.

Dickson, V. E. *Mental Tests and the Classroom Teacher.* Yonkers-on-Hudson, World Book Co., 1923. Pp. xi + 231.

Freeman, F. N. *Mental Tests; their History, Principles and Application.* Boston, Houghton Mifflin, 1926. Pp. ix + 503.

Garrett & Schneck. *Psychological Tests, Methods and Results.* New York, Harper Brothers, 1933. Pp. vi + 137 + 235.

Gaw, F. *Performance Tests of Intelligence.* Industrial Fatigue Research Board, Report No. 31. London, His Majesty's Stationery Office, 1925. Pp. iv + 45.

Gesell & Thompson. *Infant Behavior; its Genesis and Growth.* New York, McGraw-Hill, 1934. Pp. viii + 343.

Goring, C. *The English Convict: a Statistical Study.* Abridged Ed. London, H. M. Stationery Office, 1919. Pp. xvi + 275.

Hart & Spearman. "General Ability, its Existence and Nature." *Brit. Jour. Psychol.,* Vol. V (1912–13), pp. 51-84.

Herring, J. P. *Herring Revision of the Binet-Simon Tests: Examination Manual, Form A.* Yonkers-on-Hudson, World Book Company, 1926. Pp. 56.

Hollingworth, H. L. *Mental Growth and Decline.* New York, Appleton, 1927. Pp. xii + 396.

Holzinger, K. J. *Statistical Résumé of the Spearman Two-Factor Theory.* Chicago University Press, 1930. Pp. 43.

Hunt, Thelma. *Measurement in Psychology.* New York, Prentice-Hall, 1936. Pp. xx + 471.

Irwin & Marks. *Fitting the School to the Child.* New York, Macmillan, 1924. Pp. xxvi + 339.

Kelley, T. L. *Crossroads in the Mind of Man.* Stanford University Press, 1928. Pp. 238.

Laycock, S. R. *Adaptability to New Situations.* Baltimore, Warwick and York, 1929. Pp. xi + 170.

Learned, W. S. and Wood, B. D. *The Student and his Knowledge.* New York, The Carnegie Foundation, 1938. Pp. xx + 406.

MacPhail, A. H. *The Intelligence of College Students.* Baltimore, Warwick and York, 1924. Pp. 176.

Murchison, C. (Ed.) *The Foundations of Experimental Psychology,* Worcester, Clark University Press, 1929. Pp. x + 907.

National Society for the Study of Education. *Twenty-first Yearbook,* Parts I and II, "Intelligence Tests." Bloomington, Ill., Public School Publishing Company, 1922. Pp. 270.

National Society for the Study of Education. *Twenty-seventh Yearbook,* Parts I and II. Bloomington, Ill., Public School Publishing Company, 1928. Pp. ix + 465 ; and xv + 397.

Paterson, D. G. *Physique and Intellect.* New York, Century, 1930. Pp. xxvii + 304.

Pearson, K. "On the Relationship of Intelligence to Size and Shape of the Head." *Biometrika,* V, 1906.

Peterson, J. *Early Conceptions and Tests of Intelligence.* Yonkers-on-Hudson, World Book Co., 1925. Pp. xiv + 309.

Pintner, R. *Intelligence Testing: Methods and Results.* New Edition. New York, Holt, 1931. Pp. xii + 555.

Proctor, W. M. "Psychological Tests and Guidance of High School Pupils," *Jour. Educ[l]. Research Monograph,* No. I, October 1923, pp. 125.

Psychological Tests of Educable Capacity. Report of English Board of Education Consultative Committee. London, H. M. Stationery Office, 1924. Pp. xi + 248.

Ruch and Stoddard. *Tests and Measurements in High School Instruction.* Yonkers-on-Hudson, World Book Co., 1927. Pp. xix + 375.

Scottish Council for Research in Education. *The Intelligence of Scottish Children: A National Survey of an Age Group.* University of London Press, 1933. Pp. x + 160.

Spearman, C. "Some Issues in the Theory of G." *Proceedings, British Association,* Section J, Southampton, 1925.

Spearman, C. "General Intelligence, Objectively Determined and Measured," *Am. J. Psy.,* Vol. XV, 1904, pp. 201-293.

Spearman, C. "The Theory of Two Factors," *Psy. Rev.,* Vol. XXI, 1914, pp. 101-115.

Spearman, C. *The Nature of Intelligence and Principles of Cognition.* London, Macmillan, 1927. Pp. xii + 362.

Spearman, C. *The Abilities of Man: their Nature and Measurement.* London, Macmillan, 1927. Pp. viii + 415 + Appendix, pp. xxxiii.

Stutsman, Rachel. *Mental Measurement of Pre-school Children.* Yonkers-on-Hudson, World Book Company, 1931. Pp. x + 368.

Symposium on Intelligence. *Jour. Educ. Psychol.,* XII, 3 and 4, 1921, pp. 123-147; 195-216.

Terman, L. M. *The Measurement of Intelligence.* Boston, Houghton Mifflin, 1916. Pp. xviii + 362.

Terman, L. M. *The Intelligence of School Children.* Boston, Houghton Mifflin, 1919. Pp. xxii + 317.

Terman et al. *Intelligence Tests and School Reorganization.* Yonkers-on-Hudson, World Book Company, 1923. Pp. vi + 111.

Terman et al. *Genetic Studies of Genius,* I. Stanford University Press, 1925. Pp. 80 + 648.

Terman and Merrill. *Measuring Intelligence.* Boston, Houghton Mifflin, 1937. Pp. xiv + 461.

Thomson, G. H. "General *versus* Group Factors in Mental Activities," *Psychol. Review,* Vol. XXVII, 1920, pp. 173-190.

Thomson, G. H. *Instinct, Intelligence and Character.* New York, Longmans, Green, 1925. Pp. 282.

Thorndike, E. L. *Educational Psychology,* Vol. III. New York, Teachers College Bureau of Publications, 1921. Pp. x + 408.

Thorndike, E. L. *Adult Learning.* New York, Macmillan, 1932. Pp. x + 335.

Thorndike et al. *The Measurement of Intelligence.* New York, Teachers College Bureau of Publications, 1927. Pp. xxvi + 616.

Thurstone, L. L. *The Nature of Intelligence.* New York, Harcourt Brace, 1924. Pp. ix + 167.

Tredgold, A. F. *A Text-book of Mental Deficiency (Amentia).* London, Baillière, Tindall and Cox, 1937. Pp. xvi + 556.

Varon, Edith J. "The Development of Alfred Binet's Psychology." *Psychol. Review Monogs.,* XLVI, 3, 1935. Pp. 129.

Webb, E. "Character and Intelligence," *Brit. Jour. Psychol. Monogs.,* No. 3, 1913.

Wood, B. D. *Measurement in Higher Education.* Yonkers-on-Hudson, World Book Co., 1923. Pp. 337.

Woodrow, H. *Brightness and Dullness in Children.* Philadelphia, Lippincott, 1919. Pp. 322.

Yerkes, R. M. "Psychological Examining in the U. S. Army," *Academy of Science Memoirs,* Vol. XV, 1921. Pp. 890.

CHAPTER VI

PERSONALITY: ITS NATURE AND MEASUREMENT

The Meaning of Personality. — Personality is a word which has scores of meanings attached to it. It is, therefore, very difficult to use as a scientific concept. However, since it enters into popular use so frequently and has become part of the vocabulary of the common man, attempts should be made by psychologists to use it with technical precision. In some ways it would be better for psychologists to do as the medical men have done, namely, develop a technical language of their own for communication among themselves, and to preserve the terms of common speech for simple use with laymen. If common terms such as sensation, intelligence and personality are to be used with scientific accuracy, then there must be no dubiety in regard to their meaning. Unfortunately, this is not the case, although Warren's *Dictionary of Psychology* has improved the situation immeasurably. We saw in our last chapter that there were difficulties with the word "intelligence." With "personality" the difficulties are still greater. For measuring intelligence, at least there are fairly good instruments, but nobody at present knows how to measure personality accurately. Since measurement leads to better definition of the thing measured, we may hope, when the scientists have devised accurate measuring instruments for personality, to define it with accuracy and precision in terms of the results that have been obtained.

There is little doubt that personality, like intelligence, is rooted in original nature and develops through interaction with the environment. The chief stimulus for the growth of personality is the social milieu; people rather than things constitute the environment in which personality develops.

Allport,[1] in the most critical study of personality so far made, has divided the definitions of personality into seven groups, namely,

[1] Gordon W. Allport, *Personality; a Psychological Interpretation*, 1937.

(1) Early derivative meanings of Persona (the Mask)[2]
(2) Theological meanings
(3) Philosophical meanings
(4) Juristic meanings
(5) Sociological meanings
(6) External appearance (biosocial definitions)
(7) Psychological meanings

Personality has to do with persons. A man's personality is what he really is; it is the state of being a person. Allport insists that it must be defined in biophysical terms and considers the following definition to represent a synthesis of contemporary psychological usage:

Personality is the dynamic organization within the individual of those psychophysical systems that determine his unique adjustments to his environment. (p. 48)

Compare this excellent definition with those that have been given by other well-known workers in the field. For example,

(1) *Kantor.* Personality may be defined as the totality of a particular individual's reactions, in sum everything the individual does or can do.

(2) *Brown.* Personality is the final differentiation which the individual has made, as it were, and produced in himself and superimposed upon all that he has inherited from past generations and lower forms of mental evolution. It can best be thought of as mental unity.

(3) *Campbell.* The personality is the expression of the total forces of the individual; it is the product of their integrated activity; it is the man in action as seen by the outsider and known to himself.

(4) *Berg.* Personality is an integrated psycho-physical pattern; it is the totality of the individual formed by the action of the

[2] According to philologists the word personality is derived from the Latin *persona,* the name for a theatrical mask through which the actor spoke. The Greek name for the actor's mask was prosôpon, but it is unlikely that persona was derived from prosôpon. The best guess is that persona was derived from *per sonare* (to sound through), which was actually what the actors did with their masks—they spoke their lines through them. In course of time, persona became attached to the speaker behind the mask rather than to the mask itself. This is seen in our use of *dramatis personae* and *persona grata.* We still have personages, person in grammar, parsons etc., all derived from the root persona.

environment upon his hereditary potentialities. It signifies the sum total of his own and his ancestral past; his physique, his emotions, his brain patterns and his abilities. We do not see or feel an individual's personality, but we know it through behavior.

(5) *Watson.* My personality is but the sum total of my habit systems, my conditionings. What I am at any age is just what I can do at that age.

(6) *Gordon.* Personality is the emergent synthesis of the bodily and mental attributes of the individual in relation to the environment in the most comprehensive sense.

If we study these seven definitions carefully we find many excellent features. We note the emphasis on the hereditary elements of personality and the interaction of these with environment. Integration, the unity of the personality, is also stressed. But above all, the definitions are practically unanimous in insisting that personality is the expression of behavior. While it is true that personality may only become known to others through behavior, the definitions give one the impression that personality somehow or other disappears when it is not being expressed. This is a false view. The personality, the self, the person or whatever we care to call it, is still there. When a person gives rapt attention to a performance of beautiful music there are few overt acts which give outsiders a clue to the ecstatic bubblings of the personality within, yet the personality is undoubtedly there and, as Campbell states, is known to himself.

If personality is what a person really is, then the term must be restricted to persons, to human beings, and cannot be applied to animals. Dogs and cats have individualities but never personalities. Further, every person must have a personality, be it strong or weak, social or anti-social, balanced or unbalanced. And every personality is necessarily unique; no two persons can have exactly the same personality. Personality is a quality of persons exhibiting sufficient unity to be described and appraised.

If personality is more than its overt expression in behavior, it still remains true to say that it can only be known to outsiders and evaluated by them in terms of behavior. But any given form of behavior may affect different observers in different ways. In technical language, it may have a different stimulus value for each beholder. Thus the same personality may appear to be a different personality to different observers. Each individual, in this sense, may seem to have a multitude of personalities. Of course, his personality may really exhibit different aspects at different times, but it is sufficiently unitary to be described rather faithfully.

Not all of our behaviors or actions are clues to our personalities. Our pupillary reflex to light does not tell anybody very much about our personality. Some forms of behavior have much more significance, more stimulus value than others, in the identification of a personality. In school, the teacher may ask the children to spell "wood." Any normal and ready response — W, O, O, D — is relatively insignificant as a mark of personality. But if one of the pupils stammers or is emotionally upset when asked by the teacher to spell a word, the stammering or the emotional upset may be an important cue for the teacher; it may, in fact, have a unique stimulus value for him in the identification of the pupil's personality. Multiply this unique response by hundreds and we see that for the outside observer, the total personality is made up of those responses which have value in singling it out from all others. Personality in this objective evaluation is an abstraction, as it were, derived from significant acts of behavior. Some actions are profoundly significant as signs of our personalities because, as our acquaintances say, they "give us away" every time.

Since personality is a word used by the common man, it is likely to be given meanings that run counter to a scientific definition. Most of the popular misconceptions, when examined, seem to be due to special and partial usages. Thus personality is sometimes used as if it meant merely the superior qualities of mankind. But inferior qualities also enter into personality. Thus a gangster has a personality, often a dominating one, and even an idiot or an imbecile has a personality of a kind.

Other partial meanings or outright popular misconceptions are listed below:

(1) Regarding personality as merely anatomical traits, such as tallness, slenderness, fine complexion, beautiful hair, rotundity and so forth. Undoubtedly, bodily traits influence our judgment of a given individual's personality, but per-

sonality is more than anatomical traits. Still, it is illuminating to see how beliefs of this kind persist. Shakespeare, voicing a common belief of his time, wrote

> "Let me have men about me that are fat,
> Sleek-headed men, and such as sleep o' nights:
> Yond Cassius has a lean and hungry look;
> He thinks too much: such men are dangerous."

Yet history is full of fat villains and slender saints. Of course, owing to the desire to seek compensation, a defective physique may twist the personality in some way or other. Some small men are undoubtedly cocky through compensation; but most small men are probably timid and retiring. Some of the world's greatest men, for example, Socrates and Darwin, were hardly renowned for beauty, yet their sterling personalities remade the worlds in which they lived.

(2) Regarding personality as merely good grooming. However, the downcast wife who goes out and buys herself a new hat is using a sound psychology.

(3) Regarding personality as magnetism and charm, or even as "it" of the movies. Good manners are elements of value in the evaluation of a personality and we like to see people behaving nicely. They make the world a pleasanter place to live in, but manners should not be a mere accomplishment but a true reflection of the personality within. It should be noted, however, that manners vary with time and place. Good manners in America are bad manners in China and *vice versa*, yet we should never mistake a boor either in China or America.

(4) Lastly, we should not regard personality as mere trustworthiness, honorable behavior, pleasing speech and good carriage, estimable as each of these may be. The English Public School is said to cultivate these virtues. Sometimes, however, it results in worship of good form and conformity to type, which are not obvious characteristics of strong personalities. As a matter of fact, the strongest personalities seem to resist the tendency towards assimilation in the crowd; they stand out as prominently as the wart on Cromwell's nose.

If personality is what a person really is, we may have difficulty in judging it fairly. We normally judge persons scientifically from many angles — their build, their physiology, their bio-chemistry, their psychology and so on. When we study personality we emphasize those psychological elements that are of significance in a person's make-up. We look for a unity, an integration, a pattern in his many-sided behavior. His personality may change in its outward expressions from day to day and hour to hour, yet it is sufficiently stable and enduring to be studied, compared, contrasted and criticized. The gay person may have his sober moments, yet the general picture of him we carry away is one of lightheartedness. This means, of course, that the average behavior remains fairly constant with the passing of time, that the average expression of personality is a true reflection of the personality within. This personality pattern begins to show itself early in life. Even babies have personalities as mothers and nurses can testify. Those who have studied the Dionne quintuplets are certain that they have markedly different personalities. So pervasive is this integrated pattern of personality, that the investigation of it as the central feature of their field of study has commended itself both to organismic and gestalt psychologists.

If, however, personality is regarded as the central subject of inquiry by psychologists, they will have to ask themselves the questions — Does the personality pattern remain constant throughout life? And if it changes with the years, what is the extent of the change? Unfortunately, we do not know the answer to these important questions, but we may hazard the guess that the main outlines are drawn early and all that life does is to fill in the pattern. It is the old riddle of heredity and environment once more. Both contribute to the total pattern of personality, but we do not know the amounts of their respective contributions. One school of thought regards personality as almost completely determined by environmental factors; another school would give much more weight to nature's contributions. Neither the extreme hereditarian nor the extreme environmentalist position should be taken, since personality is the product of both nature and nurture. It must be admitted, however, that personality seems to be more fluid than, say, physique or even intelligence, and therefore is more open to change by environmental influences. There are personalities which seem to be completely reversed by the happenings of life, a state of affairs which is relatively infrequent in regard to physique and intelligence.

In studying personality, we try to find out what distinguishes one personality from another. The traditional method that science employs would compel us to select some single function or variable, experiment with it, measure it, and interpret our findings. The weakness of this approach as far as personality is concerned is that the individual person does not seem to be merely a conglomeration of such things as general intelligence, perception, mechanical aptitude, linguistic ability, perseveration, muscular tonus and the like. He remains uniquely a person. True, Allport makes out a good case for traits as the identifiable and usable elements in the study of personality, but even he has his difficulties. It may be that we shall have to wait until psychology has devised methods of studying persons as wholes rather than as parts or elements, but that is not the way in which other sciences have progressed. The search for recognizable elements proceeds apace and undoubted progress is being made. Even the stumbling and halting methods that have so far been made in the measurement of personality have brought us a little nearer the goal.

Whatever view we take of the theoretical problems of personality, its importance for practical life cannot be overlooked. People in general appraise it; the employer looks for it when selecting his employees; clubs try to secure members possessing it abundantly; and its importance in politics, law, teaching and other occupations cannot be denied. The fact that, up to the present, it has resisted most of the onslaughts of the scientific investigator, and has led to the emergence of that cancerous growth on the body scientific — the psychological charlatan — should not dismay us. We may deplore the presence of astrologers, tea-cup readers, bump-feelers, palmists and character-readers among us, but we regain perspective when we remember that other sciences have had their charlatans. Chemistry outgrew alchemy, astronomy outgrew astrology and the science of personality will outgrow its hangers-on. If, as we believe, personality does not lie outside physical and mental law, careful investigation should enlighten us as to its nature and function. Genetic studies show that we tend as we grow older to integrate a great core of habits which undoubtedly stabilize the personality. It may be here that the solution of the problem lies. If to our studies of the integration of habits, we add those which trace the integration of our emotional tendencies, beliefs, attitudes and interests, a corpus of knowledge will be secured which may have both theoretical and practical value. Or we may continue the search for elements and find that traits are the elements that have significance for personality. By defining them in scientific terms we may find them usable and valuable in our study.

The reader who has got as far as this in his reading, may not have a very clear idea of the meaning of personality, but the fault lies in the subject. New ground is being broken, and our present knowledge of personality is admittedly meager. We must not, however, take a defeatist attitude, but go confidently on in the belief that the scientific methods which have led to victories in other fields, will lead to victories in the difficult field of personality.

The Relationship of Character, Temperament and Disposition to Personality. — *Character* and personality originally meant about the same thing. The character was what was engraved on the individual by his dominant traits. Later it came to have a motor and a social emphasis. What a man habitually did, how he responded to social situations, became the mark of his character. However, it was inevitable that these actions should be judged according to the ethical code of the time and place, hence character came to mean the moral evaluation of an individual. Since scientific psychology is not concerned with ethical problems as such, character should be relegated to courses in ethics. Contributions similar to those that the study of character made in the past, can now be more surely achieved by the investigation of drives, controls, etc., in connection with the psychology of behavior.

Temperament is usually regarded as an inborn type of emotional response. According to the classical doctrine, the vagaries of temperament could be ascribed to excesses or deficiencies of one or other of the bodily humors. Through endocrinology, the doctrine has been revived in a new form, and now these "modern humors" are regarded as the internal environment in which personality develops and flourishes. Since endocrine imbalance generally has an hereditary basis, further ground for regarding personality as being hereditarily determined is secured. "Glands Regulating Temperament" would probably be a more scientific title than "Glands Regulating Personality." Every personality has its temperament. Temperament may best be regarded as the emotional constituent of personality.

By *disposition* we mean a mental tendency resulting from past experience or from ancestral conditions. An organic tendency to a specific line of growth and development is also called a disposition. In many respects, a disposition resembles the generalized habit of Colvin and Dewey. According to McDougall, disposition is one of the five elements of personality, the other four being temperament, temper, character and intellect.

Thus, according to the view we take, temperament, disposition and character may each be regarded as elements in the constitution of personality, or temperament alone may be so regarded. The second view is the one now generally adopted.

The Elements of Personality.— Psychology has not been very happy in the selection of the mental elements it has chosen to study. At various times in its history, it has selected elements such as faculties, sensations, reflexes, ideas, images, traits, motivations, capacities, factors and many others, depending chiefly on the interests of those who selected them. We have to confess that mental elements have not been identified or segregated for study. However, we need not be too self-depreciatory, for a similar state of affairs exists in such well-established sciences as physics and chemistry. Chemistry made astounding progress during the nineteenth century with its elementary atoms and combinations of them in the form of molecules. If, later, atoms proved to be little worlds composed of electrons, protons, neutrons and the like, no harm has been done. But at the chaos of mental elements in psychology, psychologists themselves began to rebel. The rise of the organismic and gestalt schools is a testimony of this rebellion. The categories chosen for study by psychologists were not mutually exclusive and therefore could not be elements in the true sense of the word. The present-day shift in psychology is towards mental structures and away from psychic atoms. It may be, that these structures are sufficiently integrated and organized to repay our study of them. Further, this study may reveal sub-structures of a still more elementary nature.

What possible mental structures enter into the unitary whole called personality? Suppose we list some of them that have received consideration.

1. Physical or anatomical characters — height, beauty, hair color, bodily build, health, etc. It is obvious that some of these enter into our evaluation of a personality, but they seem relatively insignificant, since there are strong personalities which seem to lack most of these gifts of nature.

2. Intellectual abilities such as native intelligence and educational achievement. In selecting these we seem to be on more solid ground, yet some geniuses seem to be lacking in personality, and some ill-educated persons have dominated vast areas of the world.

3. Physiological traits — basal metabolism, blood pressure, blood groups, coagulation time, acid-base equilibrium, blood sugar, blood calcium, blood phosphorus, opsonic index (resistance to infection), endocrine balance and many others. Recent studies point to the immense importance of some of these, especially the endocrine balance, in the determination of the emotional life of the individual, and therefore of his personality.

4. Capacities — musical capacity, mathematical capacity and the like, determined primarily by inheritance but modified by training.

5. Aptitudes — ability to acquire through training such things as proficiency in a foreign language or skill in carpentry.

6. Skills — acts easily and precisely performed, such as typewriting, billiards, tennis, basketball, or the playing of a musical instrument.

7. Accomplishments — traits placing individuals in a class above others — playing a musical instrument or speaking a foreign language.

8. Habits — acquired responses relatively invariable and readily elicited such as spelling, writing, walking and swearing.

9. Disposition — mental tendency resulting from past experience or from ancestral conditions; an organic tendency to a specific line of growth or development. We generally de-

scribe dispositions by adjectives such as sweet, charming, ugly, and so forth.

10. Temperament — the general affective nature of an individual as determined by his inheritance and life history. Temperaments in the past were attributed to the bodily humors; today they are usually attributed to the functioning of the endocrine glands. In persons of nervous temperament there seems to be a high excitability of the nerves.

11. Manners and mannerisms — shyness, boldness, aggressiveness, timidity, gentleness.

12. Faculties — a power or agency of the mind through whose action mental phenomena could be explained — intellect, feeling, will, reason, judgment, observation, memory, attention, etc.

13. Motivations or Needs — the things which serve as incentives to action — hunger, sex, dominance, abasement, seclusion.

14. Bonds — the thing in the organization of the individual that is responsible for his making, more or less regularly, a certain response to a given stimulation, hence the S-R theory. Bonds are elemental and specific. The total intellect or personality is the collection of bonds composing it.

15. Factors — units of mental organization, discoverable by mathematical analysis based on certain relationships among correlation coefficients, and apparently the modern equivalent of faculties. The commonest factor discovered by factor analysis is the verbal factor; but mechanical, numerical, practical, sociability, self-confidence and many group factors have also been obtained.

16. Traits — distinctive modes of behavior, of a more or less permanent nature, arising from a person's native endowments as modified by his experience. Ascendance, persistence, extraversion, self-assurance, tact are typical traits studied by the student of personality.

Even a casual inspection of the above list reveals many cases of overlapping. Several of the illustrative examples are listed in two or more of the categories. It may be that personality is of such a fused nature that overlapping of this kind is inevitable. But common sense dictates that the elements we use should be comprehensible, unitary and consistent. They need not be independent, for personality is not simply the sum-total of a number of independent factors, but the consolidation and integration of our various "selves" into a united personality.

After examining the various possibilities, Allport thinks that the hypothesis of traits best fills the need of psychologists. "Far better than any other doctrine of elements this hypothesis helps to account for consistency in personality wherever consistency is found, and for inconsistency whenever conflict and discordance prevail. . . Most significant of all the attributes of traits for the problem of unity is their interdependence . . . With the assumption of *over-lapping* traits the task is easier, for the very conception itself contains the idea of *fusion*. Unity lies in the overlap of the traits with one another." (p. 347)

Yet there are lions in the way. Even if we define trait, as Allport does, as "a generalized and focalized neuropsychic system (peculiar to the individual), with the capacity to render many stimuli functionally equivalent, and to imitate and guide consistent (equivalent) forms of adaptive and expressive behavior," our difficulties are not at an end. There is the problem of naming traits. Traits have been named from time immemorial, and now a large dictionary will contain about 20,000 trait-names. Which of these shall we select? Which are significant in the evaluation of personality? If we stick to common traits, which when tested can be scored on a continuous scale, we get such a selection as shown in the sample below:

Extraversion	—	Introversion
Persistence	—	Vacillation
Ascendance	—	Submission
Self-assurance	—	Self-distrust
Gregariousness	—	Solitariness
Altruism	—	Egoism
Generosity	—	Selfishness
Tactfulness	—	Tactlessness
Stability	—	Instability

There is much overlapping and this is inevitable, but if such traits as listed are important in the evaluation of personality, they should be used in interviewing, in testing programs, in rating scales and in a host of other ways. Not that they will give a complete picture of the personality. The outlines will have to be filled out by tests or evaluations of health, intelligence, temperament and the like.

There is also the problem of common as contrasted with individual traits or as Lewin[3] calls them, genotypical and phenotypical attributes. There are surface, here-and-now traits, and there are underlying motives and stresses. External conduct is phenotypical, but the underlying causes of this behavior are genotypical. Obviously, when external conduct does not "square" with the underlying personality, the truer view is the genotypical, but it is rather difficult to discover what an individual is trying to do, to learn what is the true motivation of his conduct, when we have only his external behavior to guide us. Sometimes, however, it is possible to bring many phenotypical behaviors into a single genotypical classification.

Thirdly, there is the problem of the distribution of traits among the population. Are traits normally distributed? If extraversion and introversion are simply the extremes of a continuous distribution, it is sensible to expect the majority of people to be neither markedly introvert nor extravert. Evidence accumulates which lends color to the view that common traits are normally distributed in an unselected sample of the population, with the majority of individuals exhibiting no marked variations one way or the other.

Personality testers have apparently decided that their chief job is to measure traits, especially the common traits that are normally distributed in the population. But it is one that must be supplemented by other measures and evaluations, and above all by consideration of those individual traits which are unique in each person examined. The present status of traits as the elements of personality is confessedly unsatisfactory. There has been too much of what Lorge has described as determination of "traits by fiat," but experimentation will weed out those which are not unitary or do not help us in judging a personality. Such traits as we accept for purposes of study must have both a demonstrable existence and unitary character.

Sample List of Personality Types.—The vitality of the doctrine of personality types is an astounding feature of psychology. From the time of Hippocrates, who proclaimed that personality was dependent upon the humors of the body, through various phases of characterology, through

[3] Kurt Lewin, *A Dynamic Theory of Personality*, 1935.

many classifications according to physique right up to modern psychoanalytic types of personality, the doctrine of types has enjoyed an unbroken succession. Modern scientific psychology, which insists upon measurement, has cast doubts upon the validity of the doctrine, but an idea which persists as valiantly as this has done leads one to suspect that there may be more than a grain of truth in it. The appended list does not pretend to be exhaustive, nor is it arranged in historical order. Those who wish to delve more deeply into the subject, especially into types of character, should consult the scholarly work on the subject by Roback.[4]

A. *According to Bodily Structure.*

1. *Stockard's* Linear and Lateral Types. This classification arose as an outgrowth of Stockard's[5] experimental researches on the crossing of breeds of dogs. The various breeds of dogs seemed to have different and heritable temperaments, as well as hereditary sizes and shapes. These Stockard showed to have their bases chiefly in hereditary modifications of the endocrine glands. Arguing chiefly by analogy, he inclines to the belief that the linear and lateral types of men represent true qualitative differences, just as the St. Bernard, the Pomeranian, and the bulldog represent not only differences in breed but also differences in their manner of behavior. Their individualities differ, some breeds being noted for their friendliness and others for their shyness, some for a dignity of bearing and others for their frivolous foolishness.

Stockard's linear and lateral types of men closely resemble the dolicho-cephalic (long-headed) and the brachy-cephalic (short-headed) classifications of the anthropologist. The linear type is thin, though not necessarily tall; the lateral type is wide and thickset with all his organs voluminous instead of linear. The linear is the typical hyper-thyroid; the lateral the typical hypo-thyroid. Since thyroxin is a growth-stimulating substance, and since length is achieved before volume in all organisms, it may be that the linear and lateral types are simply manifestations of a differential rate of growth. A hyper-active thyroid will result in fast growing, rapidly differentiating structures of the linear kind.

[4] A. A. Roback, *The Psychology of Character*, 1928.
[5] Charles R. Stockard, *The Physical Basis of Personality*, 1931.

Since glandular imbalance is an inherited feature, it follows that the linear and lateral are natural types. Further, there is evidence to support the contention that the lateral type is of later evolution than the linear, and that it was developed in inland regions far removed from coastal plains rich in iodine.

In personality characteristics, the linear type is active, energetic and nervous, quite self-conscious and therefore constantly forced to exert nervous control. The linears have large Adam's apples, bass voices, and are rather solemn and seldom laugh. The lateral types are exactly the opposite. They sing tenor, are less adventurous than the linear types, and choose fatty foods and much sugar for their diets. The typical Englishman, according to Stockard, is linear; the typical German lateral in type.

2. *Kretschmer's* Asthenics (slight), Pyknics (plump), Athletics and Dysplastics (disproportionate). These classificatory types were derived from a study of the inmates of mental hospitals. Briefly, he found that the asthenic physiques provided the majority of cases of dementia praecox, while the pyknics supplied the manic-depressive cases. His results are summarized in Table XLVI.

TABLE XLVI.   PHYSICAL AND PSYCHIC DISPOSITIONS.
(Kretschmer)

Physical type	Circular	Schizophrene
Asthenic	4	81
Athletic	3	31
Asthenico-Athletic mixed	2	11
Pyknic	58	2
Pyknic mixture	14	3
Dysplastic		34
Deformed and uncataloguable forms	4	13
Totals	85	175

Two hundred and sixty cases from mental hospitals are too few to base a theory of personality upon. True, the pyknic physiques were mostly found among the manic-depressive patients (cycloids, circulars), while the asthenic, athletic and dysplastic physiques were found most frequently among dementia praecox patients (schizoids, schizophrenes) as the table indicates, but Kretschmer was not satisfied with this. Arguing that the abnormal is but an exaggeration of the normal, he developed his theory of the cycloid and schizoid temperaments and extended it into a classification of normal personality. Thus he states that asthenics who, because of their build, have the schizoid temperament, must also exhibit the schizoid qualities of introversion, formalism, idealism and romanticism. Similarly, the pyknics must be jovial, extraverted, realistic and objective, because these are the characteristics of the cycloid temperament. In studying the geniuses of the world, Kretschmer finds that they fit neatly into his classification. Kretschmer's theory requires that personality, temperament and character be innately determined. Heredity, in determining our bodily physique, also determines at the same time our temperament and character. Unfortunately, studies among normal individuals do not bear out this claim. He has stretched his theory beyond its breaking point.

B. *According to character and temperament.* There are so many literary studies of characters from Theophrastus onwards that only a summary can be given. However, the work, as previously stated, has been done so thoroughly by Roback, that anyone seeking further information should consult his writings.

1. *Theophrastus's characters* — the flatterer; the boor; the loquacious; the news-maker.

2. *Earle's characters* — the antiquary; the sceptic; the drunkard; the meddling man; the rash man.

3. *Ribot's character types* — the humble; the contemplative; the emotional.

4. *Paulhan's characters* — balanced and unbalanced; coherent and incoherent (or unified and not unified).

5. *Queyrat's characters* — the pure; the mixed; the balanced; the irregular or abnormal; the psychopathic.

6. *Lévy's classification* — the exclusive or unilateral type; the mixed or intermittent; the perfectly balanced or harmonious.

7. *Apfelbach's* sex types of character — the masculine; the feminine; the sadistic (ascendance); and the masochistic (submissiveness).

8. *Malapert's* — the intellectual; the affective; the active; and the voluntary; with supplementary ones — the apathetic and the perfectly modulated.

9. *Ribery's* classification
   1. amorphous
   2. sensitive
      - affective
        - stable
        - unstable
      - apathetic
        - slight
        - deeper

10. *Bulliot's* types — primitive man (self-preservation); the imaginative; the affective; the active or combative; the intuitive; the reflective (reasoner); the practical (balanced); the radiator (leader of men).

Many of these classifications have no scientific foundation at all, and the rest are little better than shrewd guesses. One historical classification, that of *Hippocrates*, which was passed on to western civilization by *Galen*, has been revived in modern times. The classification referred to is the doctrine of humors, excess or lack of which influenced the personality. Just as the Greeks derived their four elements — fire, air, earth and water, from the four qualities moist, dry, hot and cold, so Hippocrates derived his four humors (temperaments) from four qualities found in mankind. The following arrangement shows how his types are derived.

	Strong	Weak
Quick	yellow bile *choleric* (angry)	blood *sanguine* (happy, gay)
Slow	black bile *melancholic* (pessimistic)	phlegm *phlegmatic* (unexcitable)

Quickness and strength resulted in yellow bile. Yellow bile in excess made a man choleric or, as we should say, easily aroused to anger. Slowness and weakness produced phlegm, which made a man phlegmatic or stolid and unexcitable. Naturally, there is no more foundation for these humors or temperaments than there is for the four elements. But endocrinology teaches us that the endocrines (the modern humors), which are the secretions of the ductless glands, can and do affect our emotional life profoundly.

A modern statistical investigation by *Heymans and Wiersma* led to the following classification of temperamental types — the amorphous; the apathetic; the nervous; the sentimental; the sanguine; the phlegmatic; the choleric; and the impassioned.

C. *Other classifications.*

1. *MacAuliffe's* — round type (tissues are hydrophilic, water intaking); and flat type (opposite to round type).
2. *Kollarit's* — Personality depends upon the physico-chemical properties of the nervous system, especially the autonomic nervous system.
   (1) euphoric, the pleasantly-toned
       (*a*) calm euphoric
       (*b*) excitable, exalted euphoric
   (2) indifferent
   (3) depressive, the unpleasantly-toned personality
       (*a*) calm depressive
       (*b*) excitable, despondent depressive
3. *Perez's* classification based on activity and movement — the active; the slow; the vehement and passionate; the actively intense; the slowly intense; the balanced.
4. *Sigaud's* physiological classification — the respiratory; the digestive; the muscular; the cerebral.
5. *Gurevitch's* motor types
   (1) fluent, balanced, dexterous (cycloid, pyknic)
   (2) crude, with angular movements (athletic)
   (3) feeble and awkward movements, but with manual dexterity of a high order (schizoid, asthenics)
   (4) childish, graceful (hypoplastics)
6. *Jaensch's* psychological types
   (1) eidetic, T, Titanoid, calcium deficient
   (2) memory, B, Basedowoid, thyroid excess
7. *Spranger's* sociological types — the theorist or intellectualist; the economic — the man who prefers utility; the aesthetic; the social; the political-power seeking type; the religious.

8. *Endocrine types*
   (1) hyper-thyroid — over-ambitious and domineering
   hypo-thyroid — lazy and intellectually dull.
   (2) pituitary type — good-humored, patient, considerate,
   docile, diffident, tolerant of physical and mental pain.
   (3) adrenal cortex (cortin) — the prematurely developed;
   in females leading to adiposity and beards.
   (4) parathyroids (calcium metabolism) — the explosive
   type showing aggressive conduct.
   (5) gonads, hyper-active — the more aggressive personality.
   hypo-active — the less aggressive personality interested
   in art, literature and music.

9. Types dependent on the functioning of the *autonomic nervous system.*
   (1) the sympathico-tonic individual (violent)
   (2) the vago-tonic individual (timid)

10. *The psychoanalytical school*
    (1) *Freud*
        (a) the repressed
        (b) the balanced, normal, and wholesome
    (2) *Jung*
        (a) the introvert
        (b) the extravert
    (3) *Hinkle's* modification of Jung's classification
        (a) simple introvert
        (b) objective introvert
        (c) subjective introvert
        (d) simple extravert
        (e) objective extravert
        (f) subjective extravert
    (4) *Adler*
        (a) inferiors
        (b) superiors

The Problem of a Scientific Basis for Personality Types.
When a trait is measured, it is generally found to be distributed in normal fashion over an unselected sample of the
population. Personality traits are no exception to this general rule. Thus introversion and extraversion, ascendance
and submission, etc., seem to be merely the extreme variants
of continuous scales. Most people are neither extremely
introvert nor extremely extravert, but cluster around the

center of the scale. As Thorndike says, if there is one type in nature, it is mediocrity. However, taking these traits as the extreme variants of a continuous scale, it is possible to use them in measurement. In measuring height, we may divide people into the tall and the short, but a better picture is obtained if we use a scale of inches and find out how many fall within the given inch range. Similarly with handwriting, we may classify it as good or bad, but if we devise a scale, we can find out where this sample falls and also how many different samples of handwriting fall within each segment of the scale. Spelling may range from very bad to very good spelling, but it is more informative to know how many can spell twenty, thirty, forty or fifty words of a given spelling list, that is, where they fall on a spelling scale. What we are trying to emphasize is this — dichotomous classifications may have a usefulness in the infancy of a science, but as the science advances and devises new instruments of measurement, these coarse classifications inevitably give place to finer ones. . So it will be with personality types. As soon as accurate measuring rods for introversion and extraversion are invented, we shall not be content to use this crude dichotomous classification, but shall be forced to say, for example, how far a person deviates, plus or minus, from the central tendency of the introversion-extraversion scale.

If these facts be borne in mind, then some of the dichotomous classifications found in the preceding sections may be regarded as having a scientific basis. But we must first be sure that we are dealing with a real trait. There seems to be neither rhyme nor reason about some of the classifications given in the preceding lists. They do not seem to be naming real things. Are introversion or extraversion, to stick to our illustration, realities or merely the shrewd guesses of some more or less competent observer? At present, all that we can say is that they seem real enough to be used. People can be taught to use the terms in a rational manner. They may even represent a scientific fact. It has been known for many years that the extravert when mentally ill is more likely to have the manic-depressive type of mental disease, while the introvert in a similar situation usually develops a split personality or dementia praecox. There is apparently a close relation between the position that a person holds on the introvert-extravert scale and the type of insanity he is likely to exhibit if he should become mentally ill. Moreover, some interesting results have been obtained by Gottlober by use of the new techniques which have been developed to record brain waves, that is, electric waves originating in the human brain. The records apparently distinguish between the introvert and the extravert. Hence it is likely that Jung's classification, based upon the observance of both normal and abnormal individuals, is founded on a scientific reality.

There may be more dubiety about the uniqueness of some of the other traits which have been named and classified, but so long as they serve a useful purpose, psychologists will continue to use them.

Personality types based on endocrinology seem to have securer scientific foundations. We need not be disturbed by the fact that some individuals have made interpretations that are scarcely warranted by the facts, at least at present. Such a person is the American biochemist, Louis Berman,[6] who has given a highly speculative but also interesting and thoroughgoing account of the mental and physical traits associated with excessive and deficient activity of the various endocrine glands. Cannon's work on adrenalin lends support to the theory that excessive secretion of the adrenal medulla may lead to the development of the fearful or angry type of personality. Endocrinology definitely affirms that certain personality traits are associated with the functioning of one or other of the endocrine glands. Excessive deficiency in thyroid secretion, for instance, is associated with the easily recognizable defects known as cretinism and myxedema, but whether or not a milder thyroid deficiency is associated with laziness and intellectual dullness is still unproven. One of the major difficulties confronting the research worker is the fact that the glands are intimately related or, as Berman puts it, form an interlocking directorate. It therefore becomes exceedingly difficult to assign with scientific precision a personality trait to a mild dys-functioning of any particular gland. Hyper-functioning of the thyroid gland leads to an increase in the rate of metabolism and this may, of course, have repercussions on the personality. But to say that hyper-

6 Louis Berman, *The Glands Regulating Personality*, 2nd ed., 1928.

thyroidism is associated with an over-ambitious and domineering personality is to make a statement which is simply unscientific in our present state of knowledge.

In much the same way, we know that the gonads are responsible for the primary and secondary sex characters. We also know that all human beings, whatever their sex, lie somewhere on a continuous masculinity-femininity scale. Most of the males lie on the masculine side of the central tendency, most of the females on the feminine side, but some males are feminine and some females masculine. We also know that if the male animal is deprived of his testicular secretions his reactions become less masculine, less aggressive in character. It is, therefore, reasonable to suppose that hyper-active gonads would tend to make the male swing towards the extreme end of the masculine scale. But we are merely in the realm of guesswork when we assert that males whose gonads are hypo-active are those who become interested in art, literature and music. In fact, the history of many artists, musicians and literary men does not seem to indicate that they were lacking in sexual energy or any other form of aggressiveness.

So long as we stick to the proven facts of endocrinology we shall not go far astray; the facts so far secured prove indisputably that some forms of disordered personality are linked with certain forms of glandular disturbances. But to make speculative statements about the linkage of the more elusive personality traits with the workings of still obscure glands is to render a disservice to science.

When we consider the types — violent and timid — supposed to be dependent on the functioning of the autonomic nervous system, we again run into a mixture of fact and speculation. The facts are: that the autonomic nervous system is closely associated with emotional expression. The sympathetic section has wider connections than the cranial and sacral divisions, and has especially close associations with the functioning of the adrenal medulla, which, in turn, has been shown to have connections with the expressions of fear and anger. Kempf[7] shows "that emotions are not experienced upon the cerebral changes that precede the autonomic changes, but that an emotion only comes into existence as the

[7] E. J. Kempf, *The Autonomic Functions and the Personality*, 1921.

peripheral autonomic reactions become active." (p. xiii)   At every segment of the autonomic nervous system there is antagonism between the sympathetic and parasympathetic divisions, with the tendency to establish a normal, workable balance between them.   When this balance is upset by either a hypertonicity or a hypotonicity of either system, a "segmental craving" arises.   Furthermore, any variation in the physiological condition of the body, due to such processes as assimilation and excretion, also results in this segmental craving.   Hunger, for example, is caused by the spasmodic contractions of the muscular walls of the stomach.   This disturbance compels the central nervous system, which is the servant of the autonomic, to adjust its receptors until stimuli are found which relieve the distress of hunger.   These segmental cravings vary from individual to individual and are at the very foundation of personality.   Personality is thus the expression of this characteristic segmental imbalance.   Repeated actions become habitual and the core of habits thus formed determines the personality.   As Kempf states:

"Whenever the autonomic or affective sensori-motor apparatus is disturbed or forced into a state of unrest, either through the necessities of growth, metabolism, or endogenous or exogenous stimuli, it compels the projicient sensori-motor apparatus to so adjust the receptors in the environment as to acquire stimuli which have the capacity to produce adequate postural readjustments in the autonomic apparatus.   In this manner, only, the disturbance of function may be neutralized.   The constant tendency of the autonomic apparatus is to so organize the projicient apparatus into a means as to acquire a maximum of affective gratification with a minimum expenditure of energy or effort.

"This continuous dynamic pressure determines the tendency towards perfection through practice, eliminates the useless and stabilizes the useful.   It determines the evolution of organic structure, of personality, behavior and achievement." (p. 1)

This dynamic pressure finding release via the sympathetic system leads to the development of a violent personality; but if the release is chiefly via the vagus nerve of the cranial division, then the timid personality results.   This may or may not be true.   The established facts are that the sympathetic system is closely associated with the coarser emotions of fear and anger, while the cranial division works in opposition to it. The rest is mere speculation.

Finally, we may ask if there is any scientific justification for the classifications used by the leaders of the psychoanalytical schools — Freud, Jung and Adler.

Perhaps a summary of the development of psychoanalysis will throw light on the subject. Psychoanalysis may be traced to the Herbartian doctrine of ideas. According to Herbart, ideas were separate dynamic entities, much given to moving backwards and forwards in clusters (apperception masses) across the threshold of consciousness. Freud's theory of repression demands that unwelcome ideas should be forced into the unconscious by the "censor." More directly it can be traced to the practice of mesmerism by Mesmer (1734–1815) and of hypnotism by Elliotson (1791–1868), Braid (1795–1860), Esdaile (1808–1859), Charcot (1825–1893) and Janet (1856–   ).

Freud (1856–   ) was a pupil of Charcot. In Freud's presence at dinner one night, Charcot is said to have remarked that there was always a sex element in neurosis. Charcot denies having said this, but the fact remains that Freud was profoundly influenced by it. He immediately applied the theory to one of Breuer's hysterical patients whose symptoms had grown out of a forgotten incident in early life. This first patient was healed by catharsis or abreaction, under hypnosis, in which the dammed up emotion was brought to the surface, to the consciousness of the patient, and relieved. Later, hypnosis was dropped and the "talking-out" method adopted. Catharsis was still part of the therapy.

At this stage one may notice two difficulties confronting Freud which led later to the concepts of *resistance* and *transference*. In transference, the patient developed, through long association with the physician, a strong emotional attachment. Breuer objected to Freud's emphasis on sex and to the use of transference in the therapy. A pupil of Freud's (C. G. Jung) developed a word association test and applied the adjective "complex" to those words which either caused the patient to hesitate or made him visibly embarrassed. Freud noticed that during the forming of free associations a point is often reached beyond which the patient will not go.

He refuses to discuss the matter but will talk about anything else. This was regarded by Freud as a good diagnostic sign. The idea of *repression* arose. The object of the treatment was to make use of transference in overcoming resistance in the talking-out situation. Thus the cause of the trouble was brought to consciousness. The trouble was frequently some childhood incident which had left a trauma or psychic shock. The catharsis released the psychic tension and healed the psychic wound. In course of time, this type of analysis became elaborated and the system became known as psychoanalysis or depth psychology (to distinguish it from the therapy). His pupils Jung and Alfred Adler broke away and founded schools of their own — Jung developing analytical psychology and Adler individual psychology. Jung said hunger, not sex, was the main drive in human life, while Adler maintained it was the desire for power.

Freud's other contributions are his (1) theory of dreams (wish-fulfilment, affording satisfaction in things which are repugnant in waking life); (2) theory of infantile sexuality; (3) insistence on the importance of memory lapses, slips of the tongue, slips of the pen and so forth; (4) theories of symptomatic actions; (5) traumatic theory; (6) and enrichment of the vocabulary by naming the mechanisms — symbolism, rationalization, sublimation, compensation, transference, projection, introjection, conflict, and identification.

Psychoanalysis is a theory of personality or self-psychology, since it claims to remake personalities with values that are biologically sounder than before. Much of it is illogical in that it is expounded in terms of the primitive and autistic; in wishes, chance association, analogy, purpose and desire rather than in terms of fact, observation, correlation, experiment, and congruity with other findings. Much of it is purely verbal fiction; analogy, not demonstrated fact. To this group belong such terms as censor, catharsis, libido, sublimation, projection and the like. Simpler and more truly psychological explanations can be given of the storage of memories, and also why some memories are more accessible than others. We do not need a mythical censor to explain phenomena that can be more readily explained by conditioning. Drugs (alcohol, morphine, tobacco, strychnine) and fatigue or sleep or hypnosis may kill the censor, but there are psychological and physiological explanations that seem simpler and truer. Undoubtedly "analysis" is a type of learning experience which has often led to marked changes in the personality, but we must also remember that some analyses have had disastrous results. Ideas have been introduced into the minds of patients which normally would never have found a place. Suppose, in analysis, a patient reports a persistent and consistent feeling of inferiority. We could probably get the same kind of evidence by observing his posture and general demeanor or by giving him a test of some kind. We can check our observations or results and do something to alleviate the condition. But there is no magic in it. Freud's contribution to genetic psychology is, however, a valuable one, namely, that present troubles have a history. He is really the originator of much of the present work on child study, although he is usually not credited with it.

Psychoanalysis deals with disordered personalities and we must beware of twisting its findings to fit the normal, wholesome personality. The psyche, according to Freud's first teachings, was structurally composed of the following kinds of stuff. It works, as it were, at three different levels.

(*a*) *The Unconscious:* known only through translation of its material into consciousness by a special analytic technique. In the unconscious there is no negation, no variation or degree, no order. It is but slightly related to reality and its processes are limitless. In it, the life and death urges strive for mastery.

(*b*) *Preconscious:* the part of mental life which by an appropriate stimulus or by "will power" can be brought up into consciousness. (Cf. Herbart's teachings). It merges on the one side into the conscious and on the other into the unconscious.

(*c*) *Conscious:* of which the individual is at any one time aware. This is the last in phylogenetic development. It is relatively non-essential and is subsidiary to the unconscious. Its function is to mirror the external world.

These concepts, suggested from a mass of evidence from dreams, mental diseases and hypnotic states, represent the various levels at which mental processes function. They constitute the framework of analysis. Useful in psycho-therapy, the above distinctions were found to be inadequate when Freud extended his theory into a general system of psychology. The unconscious was made over into the "Id" and now the pleasure principle is broadened to include a wider circle of instinctive urges, individual aims and racial acquisitions. His new system of psychology is more than ever a theory of personality. He divides personality into three arbitrarily conceived parts. These are as follows:

(*a*) The *Id* (called by ordinary psychologists *emotional impulse*). The Id represents the reservoir and the abode of the pleasure-principle. It is the battle-ground of Eros and Death and the depository of racial memories. The Id is illogical, unmoral, and unordered.

(*b*) *Ego* (corresponds almost to consciousness). The Ego is derived from the Id by external modification but is never independent of it. It is rationally organized and represents external reality, reason and sanity. Partially conscious, partially unconscious, it tries to be moral and serves the external world by checking the Id. This it does by permitting sublimation of the libido. The Ego must also accommodate the demands of the Super-Ego.

(*c*) *Super-Ego* (conscience). This is a modification of the Ego, arising in the Oedipus Complex and having the capacity to rule the Ego. It is a sort of secret service, functioning dominantly and critically and hypermorally towards the Ego, since it knows more about the Id than does the Ego. It is unconscious and farther removed from consciousness than the Ego.

Dynamically, the mental processes tend to shift about the following polarities — activity-passivity; self-object; pleasure-pain; life-death; love-hate; and masculine-feminine. The emotional attitudes also shift about these poles and, in children, two opposed attitudes are often directed toward the same object.

Functionally, the mental processes obey four fundamental principles: (1) the *pleasure principle* or the tendency for the unconscious to strive for pleasure and to withdraw from pain. The behavior of young children exhibits this principle in its purest form. Secondary to this is (2) the *reality principle,* the tendency to adapt to external requirements, acquired during life, which finally becomes superior to the

pleasure principle.   It is the maturing of the personality.
(3) The *Nirvana principle*, the tendency to secure a condition of minimum psychic tension.   (4) The *repetition-com-
pulsion principle*, or the tendency to re-enact some earlier
emotional experience, both in waking and dreaming.   It is
minor in importance to both the pleasure and reality principles.

We have given far too much space to the description of
Freud's views.   The reader will see that they are a curious
mixture of sound common sense and unfounded speculations.
Since, however, they have had wide influence throughout the
world, they have to be reckoned with in any discussion of
personality.   The basic mistake that psychoanalysis makes
is to conclude that since some abnormal personalities have
certain abnormal forms of behavior, especially sex behavior,
then all behavior is influenced by these same forces.   As
Allport [8] says:

"In any two personalities sexuality never seems to play the same
rôle.   Its attachments, its significance, and the conduct associated
with it are among the most individualistic of all the phenomena of
mental life.   In spite of its biologically uniform aspects, in its psychological organization it is a remarkably idiosyncratic matter.

"And this is why sex, as such, cannot be regarded as a single factor of motivation, nor as the basic element in personality.   A life is
not simply a variation on a uniform pattern of psychosexuality, but,
on the contrary, the sexuality of a life can be understood only if it is
regarded as one of the variations within the total and complete pattern of personality.   Excepting in the most infra-personal sense there
is no such concrete fact of sex; when one speaks of sex-habits and
sex-adjustments one can only mean *personal* habits and *personal* adjustments, having partial but not exclusive reference to the segmental
biological functions of sex.   Personality, then, is not a system of
formations within a matrix of sex.

"What is true of sex is true of every other so-called instinct."
(pp. 188-189)

As science is commonly understood, there are few scientific
foundations for psychoanalysis.   However, it would be fool-
ish to overlook the real contributions that psycho-analysis
has made to the science of personality.   We have previously

[8] G. W. Allport, *Personality, a Psychological Interpretation*, 1937.

mentioned the importance of the genetic approach to the study of personality which was directly inspired by the work of Freud. The pleasure principle is also well-founded in biological science. Even reputable scientists of today talk about unconscious drives without, however, subscribing to the Freudian doctrine of the unconscious. Our parents profoundly interest us all our lives, and it is well that Freud has brought it to our attention, but we need not believe in the necessary attachment of the daughter to the father, and of the son to the mother. As a matter of fact both sons and daughters are normally more attached to the mother than to the father. The theory of a dynamic personality, which can be traced to Freud, is a valuable one, even if its scientific bases are still obscure.

Jung's (1875–   ) scientific contributions to psychology are more easily recognized. His word association test is of permanent value. As shown previously, his conception of introversion-extraversion has apparent scientific validity. It is doubtful, however, if his elaborations into the thinking introvert, the feeling introvert, the intuitive introvert, etc., are justified. Experiments with rats show that Jung's preference for hunger, rather than sex, as the dominant drive is justified.

Adler's (1870–   ) desire for power as the chief motivating agent in human life is significant. Every human being likes to be successful, and without some form of success no normal life can be lived. Powerlessness, weakness, inadequacy cause us to feel inferior, and to seek some form of compensatory success. We may be derided as unscientific, say the "individual psychologists," but you use a scientific method which does not result in practical social help and is therefore valueless. Individual psychology does not pretend to be a science; it is a technique which applies natural laws that are already well-known. It must therefore be judged pragmatically on its ability to predict and to influence human conduct. And judged in this fashion it is eminently successful.

Personality and the Environment.— Campbell[9] is one of the few writers on personality who has discussed the problem of the influence of the environment on personality. Of

[9] C. M. Campbell, *Human Personality and the Environment*, 1934.

course, personality must exist in some environment and be influenced by it, but what Campbell discusses is the environment of air, food and water, things absolutely necessary for man's tissues and, therefore, for his survival.

Wild animals are peculiarly sensitive to this particular sort of environment. They seem to know, for instance, when a storm is brewing or when any other rapid change of weather is in the offing. Semi-hibernating animals such as squirrels are awakened by a rise of temperature and take the opportunity of securing a little additional food. Some human beings are affected by a coming electrical storm. They can "feel it at the top of their heads," and become changed in their behavior. All of us are aware that long deprivation of food or drink changes our behavior and personalities. Most of us tend to become short-tempered when hungry, but the personality is restored to normal after eating. A stuffy room changes the personalities of the occupants, and excessive humidity is very trying for most persons.

Campbell has collected the records of the feelings of men deprived of oxygen, food and water. Mountain climbers, balloonists and aeronautists quickly reach high altitudes in which there is a permanent oxygen famine. The following summary of records shows that, on the whole, the personality suffered deterioration at high altitudes:

Maw	Andes	1827	2190 metres	spirits elevated
Pieppig	Andes	1827–32	4350 "	anxiety and discouragement
Meyen	Andes	1831	5640 "	nausea, fury, fainting
Laverrière	Mexico	1857	5280 "	anxiety, disquiet, dread
Saussure	Alps	1788	3360 "	irritable, angry
Auldjo	Alps	1827	4200 "	exhausted, downcast, discouraged
Ramond	Pyrenees		3350 "	stimulated
Tissandier	Balloon	1875	7500 "	inward joy, glad to be rising
Douglas				senses dulled, memory affected
Haldane	Pike's			unreasonable, judgment impaired
Henderson	Peak	1912–13	4295 "	uncontrolled emotional outbursts
Schneider				

Such conditions of oxygen scarcity do not usually confront the ordinary individual, but a stuffy room with its excess of carbon-dioxide, water vapor, bodily odors and lack of oxygen seems to have very similar effects on the personality.

Deprivation of water is profoundly disturbing to the personality. Sven Hedin in his journey through Asia when almost perishing for want of water said "Our throats were on fire with hot dryness. We fancied we could hear our joints grating and thought they would catch fire from the friction of walking." Relief of this extreme thirst caused a feeling of ecstasy and of a reaction in feeling-tone. While suffering from extreme thirst, the thoughts of the sufferers were continually directed to fountains, waves, and the refreshing quality of cold water.

Extreme hunger apparently affects the personality more profoundly. Starving explorers in the Arctic and Antarctic tend to become petulant, and rambling and fitful in their talk. The conventional social amenities are difficult to preserve and everybody feels that his meager ration is somehow or other smaller than that of his fellows. Such conversation as there is always revolves around food, and the wonderful banquets they will eat on their return to civilization.

In famines, the sufferers generally show extreme apathy, but cannibalism, suicide, and wholesale flights of populations to regions unknown, have also been recorded. Starvation has been the forerunner of many a revolution, and every statesman knows that a well-fed population is generally a satisfied one. Religious ecstasy may be induced in some people by prolonged starvation. Tantrums in some young children have been improved by the addition of carbohydrates to their diets.

The environments of air, food and water may be regarded as the external environments, although changes in them, of course, alter the physiological states of the body also. There are many internal environments which affect the personality. Of the endocrine balance and its importance for the personality we have already written. But there are toxic poisons from infections of the teeth, from colonic stasis, and from various diseases which profoundly affect the personality. Drugs have also a disturbing influence on the personalities of those who use them. Best known to us is the effect of alcohol. It has a depressing action upon the cerebral cortex; and with the loss of self-control, poise and discretion disappear. The thalamic centers are then more active and there is emotional instability. When the intoxication is excessive, the centers governing the co-ordination of movements are affected, with the result that the gait is unsteady and the speech is slurred. The subsequent memory of such a condition is indistinct and fragmentary. Alcoholic intoxication, therefore, retraces the steps taken in the evolution of brain function. The first effect is the disturbance of the intellectual processes, then there is an increasing emotional display, and finally an interference with the mechanical aspects of speech and locomotion. This degeneracy of the personality, and especially the loss of judgment through drinking alcohol, is causing one of the greatest problems of modern times, namely, the increasing toll of motor car accidents. While it would be absurd to regard alcohol as the cause of all the increase, undoubtedly a great many accidents can be traced to this source.

Diabetics are notoriously crusty, and tubercular patients notoriously optimistic. Excessive doses of insulin cause amnesia and other features similar to those of alcoholic intoxication. Insulin shocks, that is, excessive doses of insulin, are now being experimented with in certain mental disorders (dementia praecox) and the results are encouraging.

But enough has been said to show the importance of normal amounts of food, air and water for the preservation of a wholesome personality, and how easily the personality may be upset by changing the internal environment by various toxic substances, whether taken in the form of drugs or derived secondarily from infections.

The Growth of Personality.— Personality grows. As it grows it changes, but somehow or other maintains a recognizable unity. In this respect, it is like the body. A photograph of an individual taken thirty years ago shows that time has wrought changes, but, generally speaking, the person can still be recognized from the ancient portrait. Changes in personality are probably more pronounced than changes in feature, but the analogy is a sound one.

At the basis of personality, as of physique, lies the biophysical inheritance. These bio-physical determiners of personality, as we have seen, are extremely important. Next in importance, are the habits developed through life in society. Continuous adjustments are being made which modify the personality. In any study of the growth of personality, we may profitably inquire into such things as the social life of children, the nature of the social groupings which any individual may be normally expected to meet and enter into, the failures to adjust to social groups, and the ways of resolving the conflicts aroused by failing to adjust to the surrounding social groups.

A. *The social life of children.* In this group of studies are included plays, games, leadership among children, and the changes brought about by adolescence. The importance of play in the development of the individual has been recognized by educators ever since Karl Groos drew their attention to it a generation or more ago. In the modern pre-school nursery, a great amount of observational and experimental work on children's play activities is being undertaken. The social reactions in play — attraction and avoidance (repulsion) — have been subjected to statistical analysis, and have also been permanently recorded in moving pictures. Careful studies of the kind and frequency of emotional upsets during group plays have also been made. In genetic fashion, the change from the individual play of early childhood to the group games of later childhood has been traced. Leadership has been investigated and attempts have been made to discover why some children naturally develop into leaders while others become disciples or followers. What are the characteristic traits of leaders and of disciples? Can we train children to become leaders, or are leaders born that way? The importance of all these studies in regard to the integration of personality cannot be over-emphasized.

With the onset of adolescence, social life and contacts increase in importance. Necessary friendships are formed and the adolescent begins "to go out with the crowd." This "crowd" is probably more potent in promoting the social growth of the adolescent than either the home or the school. Yet the school, especially through its extra-curricular activities, recognizes these imperative demands for social companionship of the adolescent and tries to supply them in a wholesome fashion.

B. *The nature of group life or social groupings in general.* Among these social groups may be included the family, neighborhood groupings, religious groupings, economic groupings, fraternal groupings, and political groupings, both large and small. While the sociologist has pre-empted this field, psychologists are becoming more interested in it. Every individual is a member of some social group or groups. During infancy, the family is the only group to which the child belongs. As infancy is the period when the personality assumes its characteristic outlines, the importance of the family in the development of personality is clearly seen. The first loyalty of the child is to his family. So dominant a rôle does the family play, that characteristic personality traits have been known to run down several generations of certain families.

As the child grows, his environment widens and he begins to make social contacts outside the family circle. The first of these are usually with some near-by playmate of about the same age. When the child goes to school his social horizon is immensely widened. The influence of teachers and schoolmates on the development of personality is profound, but not many exact studies have evaluated it. Loyalty to the school is normally added to that of the home.

Of the widening circle of church, secondary school, university and various political groupings little need be said. The impacts of these on the growing personality are profound. If the individual can adjust himself to all of them, he becomes a well-balanced citizen of the world, loyal to his family, school, city and country, and at the same time maintaining a broadminded outlook on the whole world. If, however, circumstances arise which prevent this natural and expanding integration from taking place, the personality becomes atrophied at a lower level than it should have been. Probably most of the lack of international goodwill can be traced to the atrophy of personality on these lower planes.

C. *The individuals who fail to adjust to the social groups — the abnormal or disordered personalities.* Studies of this kind lead us into the field of psychiatry. So numerous are these that it is difficult to prevent the impression from arising that abnormal personalities outnumber the normal ones. Such, however, is not the case. The abnormalities force themselves on the attention, while the normal cases are taken more or less for granted.

The maladjustments are usually classified by psychologists in such simple fashion as the following:

1. The psychoneuroses — emotional maladjustment.
   (*a*) neurasthenia
   (*b*) hysteria
   (*c*) psychoasthenia
2. The psychoses — personalities in flight.
   (*a*) schizophrenia and dementia praecox
   (*b*) manic-depressive psychoses
   (*c*) paranoia
   (*d*) organic psychoses

However, psychiatrists go into much greater detail in their classifications of mental disease. For example, the American Psychiatric Association has adopted the following classification:

1. Traumatic psychoses
2. Senile psychoses
3. Psychoses with cerebral arteriosclerosis
4. General paralysis
5. Psychoses with cerebral syphilis
6. Psychoses with Huntington's chorea
7. Psychoses with brain tumor
8. Psychoses with other brain or nervous diseases
9. Alcoholic psychoses
10. Psychoses due to drugs and other exogenous toxins
11. Psychoses with pellagra
12. Psychoses with other somatic diseases
13. Manic-depressive psychoses
14. Involution melancholia
15. Dementia praecox
16. Paranoia and paranoic conditions
17. Epileptic psychoses
18. Psychoneuroses and neuroses
19. Psychoses with constitutional psychopathic inferiority
20. Psychoses with mental deficiency
21. Undiagnosed psychoses
22. Not insane — epilepsy, alcoholism, drug addiction, mental deficiency, etc., without psychosis

All that we need to note here is that these classes represent persons whose personalities have not developed in normal fashion. Formerly, with the treatment and techniques available, little could be done for them. Today, a large percentage of those suffering derangement of their personalities can be cured, especially when early diagnosis of their condition is made.

D. *The ways of meeting difficulties and resolving conflicts of personality (the problem of mental hygiene).* Of greater interest to the educational psychologist is the way in which persons solve the problem of their difficulties and their maladjustments to the world around them. These solutions may be divided into five groups, as follows:

1. *The method of direct attack:* solve the problem. This is incomparably the best way of meeting difficulties. It is the method that well-balanced persons always adopt. The difficulty is present: what is the best way of overcoming it? Facing a clear-cut issue in such a bold fashion leads to the development of strong personalities who can weather life's storms. The difficulty is to devise educational techniques which will lead to this desirable state of affairs. One school of thought maintains that if children are taught from the beginning to face the consequences of their particular choices of conduct, it will lead them in later life to choose this method of direct attack. In the home and in the school, alternative lines of conduct can be clearly placed before the children. The children then accept one of the alternatives, and having thus accepted, are forced to abide by their decisions. In the nursery school, for instance, the pupils can either play with the scooter or build with bricks, or play in the sand-pile. Having decided, they are not allowed to change their minds later. If they choose the bricks for building, they are not allowed to ride the scooter or play in the sand-pile. Later, of course, another choice can be made. In the home, if the dessert is rice-pudding, and the child does not like rice-pudding, he is told that he need not eat it, but he cannot have a substitute. No fussing or coaxing to eat ever takes place. Such a method undoubtedly works well with young children in the home and in the nursery school. In ordinary classrooms, where the teacher is confronted with thirty to forty pupils, the application of the technique presents greater difficulty. What its ultimate effect will be, we do not know, since the nursery school products have not grown to manhood and womanhood. But it can scarcely be worse than the older methods (corporal punishment in many cases) which it is supplanting.

2. *Negative adaptation* — surrender to the inevitable. This obviously is not a real solution, since the difficulty has never been squarely faced. What is, must be, is its underlying philosophy, and this is not the way that progress has been made. It leads, inevitably, to a weakening of the personality.

3. *Securing substitute satisfactions,* for example,

(*a*) compensation — overacting in another direction.
(*b*) sublimation — motive transformed and energy directed into new and socially acceptable channels.
(*c*) rationalization — making things and behavior reasonable to one's self.
(*d*) day-dreaming and autistic thinking (thinking that is inordinately subjective or directed towards oneself).

Some of these substitute satisfactions are normally accepted by society. The young maiden who is jilted by her lover and devotes the rest of her life to social work or nursing, engages in a course that receives social approval. So also does the childless wife who adopts a child, but not if she lavishes her affection on a lap-dog. Sublimation, therefore, may or may not be a socially acceptable substitute satisfaction, but the world would be a poorer place were it not for the great souls who have secured satisfaction for their troubles in a life devoted to the welfare of others.

Rationalization is so common with all of us that we may regard it almost as a natural phenomenon of mind. We can find reasons or excuses for any line of conduct we wish to pursue. But if the rationalization takes the form of a simple way out of a difficulty we have not the courage to face, then it leads to a degenerate softening of the personality, and for that reason, should be discouraged.

Two other substitute satisfactions — seeking compensation by overacting in another direction, and seeking release from reality through day-dreams — are both regarded rather seriously by the mental hygienist. All of us, especially when young, do a certain amount of day-dreaming, but in normal personalities it decreases with age. The danger in day-dreaming lies in the fact that it may be used habitually as an escape from the unpleasantness of life. The adult, normal, wholesome personality demands that life's trials and difficulties be squarely faced, not evaded by day-dreaming or by false displays of power in other directions.

4. *Defence and escape mechanisms.* To the psycho-analyst, a defence reaction is a force or resistance which keeps from consciousness mental processes that are unacceptable to the ego or to the superego, but more usually it denotes behavior which tends (whether intentionally or unconsciously) to guard some aspect of the individual's personality or life history from scrutiny by others or by oneself, often calling into play a disguised act. A defence mechanism, therefore, is simply a defensive or self-protective type of action. Usually, there is something in the individual's past history or make-up of which he is ashamed. Instead of meeting the difficulty, he either hides it or runs away from it, which does not settle the difficulty at all.

5. *Retreat from reality in disease.* This is the resolution of a mental conflict by means of the adoption of a disease symptom. Technically, it is a symptom of hysteria. It is not a deliberately planned and conscious way out of the difficulty. Rather, it is the trick of a spoiled person who, more or less accidentally discovering that disease proves a way of escape, and being too honest to malinger, unconsciously adopts the ruse as a permanent escape from all difficulties that arise. This spoiled child trick of becoming ill in order to get what one wants or to escape from reality is essentially the act of a selfish personality. The situation is very difficult to remedy, but the individual in some way or other must be made "to face up to things." He must not be allowed "to get away with" his unconscious malingering, but every time he makes an effort to face his difficulties he must receive encouragement. In this, as in every other derangement of the personality, the early diagnosis of symptoms is imperative. Prevention is both easier and better than cure.

E. The modern concept of abnormal personalities is in marked contrast to the older ones. Instead of regarding the criminal, insane, mental defective, delinquent, genius, etc., as classes apart, they are now regarded as extreme deviates of a normal distribution. R. L. Stevenson said "Every man has a sane spot somewhere." It would be truer to say that every man has an insane spot somewhere, meaning by this, that no personality is integrated on the positive side of the scale for all traits. Such an outlook makes us more humane in dealing with all forms of abnormality, and less cocksure of the permanence of our present superiority. We take the attitude of John Bunyan who is reported to have said as he watched a murderer on his way to the scaffold, "There, but for the grace of God, goes John Bunyan."

The Measurement of Personality. — In a brief treatise such as this, it is obviously impossible to enter into the practical details of tests and measurements. For such details, the reader should consult the monumental work by Symonds.[10] Nor will it be possible to enter exhaustively into a history of the testing movement. But what should be done and what we shall try to do, is to discuss, in summary fashion, the theories underlying the various measurements, and the manner in which measurements contribute to an analysis of personality.

A. Of the *pre-scientific methods* — astrology, physiognomy, phrenology, graphology, listing of stigmata (Lombroso school) — little need be said. Unfortunately, in the hands of charlatans, they survive to this day. The ancient belief that the stars in their courses influenced human destiny and personality, accounted for the rise of astrology. Persons were born under lucky (or unlucky) stars, and definite sets were given to the personality. There is, of course, no truth in such a theory. But the modern versions of astrology have scientific foundations. Sun-spot cycles are undoubtedly related to climatic cycles, and it is suspected that cosmic rays may play a part in evolution by their action on genes. Both of these would influence the personality, one through environment, and the other through heredity.

Physiognomy, the art of discovering characteristics of personality from the features and expression of the body, especially of the face, is as old as mankind. In ancient times, the man who looked like a donkey, must be stupid. The practicers of the art were generally shrewd men and used the facial play, postures and manners of their subjects to help them in their diagnosis. The modern theory is based on the fact that personality is a unified whole and that all features and expressions must be congruent and consistent with the personality within. However, it is difficult to see how bone

[10] Percival M. Symonds, *Diagnosing Personality and Conduct,* 1931.

structure and, to some extent, how muscular structure, can reflect the inner personality. That both may be due to the physiological constitution is within the range of probability. And that well-formed, well-developed bodies lead to a vigorous and active life is a commonplace. But the actual relationships have not been worked out scientifically.

Phrenology, the doctrine that specific mental faculties are localized in definite cerebral regions, and that the development of these parts caused protuberances of the skull, we owe to Gall and his pupil Spurzheim. Unfortunately, Gall's guesses relative to localizations of brain functions were wide of the mark, although he selected them by observing the characteristic protuberances of his friends who exhibited the characteristics in question. Secondly, the bumps of the cranium do not correspond to the bumps of the brain; under a cranial bump there may be a depression of the brain. Yet he must be credited with the aim of searching sincerely for true units of personality and character, and of advancing the science of psychology by insisting on the importance of individual differences. It was primarily due to Gall that search for localizations of function resulted in Broca's success later in the century. Gall's search for faculties is not so far removed from the modern search for personality traits as some writers would lead us to suppose.

Graphology, the scientific study of handwriting, has been twisted by the modern charlatans to mean the discovery of personality traits from the form of the letters. Handwriting may give clues to degenerative diseases; handwriting may be predominantly masculine or feminine, but, so far, the relationships established are too insecure for diagnostic purposes. For instance, most groups of judges can judge correctly whether handwriting has been written by male or female in only 60-70 per cent of the cases. This being true, the chances of interpreting personality traits from handwriting seem rather slight.

Lombroso's theory of stigmata has been discussed in the previous chapter and its weaknesses need not be pointed out again.

B. *Rating scales.* Rating is the name given to the subjective estimate of the strength of some quality or trait possessed by an individual and the assignment of a rank, score or mark for it on a scale of values. It is an attempt to secure finer scalings than the traditional dichotomous ratings, and to improve their reliability. Obviously, the rating can only be made by judges who are well acquainted with the persons they are rating. Although the method, at first glance, does not seem to be very scientific, nevertheless, it is the only one that can be used under some circumstances, and anything that helps to improve judgments should be welcomed.

The normal method of rating is to use a ruled sheet, dividing the horizontal lines representing the range from extremely high to extremely low, into as many degrees of value as is deemed convenient. . Theoretically, the number of these intervals is infinite; in practice it is found that seven categories give the best results. On the left, the names of the individuals to be rated are given. The judge is required to mark the interval into which the subject falls. To aid the judge, the intervals are described in some way or other. Thus, in a rating for general health, the descriptions for the seven ratings might be — bad, very poor, poor, average, good, very good and excellent. Further descriptions or illustrations of just what "bad" health is supposed to mean are sometimes given. These seven ratings can be transmuted into scores and analysed statistically.

Several refinements and modifications of this general system of rating have been made. Among them we find that of *ranking* the group of subjects *in order of merit* for the trait under consideration. The difficulty with ranking is that it is not amenable to simple statistical treatment since the intervals between the rankings probably differ for every successive pair. The *graphic rating scale* is another refinement. This is a method of securing and recording a judgment regarding the degree to which the individual possesses the trait or quality in question, by placing a mark at an appropriate position on the scale representing the possible range of the trait. Finer distinctions can be made in this way than the 7-category plan permits. It is simple, universal, and frees the judge from consideration of direct quantitative terms. The scoring for statistical treatment can be altered at will, yielding scores of any degree of fineness desired, although, in practice, the lower ranges such as 1 to 7 and 1 to 15, are more frequently used and are more valuable than the higher ranges, such as 1 to 50. The *man-to-man rating scale* is a modification that has not been widely used since it was first introduced into the Army testing program of the United States. It is a scale designed to facilitate the ease and accuracy of estimating the degree to which a person possesses a given trait, by providing as standards of comparison a list of persons selected as possessing different degrees of the trait in question. The judge compares the person to be rated with these individuals, decides which of them he most resembles in the given trait, and assigns him the rating that has previously been assigned to that individual on the master scale. The main difficulty with the man-to-man rating scale is the preparation of a suitable list of persons to compose the master scale. Further, different master scales are needed for different groups, and these, having different values, cannot be compared directly.

All rating scales suffer from the defect that the majority of the subjects rated fall in the middle sections of the scale. They cannot be as reliably rated as the comparatively few that fall at the extremes. The reliability of the ratings depends, of course, on the extent of agreements among the judges. Such agreements are improved by training the judges. Especially must they be cautioned about the *halo-effect* — the tendency, when one is rating a person for a certain trait, to be influenced by the general impression he creates, or by his rating on a trait which has previously been estimated. The halo-effect may be minimized, but never completely obviated, by rating one trait for the entire group of persons before passing on to the second. Reliability of ratings is increased if the categories into which the scale is divided are defined objectively rather than subjectively. When all possible precautions are taken, it is found that the ratings of a single judge are too unreliable to be useful, although the combined ratings of three or more are generally reliable enough for most practical purposes. There is also the tendency among all judges to rate too frequently in the upper half of the scale. Conrad found that the reliability of ratings about which the judges feel certain is higher than for those that they are less certain about. Certain traits can also be more reliably rated than others. Among these we find emotionally and socially acceptable qualities in contrast to anti-social traits.   The reliability of ratings, and their usefulness also, is greatest when the investigation from start to finish employs the same group of subjects.

C. *Personality testing.*   The main testing devices used in the analysis and diagnosis of personality are the *questionnaire* and the *performance test.*

The Questionnaire.   In the personality questionnaire, the main consideration is not whether an individual can answer the questions asked, but whether he will answer them truthfully.   The examiner, as a rule, cannot check the answers, since they ask the subject to report how he thinks or feels or believes.   These answers are subjective and may be incorrectly reported, but it is believed that the answers to a large number of items may show significant trends.   As fact-finding devices, personality questionnaires have little reliability, but, if well designed, may throw light on the personality characteristics of the subjects answering them.

The difficulty of constructing standardized personality questionnaires is very great, and sometimes questionable methods have been employed.   Suppose, for example, a test to measure introversion-extraversion is desired.   First of all, the test-maker draws up a list of characteristics of introversion.   He may believe, with Schwegler,[11] that the introvert in the presence of a single familiar uncomplicated situation is characterized by being

(*a*) slower in verbal response
(*b*) less freely productive of words, ideas, and movements
(*c*) slightly more tenacious in holding to the evidence of his own experience
(*d*) less given to superficial automatized responses
(*e*) more inclined to morbid anxieties, to autistic trends, and to psychasthenia, obsessions, and phobias
(*f*) less inclined to admit the presence of a rich emotional life than is the contrasted extravert.

Or he may believe, with Freyd,[12] that he can list 54 characteristics of introversion.   On the basis of his convictions, he then constructs a number of items for his questionnaire which

[11] R. A. Schwegler, *A Study of Introvert-Extravert Responses to Certain Test Situations,* 1929.

[12] M. Freyd, "Introverts and Extraverts," *Psychol. Review,* 1924.

he hopes will differentiate between the introvert and the extravert. To find out if they will do so, he needs subjects on which to try them out. He therefore goes to the schools and asks the teacher to pick out the introverts and extraverts in his class. Perhaps the teacher has never heard the terms, so the characteristics of the introvert and extravert are described. Then the teacher, by observation of the behavior of the pupils and by asking questions designed to test introversion and extraversion, selects from his class the subjects asked for by the investigator. These are given the questionnaire, and lo and behold, the answers they give show that the questionnaire has a very high reliability. How could it be otherwise? They are now answering on paper questions similar to those put to them orally by the teacher. They were selected for answering them in a certain way, and continue to do so on paper. The questionnaire is printed in alternative forms and sold, maybe, by the thousand. However, the sceptical person who tries out the two forms at an interval of two weeks on the same subjects, discovers that introversion is not as constant a phenomenon as it was purported to be. Some people who were introvert on the first form are extravert on the second. This account, slightly exaggerated for purpose of illustration, explains some of the demonstrable weaknesses of a great many of the standardized personality inventories. Those who have constructed the questionnaires have really been running around in a circle. However, the problem is not insoluble, for continued experimentation with items has led to the selection of a group which have rather high validity and reliability.

With all questionnaire studies, the question of truthfulness with which the items are answered arises. Incorrect answers may be due to lack of knowledge and to deliberate deceit. When the pupil tested wishes to make a good impression, he is tempted to color his answers accordingly. Yet, on the whole, when veracity has been checked, it is found that the majority of subjects are truthful, especially if the questionnaire has been given an innocuous but misleading title. However, the preferable way is to secure the hearty co-operation of the pupils answering the questions.

Standardized interest questionnaires, such as Cowdery's and Strong's, seem to be in a different category. They simply take occupational groups, find how these groups answer the items, and compute norms. Since interest in a vocation is the best criterion for subsequent success in it, and since interests tend to become stabilized in mid-adolescence, Strong has been able to turn his list into a "Vocational Interest Blank." A pupil answering this questionnaire can be told that his interests are similar to those of a lawyer, engineer, salesman, or carpenter and be advised accordingly as to the choice of a career. This type of vocational guidance, from the cumulative evidence of many questions, is undoubtedly superior to the kind which simply asks the subject what he would like to do when he grows up.

Performance Tests. In regard to personality, performance tests are really scales of behavior — what a person does or would do in a prescribed situation. The classical investigation in this field was undertaken by Hartshorne and May [13] and reported in three volumes. The techniques used in testing were very ingenious. In the deceit series, the general plan was to place pupils in situations conducive, say, to cheating and by special devices used in the administration of each test, discover and score the amount of cheating that had taken place. For example, the pupils took tests in information, disarranged sentences, reading, completions, spelling, word knowledge and arithmetic and were carefully supervised as they worked. The papers were collected and copied in the office. Later, the papers were returned to the pupils and the following directions given: "We are giving this school and ——— (naming the other school) certain tests. The children at ——— have had the same tests that you have taken. They corrected their own papers, so we are going to have you correct the tests you took last week." The papers are then passed out. "We shall now pass out a key or answer sheet for each test. You are to use these only for the purpose of correcting the work already done. Make no changes whatever in your papers." The children are then left to score the papers and any changes made can be detected by comparing the new answers with the original ones.

Besides the duplicating technique, Hartshorne and May used the copying technique, the improbable achievement tech-

---

[13] Hugh Hartshorne and Mark A. May, *Studies in Deceit,* 1928 ; *Studies in Service and Self-Control,* 1929 ; *Studies in the Organization of Character,* 1930.

nique, and the double testing technique. They devised methods for measuring the cheating type of deceptive behavior not only in classroom situations, but also in work done at home, in athletic contests, and in parlor games. They also used tests for measuring the stealing and lying types of deception.

Some of the outstanding results are as follows:

1. The older pupils are slightly more deceptive than younger ones.
2. Sex seems to make no difference.
3. Honesty is positively related to intelligence.
4. Children who show symptoms of emotional instability or maladjustment are more likely to deceive than the better adjusted pupils.
5. Physical condition has no effect, even in athletic contests.
6. Children from homes of higher socio-economic levels cheat less than children from lower levels.
7. Children of parents born in North Europe and America cheat less than children of parents born in South Europe. Colored children cheat more than most white groups.
8. Deception runs in families to about the same extent as eye color, length of forearm and other inherited structures.
9. Retarded children cheat more than children who are of average age for their grade.
10. Those who get high marks in school cheat slightly less than those who get low marks.
11. There is a considerable resemblance in amount of cheating between classmates and between friends.
12. Cheating correlates slightly with attendance at movies.
13. There is less cheating in classes in which the teacher has secured the good will and co-operation of the pupils.
14. Pupils from progressive schools cheat less than pupils from conventional schools.
15. Children who attend Sunday-school regularly cheat in day school about the same as those who rarely or never attend.
16. Children who belong to certain organizations purporting to teach honesty deceive about the same (and in one case more than) children who do not belong.
17. Deceit and honesty are not unit traits. Most children will deceive in certain situations and not in others.
18. The most common motive for cheating in the classroom is the desire to do well.

Measures of studiousness, of will-temperament (Downey), aggressiveness, speed, caution and the like all belong to this group of performance tests. While the results from comparison of different groups of pupils are interesting, the tests are not very valuable for the diagnosis of individual personalities. Conduct such as is measured by most of the tests seems to be so highly specific, that all that can be hoped from the tests is to use a battery of them for the measurement of a general trait. However, we may know that a person is generally honest, but be unable to predict how he will react in a given situation.

D. *Free Association Tests.* In the diagnosis of personality, the free-association method, giving the first word thought of (aroused) by the stimulus word, has played a unique part. It has been used successfully for the detection of guilt, but today is mainly used for the detection of emotional complexes and of insanity. Several lists of 100 words each have been compiled. The Kent-Rosanoff list avoids words that "are especially liable to call up personal experiences," while the Jung list (modified by Eder) has been designed to locate the common complexes. Tables of frequencies of the common responses to the Kent-Rosanoff list, together with lists of juvenile reactions, and of rules for judging whether or not a reaction is to be considered normal, have been prepared.[14] (pp. 552-620) Rosanoff has collected evidence which shows that the insane give an abnormal percentage of unusual words, that is, of words not found in the lists. The length of the reaction time to the words is considered significant. In the detection of lying, the reaction to a crucial word is usually longer than to a neutral one, probably because the subject tries to substitute a second word for the first one aroused, fearing that it will disclose his guilt. In psychoanalysis, the words with long reaction times are specially noted, since it is around these that emotional complexes and repressions cluster. They are supposed to be valuable clues for further analysis. Luria's[15] modification of the technique, which combines motor responses both of a voluntary and involuntary nature with word associations, produced remarkable results when it was tried on Russian criminals. Attempts to classify individuals according to their verbal reactions on free association tests, have usually proved abortive.

[14] A. J. Rosanoff, *Manual of Psychiatry*, 1927.
[15] A. R. Luria, *The Nature of Human Conflicts*, 1932.

E. *Experiment.* Experimenting with personalities at first glance seems a dangerous proceeding. When we have an obviously sub-normal personality, such as the cretin or schizophrene, experiment is the indicated expedient. So the cretin was given extract of sheep's thyroid and was found to improve in physique, mentality and personality. Excessive doses of insulin, sufficient to produce the so-called insulin shock, have been used with success on a number of schizophrenic patients. But what is usually meant by experiment in personality is the kind that Allport and Cantril[16] carried out with judgments of personality from the quality of the voice. Three persons carried out ten experiments using identical pieces for testing the voice. Two were regular radio broadcasts, six were simulated broadcasts in the laboratory, and two compared the natural voice with the same voice heard through a loud-speaker. The student groups who heard them were required to match the voices against such objective things as photographs, handwriting, descriptions of complexion, accounts of political preferences of the speakers, scores on extraversion-introversion and on ascendance-submission scales, and summary accounts of the speakers made up from the previous items. Needless to say, students could not match handwriting or photographs successfully with voices, and the only matching that ran higher than .4 (contingency coefficient) was voice *versus* summary sketch of characteristics. This, of course, is to be expected from theoretical considerations of halo-effect. Listeners to the actual voice gave results about 7 per cent better than listeners to the radio voice.

Similar in character are the attempts to judge the emotions from facial expression. For this purpose, posed photographs or drawings of posed photographs are usually used. Excellent summaries of studies in the field have been made by Landis,[17] Ruckmick[18] and others. Laughter, pain, disgust or contempt, fear or horror can generally be recognized by 50 per cent or more of the judges, but the agreement on

[16] G. W. Allport and H. Cantril, "Judging Personality from Voice," *Jour. Social Psychology*, 1934.

[17] Carney Landis, "The Expression of the Emotions," in Murchison's *Foundations of Experimental Psychology*, 1929.

[18] Christian A. Ruckmick, *The Psychology of Feeling and Emotion*, 1936.

hate, anger, surprise, suspicion, etc., is much less. Landis criticizes the technique of such experiments as follows:

"These studies all smack of guessing games. The game is that of attaching a label to a photograph so that the label will agree with the notion which the experimenter held concerning the picture. They are in no sense true studies of the expressions of emotion but are investigations of the socialization of the perception of facial contortions. Their value lies in the fact that they show clearly that even the most conventionalized of social expressions is very poorly interpreted by the average observer. So poor are the judgments, that little trust or reliability may be placed upon the judgments when the observer has *only the face* to guide him. Note the phrase 'only the face,' for it is practically certain that if the observer could see the entire situation his judgment would be much more accurate." (pp. 494-495)

With this we agree. In actual life we seldom confuse a sorrowful with a joyful expression. But in these situations, it is not only the facial expression that influences our judgment but all sorts of accessory behavior as well.

Any investigation of the experimentation on personality that has been done to date, shows that a great deal of it has been concerned with somewhat trivial, comminuted elements of personality. If, as Allport maintains, it is only in the complex patterned forms of behavior and thought that personality can be said to exist, then it is with these that experiment must be concerned.

The Most Significant Elements in Personality. — While it is undoubtedly true that — (*a*) the physiological and psychological organism is the central fact of personality, (*b*) the biological individual is primary, and (*c*) the individual personality is derived from the interactions of the biological organism with its environment (chiefly social), it nevertheless remains true to say that certain aspects or traits give a more pronounced stamp to personality than others. Among these may be noted —

1. The intensity of the urge for self-expression and the direction this urge takes. The artist in words or paint seems insatiable in his desire to express himself. Neither poverty nor sickness seems able to destroy this urge. The poverty-

stricken George Gissing and the sick R. L. Stevenson were at one in their desire to write. Scientists, like Darwin, who never enjoyed ebullient health, have been noted for their enormous capacity for work. And the urge towards work exhibited by some of our colleagues of the genius variety is a never-ending source of wonder to the less-gifted members of the staff. The artist may starve in his garret, but he never ceases to paint. The money-maker may make his millions but he goes on piling up his wealth. This urge seems to be the determinant of the personalities of these individuals as they are, or were, known to their contemporaries.

2. The range and intensity of an individual's curiosity and interest. The person who is full of curiosity and interest seems to be more alive, to have a more dynamic personality than the apathetic and incurious individual. True, the interest and curiosity may be directed towards frivolous and inconsequential ends, but without them, the personality remains pale and colorless.

3. The importance of the rôle of feeling and emotion. From the earliest times, the part that sentiments and emotions play in personality and character has been widely recognized. The artist, the man of feeling, above all others possesses a striking personality. Probably this is because the emotions are more deep-seated than the intellect. They seem to have evolved at an earlier stage and proved themselves admirable instruments in what has been described as mere biological survival. Today, their fundamental importance in life is increasingly realized, and attempts are being made to train them to social ends. Without trained emotions, the personality seems to be cold, even to be atrophied in some degree.

4. The sensitiveness to the concept of value. The great personalities seem to place high value on the important things of life; trivial matters do not command their interest. In education, the problem is an ever-present one, since it is the aim of educators to bring children into contact through schooling with the eternal verities of life. What these are, is the subject of never-ending controversy, but all builders of curriculums are sure that their particular selection is the right one. To select things that are right and good for everybody on earth, things that are independent of time,

space, race, color and nationality, is no simple task, but the following list commands respect: (*a*) Communication of one with another. Since language is now our chief means of communication, children should be taught to be accurate and precise in the use of their mother tongue, and to learn as many foreign tongues as they have time and ability to learn. (*b*) Loyalty to one another. We should inculcate loyalty to the family (presuming, of course, that the family is worth being loyal to), to the school, to the city, to the state, and, as age increases and knowledge widens, to humanity at large. For we cannot be truly loyal to any wider group without being loyal to a narrower one, but we should take care that our loyalties do not atrophy at too low a level. (*c*) Ability to weigh evidence, to know when a thing is proven or disproven. This ability marks off more surely than any other the educated from the uneducated person; it is also a distinguishing feature of personality. It is useful in every walk of life. It is needed by the historian and the politician, by the manufacturer and the commercial man, by the radio-listener as well as by the scientist. (*d*) The ability to appreciate, and, if natural gifts permit, to be producers of at least one of the great arts of the world — literature, music, painting, sculpture, drama or architecture. (*e*) Unselfishness. And included in this is the ability to see the other person's point of view as well as to be able to give up the present good for future gain. Since one of the major troubles of this "Brave New World" of ours is sheer, stark selfishness, the importance of training in this eternal verity cannot be over-emphasized. (*f*) Ability to play the game. Besides fairness, this includes the ability of persons to be true to their better selves even at considerable sacrifice. It means that sometimes we may have to desert the crowd and refuse to follow the fashion. We may be called puritans, frumps and kill-joys, nevertheless there is virtue in fair dealing and clean conduct.

Given this training, we should develop richer personalities, which would be sensitive to the more important values of life.

5. Prominence of a specialized gift of self-expression. If an individual can express himself in oratory, in craftsmanship, in art, his personality is sure to stand out above that of

his fellows. Self-expression of this kind, therefore, stamps a personality in an unmistakable way.

Other Problems in Regard to Personality. — Some problems connected with personality that await solution can only be briefly mentioned.

A. *The effect of occupation upon personality.* The difficulty with this problem is to decide which is cause and which effect. For example, Terman has shown that male teachers tend to be somewhat feminine in outlook and reactions. Is this because teaching affects the personality in this way, or is it that the male with a mildly feminine personality is attracted by the profession of teaching? Again, is the danger-seeking, rather boyish personality of the naval officer due to his occupation, or does this type of personality naturally drift into the navy? Strong has shown that persons in different occupations have different congeries of interests. Do persons select occupations because they have these particular sets of interests, or do the occupations create the interests? The question is an important one, but the answer is still unknown. We are aware that lawyers, doctors, pugilists, clergymen and others seem to belong to recognizable groups. The habit of thought in the scholar is supposed to be reflected in his countenance. It would be strange if the personality did not reflect the occupation, for of all the environmental forces, occupation is one of the most constant. More work should be done in this promising field.

B. *Personality and industrial adjustment.* One of the great problems of industry is to place the round peg in the round hole. The problem is not merely one of vocational skill and knowledge, but frequently one of personality. Take the case of the young married man who wanted, more than anything else in life, to live on a farm. Being poor and married, he could not afford to buy or rent a farm, or even work on one as a hired man. So he worked in a factory and made motor cars. But all the time he was thinking of cows and green fields and was unhappy in his work. He suffered because he was in the wrong job. His personality leaned to the farm, but the demands of a family kept him at a machine in a factory. Probably personality tests are sufficiently advanced to enable us to diagnose the more obvious difficulties, but it is another thing to solve them. However, employers are beginning to realize that it is to their advantage to have employees doing jobs which not only match their technical skill, but gibe also with their personalities.

C. *Personality and marital compatibility.* This interesting and important problem has been broached by Terman and Buttenwieser.[19] In an attempt to discover what personality traits contributed to happiness in marriage, they gave the Bernreuter Personality Inventory and the Strong Vocational Interest Test to 345 married couples and to 116 divorced couples. The married couples supplied anonymous data which yielded marital happiness rates. A comparative study made of the 100 most happily married couples, the 100 least happily married couples, and 100 divorced couples with respect to the scores in the thirteen variables provided by the tests, showed low or negligible correlations with marital happiness. About one-quarter of the 545 items of the test appeared to have validity as indicators of marital compatibility. "Incidentally no correlation was found between marital happiness and age at marriage, age differences between spouses, number of offspring, or spouse-parent attachments and conflicts." (p. 288) This preliminary study indicates some of the difficulties which confront the person who endeavors to untangle the web of personality in its relationship to happiness in marriage.

D. *Sex differences in personality.* Terman and Miles, as shown in a previous chapter, devised a series of paper tests which seemed to rate people on a masculinity-femininity scale. Sex, however, may be so pervasive in character as to make its measurement by a single battery of tests quite out of the question. The personality traits designated by such terms as ascendance-submission, strong emotions-weak emotions, aesthetic-nonaesthetic, religious-nonreligious and many others, while not absolutely determined by sex, undoubtedly have a sexual basis. Instead, therefore, of taking the more inclusive sex and measuring it as a single trait, it might be more profitable to study the more elementary traits into which it indubitably enters.

Whatever conclusion we reach regarding traits, the importance of sex differences in personality cannot be overlooked.

[19] L. M. Terman and P. Buttenwieser, "Personality Factors in Marital Compatibility," *Jour. of Social Psychol.*, 1935.

The fact that some sex differences which were thought to be mainly due to heredity have been shown by Mead and other anthropologists to be mainly due to their environmental setting, does not alter the case. In most of the higher mammals, including man, the male is the bigger and stronger and built for aggression. The effect of this on human personality has determined the course of human history. Whether education can or can not change the aggressive qualities of the human male is a question that presses for an answer. The development of weapons of offence has now reached such a pitch that aggression on the part of any group may wipe out civilization as we know it, or at least set it back centuries. It may be, as Wells maintains, that education is racing with catastrophe.

E. *The personality of the artist.* We have maintained that the artist is a person who lives at a higher emotional level than the rest of mankind. This must necessarily be the case since art of every kind is, at bottom, an expression of emotions. But no studies have been made of the scientist to see whether or not the emotional pleasure he gets from his discoveries is similar to that which the artist gets from his artistic creations. For the bulk of mankind, the thrills from science remain a closed book. But if Tolstoy is right, then the only art that exists is that which has universal appeal. He overlooked the fact that mankind develops in artistic taste, just as the individual does. An artistic creation must therefore be judged by artistic peers; nevertheless it is true to say that the milestones on the road of civilization are the supreme artistic creations rather than the great scientific discoveries. If this be so, the personality of the artist should be studied intensively.

F. *The personality of the man of science, the discoverer, the man of genius, and the inventor.* In this group we place a group of men who lead the world on to a higher plane of living by means of the discoveries they make. The highest ranking members of this group are so far removed from the rest of us that they seem to be a class apart rather than the extreme variants of a continuous scale. Reputable persons have argued that genius, scientific or otherwise, is not merely a quantitative distinction, but qualitative as well, especially in its higher rankings. Against this view, we can place the demonstrated finding that whenever groups are measured for any trait the quantitative findings seem to explain all the facts.

There is, however, one common view of genius that is unwarranted by the facts, namely, that genius is exhibited along single lines. Reference to the biographies of geniuses shows that, in general, they are animated by a wide-spread curiosity and generally exhibit marked talents in several fields. The best treatise on the New Psychology, as it was called, was written by a professor of botany. The juiciness of the minds of such geniuses as Galton, Galileo, Newton and the like almost beggars description. Not only are they devoured by an insatiable curiosity, but they are also fired by a zeal and an industry that is simply indomitable. The personality traits of these leaders in science and discovery should be studied. If they are mainly the product of good stock, little can be done except to be thankful when they appear, but if they can be developed by environmental means, the world should know about it and take steps to produce them.

G. *The personality of the religious person, the ethical person.* Many studies have been made of the founders of the great religions of the world — Christianity, Mohammedanism, Buddhism, but the personalities of their adherents have not been the subject of much scrutiny. In a general way, we are aware that the Buddhist is meditative, the Mohammedan is aggressive, and the Christian meek and submissive. What we do not know is the proportion of Buddhists who are not meditative, Mohammedans who are not aggressive, and so forth. Nor do we know whether it is Buddhism that makes a man meditative or whether the meditative man becomes interested in a religion like Buddhism. That as powerful an emotional environment factor as religion can have no influence on the personalities of its adherents is unbelievable. Careful and dispassionate inquiry into the subject should be made, difficult as the work may be.

H. *Personality and the cultural pattern.* In 1937, Dr. Plant [20] published a book with this title. The book, sponsored by the Commonwealth Fund, breaks new ground. Briefly, Plant, a psychiatrist by profession, argues that the usual psychiatric formulations for children are inadequate and that

[20] J. S. Plant, *Personality and the Cultural Pattern*, 1937.

in some way or other the forces of the cultural pattern in which we live are of dynamic importance to the personality. The moment an individual makes his first and perhaps temporary break with his environment is the time we should do something for him. Certainly, as Plant shows, it is the occasion that gives us a new and so far unused source of personality data. While Plant's interpretations of the data may not meet with wholesale acceptance by the reader, we think they should be brought to his attention. Anything that bids fair to unravel the problem of personality should be welcomed.

Of the disordered personality and of mental hygiene, we shall say nothing. We have tried to restrict the discussion to the normal personality. However, the problems of abnormal people, mental disorder, and unadjusted personalities are of supreme importance, as the flood of books on the subject testifies. But after reading them, one gets the idea that "everybody is more or less cracked," and this is an unhealthy attitude for anybody to get, more especially the teacher. Far truer is the view that these represent the extreme deviates, and that the majority of mankind are normal, mediocre persons like the writer and the reader.

REFERENCES

Adler, A. *Understanding Human Nature.* New York, Greenberg, 1927. Pp. xiii + 286.

Allen, C. *Modern Discoveries in Medical Psychology.* London, Macmillan, 1937. Pp. x + 280.

Allport, G. W. *Social Psychology.* Boston, Houghton Mifflin, 1924. Pp. xiv + 453.

Allport, G. W. *Personality: a Psychological Interpretation.* New York, Holt, 1937. Pp. xiv + 588.

Bagby, E. *The Psychology of Personality: an Analysis of Common Emotional Disorders.* New York, Holt, 1928. Pp. viii + 236.

Bentley & Cowdry (Eds.). *The Problem of Mental Disorder.* New York, McGraw-Hill, 1934. Pp. x + 388.

Berg, L. *The Human Personality.* New York, Prentice-Hall, 1933. Pp. xv + 321.

Berman, Louis. *The Glands Regulating Personality.* New York, Macmillan, 1921. Pp. 300.

Brown, William. *Mind and Personality: an Essay in Psychology and Philosophy.* New York, Putnams, 1927. Pp. x + 356.

Cameron, A. T. *Recent Advances in Endocrinology.* London, Churchill, 1933. Pp. vii + 365.

Campbell, C. M. *Human Personality and the Environment.* New York, Macmillan, 1934. Pp. xi + 252.

Campbell, Langfeld et al (Eds.). *Problems of Personality.* New York, Harcourt Brace, 1925. Pp. xiii + 434.

Character and Personality: an International Psychological Quarterly. Durham, Duke University Press. (See files of)

Chassell, J. O. *The Experience Variables: A Study of the Variable Factors in Experience Contributing to the Formation of Personality.* New York, Rochester, 1928. (pages un-numbered)

Crutcher, Roberta. *Personality and Reason.* London, Favil Press, 1931. Pp. ix + 178.

Dorsey, J. M. *The Foundations of Human Nature: the Study of the Person.* New York, Longmans, 1935. Pp. xiii + 488.

Freud, S. *General Introduction to Psychoanalysis.* New York, Boni and Liveright, 1920, 1935. Pp. x + 406.

Freyd, M. *The Personalities of the Socially and the Mechanically Inclined.* Psychol. Monogs., 1924, XXXIII, 5, pp. vii + 101. No. 151.

Gordon, R. G. *Personality.* New York, Harcourt Brace, 1926. Pp. xiv + 302.

Harrow, B. *The Glands in Health and Disease.* New York, Dutton, 1928. Pp. xviii + 365.

Hartshorne & May. *Studies in Service and Self-Control.* New York, Macmillan, 1929. Pp. xiii + 559.

Hartshorne & May. *Studies in Deceit.* New York, Macmillan, 1928. Pp. xxi + 414 + 306.

Hartshorne, May & Shuttleworth. *Studies in the Organization of Character.* New York, Macmillan, 1930. Pp. xvi + 503.

Healy, W. & Bronner, A. F. *New Light on Delinquency and its Treatment.* New Haven, Yale University Press, 1936. Pp. vii + 226.

Henry, G. W. *Essentials of Psychopathology.* Baltimore, Wood, 1935. Pp. ix + 312.

Hinkle, Beatrice M. *The Re-creating of the Individual: a Study of Psychological Types and their Relation to Psychoanalysis.* New York, Harcourt Brace, 1923. Pp. xiii + 465.

Hollingworth, H. L. *Vocational Psychology and Character Analysis.* New York, Appleton, 1929. Pp. x + 409.

Huntingdon, E. *The Character of Races as Influenced by Physical Environment, Natural Selection, and Historical Environment.* New York, Scribners, 1925. Pp. xvi + 393.

Jung, C. G. *Psychological Types.* New York, Harcourt Brace, 1926. Pp. xii + 654.

Jung, C. G. *Psychology of the Unconscious.* New York, Moffat Yard, 1916. Pp. lv + 566.

Kelley, T. L. *Essential Traits of Mental Life.* Cambridge, Harvard University Press, 1935. Pp. 145.

Kempf, E. J. *The Autonomic Functions and the Personality.* New York, Nervous and Mental Disease Pub. Co., 1918. Pp. xiv + 156.

Kretschmer, E. *Physique and Character.* New York, Harcourt Brace, 1925. Pp. xiv + 266.

Krout, M. H. *Major Aspects of Personality.* Chicago, The College Press, 1933. Pp. xviii + 364.

Lewin, K. *Dynamic Theory of Personality.* New York, McGraw-Hill, 1935. Pp. ix + 286.

Malinowski, B. *Sex and Repression in Savage Society.* New York, Harcourt Brace, 1927. Pp. xiv + 285.

Miller, E. *Types of Mind and Body.* New York, Norton, 1927. Pp. 132.

Morgan, J. B. *The Psychology of Abnormal People: With Educational Application.* 2nd Ed. New York, Longmans, 1937. Pp. vii + 605.

Morris, Elizabeth H. *Personality Traits and Success in Teaching.* New York, Teachers College Bureau of Publications, 1929. Pp. 75.

National Education Association, Department of Superintendence. *Tenth Yearbook, Character Education,* Washington, D. C., N. E. A. 1932. Pp. 535.

Paterson, D. G. *Physique and Intellect.* New York, Century, 1930. Pp. xvii + 304.

Plant, J. S. *Personality and the Cultural Pattern.* New York, Commonwealth Fund, 1937. Pp. x + 432.

Reymert, M. L. (Ed.). *Wittenberg Symposium: Feelings and Emotions.* Worcester, Clark University Press, 1928. Pp. xvi + 454.

Rivlin, H. N. *Educating for Adjustment.* New York, Appleton-Century, 1936. Pp. xiv + 419.

Roback, A. A. *The Psychology of Character.* New York, Harcourt Brace, 1928. Pp. xxiv + 603.

Rosanoff, A. J. *Manual of Psychiatry.* 6th Ed. New York, Wiley, 1927. Pp. xvi + 697.

Rosanoff, A. J. "A Theory of Personality Based Mainly on Psychiatric Experience." *Psychol. Bulletin,* 1930, XXVII, pp. 281.

Shaffer, L. F. *The Psychology of Adjustment: an Objective Approach to Mental Hygiene.* Boston, Houghton Mifflin, 1936. Pp. xix + 600.

Shand, A. F. *The Foundations of Character.* 2nd Ed. London, Macmillan, 1920. Pp. xxxvi + 578.

Shuttleworth, F. K. "The Measurement of the Character and Environmental Factors involved in Scholastic Success." *University of Iowa Studies in Character,* I, II, Oct. 1927. Pp. 80.

Stagner, R. *Psychology of Personality.* New York, McGraw-Hill, 1937. Pp. xi + 465.

Stockard, C. R. *The Physical Basis of Personality.* New York, Norton, 1931. Pp. xviii + 320.

Strong, E. K., Jr. "Interests of Men and Women." *Jour. of Social Psychol.,* 1936, VIII, pp. 49-67.

Symonds, P. M. *Diagnosing Personality and Conduct.* New York, Century, 1931. Pp. xvi + 602.

Symonds, P. M. *Psychological Diagnosis in Social Adjustment.* New York, American Book Company. Pp. ix + 362.

Terman, L. M. "The Measurement of Personality." *Science*, 1934, LXXV, pp. 605-608.

Terman and Buttenwieser. "Personality Factors in Marital Compatibility," I and II. *Jour. of Social Psychol.*, 1935, VI, pp. 143-171; 267-289.

Terman, L. M. & Miles, Catherine C. *Sex and Personality; Studies in Masculinity and Femininity.* New York, McGraw-Hill, 1936. Pp. xi + 600.

Wood, C. R. *Does Personality have a Definite and Consistent Use in Education?* Nashville, George Peabody College for Teachers, 1929. Pp. 77.

Woodworth, R. S. *Contemporary Schools of Psychology.* New York, Ronald Press, 1931. Pp. vi + 232.

Zachry, Caroline B. *Personality Adjustments of School Children.* New York, Scribners, 1929. Pp. xii + 306.

INDEX

Abilities of various races, 141 ff.
Abnormal personalities, 427 ff.
Abnormal psychology, 9, 30
Absolute refractory period of nerve, 247
Abstract intelligence, 346
Achievement, measurement of, 33
Acquired characters, non-inheritance of, 41 ff.
Acromegaly, 233
Action current, 246, 247, 248
Actions, physiological, 261 ff.
Activities, list of animal, 273 ff.
Activity stream, Watson's, 287, 292 ff.
Adler, 26, 28, 310, 412, 418
Adler's theory of personality, 423
Adolescence, ratio of longevity to, 210
Adrenal glands, 230 ff.
Adrenalin, 228
Adrenalin, action of, 231 ff.
Adrenalin, formula for, 230, 231
Adrenal medulla, 246
Adrian, 249, 250, 251
Age and brain-weight, 168
Age and grade norms, 365
Age and physiological gradient, 224
Age and variability, 196 ff.
Age of maturity of intelligence, 373 ff.
Alcohol and personality, 425
Allelomorph, 58
All-or-none law, 247, 248
Allport, F. H., 315, 318
Allport, 394, 395, 400, 405, 421, 441, 442
Amblystoma, development of behavior in, 171, 216 ff.
Aments, 30
America's contribution to intelligence testing, 358 ff.
Analysis, 26 ff.
Analysis and gestalt psychology, 218
Analysis, factor, 343, 345
Analysis, necessity for, 22
Analytical psychology, 418
Anastasi, 138, 197
Anatomical age, 173, 174
Ancestry and individual differences, 138 ff.
Ancestry, effect of, 148 ff.
Anemotropism, 263
Animal activities, list of, 273 ff.
Animals, mendelian inheritance in, 60 ff.
Animal psychology, 31
Anoegenetic principles, Spearman's three, 337
Antithesis, principle of, 278
Apfelbach, 410
Applied psychology, 31 ff.
Arc, reflex, 265
Archer, 307
Archipallium, 312
Aristotle, 1, 305, 348

Army Alpha, 360
Army Beta, 360
Artist, personality of the, 447
Association by contiguity, 305
Association tests, free, 440
Associative shifting and conditioning, 302 ff.
Asthenics, 408 ff.
Astrology, 432
Athletics, Kretschmer's, 408 ff.
Atomism, 26
Attributes of intelligence, 347 ff.
Audiometric survey, 182 ff.
Autistic thinking, 430
Autonomic nervous system, 240, 243 ff.
Autonomic nervous system, divisions of, 244, 245
Aveyron, wild boy of, 130, 357
Axon, 242

Babinski reflex, 287, 293
Bach family, 128 ff.
Bagley, 89, 90, 333
Baldwin, 369
Banting, 234
Bard, 245, 309, 310, 313, 315, 319
Barger, 229
Barotropism, 263
Bayliss, 234
Bean, 173
Behavior and age, 209
Behavior and environment, 206
Behavior as a response, 205
Behavior, factors affecting complexity of, 208 ff.
Behavior, forms of non-variable, 261 ff.
Behavior, genotypical and phenotypical, 406
Behavior, integrative, 212
Behavior, intrinsic, 212
Behavior, level of biological development and, 208 ff.
Behavior, maturation and, 169 ff.
Behavior, meaning of, 205 ff.
Behavior, mechanisms of, 226 ff.
Behavior, organismic, 214 ff.
Behavior, parental, 274
Behavior, principles of, 213 ff.
Behavior, protoplasmic, 219 ff.
Behavior, self-maintaining, 226
Behavior, social, 276
Behavior, structure and, 207
Behavior, unit of, 212 ff.
Behavior, unlearned, 257 ff.
Behavior, variable and non-variable, 225 ff.
Bekterev, 309, 314
Bell, 217
Bentley, 18
Bentley and *Day*, 259
Berg, 395

Bergson, 18
Berkeley, 18
Berman, 192, 234, 414
Bernheim, 26
Bernreuter, 446
Best, 234
Bibliographies of tests, 363
Bi-focal theory of intelligence, 337 ff.
Binet, 103, 348, 353 ff.
Binet's contributions to intelligence testing, 354 ff.
Binet-Simon test, 353 ff.
Binet test, American revisions of, 354
Biological level and behavior, 208 ff.
Biological list of unlearned responses, 295
Biometricians and geneticists, 136
Blanton, 284, 285
Blatz, 121, 125, 127, 323
Blin and *Damaye*, 354
Blind, education of the, 180 ff.
Blind, intelligence of the, 389
Blood pressure and emotion, 322 ff.
Blood volume and emotion, 322 ff.
Bobertag, 358
Bodily structure and personality, 407 ff.
Boring, 238, 249, 321
Boyle, 4
Braid, 417
Brain, evolution of, 237
Brain functions, localization of, 251 ff.
Brain, parts of, 312
Brain waves, 243
Brain-weight and age, 168
Bray and *Wever*, 249
Brentano, 20
Breuer, 26, 417
Bridges, 278, 287
Brigham, 141, 146
Brown, 137, 395
Brunswick, 218
Bulliot, 410
Bunyan, 432
Burlinghame, 130
Burks, 91, 92, 94, 95, 376
Burks, J. D., 200
Burns, 196
Burt, 162, 198, 356, 357, 372, 373
Buttenwieser, 446

Calcium metabolism, 234
California, gifted children of, 86 ff.
Campbell, 303, 395, 396
Canal-boat children, study of, 95 ff.
Cannon, 21, 192, 231, 278, 279, 309, 310, 315, 316, 318, 324, 325
Cantril, 441
Carmichael, 170, 266
Catharsis, 26, 417, 418
Cattell, 84, 85, 137, 159, 193, 358
Cattell, Psyche, 173
Causation, 15
CAVD, 348, 358, 369, 370, 371, 374
Cell-body, 242

Cell, description of, 44 ff.
Cell division, 44 ff.
Censor, 418
Central nervous system, subdivisions of, 240
Central theory of emotion, 315 ff.
Cerebellum, 312
Chamberlain, 210
Chapman, 197
Character and personality, 401
Characteristics of emotion, 272 ff.
Characters, independent assortment of unit, 59 ff.
Characters, mendelian, 60 ff.
Characters, non-inheritance of acquired, 41 ff.
Charcot, 26, 417
Chicago study of foster children, 91 ff.
Child, 21, 207, 217, 223
Childhood genius, 335, 336
Child psychology, 30, 33
Children, studies of foster, 90 ff.
Chromosome, description of, 44
Chromosomes, 52, 53, 54
Chromosomes in Man, 63
Chromosomes, X and Y, 62 ff.
Chromotropism, 263
Classical theory of emotion, 315
Classification of maladjusted personalities, 428
Classification of studies in heredity, 72
Cobb, 99
Coefficient of intelligence, 368
Coghill, 21, 170, 215, 216, 218
Collateral, 243
Color-blindness, 9, 62 ff.
Colvin, 337, 402
Compatibility, personality and marital, 446
Compensation, 430
Complex, inferiority, 28
Complexity of behavior, factors affecting, 208 ff.
Concrete intelligence, 346 ff.
Conditioned arc, 251
Conditioned response, 299
Conditioned stimulus, 299
Conditioning and associative shifting, 302 ff.
Conditioning as association by contiguity, 305
Conditioning as a substitute stimulus, 303
Conditioning of emotions, 279, 280, 287 ff.
Conditioning of reflexes, 298 ff.
Conditioning results, Pavlov's, 299 ff.
Conditioning, Russian studies of, 305
Conduction, 240
Conduction, absolute refractory period of nerve, 247
Conduction, path of, 242
Connecting neurons, 241
Connectors, 227, 240 ff.
Conradi, 176, 284
Conscious, Freud's, 419
Consciousness, stream of, 26
Consciousness, thresholds of, 27
Constancy of I.Q., 375 ff.

Contiguity and conditioning, 305
Convict, study of English, 96 ff.
Conway, 182
Copernicus, 4
Corning, 385
Corpora quadrigemina, 312
Corpus callosum, 312
Correlation, 70
Correlations, siblings, 102
Correlations, twins, 103, 107, 109, 110, 116, 121
Correlations, twins and siblings, 107
Correlative nature of heredity and environment, 41, 126 ff.
Correns, 54
Cortin, 230
Cortin types of personality, 412
Cortical control of emotion, 315, 316
Cortical system of sense organs, 239
Co-twin studies, 114 ff.
Co-twin studies of maturation, 170 ff.
Cousin marriages, 128 ff.
Cowdery, 457
Cox, 334
Cranial division, 244
Cretin, 441
Cretinism, 228
Crile, 315, 317, 318, 327
Criminals, study of, 95 ff.
Criteria of monozygocity in twins, 115 ff.
Criteria of native responses, 280 ff.
Crossing over, 50 ff.
Crozier, 262, 263, 264
Cultural pattern, personality and the, 448 ff.
Current, action, 246
Curriculum and values, 443 ff.
Curriculum provision for individual differences, 200 ff.
Curriculums of France, Germany, England and United States, 201
Curve of chance, 66 ff.
Curves of growth of intelligence, 369 ff.
Curves of mental growth for normal, subnormal, and supernormal children, 371, 373

Dacks, 78
Dalton plan, 200
Darwin, 36, 65, 73, 128, 151, 275, 277, 278, 284, 305, 334, 443
Dashiell, 219
Davies, 238
Day and *Bentley*, 259
Day-dreaming, 430
Deaf, education of, 184 ff.
Deaf, intelligence of, 389
Deaf, motor abilities of, 186
Deaf, number of, 182, 183
Deafness, inheritance of, 148 ff.
Dearborn, 137, 337, 374
Death, feigned, 270
Deceit, studies in, 438 ff.
De Candolle, 81, 83
Defence mechanisms, 431

Definition of emotion, 272
Definition of instinct, 268
Definitions of intelligence, 337
Definitions of personality, 394 ff.
Delinquents, intelligence of, 389
Dementia praecox, 413
Dements, 30
Dendron, 242
De Sanctis, 358
Descartes, 3
Determinism in education, 89 ff.
Detlefsen, 42
Developmental psychology, 30 ff.
Developmental schedules, 287
Development defined, 167 ff.
Development of behavior in *amblystoma*, 171, 216, ff.
Development, phylogenetic and ontogenetic, 260
De Voss, 177, 178
De Vries, 54
Dewey, 26, 402
Dewey, Evelyn, 268, 282, 287
Diabetes mellitus, 234
Diagnosis and discovery of feeblemindedness, 388
Dichotomous classifications, weakness of, 413 ff.
Diencephalon, 312
Differences due to maturation, 162 ff.
Differences, extreme individual, 178 ff.
Differences, individual, 136 ff.
Differences in rates of mental growth, 172, 173
Differential psychology, 31 ff., 136 ff.
Diiodotyrosine, 229
Dionne quintuplets, 99, 121 ff., 349, 399
Disordered personalities, 427 ff.
Disposition and personality, 402
Distribution of intelligence, 377 ff.
Distribution of traits, 406
Divisions, racial, 139 ff.
Doll, 373
Dragon-fly, instinctive action of, 269
Dreams, theory of, 418
Drosophila, 49, 51, 52, 64
Drugs and personality, 424
Dual aspect theory, 17
Dugdale, 76
Dysphoria, 244
Dysplastics, 408 ff.

Earle, 409
Ebbinghaus, 358
Ecological niche, 261
Education and variation, 70 ff.
Education as a special environment, 42 ff.
Education, limits to power of, 131
Educational provision for individual differences, 199 ff.
Educational psychology defined, 32 ff.
Educational significance of infancy, 209 ff.
Education of the blind, 180 ff.

Education of the deaf, 184 ff.
Education of the feebleminded, 189 ff.
Education of gifted children, 187 ff.
Education of morons, 190
Education of physically handicapped, 191
Edwards family, 80 ff.
Effectors, list of, 227
Effectors, 227 ff.
Ego, 420
Electrical changes in nerve action, 246
Elements of heredity, 44 ff.
Elements of personality, 402 ff.
Elements in personality, the most significant, 442
Elliotson, 417
Elliott, 37
Ellis, 84, 85, 159
Ellis, R. S., 138
Emergency theory of emotion, 232, 318
Emotion, 27 ff., 272 ff.
Emotional expression, experimental studies of, 320 ff., 441 ff.
Emotional levels and outlets, 325 ff.
Emotion and blood pressure, 322 ff.
Emotion and blood volume, 322 ff.
Emotion and pulse-rate, 322 ff.
Emotion and respiratory changes, 323 ff.
Emotion, characteristics of, 272 ff.
Emotion, conditioning of, 279
Emotion, experimental study of, 311
Emotion measured by spontaneous movement, 324 ff.
Emotion, theories of, 315 ff.
Emotions and adrenalin, 232
Emotions and glandular secretions, 324
Emotions and instincts, paired list of, 296
Emotions and nervous system, 311 ff.
Emotions and psychogalvanic reflex, 324
Emotions and sympathetic nervous system, 246
Emotions, conditioning of, 287 ff.
Emotions, History of study of, 305 ff.
Emotions, hypothalamus as seat of, 313 ff.
Emotions, James-Lange theory of, 306 ff.
Emotions, unconditioning of, 291
Emotions, Watson's list of, 278
Endocrine glands, 228 ff.
Endocrine types, 192, 412
Endocrinology, 234 ff.
Endocrinology and sex, 152
Engels, 359
England's contribution to intelligence testing, 357
English convict, Goring's study of, 352
Environment and behavior, 206
Environment and heredity, 36 ff., 41, 71 ff., 126 ff.
Environment and I.Q., 93 ff.
Environment and personality, 422 ff.
Environment as a flexible factor, 42
Environment, influence of, 82
Eoanthropus, 38
Epicritic sensibility, 238

Epinephrin, 230
Epiphenomenalism, 18 ff.
Epithalamus, 312
Esdaile, 417
Estabrook, 77
Ethical person, personality of, 448
Eugenics, 42
Euphoria, 244
Evaluation of test scores, 367 ff.
Evolution of brain, 237
Evolution of man, 38 ff.
Evolution of sense organs, 236 ff.
Evolution, emergent, 18
Evolution, evidences of, 37 ff.
Excess action, principle of, 278
Excisions of brain, results of, 312 ff.
Excitability, 240
Excitation, 224
Existentialism, 20
Experiment as controlled observation, 12
Experiment, mendelian, 55 ff.
Experimental studies of emotional expression, 320 ff.
Experiments, types of conditioning, 304
Experiments with personality, 441 ff.
Expression of emotions, 274 ff.
Expression, photographic studies of emotional, 320 ff.
Exteroceptive reflexes, 266
Extraversion, 28
Extravert, 191, 412
Eye-color, inheritance of, 60

Factor-analysis, 343, 345
Factorial hypothesis, 63
Families, degenerate, 76 ff.
Family, effect of, 148 ff.
Family histories, 72 ff.
Family, importance of, 130 ff.
Family, Wedgwood-Darwin-Galton, 74
Fay, 148, 149
Fear, 12
Fearing, 265
Fears, children's, 328
Fechner, 248
Feebleminded, 189 ff.
Feeblemindedness, inheritance of, 78 ff.
Feleky, 320
Femininity and masculinity, 153 ff.
Finger patterns of quintuplets, 123 ff.
Fiske, 210
For and against the James-Lange theory, 307 ff.
Ford, 121
Fore-brain or end-brain, 312
Formula for adrenalin, 230, 231
Formula of probability curve, 67
Formula for testicular principle, 233
Formula for thyroxin, 229
Foster children, studies of, 90 ff.
France, Germany, England and United States, curriculums of, 201
Franz, 137, 252

Free association tests, 440
Freeman, 91, 115, 119, 120, 121
Freeman, F. S., 138
Frequency, normal surface of, 66 ff.
Frequency polygon, 67
Frequency theory, 248, 249
Freud, 26, 27, 310, 412, 417 ff.
Freyd, 436
Frogs, maturation of, 170
Frois-Wittman, 321
Functionalism, 23
Function of pituitary gland, 233
Functions of sense organs, 235 ff.
Fusion of races, 141

Galen, 410
Galileo, 4, 448
Gall, 351
Galton, 70, 73, 81, 82, 83, 84, 100, 136, 137, 141, 142, 357, 448
Galvanotropism, 263
Gamete, 40, 58
Gametogenesis, 47 ff.
'g' and 's', Spearman's, 339 ff.
Garnett, 357
Garrett, 137
Garth, 139, 144, 147
Gates, 137, 281
Gene, theory of, 44 ff.
Genetecists and biometricians, 136
Genetic observation of infants, 310
Genetic psychology, Freud's contribution to, 419
Genius in childhood, 335, 336
Genotype, 58, 65
Genotypical behavior, 406
Geotropism, 263
German revision of Binet tests, 358
Germany's contribution to intelligence testing, 358
Gesell, 114, 170, 172, 173, 179, 268, 284, 362, 371
Gesell and Thompson's schedule, 362
Gestalt principles, 217
Gestalt psychology, 25 ff., 212
Gifted children, 86 ff., 187 ff.
Gissing, 443
Glands, adrenal, 230 ff.
Glands, endocrine, 228 ff.
Glands, kinds of, 227
Glandular secretions and emotions, 324
Gobineau, 141, 192
Goddard, 79, 359
Goeckel, Rudolf, 2
Goiter belts, 230
Goitrous *versus* non-goitrous children in steadiness tests, 194, 195
Golgi cells, type II, 243, 254
Goodenough, 162
Gordon, 89, 395
Goring, 96, 352
Gottlober, 414
Gradient, physiological, 207, 217, 221 ff.

Grant 141,
Graphology, 432, 433
Grasping reflex, 282
Griffith, 42
Group test of intelligence, 360 ff.
Growth defined, 166
Growth of intelligence, 369 ff.
Growth of personality, 425 ff.
Guidance, intelligence tests and, 387 ff.
Gull, instinctive actions of young, 270
Gurevitch, 411
Gypsies, study of, 95 ff.

Haeckel, 209
Hall, 209, 328
Hall of Fame relatives of Californian children, 88
Halo-effect, 435, 441
Hamilton, 15
Harington, 229
Hartshorne and *May*, 438
Harvey, 4
Hayes, 181
Head, 237
Hegel, 18
Height records of quintuplets, 125
Heliotropism, 262, 263
Henmon, 337
Hepburn, 379
Herbart, 27, 417
Hereditary genius, 137
Heredity as a fixed element, 42
Heredity as stablizing factor, 64
Heredity, definition of, 41
Heredity and environment, 36 ff., 41, 71 ff., 126 ff.
Heredity and environment, correlative nature of, 41, 126 ff.
Heredity, social, 130 ff.
Heredity, studies of, 71 ff.
Herrick, 209, 212, 217, 234
Herring, 354
Heymans and *Wiersma*, 411
Hickories, 78
Hilgard, 303
Hilgard, Josephine R., 114
Hill Folk, 78
Hind-brain, 312
Hinkle, 412
Hinsey, 243
Hippocrates, 406, 410
Hippocratic theory of humors, 192
Hirsch, 111, 112
Histogram, 67
Histories, family, 72 ff.
History of intelligence testing, 351 ff.
History of psychoanalysis, 417 ff.
History of study of emotions, 305 ff.
Hoagland, 262, 263, 264
Hogben, 197
Hollingworth, 19
Holmes, 272, 274, 275, 276
Holmes and *Jersild*, 328

Holt, 271
Holzinger, 91, 115, 118, 119, 120, 121
Homogeneous grouping, 384
Honesty not a unit trait, 439
Honesty, studies in, 438 ff.
Hooke, 4
Hormones, 230 ff.
Hotelling, 343
Hudgins, 304, 305
Hull, 304, 305
Humors, bodily, 192, 406, 410 ff.
Humphrey, 217, 357
Huxley, 18, 19, 36, 219
Hybridization, 54
Hydrotropism, 263
Hyper-thyroids, 412
Hypnotism, 26, 417
Hypothalamus, 312
Hypothalamus as seat of emotions, 313 ff.
Hypothesis, factorial, 63
Hypo-thyroids, 412
Hysteria, 428

Id, 420
Idealism, 18
Idiot, 189
Imbecile, 189
Impulse, nervous, 246 ff.
Index of brightness, 368
Individual differences, 136 ff.
Individual differences, ancestry and, 138 ff.
Individual differences, educational provision for, 199 ff.
Individual differences, extreme, 178 ff.
Individual differences in motor reactions, 193 ff.
Individual differences in motor skills, 195, 196
Individual differences in sensitivity, 192 ff.
Individual psychology, 418
Individual, variation within the, 177 ff.
Industrial adjustment and personality, 445, 446.
Infancy, meaning of, 209 ff.
Infancy, unlearned reactions of, 285 ff.
Inferiority, feeling of, 28
Inferiors, 412
Inheritance in animals, mendelian, 60 ff.
Inheritance in *drosophila*, 49 ff.
Inheritance, mendelian laws of, 57 ff.
Inheritance in man, mendelian, 60 ff.
Inheritance in peas, 55 ff.
Inheritance in royalty, 73 ff.
Inheritance of criminality, 96 ff.
Inheritance of deafness, 148 ff.
Inheritance of feeblemindedness, 78 ff.
Inheritance of musical capacity, 128 ff.
Inheritance of special traits, 128 ff.
Inheritance of talent, 81 ff.
Innate intelligence, 333 ff.
Innate propensities, 297
Insight, 25
Instincts, 268 ff.

Instinct and emotion, 257
Instincts and emotions, paired list of, 296
Instincts, examples of, 259
Insulin, 234
Intelligence, age of maturity of, 373 ff.
Intelligence and physiological age, 175
Intelligence and precocity, 334 ff.
Intelligence and sex, 159
Intelligence, area of, 350
Intelligence, attributes of, 347 ff.
Intelligence, distribution of, 377 ff.
Intelligence, growth of, 369 ff.
Intelligence is innate, 333 ff.
Intelligence, kinds of, 346 ff.
Intelligence, male and female, 149 ff.
Intelligence, nature of, 337 ff.
Intelligence, normal distribution of, 379 ff.
Intelligence, range or width of, 348 ff.
Intelligence, Scottish survey of, 379
Intelligence, symposium on, 337
Intelligence tests and maturation, 171
Intelligence of Indians, 145
Intelligence of negroes, 143 ff.
Intelligence of the blind, 181
Intelligence of twins, 103 ff.
Intelligence of various races, 141 ff.
Intelligence testing, Binet's contributions to, 354 ff.
Intelligence testing, history of, 351 ff.
Intelligence testing, national contributions to, 357 ff.
Intelligence testing, results of, 388 ff.
Intelligence tests, diagnostic value of, 388
Intelligence tests, maturation and, 171
Intelligence tests, prognostic value of, 388
Intelligence tests, types of, 360 ff.
Intelligence tests, universities and, 385 ff.
Intelligence tests, uses of, 383 ff.
Intelligence, theories of, 337 ff.
Integrative or somatic behavior, 212
Intensity of nerve impulse, 247
Inter-brain, 312
Interest blank, Strong's vocational, 438
International test of intelligence, 366
Intrinsic or physiological behavior, 212
Introspection, 3
Introspection, weaknesses of, 6 ff.
Introversion, 28
Introvert, 190, 412
Iodothyroglobulin, 229
I.Q., 356, 358, 367 ff.
I.Q. and environment, 93 ff.
I.Q. and eruption of teeth, 174
I.Q., constancy of, 375 ff.
I.Q., improvement by training of, 131
I.Q. of canal-boat children, 95
I.Q. of Chinese and Japanese, 145
I.Q. of deaf, 186
I.Q.'s of urban and rural groups, 378
I.Q., white *versus* negro, 144
Irritability, 219
Ishmaels, 78
Italian revision of Binet tests, 358

Italy's contribution to intelligence testing, 358
Itard, 357

Jaensch, 411
James, 26, 215, 287, 315
James-Lange theory of emotions, 306 ff., 315
Janet, 417
Jennings, 21, 121, 263
Jersild and *Holmes*, 328
Jones, H. B., 374, 375
Jones, Mary C., 284, 287, 291, 292, 293, 311
Judd, 217
Jukes, 76 ff.
Jung, 26, 28, 310, 325, 412, 417, 418
Jung's theory of personality, 422
Jung's word association test, 440

Kallikak family, 79 ff.
Kammerer, 42
Kant, 18
Kantor, 395
Kelley, 137, 343, 359
Kempf, 415
Kent-Rosanoff list, 440
Kepler, 4
Kilpatrick, 200, 217
Kinaesthetic sense, 236
Kinds of intelligence, 346 ff.
Kinds of norms, 363, 365
Klineberg, 146, 147
Knox, 359
Koehler, 25
Koffka, 25
Kollarit, 411
Kretschmer, 408, 409
Kretschmer's personality types, 408 ff.
Kuhlmann, 354, 374
Kuo, 270, 271

Ladd, 315
Lands, 321, 441, 442
Lange, 315
Langerhans, Islands of, 234
Langfeld, 320
Language, importance of, 24, 40
Language, lapses in, 27
Lapses of memory, 418
Larson, 323
Lashley, 21, 243, 251, 252, 253, 254
Lauterbach, 104, 105, 106, 107
Lavater, 351
Lavoisier, 4
Laws of inheritance, mendelian, 57 ff.
Learned, 386
Learning, biological, 259
Learning, conditioned and other, 304
Leeuwenhoek, Van, 4
Leibnitz, 18
Level, emotional, 325 ff.
Level of intelligence, 333, 347 ff.
Lévy, 409
Libido, 28
Lie-detector, 323, 325

Lincoln, 150
Lindemann, 4
Linear and lateral types, Stockard's, 407 ff.
Linkage, 49 ff.
Lippmann, 333
Localization of brain functions, 251 ff.
Locke, 18
Loeb, 175, 260, 262, 265
Logarithmic curves of growth of intelligence, 370, 371
Logistic curves of growth of intelligence, 372, 373
Lombroso, 96, 151, 351
Long, 186
Longevity, ratio of adolescence to, 210
Lorge, 406
Luria, 324, 325, 326, 440

MacArthur, 121, 124
MacAuliffe, 411
McCall, 359, 369
McDougall, 42, 258, 272, 282, 295, 296, 297, 307, 402
McGraw, 171, 268
McNemar, 115, 159
MacPhail, 385
Magnetotropism, 263
Maladjusted pupils, 190 ff.
Malapert, 410
Male and female compared. 149 ff.
Malinowski, 298
Man, ancient types of, 38 ff.
Man, chromosomes in, 63
Man, color-blindness in, 62 ff.
Man, distinguishing characteristics of, 36
Man, evolution of, 38 ff.
Man, mendelian inheritance in, 60 ff.
Man, races of, 139 ff.
Man of science, personality of, 447 ff.
Man's place in nature, 36 ff.
Manic-depressive psychoses, 428
Marital compatibility and personality, 446
Marquis, 303
Marriages of close relatives, 128 ff.
Marston, 323
Masculinity and femininity, 153 ff.
Mass action, 243-251
Matthew's theory of zones and strata, 140
Maturation, 47, 268
Maturation and behavior, 169 ff.
Maturation, co-twin studies of, 170 ff.
Maturation, differences due to, 162 ff.
Maturation hypothesis, 114, 167
Maturational patterns, 226
Maturity in mental growth, 373 ff.
Maze test, Porteus, 357
Mayow, 4
Mead, 298, 447
Measurement of personality, 432 ff.
Measurement of variability, 197
Mechanical ability, sex differences in, 152
Mechanisms of behavior, 226 ff.
Mechanisms, defence and escape, 431

Medulla oblongata, 312
Meiosis, 47 ff.
Membranes, permeable, 243
Membrane, plasma, 220
Memory, 27
Mendelism, 54 ff.
Mendelian experiments, 55 ff.
Mendelian inheritance in man, 60 ff.
Mendelian laws of inheritance, 57 ff.
Mental age, 367 ff.
Mental age of adult racial groups, 146
Mental age, concept of, 355
Mental growth, differential rates of, 172, 173
Mental testing, contributions of various nations to, 357 ff.
Meriam, 200
Merriman, 103, 104, 105, 106
Merrill, 359, 377, 378
Merrill-Palmer scale, 362
Mesencephalon, 312
Mesmerism, 417
Metabolism, calcium, 234
Metabolism and physiological gradient, 221 ff.
Metencephalon, 312
"Method of impression," 8
Methods, scientific, 11 ff.
Mid-brain, 312
Miles, 151, 153, 162, 446
Mill, 151
Millichamp, 127
Mind, theories of, 17 ff.
Minkowski, 268, 282
Mitchell, 91
Mitosis, 44 ff.
Monozygocity of Dionne quintuplets, 122 ff.
Monozygocity in twins, criteria of, 115 ff.
Morgan, 16, 259, 268
Morgan, T. H., 43, 50, 51, 64, 136
Moron, 189, 190
Motor abilities of deaf, 186
Motor reactions, individual differences in, 193 ff.
Motor skills, independent, 195, 196
Motor neurons, 241
Motor skill of twins, 115 ff.
Müller, 115
Multiple-factor hypothesis, 343
Multiple fiber theory, 248, 249
Multi-focal theory of intelligence, 337 ff.
Muscles, kinds of, 227
Musical capacity, inheritance of, 128 ff.
Mutations, 65
Myelencephalon, 312
Myxedema, 228 ff.

Nams, 78
Native responses, criteria of, 280 ff.
Nature, as a continuum, 19
Nature, uniformity of, 14 ff.
Nature of 'g' and 's', 342 ff.
Nature of intelligence, 337 ff.
Negroes, intelligence of, 143 ff.

Nelson, 16, 194
Neo-natal, behavior, 268
Neo-pallium, 312
Neuron, 240 ff.
Neurons, forms of, 241
Nervous impulse, 246 ff.
Nervous system, autonomic, 243 ff.
Nervous system and emotions, 311 ff.
Nervous systems, subdivisions of central and peripheral, 240
Newman, 106, 115, 119, 120, 121, 127
Newton, 4, 334, 348, 448
Nichols, 99
Noegenetic principles, Spearman's three, 337
Non-linguistic group test, 361
Non-variable behavior, 257 ff.
Non-variable behavior, forms of, 261 ff.
Norm, 363
Norms, how to secure, 364 ff.
Norms for age and grade, 365
Normal distribution, 136
Normal surface of frequency, 66 ff.

Objective psychology, 11
Occam, 15
Occupation and personality, 445
Odin, 84, 86
Ontogeny and phylogeny, 209
Optic lobes, 312
Optic thalami, 312
Oedipus complex, 420
Organismic behavior, 214 ff.
Organismic psychology, 20 ff., 212
Organs, sense, 235 ff.
Orientals, intelligence of, 145
Orientations, stereotropic, 264
Origin of species, 36
Orphans, study of, 95 ff.
Otis, 108, 357, 359, 368
Outlets, emotional, 325 ff.
Overlapping of racial distributions, 148

Pancreas, 234
Parabolic curves of growth of intelligence, 370, 371, 372
Paramecium, 225, 259
Paranoia, 428
Para-sympathetic and sympathetic, 244
Parathyroid glands, 234
Parathyroid type of personality, 412
Parental behavior, 275
Parkhurst, 200
Parsimony, principle of, 15 ff.
Paterson, 352
Pattern actions, 257
Patterns, finger, 123 ff.
Paulhan, 409
Pavlov, 42, 298, 299, 304, 305
Pavlov's conditioning results, 299 ff.
Pearson, Karl, 15, 70, 73, 96, 102, 142, 352
Pearson's goodness of fit, 382
Peas, inheritance in, 55 ff.
Peckham, 176

Peking man, 38
Pennsylvania survey, 386
Percentile rank, 368 ff.
Perception, miracle of, 8
Perez, 284, 411
Performance tests, 361 ff., 438 ff.
Peripheral nervous system, subdivisions of, 240
Perkins and *Wheeler*, 25
Persistency of emotion, 279
Personalities, abnormal, 427 ff.
Personality, alcohol and, 425
Personality, bodily structure and, 407 ff.
Personality, cultural pattern and, 448 ff.
Personality, definitions of, 394, 395, 396
Personality difficulties, treatment of, 429 ff.
Personality, elements of, 402 ff.
Personality, endocrinology and, 412
Personality, environment and, 422 ff.
Personality, fluctuations of, 399
Personality, growth of, 425 ff.
Personality, importance of, 400 ff.
Personality, industrial adjustment and, 445 ff.
Personality, marital compatibility and, 446
Personality, meaning of, 394 ff.
Personality, measurement of, 432 ff.
Personality, misconceptions regarding, 397 ff.
Personality, occupation and, 445
Personality of the artist, 447
Personality of the discoverer and inventor, 447 ff.
Personality of the religious person, 448
Personality, social environment and, 394
Personality rating scales, 433 ff.
Personality types, 406 ff.
Personality types, founded on character and temperament, 409 ff.
Personality types, a possible scientific basis for, 412 ff.
Phenotype, 58, 65
Phenotypical behavior, 406
Photographic studies of emotions, 274, 320 ff.
Phrenology, 351, 433
Phylogenetic theory of emotion, 317 ff.
Phylogeny and ontogeny, 209, 260
Physically handicapped, education of, 191
Physical monism, 17 ff.
Physiognomy, 351, 432 ff.
Physiological actions, 261 ff.
Physiological age and maturation, 175
Physiological gradient, 207, 217, 221 ff.
Physiological gradient, proof of, 222 ff.
Piltdown man, 38
Pineal gland, 234
Piney Folk, 78
Pintner, 143, 144, 148, 186, 337, 359, 374, 385, 386
Pithecanthropus, 38
Pituitary body, 232 ff.
Pituitary types of personality, 412
Pituitrin, 232
Plant, 448, 449
Plantar reflex, 268

Plasma membrane, 220
Plato, 18, 305
Plethysmograph, 322
Poffenberger, 137
Point-scale scoring, 359
Polarity of organisms, 220
Porteus, 357
Precocity of intelligence, 334 ff.
Preconscious, Freud's, 419
Pre-school children, intelligence tests for, 362
Preyer, 175, 284
Primates, subdivisions of, 37
Prince, 18
Principles of behavior, 213 ff.
Principles of emotion, Darwin's, 277 ff.
Principles, Freud's, 420 ff.
Principles of gestalt psychology, 217
Principles, scientific, 11 ff.
Probability curve, 66 ff.
Progressive education and individual differences, 199
Project method, 200
Propensities, innate, 297
Properties of genes, 45
Protestantism and talent, 83
Protopathic sensibility, 238
Protoplasm, 213 ff.
Protoplasm, composition of, 219
Protoplasm, embryonic, 220
Protoplasmic behavior, 219 ff.
Pseudo-emotions, 308
Psyche, of the Greeks, 2
Psychical monism, 18
Psychoanalysis, history of, 417 ff.
Psychoanalysis, theory of personality, 418 ff.
Psychoanalytical school, 26 ff.
Psychoanalytical school, emotion and, 310
Psychoanalytical schools, 417 ff.
Psychoanalytical types, 412
Psychogalvanic reflex, 261
Psychogalvanic reflex and emotions, 324
Psychologia, Goeckel's, 2
Psychological investigation, difficulty of, 5, 17
Psychological studies, divisions of, 29 ff.
Psychology, abnormal, 9, 30
Psychology, analytical, 418
Psychology, animal, 31
Psychology, applied, 31 ff.
Psychology, as a science, 1 ff., 34
Psychology, bond, 21, 212
Psychology, child, 30, 33
Psychology, comparative, 31
Psychology, developmental, 30 ff.
Psychology, differential, 31, 136 ff.
Psychology, educational, 32 ff.
Psychology, general human, 30
Psychology, genetic, 30, 33
Psychology, gestalt, 25 ff., 212
Psychology, gestalt and traditional, 26
Psychology, history of, 1 ff.
Psychology, individual, 31
Psychology of individual differences, 136 ff.

Psychology of learning, 32 ff.
Psychology, objective, features of, 11
Psychology, organismic, 20 ff., 212
Psychology, other sciences and, 4 ff.
Psychology of race, 138 ff.
Psychology, schools of, 16 ff., 19 ff.
Psychology, scientific lag of, 4 ff.
Psychology, social, 31
Psychoneuroses, 428
Psychophysical interaction, 18
Psychophysical parallelism, 18
Psychoses, 428
Pulse-rate and emotion, 322 ff.
Pupils, deafness among, 183, 184
Purkinje, 219
Pyknics, 408 ff.
Pyle, 194
Pyramidal cells, 243

Quantitative laws, Spearman's five, 337
Questionnaires, 436 ff.
Queyrat, 409
Quintuplets, Dionne, 99, 121 ff.

Race differences, 138 ff.
Race differences in sensitivity, 193
Race, divisions of, 139 ff.
Racial fusion, 141
Racial groups, intelligence of, 389 ff.
Racial intelligence, 142 ff.
Rage, expression of, 275 ff.
Rage, sham, 319
Range of intelligence, 348 ff.
Rat-killing instinct of cats, 270 ff.
Rationalization, 430
Rating scale, graphic, 434
Rating scale, man-to-man, 435
Rating scales for personality, 433 ff.
Ratios, mendelian, 55 ff.
Raup, 217, 327
Ranson, 243
Razran, 305
Reaction-hypothesis, 218 ff.
Reactions, stereotyped, 258
Receptors, 227, 235 ff.
Reed, 196
References, lists of, 34, 35, 132, 133, 134,
    135, 202, 203, 204, 255, 256, 328, 329,
    330, 331, 332, 391, 392, 393, 449, 450,
    451, 452
Reflex arc, 26, 242, 251
Reflex, Babinski, 287, 293
Reflexes, conditioned, 25
Reflexes, 265 ff.
Reflexes, conditioning of, 298 ff.
Reflexes, list of human, 267
Refractory period, absolute, 247
Reflexes, psychogalvanic, 261
Religious person, personality of, 448
Renshaw, 305
Repressed types, 412
Repression, 26 ff., 418
Resistance, 417

Respiratory changes and emotion, 323 ff.
Response, conditioned, 299
Results of intelligence testing, 388 ff.
Results, Pavlov's conditioning, 299 ff.
Revisions of Binet tests, 360
Rheotropisms, 263
Ribery, 410
Ribot, 409
Rignano, 217
Rivers, 237
Roback, 409
Royalty, inheritance in, 73 ff.
Royal Society, 81, 83
Ruckmick, 315, 317, 318, 321, 441
Rugg, 21

Sacral division, 244
Salamanders, maturation of, 170
Sampling, random, 363
Sampling theory of intelligence, 345 ff.
Scales, personality rating, 433 ff.
Schafer, 238
Schizophrene, 441
Schizophrenia, 428
School, child-centered, 21
Schooling and variability, 198
Schools of psychology, 16 ff., 417 ff.
Schools of psychology, organismic, 19
Schools of psychology, atomistic, 19
Schopenhauer, 149
Schwegler, 436
Scientific methods and principles, 11 ff.
Scientists of U.S., 85 ff.
Score, standard, 369
Scores, evaluation of test, 367 ff.
Scottish survey of intelligence, 379
Seashore, 195, 196
Seashore, C., 322
Seat of emotions, 313
Secretin, 234
Self-maintenance, 301
Self-maintaining behavior, 274
Segregation, 58
Selection and classification of pupils by in-
    telligence tests, 383 ff.
Selection and individual differences, 147
Sensation, sex differences in, 152
Sense organs, 235 ff.
Sense organs, cortical system of, 239
Sense organs, evolution of, 236 ff.
Sense organs, functions of, 235 ff.
Sense organs, list of, 236, 237
Sense organs, thalamic system of, 239
Sensibility, protopathic, epicritic, and deep,
    238
Sensitivity, individual differences in, 192 ff.
Sensori-motor arc, 265
Sensory neurons, 241
Sergi, 315
Serviceable associated habits, 277
Sex characters, secondary, 233
Sex differences, 149 ff.
Sex differences in personality, 446 ff.